Paths, Pals and Pints

Three friends walk and talk their way round
Scotland and the North of England

Helen Williamson

Copyright © 2022 Helen Williamson

All rights reserved

Whilst all the walks in this publication did take place, some names, characters and minor events have been partly fictionalised.

No part of this book may be reproduced, or stored in a retrieval system, or transmitted in any form or by any means, electronic, mechanical, photocopying, recording, or otherwise, without express written permission of the publisher.

Cover design by Bruce Jamieson

ISBN: 9798367399097

To the real Fiona and Liksi, without whom this book would never have come into being

Paths, Pals and Pints

18	West Island Way, south loop	Pg 199
19	St Cuthbert's Way 1	Pg 210
20	St Cuthbert's Way 2	Pg 223
21	St Cuthbert's Way 3	Pg 234
22	Ben A'an	Pg 245
23	St Cuthbert's Way 4	Pg 256
24	St Cuthbert's Way 5	Pg 267
25	John Muir Way 1	Pg 280
26	Ben Lawers and Beinn Ghlas	Pg 291
27	Glentress and Peebles	Pg 302
28	John Muir Way 2	Pg 315
29	Kinder Scout	Pg 327
30	Easedale Tarn and Thorn Crag	Pg 338
31	Scarborough to Filey	Pg 349
32	John Muir Way 3	Pg 363
33	Ben Nevis	Pg 377
34	Blairgowrie to Kirkmichael	Pg 390
35	Rubha Mor	Pg 402
	Acknowledgements	Pg 416

Contents

	Preface	i
1	The Towns	Pg 1
2	West Highland Way 1	Pg 17
3	West Highland Way 2	Pg 29
4	Helvellyn	Pg 40
5	Skiddaw	Pg 52
6	Ben Lomond	Pg 62
7	The Cobbler	Pg 73
8	West Highland Way 3	Pg 86
9	West Highland Way 4	Pg 97
10	West Highland Way 5	Pg 107
11	West Highland Way 6	Pg 119
12	Loch Katrine	Pg 128
13	Water of Leith	Pg 140
14	Ambleside and Wansfell Pike	Pg 153
15	Pentlands	Pg 165
16	Scafell Pike	Pg 178
17	West Island Way, north loop	Pg 188

Preface

Anyone who walks in the countryside will know that no two walks are the same, even for a lone walker. The seasons, weather, flora, fauna, and other hikers encountered combine to make each walk a unique experience. Multiply that by three walkers' perspectives, and their conversations en route, and each walk becomes a truly memorable occasion.

The walks in this book all took place at the times indicated, and the paths should all be easily found online or in walking books if readers want to follow in our footsteps. The pubs, hostels and guesthouses all exist, or did at the time of writing. Almost all of them can be easily identified, although there are one or two which have not been named for (usually) obvious reasons. The wonderful 'pals' are very real and were partly responsible for suggesting that our experiences should find their way into a book.

I have, however, taken liberties with the characterisation of these pals, their husbands, partners, children, parents and other individuals mentioned. Some aspects are genuine, others are fictionalised - partly to add interest, but also to preserve an element of privacy. Readers can relate to the type of conversations women have, the life experiences they might grapple with and the shared confidences; the bond of close female friendship will be familiar and essential to many.

Countless individuals discovered the benefits of walking as a way of getting through the recent pandemic; my hope is that this book will encourage others to do the same - for reasons of health, friendship, sanity and fun. Our great outdoors is rich in rewards - and also free for everyone to enjoy.

Chapter 1 – The Towns (2001-2003)

Manchester (November 2001) - Fiona

It was a relief to see the sun finally breaking through the greyness, as I didn't want the others to see my adopted city in a bad light, and I wasn't quite sure what they were expecting. Not that it mattered, we'd *so* much to talk about – after Eilidh's phone call about four months ago, I wondered why we hadn't got together years ago. I'd missed the pair of them, and their easy company.

As I walked along to Manchester Piccadilly, I found myself thinking back to how the three of us had met – almost 20 years ago now. After university in Edinburgh, one by one we'd found jobs in London. Through mutual acquaintances and the usual run of parties, we bumped into each other and started meeting up on a regular basis. It was a heady time – first jobs, well away from home and with a myriad of new friends and experiences. However, over time careers, buying our first homes, getting married and having children took us away from London and contact become sporadic.

Making my way through the crowds at the station, I got to the platform as the Edinburgh train was arriving, and craned my neck to get a better view of the passengers alighting. And there they were, right at the back. Liksi was unmistakeable, with her ash-blonde, almost white hair, cut in a sleek bob. In some ways she was an unlikely athlete, being so petite that she looked almost frail. However, her looks belied her fitness due to years of training, mainly for hockey but she was also a keen runner and was easily the sportiest of the three. And there was Eilidh, in a vivid green jacket which looked a bit too tight for comfort. However, her face was as striking as ever – a very rosy, Highland face under that unruly auburn mop.

I waved furiously, and suddenly there we were, all together again in a tangle of hugs and welcomes. When I finally broke free, I herded them into a little bistro just outside the station, and within minutes we were sitting at a table with a bottle of house red and 3 glasses in front of us.

"Och, this is the life." Eilidh sighed happily as she poured the wine. "No husbands, children, work – just us, and good old vino. Cheers!"

"Cheers!" We joined her with raised glasses. It was good to see that our joint preference for red wine, proudly developed at a time when most women drank white, had not altered over the years.

"So how's Manchester, Fiona?" Liksi set her glass down. "I'm afraid I really don't know much about it. Guess you feel quite at home here now?"

"Yip, pretty much, though I don't know if I'd want to stay here forever. Sometimes I envy you two being back in Scotland, but there's a lot going for Manchester just now."

"And how about Olly? That was a shock, him ending up here. Never thought he'd leave London." Liksi was absolutely right – even I hadn't expected my suave boyfriend to leave his lucrative job and somewhat pretentious lifestyle, and end up a permanent fixture.

"What, not even for Fiona?" Eilidh grinned. "Come on now, we always knew he was besotted with you. What *is* surprising though is that you married him - doesn't quite tie in with the Bohemian lifestyle I remember you having."

"Well, it seemed to be the next obvious move." I didn't want to go into details at this stage – my relationship with Olly had always been a bit complex. "Anyway, he got on well with the cats, so that was the deciding factor. Come on, we'd better order some food or we'll be needing another bottle – and afterwards, I'll show you Manchester."

Lunch passed in a torrent of catching up. I don't think any of us would remember what we'd had to eat – the food was incidental, although I don't think the chef would have been happy to know that.

"Right, ready to hit the town now? OK lugging these bags around?" Although it was getting on for 3 o'clock, I was keen to take them on a whistle-stop tour of the centre so that at least they could say that they'd seen some of Manchester and not just a little-known bistro near the station.

"Definitely. You need to show us what Manchester's got that Edinburgh and Glasgow don't." Liksi hoisted her small rucksack easily onto a shoulder, and Eilidh picked up her rather large bag with a slight grimace.

"It's OK, I'll manage, I'm used to hoiking things about." She had a determined look on her face, although I had my doubts. "How do you manage with so little, Liksi?"

"Och, backpacking around Australia got me used to it, I s'pose. Travelling to sports events."

Eilidh looked unconvinced, but started walking. I led them through the streets to Canal Street, guessing correctly that this would be a bit of a novelty. There wasn't really a part of the Forth and Clyde canal which went through the centre of Glasgow or Edinburgh.

"These buildings remind me of Glasgow, though they're more red brick than red sandstone." Eilidh was looking around with interest.

"Yeah, kind of imposing, aren't they?" Liksi gazed up at the top floors. "See what you mean – you've got lovely old buildings next to modern office blocks. Very Glasgow – but not Edinburgh at all."

"Good – beginning to feel at home? Come on, we'll go up to the centre now and you can see some of the main attractions." It amused me to hear what they thought of Manchester – I'd been there for so long I couldn't really see it with non-local eyes any more.

We had a quick drink in the Molly House – couldn't let them miss Manchester's best pub. Although popular with the gay scene, it was equally welcoming to anyone else, and an ideal "take the tourist" pub. Eilidh reverted to her first love, beer, while Liksi and I continued with the red wine. Before Eilidh could order another, I steered them outside and we carried on to St Peter's Square.

"This is the Manchester Central Library," I told them, as we passed by its dome and columns.

"Not quite like the building I spend most of my waking hours in." Liksi sounded regretful. "Nor like yours, Eilidh, I'd imagine."

"No, indeed." She and Liksi both worked in further education colleges, neither of which were famed for their architectural splendour.

After pointing out the Town Hall Extension and the gothic Town Hall itself, Eilidh was starting to flag with that big bag of hers, so another refreshment stop was required. I took them into the City Arms and we managed to get a seat in the cosy snug at the back, settling in amongst locals nursing their pints, and workers postponing going home. "Wonderful," Eilidh said, as she lifted her pint of Boddingtons. "I mean the Town Hall, as well as the beer. I'm so glad you didn't drag us round the shops."

"Ah well, maybe next time." I fished in my bag and produced a packet of ten Benson & Hedges, then offered one to Eilidh, wondering if she'd accept. To my selfish relief, she was delighted.

"Fiona!" She almost yelped, as she reached out for one. "I'd no idea you still smoked."

"Well, I don't really. Just sometimes. I wasn't sure whether you still did, and I know you disapprove, Liksi."

"Don't really, just that I've never smoked, though I was brought up in a smoke-filled household." Liksi was watching us with some amusement. "In fact, don't know how James's and my lungs weren't permanently damaged as a result. Go ahead."

"I gave up smoking about thirteen years ago, and just take an occasional one." Eilidh tried - and failed - to look virtuous, as she took a long, deep drag. "I'm scared that if I actually bought a packet, I'd start again."

"And I just keep these for special occasions. Honestly." We enjoyed our clandestine smoke, finished our drinks, and then it was time to head home.

"I think I told you that Olly is away on a golfing trip, and the boys are on sleepovers – we'll get peace." I got up and reached for my jacket. "Also, home means a tram to Sale – another novelty for you two."

"I've heard talk of trams coming to Edinburgh – we'll catch up with you southerners yet," said Liksi.

"Hey, none of that here – the Mancunians see themselves as northerners."

"Northerners? Manchester?" Eilidh was incredulous. "Is that because they don't count Scotland as being significant enough to bother with?" Oh, God, was she still sensitive to slights against Scotland?

"Nope, they just don't want to be lumped in with London and the south. A Mancunian is a very different animal from a Londoner – and has more in common with us Scots in many ways. Believe me."

I could see Eilidh'd take a bit of convincing, but the tram arrived and put paid to the conversation at this point. We got to Sale, called in at the King's Ransom (well, they had to see my local), and then I took them home. We were all pretty exhausted by this stage, so had a bit of 'down time' for a while. Alfie and Splurge, who'd been dreaming happily with twitching tails in front of the radiator, woke up abruptly and then thought all their Christmases had come at once, with two more people to make a fuss of them. Unfortunately, this great vision wasn't shared by Liksi, who carefully rejected their advances, apologising for not being the greatest cat lover in the world.

Once we'd recovered a bit, I took them out to a local Thai restaurant, and our sightseeing tour of Manchester/Sale finished in the same way it started – with a bottle of red wine. Eilidh joined us this time, insisting that beer was for pubs and wine for meals. Goodness knows how her insides managed with the mixture she'd had today.

"Really don't know the last time I've enjoyed myself so much." Liksi drained her glass, stretched luxuriously and leant back in her chair.

"Just like London." Eilidh drew us all in with her wide grin. "We should never've left it this long to re-group – there's still a LOT of catching up to do. So, can we do this again?"

We agreed there was no point in trying to organise anything till at least February, with all the Christmas goings-on, and the Celtic Connections festival that Eilidh said was sacrosanct. She said she'd get in touch with us again in the spring to sort something out. As we reluctantly headed home, I felt a warm glow of affection for them both, and was already looking forward to the next time – and for an excuse to be back north of the Border again.

Glasgow (May 2002) - Eilidh

How can it be so difficult to get three people together? OK, so I'd forgotten about it till March, then it was almost the Easter holidays and everyone had their own ploys, so by the time I got them to agree a date for Glasgow, it was the middle of May. We all knew Edinburgh well, having studied at Edinburgh University, but Fiona had only been to Glasgow for the occasional concert in her student days, and Liksi had just visited on occasion, mainly for sporting events.

Fiona arrived at Central Station mid-afternoon, looking glamorous as ever and with a Gucci overnight bag that I would never even have dreamt *of,* let alone considered buying. Scruffy holdalls or tatty rucksacks were more my style. And how did she manage to keep her hair looking so, so – perfect? Expensive hairdresser, probably.

"How d'you do it? You look wonderful – but when we shared a flat together you were as scruffy as me. What's changed?" I asked her, not without a hint of envy.

"Nonsense – you look fine!" She tried – unsuccessfully – to hide a rather smug smile. "I s'pose I just got more fashion-conscious over time – and Manchester has great shops. So has Glasgow, though – d'you mind if we call in at Hobbs, as they've got a sale on and I've asked them to set aside a skirt for me?"

Oh dear. On the rare occasions I'd set foot in Hobbs I found myself quickly out on the pavement again in disgust – Hobbs clothes weren't made for people my shape. I'd never been able to understand the fascination with shopping anyway – in Glasgow it was elevated to a profession, where you had to put on the 'slap' and heels and traipse round the shops at least in pairs, if not in hordes. However, ...

"Sure – Liksi isn't going to be here till 6 anyway. She's playing in a competition somewhere." I managed this statement without flinching, as if arranging for clothes to be awaiting collection in different cities was a matter of course for me too. "Fancy some lunch first?"

"It's OK, I've eaten on the train."

Needless to say, after Hobbs came Frasers, then John Lewis (with items purchased in both of them), then a look round Buchanan Galleries. I was vaguely aware that Glasgow had a good reputation for shops, but for heaven's sake, surely they'd shops in Manchester too? I wish I'd suggested that we'd gone to Lomond Shores or somewhere instead – at least we'd have had a blast of country air as well as shops.

To my great relief, when I finally found the courage to suggest a visit to the Drum and Monkey, Fiona had no objection. "Good idea." She swapped her bags to the other hand and shook her free one about with relief. "Thanks for indulging me – hope you didn't mind. It's just that I don't often get the chance to shop, so I fit it in when I can. And I really wanted that skirt."

We managed to find a corner large enough to house ourselves and all of Fiona's purchases, and settled down with our drinks into the comfy if rather worn chairs.

"Bliss." I was so glad to get off my feet. "I've always liked this pub - the variety of seating, the cosy nooks. And usually the beer's quite good though I'm not sure about this one." I took another mouthful and looked at my glass doubtfully.

"Well, the wine's lovely – I needed it after all that shopping. So tell me, how're things going with you?"

"Och, the usual. Busy at work."

"Enjoy it?"

"Mm-hm, most of the time. I'm a bit fed up just now, though, as I got turned down for a promoted post recently." I didn't want to admit that I'd actually been pretty devastated.

"Oh, well, I guess there's plenty other colleges. Good luck anyway – I'm sure you'll get something." I wish I had

Fiona's confidence.

"It's almost time for Liksi's train." I remembered this suddenly, grateful for a change of subject. "Want to stay here and I'll go and get her? I guess you'd rather not trundle that lot about any more than you have to."

"Nope, that's fine, I can check my emails." I guessed that over the years Fiona, like the rest of us, was much less self-conscious in a pub on her own than we used to be, even one in a strange city on a Friday night.

I went off to meet Liksi, leaving Fiona already engrossed in her Blackberry. Since we left London, I hadn't seen as much of Liksi as I had of Fiona. It was just one of these things that happened – no particular reason, as I was equally fond of both of them. Seeing Liksi's trim form standing by the clock was as warming as ever – there was something so likeable about this person who was currently aiming a wide smile in my direction. I'd forgotten how small she was, but in spite of that she was a great runner, and I'd been told she was pretty fierce on the hockey field. She was wearing jeans and a sweatshirt, and I was glad to see that she at least wasn't going to show me up in the dress sense.

We hugged, and I steered the way to the Drum and Monkey as soon as we cleared the post-work crowds milling about Queen Street Station.

"We'll no doubt have to prise Fiona off her phone," I started to say when we got in the door, then I realised that there wasn't going to be any need for that. One of Glasgow's worthies had struck up a conversation with her, much to the amusement of a couple of guys in nearby seats. Fiona was trying to rear back from his rheumy gaze and toothless grin.

"Hi there, Fiona, making new friends?" I couldn't help laughing at her slightly alarmed expression as she grabbed her bags and rushed towards us gratefully. So some situations *did* faze my confident, high-flying friend.

"Liksi, great to see you – where'd you say we're going

next, Eilidh?" She had us out the pub door before we could draw breath, leaving her new friend bemoaning the loss of his attractive drinking pal. "Thank God you came when you did. I got no peace at ALL in there!"

"Well, this *is* Glasgow, you know – everyone's friendly and it's a crime to be sitting on your own. You don't usually get people like that in this pub though – you were just unlucky. Come on, we'll go somewhere else and get Liksi a drink."

We crossed over Buchanan Street, and settled ourselves down in the Old Printworks, tucked away on North Frederick Street.

"It's good for real ale here." I waved my hand at all the pumps, and blackboards listing guest beers. "There's not so many real ale pubs in Glasgow, more's the pity. Remember how it was always a wine bar near Covent Garden we used to meet up in?"

"Ah, we had style in those days." Liksi gave a nostalgic sigh.

We had a few drinks there, then moved on to George Square for a meal in an Italian restaurant. Afterwards we got the train up to Bearsden – no trams here - and burst in on my husband, who was dozing contentedly over Match of the Day.

"Sorry to shatter your peace." I grabbed the bundle of papers, books and assorted other debris from the couch which he had commandeered, to make room for someone to sit, and he shuffled over and patted the seat invitingly. I'll say this for Alan – he was always, always sociable.

"I should think so, at this time of night. Good to see you two again – Eilidh, how much have you had to drink?"

"Mm? What d'you mean?" I looked at him defensively, knowing fine well what he meant but trying not slur my words.

"Oh dear." He shook his head. "And I guess you two're

just as bad. Hope you like football?"

"Depends who's playing." Liksi settled down on the couch beside him and focused on the screen. "Not if it's someone beating Rangers. Oh, good *goal* – smart thinking!"

"Why d'you support Rangers? Thought you'd be for Hibs or Hearts, being an Edinburger?" Alan was taken aback at the unexpected bonus of one of my female friends expressing *any* interest in football.

"My Dad loves the 'Gers, don't know why really. Have just followed the family tradition."

"OK, before you get too much into football, where d'you want to sleep tonight? There's the double bed in the spare room – you could both go there, or one of you on the couch downstairs."

"Fiona can have the bedroom. I'll go downstairs," said Liksi quickly - and rather assertively for her.

Fiona and I looked at each other with amusement. Wonder where that came from? We'd so much to catch up on yet. As we agreed over a hearty breakfast the next morning, we could spend a lifetime filling in all the gaps. Liksi offered to arrange our next meeting, at her place in a few months' time.

"Poor Pete – his turn for the invasion. Great for me - I'll have the place to myself that weekend without drunken harpies disrupting my peace."

I smiled at Alan affectionately, knowing full well he didn't mean a word of it.

Edinburgh (June 2003) - Liksi

"Sorry, sorry, I know, need to look at the calendar more often. I forgot, and *please, please* could you go and pick them up? Just this once – it won't happen again. Honestly. Please."

I hated having to plead with Pete like this, just as he didn't like having to give up his free time to help me out with any of my social activities. However, his curiosity regarding the other two won him over and he reluctantly agreed to pick them up from the station. He'd come across Eilidh briefly a couple of times, and had met Fiona once when she'd been up visiting the University as part of a training programme. She'd made quite an impression on him though, so at least he knew who to look out for at the station. I still remember him saying, "Well, she's a refreshing change from most of you geeks".

Anyway, not an auspicious start. How could I have forgotten that I was playing hockey in the Marie Curie charity match? It *was* on the kitchen calendar – it's just that I was probably so focused on Eilidh and Fiona coming that I forgot the two events clashed. There'd been so many things going on in the children's lives – changes of school, after-school activities, the usual – but as always Pete left most of it to me and the last couple of weeks had been particularly hectic.

As I burst into the sitting room after the game, scattering kit and boots all over the kitchen in passing, I was relieved to see both of them there, along with Pete who judging from his expression had decided to morph into the charming host.

"SO sorry not to've met you at the station – thanks, Pete." Breathlessly, I hugged them both and flung myself down on the only unoccupied chair.

"Not a problem." Eilidh winked at Fiona. "Pete saw two gorgeous females waiting on Market Street and knew us immediately. Did his street cred the world of good to be seen picking us up."

"Absolutely." Pete smiled at her then turned to me. "Makes a bit of a change from carting you and your hockey sticks around in a mad rush to get to a match on time. Maybe just once, you could try to remember a match before the last minute, when the whole house has to do triple somersaults to get you there?" I felt my face flushing – did he have to do this in front of people?

"And we were very happy to be picked up, instead of having to get the bus." Fiona followed on from Eilidh, as if Pete hadn't spoken. "How'd the game go anyway?"

"Well, not exactly our most memorable performance, but we raised over £800 from tickets, teas, etc. Pretty good, really."

"Don't worry, Pete made us at home and poured coffee down our throats – and that yummy banana cake." I looked anxiously at Eilidh as she spoke, but she was smiling at me as she pointed to an empty plate beside her chair. "Our stuff's up in Joe's room, and Fiona's going in the top bunk, so we're all organised."

Eilidh had always been good as a peacemaker; that was one of her many endearing qualities. I was also relieved that the pair of them didn't seem to mind sleeping in the same room – unlike me. I so much value my own space at the end of the day when I'm away anywhere. Don't know why, when I'm so used to being here with Pete. Maybe I just like the freedom of being able to do absolutely my own thing, for a few hours at least.

"Well, we can leave the man in peace now and hit the town. I'll just get tidied up and then we can go." I cast a surreptitious glance at Fiona's stylish outfit, decided not to even try to compete and went upstairs to change into my chinos and favourite squishy top. I think I'd got it in a charity shop somewhere. Eilidh too was dressed for comfort rather than style, I was glad to see.

There was no protest from Pete as we left him to fend for himself. Being out with three chattering females, who were largely uninterested in him, was not a selling point. He was quite happy with his bottle of Speckled Hen and the TV remote – I think.

"OK, girls, slumming it – bus OK?" I asked, as we turned the corner onto the main road. "No trains - or trams for that matter, yet."

"If my memory serves me correctly, Edinburgh's buses were always great." Fiona was heading for the bus stop. "Are they still?"

"Yeah – everyone goes by bus here. Cheap, reliable, plenty of them – here's one that'll take us down South Clerk Street." I got tickets for them all and we climbed upstairs for the views.

"Wow, Memory Lane – are we going to the Southern?" Eilidh had lived in Pollock Halls as a student, and the Southern bar had been popular with students as they made their way down South Clerk Street en route to various parties or to the Union. I'd missed all that as I'd stayed at home.

"No, wee bistro called Biblos. Cheap'n'cheerful." It wasn't long before we were settled at a table there, with a welcome bottle of Cabernet Sauvignon placed in front of us.

"Nice." Fiona poured the drinks expertly. "Strange that it never feels as if our trip starts properly until we've our first drink. What does that say about us?"

"Let's not go there." Eilidh reached out for her glass. "So, Liksi, how're the kids? Feel I've got to ask about Joe specially, since we've commandeered his room for the night."

"Doing fine, thanks. Joe's sports daft. He's away on a football tournament this weekend."

"And Julie?" asked Fiona.

"Oh, complete opposite – loves her dance classes. Bit of a pink princess but also a real bookworm. What about your two, Fiona?"

"Well, Jack's the bookworm - he has to be reminded sometimes that there's a world outside The Shire or Hogwarts. He's wanting me to queue up with him next week, to get the 'Order of the Phoenix' as soon as it's released. Joy."

"Really?" Eilidh raised her eyebrows. "Pity he didn't live in Glasgow - I'd queue up with him. I *love* the Harry Potter books – but I'd have to borrow a child to justify actually queuing for one."

"Indeed. We're all so different, aren't we?" Fiona swirled her drink, looking thoughtfully into its crimson depths. "Remember in London, we discovered that one thing we had in common was squash? Heaven knows how many different courts we played in – at least the exercise always seemed to justify a drink afterwards."

"True." Eilidh looked momentarily wistful, then brightened up again. "Now we don't need the exercise as an excuse to meet up. Although, maybe we should. Anyone still play squash?"

Fiona and I shook our heads.

"So, have we just become ladies who lunch? How boring." I laughed with them, but there was definitely a 'perish the thought' lurking there.

"You know, I've been thinking." Eilidh put her glass down and straightened up in her seat. "You two seem pretty fit, and I'm trying to up my exercise levels. I'm still a country bumpkin at heart, so not a great fan of traipsing round cities – and specially not round shops. No need to snort, Fiona!"

"Think we didn't work that one out?" Fiona gave me a conspiratorial wink, and I couldn't help laughing too.

"Ha ha. Anyway, how d'you fancy meeting up again somewhere where we could do a walk or climb? Exercise followed by justified indulgence, just like old times? What d'you think?"

"Great idea." I didn't have to think about it and noticed that Fiona was also nodding enthusiastically. "Much better than spending the *whole* weekend eating and drinking."

And so our small walking group was born. After we'd finished our meal, we continued down Memory Lane via the Beehive and the White Hart, then set the scene for our newly formed plan by walking somewhat unsteadily all the way back to my house. As we chattered and laughed our way home, enjoying the easy company and shared confidences, I found myself looking forward immensely to the start of a new (and healthier) chapter in our get-togethers.

Chapter 2 – West Highland Way 1 (January 2005) - Eilidh

The West Highland Way is Scotland's best-known long-distance walk. Officially 96 miles long, it runs from Milngavie, on the outskirts of Glasgow, to Fort William. This chapter relates to one 12-mile stretch from Drymen to Milngavie. The terrain is largely flat, with well-defined paths.

Well, I don't quite know what happened to 2004, but we didn't manage to meet up. Fiona was on a secondment to an EU-funded project and seemed to be diving about various Eastern European countries. Liksi was an IT technician in a large college and was finding everyone except herself slightly insane ... and me, well, I was still enjoying lecturing, and having finally managed to get a minor promotion I was enjoying the status that came with it, if not always the role itself.

So, when we finally arranged another meeting it was for January 2005, and our aim was to tackle the first stage of the West Highland Way. *January*, for a major walk?! Why did we do all our 'ladies who lunch'-type meetings in spring or summer, and then set out on a 12-mile walk in what was practically the middle of winter, and a Scottish winter, at that?

The decision to tackle the WHW had been unanimous. It had a romantic appeal in its route up through the Lowlands and into some of the most dramatic scenery of the Highlands. I'd been a bit wary of an actual climb for our first rural expedition, because I wasn't sure how fit I'd be compared to the other two, but the WHW had intrigued me for some time and I'd no worries at all about a long walk. I bought the official book and map for peace of mind, so that there that would be no hidden problems (the confidence of the uninitiated ...). Another advantage was that the official start in Milngavie was only two miles away from my house.

Liksi and Fiona arrived at Bearsden station within an hour of each other, and I picked each of them up as they had their full walking kit with them. Liksi arrived first, and once in the house she typically offered to sleep on the couch again.

"You don't have to, you know – I'm sure Fiona would agree that it's your turn for the bed."

"No, honestly, I don't mind – can watch the telly in the lounge anyway." Liksi was already on her way downstairs with her bag. "I'm an owl, not a lark like you two. My system can't cope with going to bed too early."

So that was sorted and, unsurprisingly, there was no dissent from Fiona when she arrived. I'd made chilli for a late dinner as I knew it was one of Liksi's favourites, and it seemed to go down well. We were lounging contentedly in the snug when Alan burst in from the pub at about 11.30 pm, bringing fresh air and beer smells in with him.

"Ha!" He flung off his jacket and aimed it at a chair. "Caught you! *Still* drinking red wine – perfect way of preparing for a long trek tomorrow - not!" He looked around hopefully, to see if any bottles were open.

"Thought you'd all be tucked up in your jim-jams, rucksacks packed, sarnies made, getting your beauty sleep before setting off at first light - oops, sorry!" As he'd plonked himself down on the sofa beside Fiona, the bowl of nuts beside her upended itself and the pair of them scrabbled about hunting down those making a bid for freedom.

"Alan! For heaven's sake, watch what you're doing." I picked up the bowl and put it on the table beside them.

"Och, at least it wasnae the wine – anyway, where's mine?" Liksi poured a glass for him and he resumed the tirade: "Don't blame me if you have hangovers tomorrow and have to call on yours truly to pick you up after a few miles!"

I glared at him. "You're a fine one to talk – I think

yours'll be a lot worse than ours, and you said you'd drop us at Drymen."

"Och, so I did. Don't worry, I'll be fine by the morning. Remind me – why on earth are you starting from Drymen and walking *backwards* to Milngavie?" He shook his head. "Doesn't the route normally go the other way, ie from Milngavie north? Something about not getting the sun in your eyes, and better views?"

"Because YOU said you'd give us a lift to Drymen early on, because you're going to Gerry's to watch the game later. Otherwise, we *would* have gone in the normal direction." I reminded him of this a bit huffily, as, being of a somewhat linear disposition, I'd wanted to follow the standard route in the first place.

"Oh, right. If you say so. Anyway, have you seen the snow outside? Ah hae ma doots as to whether I'll be able to get the car to Drymen in the first place, far less you lot walking through snowdrifts." Alan's lapses into the vernacular were more deliberate than accidental, and usually helped along by a few pints of wheatbeer.

"Och, come on, Alan, it's only wet snow and it'll be gone tomorrow." Fiona had a tendency to make sweeping statements although she'd been living in England far too long to have any insider knowledge of the vagaries of Scottish weather, but I hoped she was right.

I needn't have worried. When we got up the next morning, the snow wasn't any worse, and the roads were clear. In fact, the sun was shining and the prospect of a long walk in the fresh air was very enticing. Much better than a trek round the shops like last time ... We were getting stuck into bowls of cereal when Alan appeared, looking only slightly the worse for wear but as boisterous as ever. Fiona, being nearest the kettle, got up to pour him a cup of tea but was rudely interrupted.

"WHAT the FUCK are you wearing?! You're not going

walking in that surely?" Alan was gazing at Fiona in disbelief.

"What, don't you like my jim-jams?" Fiona did a twirl to show off her tartan nightwear.

"Is that what they are? Christ, that's a relief – I thought they were an English form of walking gear. My God, you'd frighten the natives in that getup!"

"Well, you don't need to worry on that score – they won't be going out of the house, I can promise you. Now do you want this tea or not?"

I felt a bit responsible for this trip, our first walking one and on "my" territory, so I squeezed a first aid kit into my already bulging rucksack – I never did seem to be able to master the art of travelling light. At my suggestion, we didn't take any sandwiches because the Beech Tree Inn, near Glengoyne Distillery, was en route.

Eventually all the rucksacks were packed, boots laced up and we bore a passable resemblance to seasoned walkers. Having said that, Fiona was clad in expensive branded outdoor gear, Liksi was in a colourful ensemble which she'd put together from her hockey and running clothes, and I was in my walking trousers, T-shirt and sweatshirt which had definitely seen better days. Shaking his head and hurling insults ("Drymen doesn't know what's coming to it"; "Not one of you with an ounce of sense" etc), Alan herded us all into the car and with much hilarity, drove us the relatively short distance to the eastern end of the Drymen loop on the A811, where he deposited us along with much unwanted advice.

"Told you we'd be fine, weather-wise," I couldn't resist saying to him, as I planted a kiss on his head before getting out. "Nothing on the roads. Look at that sky – it's blue. Perfect. There's not *that* much snow lying about, and it's so cold that it's likely to be good crisp walking."

"I'm sure there's another dump of snow forecast." He was

already moving the car into reverse. "You'll have the perfect excuse to pack it in and hole up in the Beech Tree till I can pick you up after the football." He grinned, as he shouted through the window. "Though you'd have to wait till I sobered up so it might be tomorrow. Enjoy yourselves!" and without waiting for a reply he drove off, leaving us in sudden peace, ready to embark on the best-known of Scotland's long-distance walks.

The surrounding fields had a layer of snow, although not as much as the Campsies, but the sky was encouraging with the few clouds in sight being small and puffy, and the sun was putting in an unexpected appearance for the time of year. The location was a very unassuming starting place (a road next to a field) – but then, as Alan had pointed out, it *wasn't* the starting place. Not that the obelisk in Milngavie's town centre constituted a memorable one either, but even so ...

Taking a deep lungful of the fresh, cold air, I led the way briskly across the road and down into the snow-covered field. I was determined to start with confidence and set a good pace. "Wonderful! Much better for us than traipsing round a city! So good to be – argh! *Bugger!*" Suddenly I was up to my ankles in an icy bog, with my boots filling rapidly with very cold water. "Watch out!" I flailed about till I managed to get myself onto a firmer patch of field, then turned round to see how the others were doing. Were they looking at me with concern? Not a bit of it - their yells of laughter had caused them to be doubled up, helpless, and I glared at this example of female solidarity.

"Oh, if only Alan could see you – can you imagine what he'd have to say?" Liksi eventually got her breath back enough to speak – just. "Two seconds earlier and he'd still have been here! Oh, my side aches."

"I can just imagine his comments about 'ladies who lunch trying to go walking' – we'd never hear the end of it." Fiona wiped her eyes, then looked at me more carefully. "Are you OK? D'you want to stop and change your socks?"

"Thanks, but no. That would be too much effort and my boots are sodden anyway. Bugger!" I rolled my trousers up a bit so that they wouldn't get any wetter. "Come on, we'd better get going – and STOP LAUGHING!" Difficult to say, when I was pretty hysterical myself.

In spite of this unfortunate start, the conditions were otherwise ideal. We were well wrapped up and far too busy catching up on life to notice the low temperature (except, perhaps, in my feet). Once we crossed the field and got on to a proper path, the going was much easier. Although there was snow in the fields, the well-worn path was frozen hard, with some icy patches, but generally free from further obstacles. It was gorgeous – if I had to live in the urban central belt, this was as good as it got – and it was *very* good. Alan and I had often congratulated ourselves on landing up in Bearsden – still on a train line for easy commuting into Glasgow, but less than an hour from Loch Lomond and nearer still to the Campsies. Lots of countryside, lots of walking opportunities. And now, in the company of my two closest friends, I felt really fortunate.

We walked past the pretty stone cottages at Gartness, but decided not to visit the Pots of Gartness as we weren't too sure of distance or time. Pity, as all those pools with the overhanging birches would be very pretty just now, laced with snow and ice. Anyway, it wasn't the time of year to watch salmon leaping their way upriver to spawn, which is what the Pots were best known for. Instead, we continued past, enjoying the gentle woodland walking. By the time we got to Dumgoyne, the first 5 miles had passed easily but we were looking forward to lunch. I pointed out the Beech Tree Inn and we turned to go inside.

"Doesn't *look* open." Liksi voiced what I was beginning to realise. "No-one about, no cars, and oh, wait – there's a notice here." We crowded round her, peering through frosty clouds of breath to see what it said:

BEECH TREE INN
Closed for refurbishing November – February
Apologies for any inconvenience

"Oh, no, I don't *believe* it!" I stared at the notice, aghast. "I've been banking on this – and looking forward to it all morning!"

"Good one, Eilidh! You've brought us here under false pretences." Fiona was laughing at my expression. "*Now* what do we do? Where's the next eating place? Didn't you say there was a distillery somewhere near here? No, I don't mean for a dram – but they must have a coffee shop?"

"No, 'fraid not – there's only Glengoyne Distillery itself. Actually, there isn't anywhere to eat at all before Milngavie." I felt really bad, not least at the receding image of a pint of something sustaining. "I'm terribly sorry, I should have known this, or at least checked it out. Some expedition leader, me."

"Well, let's see what we've got." Fiona, as always, was the practical one. A rummage in our packs produced a combined contribution of the following delicacies - one flask of coffee, one rather old bar of Kendal mint cake, and one apple of equally uncertain vintage.

"Better than nothing." Liksi laughed as she looked around. "Come on, there's a big flat stone there - picnic table or seat."

We made our way over to the stone, just on the edge of the former railway line which formed the West Highland Way at this stage. Perched uncomfortably on the bank of the path, opposite the glistening and very steep slope of the volcanic plug of Dumgoyne, we laid our offerings out and embarked on our feast with limited enthusiasm – although the two metal cups of coffee were in much demand. This was probably as much to do with the fact that they warmed our hands as anything else – although poor Liksi had to give up after a couple of sips as we didn't have any sugar.

"I don't even *like* Kendal mint cake." I gratefully accepted a second piece after 2 bites of the apple. "Och well, at least we're outdoors and the sun's out. I'll just pretend I'm not half frozen."

"It is lovely here, though. Glad that you ended up in Glasgow?" Liksi, like so many 'townies', probably couldn't imagine anyone actually preferring to live far from city amenities.

"Och, I'm perfectly happy here, but as I get older I do miss the Highlands and wish I could spend more time there. However, the jobs are here so that's that." And Alan, of course.

"What about you, Fiona? Do you miss Aberdeen?" Liksi passed the Kendal mint cake back to Fiona.

"Heavens, no! Aberdeen's not the place it used to be these days. In any case, I don't know anyone there now. I do miss Scotland though sometimes, and wonder if I'll move back up eventually."

"What do you miss?" I asked with interest.

"Oh, I don't know – the people? The – the places? I don't really know – Manchester is home now, but I'm *from* Scotland."

"Well, I'm very glad I live in Edinburgh, but if we don't get a move on I'm going to freeze to death right here and never get back." Liksi started gathering the coffee cups and putting the flask back together. Fiona pocketed the remaining square of mint cake, threw the apple core away and we started on our way again, moving briskly to warm up.

The railway line ended at a small bridge and after that, the path reverted to a more natural winding track, with a few bare skeletons of oak trees dotted about. We skirted round the thickly wooded mound of Dumgoyach, trying not to disturb the cows, who were munching quietly on a bale of hay in the neighbouring field.

"Looks like a tarmac road ahead." Liksi was pointing ahead.

"Yes, pity." I swerved to avoid an icy bit. "It always feels like a cop-out on a walk, somehow. Oh, wait a minute – if you go right you get to the Carbeth Inn."

"An inn? You mean somewhere that sells food and drink? We could have had our lunch there!" Fiona's slightly accusatory voice irked me as, I have to confess, I'd forgotten about the Carbeth.

"Maybe, but it's now almost 2 o'clock and I don't think we'd have lasted all this time without *anything*." I ignored her disbelieving look. "Anyway, it would take us slightly out of our way, and I don't know if we'd want any extra mileage at this stage? We've still got about 5 miles to go."

"Yeah, I think we should press on." Liksi wrapped her scarf more firmly round her neck. "Coffee and cakes in Milngavie?"

This cheery thought saved the day, and we turned left onto the road instead. After half a mile or so we turned right to go back onto a path, with a ramshackle collection of chalets and huts on either side, visible through the bare branches of the trees.

"Where's this?" Liksi was peering at a wooden sign which had been overtaken by lichen. "I can't decide if it's all a mess, or if it's somehow in keeping with the landscape."

"These are the Carbeth huts, where the 'hutters' live." I stopped for a better look. "The first ones were built after the First World War as places to encourage outdoor activities. More sprung up during the Second World War, and evacuees from Clydebank moved there."

"And now?" Liksi was having a good look at one of the buildings. "There's a light in this one."

"Some of them have become permanent homes, and there's a real community there now. There was even a pool known as the Carbeth Lido here at one time, believe it or not, equipped with a rail and a diving board."

"Brr!" Fiona shivered and wrapped her arms round her body. "They must have been hardy in those days. Nice idea though."

We passed Carbeth Loch on the right, and then the larger Craigallion Loch on the left. Both looked very attractive in the crisp winter sunlight, sparkling on the icy edges of the water. Rushes, frozen into unlikely shapes, framed the lochs and the odd wader strutted about, probing half-heartedly into any nooks and crannies below the water. Not the best time for fishing.

As we crossed the road and entered the main part of Mugdock Country Park, it was evident that we were nearing the end of the route. In spite of the chilly air and slowly fading light, dog-walkers abounded, as did families and couples out for a stroll – unencumbered by backpacks.

"Do you know *everyone* here?" asked Fiona suddenly, looking at me strangely.

"No, of course not – what do you mean?" I was puzzled by this. "I've not known anyone we've passed."

"You've said hallo to practically everyone we've met. In fact, you seem to know some of them too, Liksi."

I laughed as I realised what she was getting at. "Fiona! I was only saying hallo - we *speak* to people when we pass them. Don't you do that down south?" It's one of the things I like about walking – you feel you're a member of a large outdoor community, with something essential in common, and a brief 'hallo' acknowledges that.

"'Specially around the west of Scotland." Liksi reminded me. "It's true what they say about it being friendlier over here than in Edinburgh."

"Mm." Fiona looked unconvinced.

"Methinks you need an injection of Caledonian air every so often to boost your Scottishness. Can't have people thinking of you as *English*!" I couldn't resist teasing her.

"No, that would never do." Liksi moved into the left of the path. "Here, there's a couple of guys coming – you need to start practising."

"It's all right," said Fiona hastily. "I'll work it through in time."

I confess to having been very slightly pleased by this exchange. Fiona seemed so successful, so sure of herself, and so confident that it was reassuring to catch her on the wrong foot occasionally. Or did that make me a bad person ...?

We were getting tired by now and the focus became very much on getting to the end. Once we reached the outskirts of Milngavie it wasn't long before we skirted the library and its decidedly unappealing concrete surroundings. Even the pond looked sad and overgrown. Shortly afterwards, we were walking up the steps to the precinct.

"Look, there's the obelisk over there. Where most normal people would have *started* the walk!" I led them over so that we could get the obligatory photo in front of the granite monolith. "Well done, ladies – we made it. Our first walk!"

Genteel Milngavie was resigned to having its pedestrian areas tramped on by muddy boots en route to the WHW, although I'm not sure the Tea Cosy was quite so at ease with this type of customer. We felt rather self-conscious as we piled our rucksacks in the corner and peeled off a couple of layers of sweaty jackets and fleeces, receiving some condescending smiles from some of the well-dressed elderly ladies. However, the sight of the cakes banished all these thoughts and we were soon enjoying our first real food since breakfast.

"And you know something," I said in between mouthfuls, "I don't feel too bad at all. My feet're a bit sore, and I'm pretty whacked, but that's it. I thought you two might run rings round me."

"Not at all." Liksi, as always, kindly re-assuring. "Haven't really done this kind of walking before, so I'm tired too."

"Me too." Well, maybe, but Fiona hadn't shown *any* signs of fatigue or discomfort as far as I could see. "So, are we up for this again? What's the next stage?"

We agreed to tackle Drymen to Rowardennan some time during the summer. It was difficult to do more than one day's walking at a time, unless we used holidays, but that wasn't suitable for the others and their children, and I guess Alan wouldn't be too happy if I started using up holidays without him either.

Later on, over curry at the Ashoka, that warm, post-exercise feeling of contentment and well-being settled over me.

"Can I just say," I stopped to put my glass down, "it is *so* much better to have feet sore from this kind of walking, than from tramping round shops."

There was a loud snort from Liksi. "Bet you weren't thinking that when you fell in the bog ..."

"I didn't *fall*, I just – oh, I give up ..."

Chapter 3 – West Highland Way 2 (June 2005) - Liksi

This 14-mile stretch of the West Highland Way is from Rowardennan to Drymen. The route follows the eastern shore of Loch Lomond, along rough paths above the water, or alongside the road, then moves inland to skirt the side of Conic Hill as it heads towards the village of Drymen.

"Rowardennan to Drymen? If you were going to do the West Highland Way backwards *properly*, you'd start at Fort William. Guess you amateurs haven't been able to work that out."

"Oh, Pete, it doesn't *matter*! I don't care where we walk, it's just really good to get out in the fresh air. Anyway, the main point is to see each other – *anywhere*." It was Eilidh who had decided that our next walk would be another chunk of the WHW, and I was happy to go along with doing it any which way.

"Don't know why you think so much of those two anyway – although I suppose Fiona's OK."

Pete's barbs came so often that they'd lost their ability to hurt. It was only really when we were in company that I found it upsetting, weighing up whether or not to challenge him. I hated confrontation, but being constantly put down wasn't great either. He had point-blank refused to take Julie to her dancing competition in Glasgow tonight, probably just to make my life difficult more than anything else. I'd thought at one stage that I'd have had to drive her back to Edinburgh, and miss the Friday night in Glasgow with the others. However, having phoned around I managed to arrange a lift home for her with Shona's mum and she was invited to stay the night there, so at least I'd be able to join the others later on.

As I waited in the Kelvin Hall for my daughter to perform, I mused over how my life had turned out. I'd been very happy in London - a promising job, great social life, lots of opportunities to play hockey and squash – and had fully expected to spend the rest of my life there. Then along came Pete, with his casual good looks and easy charm, turning up in the pub after a hockey tournament run by my local club. We discovered a shared love of hockey, and had both spent time working in Australia, and that was all it took. Six months later, when he announced that his company was moving him to Edinburgh, but that he wanted me to go with him as his wife, I accepted immediately. These days, I found myself wondering more and more how different things might have been if I'd refused.

Shaking myself out of this train of thought, I concentrated on Julie's performance, wondering as always how I could've produced such a graceful child. Hugging her tightly afterwards, I reluctantly handed her over to Shona's mum, before driving up Crow Road and the Switchback to Eilidh's. The ever-present guilt at leaving my children – Joe was also staying with friends – was compensated by the prospect of a couple of days of freedom. Eilidh and Alan were always good hosts, and their large house was quirky and comfortable.

Alan met me at the door with a "Oh, no, no' another one – can a man no' get any peace on a Friday night?" and then swept me into a bone-crushing bearhug. "Good to see you again. Still some curry left, come on in before these gannets polish it off." He herded me into the dining room, where Eilidh and Fiona were sitting over the remains of their meal.

"How'd the competition go?" Eilidh passed a generous helping of curry my way.

"Good thanks; two second places."

"That's great, good for her. How're Nathan and Jack – are they sporty too?" Eilidh turned to Fiona.

"Jack's football daft, but enthusiastic rather than skilled.

And Nathan, he doesn't seem to be interested in anything much these days." I glanced at her sharply - Nathan had always been a rather diffident child, and I got the impression that Fiona found it difficult to talk about him sometimes.

"I hope Jack's keeping an eye on the Scottish results too." Alan put another spoonful of curry onto his plate. "Or have you turned these two into wee Sassenachs by now?"

"Ha ha – no chance. Football? I've given up trying to work it all out."

"Aye, it takes a skilled brain to do that – not for you girls at all – hey!" Alan yelped as he dodged a well-aimed coaster from Eilidh.

"Skill? Football? Football is for those who don't have the brains to use them elsewhere." Eilidh threw her husband a mock-scornful look. "It's also a convenient excuse when there's chores to be done ..."

"Och, here we go again – re-run of the battle of Culloden – you've no idea what it's like being married to a Highlander." Alan tried – and failed – to look put-upon as he made a big show of getting up and collecting the dishes.

"You don't know how lucky you are." Eilidh grabbed the coaster before it disappeared under the sofa.

I envied them their gentle banter. Although they were both liable to flare up on occasion, the flares were quickly dimmed and they were obviously very fond of each other. Their easy, companionable relationship made their home so welcoming that it was a real haven at times.

The next morning was more or less a replay of the last time we met up, with Alan lavishly throwing insults about and complaining about his house being over-run with harpies.

"For Christ's sake." He fiddled impatiently with the car keys. "Can none of you speak below the threshold of pain? It's like Act 1 Scene 1 of Macbeth in here. Just a pity it's *my* house that's the blasted heath."

"Maybe you should remember what happened to Macbeth." Eilidh warned him as we got all our stuff together and loaded it into the car.

In spite of his rants, Alan had offered to drive us to Rowardennan. The relatively good road from Drymen and through Balmaha became narrower and twistier at a sharp right bend as it wound its way round the loch, through dense woods of oak and birch. As we got out of the car, hordes of midges enveloped us, quickly making their presence felt on any exposed skin. We grabbed our rucksacks and slammed the boot shut, and Alan quickly headed off. These bloody insects ruined tourism in Scotland for some people – thank God we didn't see many of them in Edinburgh. Although, come to think of it, they might be useful during the Festival …

"Why does something bad happen whenever Alan leaves us?" I joined Fiona in a manic dance intended to drive off the miserable biters, while slathering on something intended to repel them but getting most of it (and them) in my eyes. "It was Eilidh and the bog the last time."

"I'd rather have the bog again," said Eilidh with feeling, zipping up her jacket to her neck and pulling the cords of her hood so that as little of her face as possible was exposed. "Come on, we need to move."

We set off on the pleasant stretch between Rowardennan and Drymen, which follows Loch Lomond for the first half, then moves inland towards Drymen. Ben Lomond loomed above us on the left from its 3,195 ft summit, looking tempting but we'd have to leave it for another time. Fourteen miles were quite enough without adding a Munro. It was warm but airless and rather unpleasant at the beginning, but once we were on the move and a slight breeze from the loch started up, our fiendish insect companions dispersed and we started to enjoy ourselves.

"New boots, Eilidh?" I was asking the obvious, really –

they looked as if they'd just come out of the box.

"Uh-huh. I've had them on for a couple of short walks recently, but this is their first real test. I hope they're going to be OK."

I'd bought my own boots in a children's department somewhere. Being a size 3, I sometimes found really good bargains and anyway I'd never seen the sense in buying expensive things if I didn't have to. It gave Pete something less to moan about if I didn't spend money 'wastefully'. Funny how that activity seemed not to apply to him ...

We made good progress through the dense shrubs and trees of Ross and Sallochy Woods, scrambling up and down over tree roots and taking care where the rocks dropped down to the water. One of the shingle shores looked just too inviting, and as no-one else had commandeered it yet we stopped for an early lunch. It was very muggy, and the surrounding hilltops weren't as clear as they could be, but they were still comfortingly *there*. The water lapped peacefully at our feet, rolling its way over the stones, but at this time of year you could also hear the low growl of the traffic on the other side of the loch, and the deeper roar of outboard motors and jet-skis. We could see across to the purple slopes of Glen Luss, and as I ate my cheese and ham roll, I couldn't help feeling a bit smug that we were on the quieter side of the Loch.

"So, Liksi, how's the IT department going these days?" Fiona leaned back on her elbows.

"Oh – OK, I guess." I was abruptly brought back to the world of work. "I'm still the only female there, and the guys are only interested in their equipment and have no social skills at all. I really, really hope that no-one would describe me as a typical technician, ever."

"What's your job title, Liksi?" asked Eilidh through a mouthful of sandwich.

"I'm just the Art Department's technician. Although if

they're short in another department, I get called in. Jack of All, I suppose."

"Every technician I've worked with thinks he or she is a technical genius." Fiona shuffled to get more comfortable. "They work in the bowels of the building, a nice safe cave where they can escape from the real world. They don't speak unless they have to. Just like Liksi, really." Fiona swerved out of reach of my half-hearted swipe with the map.

"Don't *dare*! Most of the ones I know are off their heads." I put the map back safely in my rucksack. "One of them in my place has a collection of false teeth in his drawer – I kid you not – and that's not the worst example."

"Eh? You're kidding? *Why?*" Eilidh looked at me incredulously, and I shrugged.

"Tell me about it." Fiona shrugged. "Problem is, they like being considered essential to the operation of the place, and that gives them an inflated sense of their own worth. They fix the simplest things with great fuss and secrecy so their expertise is admired – they're scared that their skills will no longer be acknowledged or required."

I winced at the thought that Fiona might think I shared these characteristics too, so blurted out, "There's a team leader post coming up soon, for the departmental technicians. I just wonder if I should have a go at it." I surprised even myself by suggesting this – I quite liked my busy and undemanding job but was becoming increasingly aware that I should move on or I might become one of these extreme caricatures myself. Eilidh, who'd been yawning and looking a bit spaced out, suddenly appeared interested again.

"Of *course* you should." Fiona turned to me with enthusiasm. "You'd be great at it, and anyway you'd be unlikely to stay there for too long – it should be a stepping stone to other things. You don't need to stay in further education all your life."

I liked her confidence, but I wasn't going to take anything

for granted. Anyway, as long as it paid the bills, my job wasn't the central thing in my life. I'd never been ambitious – in fact, along with my parents I still sometimes marvelled at the realisation that I'd actually managed to get a degree – and was much more concerned with my children, and my hockey. At one stage Pete had featured in this list too.

"Right, enough chat – up you get!" Fiona was never one for losing time, and anyway, the midges had found us again and were making their presence felt. We zipped up jackets, and waved our arms around as we set off, and it wasn't long before we were free of them again.

"This is so different from the first part of the walk that we did last time." I looked round at the birches and oaks, with their full summer leaves. "It's good to see the loch today, and the woods – last time it was country park, farmland, old railway line and rivers. Oh, and closed pubs."

"No need to remind me, thank you." Eilidh's smile belied her clipped response. "I can promise you an open establishment for the next stop – definitely."

"We'll believe it when we see it. By the way, is your leg OK, Eilidh?" Fiona was looking at her curiously. "You seem to be limping."

"My knee's a wee bit sore." Eilidh looked a bit embarrassed. "I don't know why, but I'll be fine, honestly."

"Can go more slowly if you want?" I ignored the hint of exasperation on Fiona's face. Actually, I was pretty sure Eilidh would get on better if she lost a bit of weight – she was by far the heftiest, and the most unfit, of the three of us. "Why don't you go in front for a while?"

Eilidh took the lead for the next section, moving slowly through more woodland but also up and down steep gnarled paths, culminating in a viewpoint called Craigie Fort, where we stopped to gaze over Inchcailloch Island and give Eilidh a rest.

"You can get a boat out there during the summer

months." Eilidh pointed to the island. "They take you over, leave you for an hour or so, and then bring you back. It's actually a really nice way to spend a leisurely afternoon, and have a picnic."

The island looked deserted and rather small, but Eilidh assured us that it was an interesting spot. "It's also on the Highland Boundary faultline – it marks the line between the Highlands and the Lowlands," she added.

"We should get a better view as we go up the side of Conic Hill." Fiona was looking up at the hills behind us. "We can't be far off there now."

"Beer stop first," said Eilidh firmly. "I promised you a pub this time, and the Oaktree Inn is in Balmaha – just down there."

"I guess a *quick* half pint wouldn't hurt." Fiona laughed. "I could murder a drink."

The Oaktree Inn proved to be a very pleasant spot right enough, and I sighed happily as we settled down with our drinks at an outside table and rested our feet. "This is the life!"

"Aye, it's good to mix exercise with pleasure." Eilidh rubbed her knee with relief.

"What, you mean walking *isn't* pleasurable?" I couldn't resist teasing her. "So remind me, why are we walking 14 miles to get to a couple of pubs? Assuming we do find an open one in Drymen at the end?"

"Good question." Eilidh looked as if she could have stayed there happily all day. "Guess we're a bit mad. Or deluded. Or something. At least we're over halfway there now – though we'll be moving up to higher ground now."

We finished our drinks and set off again, crossing the road and walking through the car park to re-connect with the official route. The path took us through woodland which ended at a gate, through which there was open moorland and a steep climb, although the WHW did not officially include the actual summit of Conic Hill. As we reached the spot where the path split to go to the summit, Fiona and I waited for Eilidh.

"Sorry." She grimaced slightly as she caught up with us. "This knee is giving me gyp. Thank goodness we don't need to go up to the summit."

I caught Fiona's eye and she said, "Well, I'm going up – Liksi, are you game?"

I was, and Eilidh seemed happy enough to sit it out and nurse her knee. She said she'd been up to the top recently, so didn't feel she was missing anything. Having said that, for me the short climb to the summit was well worth it, giving us by far the best view we'd had all day. The long expanse of water stretched out in both directions, and straight down from us we could see the islands spaced out along the width of the water. I guess that was probably the fault line that Eilidh'd mentioned. The climb was obviously a popular place for a summer stroll, and several clumps of walkers were settled down with a picnic, or posing for photos with a scenic backdrop.

We didn't stay long though, and jogged down to pick up Eilidh, who got to her feet reluctantly. We'd a steady walk down the side of Conic Hill now, through open moorland and bracken and then into more woods. In spite of the easy walking, Eilidh began to trail further and further behind, and I called ahead to Fiona to wait for her.

"Knee still bad?" Fiona made an attempt to be sympathetic.

"Aye, but it's my ankles that are hurting now – these boots are chafing them. I need to take them off and have a look." The next minute she was sitting down in the middle of the track, hauling off her boots, rolling down her socks and investigating the damage. Her lower calves were red and fiery, and must've been pretty sore.

"It's these new boots." She ran her hand over her shin. "I

did try and wear them in, but I guess not enough. I'm OK, honestly – but I'm not putting these bloody things on again." As we looked rather incredulously at her, she got to her feet and announced, "I can walk in my socks – we're almost in Drymen now."

And so she did. With a gait that John Wayne would've been proud of, and her boots tied on to her rucksack, she managed to cover the last 2 miles in her socks. Slowly, but determinedly. I felt so sorry for her, as she was obviously in quite a lot of discomfort, but she made it down into the village – and cheered when we saw the welcome sight of the Clachan pub ahead. Stumbling inside, she made for the nearest free table and collapsed into the corner seat, ignoring the amused looks she got from some of the regulars.

"I'll get the drinks." I grinned at her. "Don't think you're capable of standing at the bar somehow!"

"You're dead right – but a pint of whatever the guest beer is might revive me. Oh yes please, one of these too. Thanks, Fiona." She accepted Fiona's offer of a cigarette, and lit up and inhaled with obvious enjoyment. Nasty habit – at least they didn't seem to indulge often.

"Let's have a proper look." Fiona bent down as I came back with the drinks, and Eilidh obediently held up one leg. "It looks like either the boots are too small, or you've laced them up too tightly."

"Try leaving the top loops unlaced – in fact, see if you do it this way it allows a bit more 'give'." I showed her mine. "Could also try asking a cobbler to stretch them a bit."

"Thanks, guys, I'll bear all that in mind before the next time. It was too good to be true to begin with – they were SO comfy – but at least I don't seem to have any blisters."

I was relieved to see Eilidh looking a lot less miserable as we relaxed and enjoyed our drinks. I'd been worried that her boot problem would put her off future walks – just as I was getting into the way of walking, and really enjoying what we'd done so far. These weekends away were also a wonderful opportunity to escape Pete's hurtful comments for a while. Any personal comments in this company took the form of gentle teasing, or genuine interest or concern. How different from everyday life at home; how much I savoured being able to be myself with these two, instead of having to build a protective force field around me.

And, as Alan barged into the pub in his usual ebullient form to collect us, mumbling something about 'toil and trouble', how much I wished ... oh, God, what exactly *was* I wishing for?

Chapter 4 – Helvellyn (June 2007) - Fiona

Helvellyn in the Lake District is England's second-highest mountain at 3,117 ft. This is a circular route of approximately 10 miles, starting and finishing in the village of Glenridding. It includes the Red Tarn, the ridges of Swirral Edge and Striding Edge, and the village of Patterdale. The ridges make this quite a challenging climb.

Well, we'd certainly have plenty to talk about this time, I mused as I turned into the parking area outside Penrith railway station to pick up the other two. In spite of all our good intentions, our lives had caught up with themselves and 2006 had come and gone without us managing to meet up for a walk at all. Liksi and I had bumped into each other briefly at a Cisco conference in Birmingham, but hadn't had the chance to exchange more than a few words. She'd got her promotion to team leader (no surprise), I'd been busy with all the travelling involved in my secondment, and Eilidh had been away with the college a couple of times too, as well as enjoying her usual exotic holidays with Alan.

It was maybe just as well – I really didn't want to get into a conversation which mentioned Pete. In fact, just thinking about him made me shudder. The night Eilidh and I had stayed at Liksi's, I'd got up to go to the loo and found Pete lurking about when I came out. He'd grabbed hold of me as I passed and tried to kiss me – what on *earth* had he thought he was playing at? I didn't even feel like talking to Eilidh about it – it was so, so *sleazy*. Part of me wanted to confront Liksi with the evidence of what an absolute shit she'd married, in the vague hope she'd kick him out; part of me hoped she'd never know and could continue in blissful ignorance.

We'd wanted to do the next bit of the West Highland Way, but we all felt that we'd need to stay overnight somewhere next time, and the logistics of doing that over a weekend or long weekend were tricky – especially as Eilidh was limited to college holidays. I should've been more on top of things and suggested a date soon after the last meeting, but got waylaid by work. Anyway, we'd decided to shelve the WHW for the time being, and have a go at the Lake District peaks instead – the others felt that it was only fair that I didn't have to do the bulk of the travelling each time.

It was great to see them again – both looking well, and in good form. I stuffed all their gear into the boot and drove down through Pooley Bridge, then along the side of Ullswater towards Glenridding.

I'd wanted to stay as near as possible to the beginning of the walk tomorrow, so we checked in at the Fairlight Guest House in Glenridding. Somehow, without even discussing it, we all knew that Eilidh and I'd share the double, giving Liksi her own room. Even after a gap of over 20 years, now that we'd got together again we were prepared to accommodate each other's foibles without question. The old cliché relating to a comfortable pair of slippers was not far wrong - if only *all* relationships could be so cosy.

"What's Olly up to this weekend, Fiona?" As if on cue, Eilidh raised her head from sorting through her rucksack. "Does he mind you deserting him again?"

"Oh, he's down in London – he's been there for the last couple of weeks actually." I said this airily, fully aware of the effect it was likely to have. Eilidh looked at me with concern.

"It's OK, we both like the space. I don't ask what he gets up to down there, and he doesn't ask me. Suits us both." Actually, I was pretty sure Olly had had affairs over the years, but as long as he was around when I needed him, or more importantly when the children did, that was fine with me.

"Sounds a great arrangement to me." Liksi smiled rather

sadly. "Wish Pete could get regular breaks away." Poor Liksi, I don't know how she put up with him. The difference with us was, I really, really *liked* Olly. Seems a strange thing to say about your husband, but there it was.

I was spared further questioning, as everyone was keen to get back outside. It was a glorious evening, and it wasn't long before we found ourselves in front of the Inn on the Lake, just a few yards back up the main road.

"Tables outside, great." Liksi made a beeline for one of them. "Not many chances to sit outside in Edinburgh at this time of year." Eilidh and Liksi seemed to view England as a foreign country sometimes – conveniently forgetting that they'd both spent the best part of 5 or so years in London.

We settled down with our drinks and I brought out a pack of 10 Benson & Hedges which I'd bought specially.

"Mmm." Eilidh lit one, breathed in deeply then exhaled appreciatively, throwing her head back. "This's a rare treat – we can't do this in pubs in Scotland now."

"Oh, yes, your ban came into place last year, didn't it? Better make the most of it – we won't be able to do this south of the border either, from next month. Well, not *inside* pubs or restaurants, anyway."

"Contrary to current appearances, I'm all in favour of the ban, and proud of Scotland for getting in before England. Typical that only the Scottish Tories opposed it." Eilidh never missed an opportunity to deliver a political point. "This is just a wee indulgence of ours, isn't it, Fiona?"

"Yip, absolutely." I grinned conspiratorially at her, whilst Liksi shook her head in mock despair.

"Och well, the beer's so good down here that anything else is secondary anyway." Eilidh polished off her pint of Marston's with relish. "I *really* envy you that."

"Talking of which – food." I knew if we didn't move now, we'd probably end up drinking too much. "The Travellers Rest gets good reviews for hearty walkers' fare, and it's just up that hill there so we might even get a view of the lake. Good practice for tomorrow. Ready?"

They didn't need a second telling, and in spite of the gradient it wasn't long before we were seated at the wooden tables outside the Travellers Rest, enjoying the views as well as the food and drink. Eilidh was reading bits out of her walks book – I think she felt she had to check the literature in case we attempted anything she felt was foolhardy.

"Have you guys ever heard of a "Furth Munro"?" she asked suddenly. When we looked at her blankly she continued, "Apparently it's a UK peak of 3,000 ft or more *outside* Scotland. Well, well, you learn something every day."

"So, guess Helvellyn is a Furth Munro then?" Liksi leaned over to read the page.

"Yes, and apparently it's also a Birkett, Historic County Top, Wainwright, Marilyn, Nuttall and a Hewitt. A Birkett is a –"

"For heaven's sake, Eilidh!" I couldn't help laughing. "If you start on all of those we'll be here all night."

"Just trying to educate you." Eilidh put on her offended look. "OK, let's see what it says about the best route."

"Look, that's the way we go up tomorrow." I pre-empted her by pointing up the hill behind us. Even on this warm June evening, the top of the mountain was shrouded in a wispy blanket of mist.

"It says here that the route from Thirlmere is easier than the one from Glenridding." Eilidh frowned.

"Yes, but this is THE one to do, as it takes in Striding Edge and Swirral Edge in a horseshoe."

Eilidh looked dubiously at me. "I guess that means that the one from here is a harder one, then?" Taking my smile for an answer, she said, "Huh. It sounds like something out of an Alan Garner novel. Hope it won't be quite as exciting as that ..."

"Oh, did you read him too? *The Weirdstone of Brisingamen*? Great books, loved them as a kid – weren't they set down your way, Fiona? Alderley Edge?" Liksi turned round to look up at the ridges. "Yeah, I see what you mean." Even in the bright weather, they still looked quite challenging. We stayed outside with our drinks, watching the peaks dimming as the dusk gathered round them, and only when it became too dark to see them at all, did we head back to the guesthouse.

The next morning was glorious, when we set off after breakfast and followed the route out of Glenridding and onto a farm track. It didn't take long for a steep incline to kick in, and I set off at a good pace, enjoying the sense of well-being from the stiff exercise. *This* was why I loved being in the mountains. Liksi was just behind me, but after a short while we stopped at a stile to let Eilidh catch up. She stopped, panting, and gasped out, "Far too hot. Need to take some clothes off. What did you two have for breakfast – rocket fuel?" Tearing off her jacket and then her sweatshirt, she gulped down some water and joined us in looking back over Glenridding and the long glistening strip of Ullswater.

"How're your boots now, Eilidh?" Liksi looked down at them. "I'll never forget you struggling into Drymen in your socks last time."

"Neither will I, I can assure you." Eilidh shook her head at the memory. "I think they're fine – I lace them up the way you showed me, and I've given them a few airings. Don't worry – I won't be doing that again in a hurry. I was just a bit hot just now. Any chance of going a *bit* more slowly?"

Liksi tried to slow the pace down, but we soon got engrossed in talking about work, and Eilidh fell steadily behind. After a while we stopped to wait for her at the top of a rise.

"Anyway, tell me." I turned to Liksi. "How're you getting on with the team leader post now?"

"Well, glad I went for it as I'd have gone mad if I'd stayed doing what I was doing for much longer. As it is, everyone around me is mad instead, and I'm the sane one trying to oversee all their peculiarities."

"I know, techies are a strange breed. When I go to a conference and look around me, I think 'am I really one of these people?'" If I thought about the answer for too long I think I'd go mad too.

As our red-faced and breathless friend drew level with us, we all sat down – or collapsed, in Eilidh's case – on a strategically-positioned boulder.

"So what've you two been talking about?" Eilidh looked at each of us in turn, as she wiped her sweaty face with her buff. "Work? The intriguing, other-world of technology?"

"Well, yeah." Liksi had a mischievous smile on her face. "In fact, we need your opinion on a *very* important point – would you say that we were typical techies?"

Eilidh turned to look at us suspiciously. "D'you mean, d'you *look* like techies, or d'you *act* like them?" Good question.

"Both," we said in unison, laughing.

"Well, maybe. You've a certain bohemian style of dress, Liksi, which *might* qualify, but your new glasses make you look *very* bookish – intelligent, I mean." Liksi gave her a questioning look, frowning slightly. "Fiona, you're too much of a sharp dresser – most technicians I know go around in black T-shirts and ripped jeans."

"Unique." I tried not to look smug. "We're all unique."

"Of course, of course! But you share one thing – you both speak in another language. I don't know what you're talking about half the time. Cisco, networking, configurations – it's another world to me. Is that normal?"

"Probably," admitted Liksi, "if that recent conference was anything to go by. You know, I wish I actually got a chance to be bookish at work sometimes. There's always something new to learn, and never enough time or space to actually sit down and study something. It seems just now that work is *all* about systems, networking and firefighting."

"Yip, I know what you mean. At least I'm getting a chance to travel while looking at other systems, so it's not so bad."

"Secondment seems to have lasted a long time?" Liksi looked up from tying her shoelace.

"S'pose it has; sometimes I think they've forgotten me." And I had no complaints about that, at all. "Seriously though, I think my Slovenia trip at the end of this year might be the last one. Then I'll have to look for something else at home. I couldn't bear going back to what I had." Dead right – the last thing I wanted was to go back into a bog-standard technician job. I don't know how Liksi could stand it.

"Right, I've recovered. I'm off - going to get a headstart." Eilidh broke in as she stood up suddenly. "You two can catch up with me for a change – it won't take you long, I'm sure."

We followed her up and stopped again when we reached the Hole in the Wall. This gap in a long drystone wall was bridged by a stile; once over we could see that it served as a hub for a myriad of paths leading to the summit of mighty Helvellyn, which was now displayed before us in all its glory. Its forbidding and striking horseshoe ridges surrounded a dip, which contained the Red Tarn.

"I remember this now." Eilidh reached out to steady herself as she set both feet on the ground again. "Alan and I climbed up here years ago, but we didn't get further than the tarn there, as we landed up in a bog and it was too icy to continue any further."

"You seem to make a habit of falling into icy bogs when Alan's around?" Liksi laughed as she pulled herself up the wooden up-and-over ladder. Once on the ground on the other side, she held out her hand for Eilidh's rucksack while she climbed over after her.

"Ha ha. Thanks." She rested with her back to the stone wall to get a better look at what was ahead. "Impressive, isn't it? Almost a perfect circular ridge. Fierce, mind you." It was indeed. From this angle, the summit itself seemed less important than the picture-book setting of the small tarn, almost encircled by reddish slopes topped with jagged spurs and outcrops. Most people seemed to be moving in a clockwise direction over the two ridges, but having had a look at the map I felt we should do things differently.

"Swirral Edge – that one there," I pointed to the less fearsome ridge, "is easier than Striding Edge. If we go round anti-clockwise over Swirral first, we can have a rest at the summit, before tackling Striding Edge on the way down, and we can come back via Patterdale."

"Well, OK, but Striding looks a bit dangerous to me. Can't we just go up Swirral and back the same way?" Eilidh had her hand up to shield her eyes from the sun.

"No, no – if we've come all the way up here, we need to do Helvellyn properly. Wouldn't want to miss out on the fun bit!" I grinned at Eilidh, knowing that she was nervous but I was determined not to miss the opportunity to tackle both ridges.

We continued on up and began the scramble over Swirral. It was arduous, but not difficult, although Eilidh obviously found it quite challenging. She was very careful where she put her feet, and she just wasn't as supple as Liksi and I. I found it pretty straightforward really, enjoying the challenge of clambering over the boulders. The momentum propelled me on, and I soon reached the summit, where I sat on a relatively smooth boulder and watched the other two coming up. Liksi was doing fine, but she would stop and wait for Eilidh to catch up every so often, and I could see them admiring the view each time. It was certainly breathtaking, and although there was a slight haze, it seemed as if the whole of the Lake District was on show. The length of

Ullswater was revealed, snaking through the valley with Glenridding nestled near the bottom. Thirlmere, also a long thin stretch of water, was to the left, with the wider Derwentwater just below the town of Keswick. Further still was the sea, and on a day like this it just felt so good to be here. I felt like a queen surveying her realm.

Eilidh's red and sweaty face finally appeared over the ridge, with Liksi just behind her – probably for reassurance. After a short rest while they got their breath back, I joined them and we kept going till we got to the cairn, which Eilidh hugged reverently before leaning against it and looking round at the glorious vista.

"Great views." She ran her fingers though her curls to feel some cooling air. "D'you remember the picture we've got in our lounge? The big one over the sofa? It's of Ullswater, by Heaton Cooper. Good to see the real thing again."

"Yeah, that's a great painting. It's some lake, isn't it? *Almost* as good as our home-grown ones!" Liksi laughed as she looked around with awe.

"Ullswater is the second largest lake in England – well, in the Lake District anyway. It inspired Wordsworth to write his daffodils poem, so you need to appreciate it, you Philistine." I shook my head at her.

"Argh. Please don't mention Wordsworth. I had to study him at Uni, along with Pope, and Donne, and heaven knows who else. Put me off poetry for life." Eilidh made a face. Although she was the only one who had undertaken an Arts degree, all three of us had always been great readers, but none of us were fans of poetry.

"Anyway, it's worth the pain – I think." She led us to the edge of the plateau where we'd a well-earned stop for lunch. Eilidh and Liksi made short work of their sandwiches, while I nibbled on my nut and yoghurt health bars. We were sitting there happily, legs dangling over the edge and looking back over the route we'd come, when we became uncomfortably aware of being in a cloud of small black flies.

"Yuch!" Liksi frantically tried to swat the little beasts away with no success whatsoever. "Thought you only got midges in Scotland! Want my money back!"

By this time we were all on our feet, making a futile attempt to ward off the attack. Midges or flies, I didn't care – the original invaders seemed to have called in reinforcements, and it was thoroughly unpleasant.

"We're going to have to keep going." I stuffed everything back into my rucksack as quickly as possible. "They're just not going to go away." We weren't the only ones picked out for special treatment – the summit plateau was full of little groups of walkers who'd hoped to have a pleasant picnic to recover from the climb and were getting to their feet in a hurry, flapping towels or T-shirts around trying to fend off the clouds of assailants.

"Wee buggers, I hate them! Oh my God – are we supposed to go down there?" Eilidh gazed in horror at the jagged spikes of Striding Edge before us. "Surely that's for *experienced* climbers?"

"It's OK, we'll stay with you and you'll be fine." Liksi tried to re-assure her. "We'll take it slowly." She led us down the first, very steep, descent over the boulders to the saddle before the start of Striding Edge.

Thankfully, the flies soon deserted us, as we certainly didn't have hands free for fending them off. After that, I overtook them and checked out the path that led down the side of the ridge, just in case it was any easier, but I didn't like the look of it either – it was narrow in places and there was too much of a drop. So we headed over the top, giving Eilidh a hand from time to time. She could actually do it perfectly well, it was just that she was lacking in confidence. Even I had to admit – to myself – that it was hard going. You couldn't take your eyes off the trail for one minute, and had to think carefully about every step. This must be a nightmare – or the height of stupidity – in misty or windy weather. In fact, as we approached the end of Striding Edge there was a sobering memorial overlooking yet another sheer drop. A white metal plaque on top of a black plinth proclaimed:

> '*In memory of Robert Dixon of Rooking, Patterdale who was killed on this spot on the 27th day of November 1858 following the Patterdale Foxhounds*'.

As we looked at it sombrely, Eilidh snorted. "Serves him right for chasing foxes. Nasty way to go, though."

"Absolutely – but we made it. Look – dead easy now." Liksi was pointing down towards Glenridding.

"Yes, but we're going down via Patterdale – makes more of a circular walk." I pointed over to the right. I was determined to get as much mileage as possible out of the day.

"But doesn't that make it longer?" Eilidh queried. "Liksi raised my hopes there."

"Maybe very slightly longer, but really, there's not much in it. We could always have a drink in Patterdale before the last bit along the road to Glenridding." Eilidh gave me a look that showed she didn't quite believe me, but she didn't make a fuss, and began to plod downhill. Liksi tried to hold back for her, but the momentum carried her down and we waited for Eilidh at Grisedale Bridge, just before Patterdale.

"I'm sorry." Eilidh winced as she rubbed her knee. "I honestly couldn't go any faster. You two were like bloody fell runners while I was doing a crab impersonation. It's no fun, this. If it's not boots, it's knees."

"But you made it, Eilidh – that's the main thing." Liksi looked round at the surrounding buildings of the small hamlet. "What about this pub – looks good with everyone sitting outside?"

It sure did, and we were soon sitting with brimming

glasses at the wooden tables. Liksi had her summer drink, ie a shandy, which was the only drink I'd seen her with other than red wine. Eilidh was doing her best to revive her knee with a pint of Wainwright's, and I bowed to her superior knowledge and joined her with a half pint.

"What's wrong with your knee, Eilidh?" asked Liksi. "Have you had problems before?"

"Not really. It wasn't really a problem till we started coming down, and then it was agony at times. I guess I'm just not as fit as I should be, and I really must lose some weight. I can't keep holding you two back."

"Don't mind in the least." Liksi was quick to reply, although I was glad she didn't look at me for agreement. "Gives us a chance to talk about IT stuff without you falling asleep listening to us."

"True; there's always a bright side to things. Now, if you two would like another drink here's a tenner, if one of you can go up and get them. I need to conserve my energy for the walk home." She slouched back against the chair, wiping down her face with the buff she'd had round her neck.

We took her up on her offer, savouring our drinks with that warm and satisfying post-walk feeling. It'd been a good day. It would've been easy to stay there, having another drink and even an early meal, but I was glad when Liksi suggested that it would be more sensible to walk – or hobble – the 1.5 miles back to Glenridding rather than leave it till later. We were all pretty weary by the time we got back to the hotel and took our time to peel off boots and sweaty T-shirts, and to relax while waiting our turn for the shower.

Once we were presentable again, we trekked up the hill to the Travellers Rest for another substantial meal – and for Eilidh and I, a last chance to indulge in our decadent addiction in an English pub, as we watched the sun going down at the end of a glorious day.

Chapter 5 – Skiddaw (January 2008) - Eilidh

Skiddaw, at 3,054 ft, is the third highest mountain in England (although there are other slightly higher peaks in the Scafell Pike massif). It is a relatively easy climb from Keswick, following the Jenkin Hill Bridleway; the distance is approximately 10.5 miles.

"I suppose that if this weather keeps up, at least we could find a pub to keep dry in, as I don't suppose the hostel will let us in during the day." From the back seat of the car, I peered gloomily through rain-lashed windows as we drove from Penrith station to Keswick.

I'd had my reservations about Fiona's choice of accommodation for this trip. For some years now she'd been hostelling with Olly (occasionally) and the kids, and was full of praise for the whole thing. It seemed a bit incongruous to me – Fiona, with her smart clothes and comfortable lifestyle, an advocate of youth hostels?

She glanced at me with amusement in her windscreen mirror. "Plenty of good pubs around, certainly, but no problem getting into the hostel. Are you thinking back to the old days again? I keep telling you, there've been lots of changes since then."

"Mind you." I perked up at a thought. "I guess I'm still in the *youth*ful category, being still in my 40's. Not like you two." Liksi and Fiona had celebrated their 50ths last year, whilst mine wasn't till July.

"Ha. Not even a full year between us, so don't start!" Liksi's grin belied her mock indignation.

"Well, I can assure you that this is an impressive hostel." Fiona parked on the road, a short distance up from the hostel sign. "Anyway, we won't *be* spending all our time in pubs. We're here to *walk*, Eilidh, remember? And the forecast's fine for tomorrow."

Pulling on jackets and hoods before getting out of the car, I was still unconvinced. The hostel was located right by the river, with only a wall and paved walkway separating them. We crossed the bridge and walked down the steps to the walkway, juggling rucksacks with trying to avoid the rain and wind. I looked at the swollen river with concern as it rushed angrily along below us, swirling over hidden obstacles, and forcing its way up the grassy bank.

"It's almost up to the level of the path." I shouted above the roar of the elements, as I pulled my jacket even more tightly round my neck - as if that would protect me from anything. "If it keeps raining like this we'll have to swim to get out in the morning."

"Eilidh, for heaven's sake! It'll be fine." Fiona pushed open the hostel door and we stumbled thankfully inside. I thought – and not for the first time on these walks - it might be wiser to keep some of these thoughts to myself. Fiona was always *right*. Anyway, who was I to say that was a bad thing? Liksi was so laid back she was horizontal, and I'd spent much of my life wishing I was more assertive. At least Fiona got things done.

However, first impressions of the hostel were promising. Lots of wood – walls, floors - and a pleasant and homely reception area. Not to mention a *very* attractive guy at the desk, who shook back a mane of honey-coloured hair as he looked up with a welcoming smile.

"Three of you, is it? One room? Any of you YHA members?"

"Yip, me." Fiona handed over her card.

"Discount for you then. What about you two?"

"No." Liksi was getting her purse out. "How much to join? Can we join now?"

"Ah, I detect an accent from over the Border. No – only bona fide English or Welsh members accepted here, sorry."

He shook his head with mock sadness.

"That's racist." Liksi's laugh softened her words. "Anyway, don't let her fool you - she's Scottish too, but she's lived in England so long now that she's got a funny accent."

"It's all right, only joking." He held his hands up, noticing Fiona's half-serious glare. "Of course you can join – but membership would only be valid for hostels in England and Wales." That devilish grin was just *so* sexy.

Liksi and I eventually decided not to bother, and we all paid up.

"OK, guys, enjoy your stay. Here's your keys – room's up the stairs and turn right. If you need any help, I'll be here tonight and tomorrow – name's Mark. "

Reluctantly, we left Mark, took the keys and headed upstairs to the room, which again didn't disappoint. It was bright and fresh, with 2 sets of bunk beds adorned with crisp green bedding. I looked at Liksi anxiously.

"Are you sure you're OK with this, Liksi? I know you prefer your own room." As soon as I said this, I wondered if Fiona had checked with her before booking, or just gone ahead.

"No, this is fine, honestly." Liksi smiled at us reassuringly. "Great price compared with B&Bs. As long as I've got a light to read by I'll be fine." She paused. "Anyway, I've worked out by now that I might miss out on any gossip if I'm in a different room."

"Good, the lights are at the top, so that means I can get a bottom bunk." I worked this out with relief. "I don't fancy scrambling down a ladder to get to the loo in the middle of the night – especially after a few drinks."

"Well, you don't need to drink so much beer." Fiona claimed the other bottom bunk by plonking herself down on it.

"Yes I do – you don't get beer like this in Scotland. By the way, Fiona, if every hostel has this standard of receptionist, can we stay in them on all our trips?"

"That was a quick conversion." Fiona gave me a smug look. "I can't promise you, but I'll see what I can do."

Shortly afterwards, and braving the rain, which was still coming down relentlessly, we made our way down the street to the Dog and Gun, and managed to squeeze into a table at the wall opposite the bar. After shedding her dripping jacket, Liksi went to the bar to get the drinks, and I was pleased to see that they had Old Speckled Hen. Fiona tried an IPA this time, and we swapped glasses to taste them both.

"Wish I liked beer." Liksi turned her gaze to her Cabernet Sauvignon.

"D'you know how Old Speckled Hen got its name?" They looked at me blankly. "It was produced to celebrate the 50th anniversary of MG cars. The factory had an old car covered in splashes of paint, and they referred to it as the 'Owld Speckl'd Un'. There you are now – bet you're glad of that piece of useful information."

Liksi and Fiona shook their heads. "The things you come out with, Eilidh," said Fiona – but by this time I'd spotted the most gorgeous collie and it wasn't long before I'd gone over to speak to its owners. In between stroking her silky coat and murmuring dog-talk into receptive ears, I discovered she was called Ellie, was very smart and had walked all over the Lake District. It was with great reluctance that I dragged myself away before outstaying my welcome, and returned to the others.

"Sorry, just love dogs," I said, unnecessarily. "I'm so used to the collies on my aunts' crofts in Lewis that I can't see past them."

"So we see." Liksi grinned at me.

"Indeed. Right, time to go." Fiona got up and reached for her jacket. "We need to get her out of here before she kidnaps that animal. How about trying the Pack Horse for a last drink?"

Reluctantly, I gave Ellie a last glance – she'd her head on her paws but was watching us closely, with her ears still pricked up – and out we went. The Pack Horse wasn't far away, and was slightly nearer the hostel anyway. Inside, it was cosy, with a mesmerising log fire and a good selection of real ales. We just had the one drink, then went back to the hostel, which I was relieved to see was still comfortably above the water line. Sadly, our friend at reception was no longer there, so we made our way up to the room and bed. I've no idea when Liksi finally put out her light, as I slept fitfully with snatches of dreams about collies, crofts and flooding.

The next morning, fully fortified after a substantial breakfast and waved off by Mark, we set off to climb Skiddaw. The sky was grey, but the rain had stopped at last and the weather was as good as you could hope for at this time of year. As we crossed the river, the level seemed to be down quite a bit from the night before.

The route led round the back of a leisure centre, through a residential street or two, then turned left onto a path which crossed the A66 and led steadily uphill. As we climbed, and the cleansing country air made its way into my lungs, I felt that I was escaping worldly cares and giving myself up to the elements. It was always like this – it didn't matter what the weather was, or how unfit I felt, the feeling of escape and release was always there.

Even though I quickly fell behind, as usual, and was missing out on a substantial amount of the chat, I was sure that a lot of their conversation when I wasn't there was about the mysterious world of systems and networks. When I dared to look up to see how far ahead they were, I realised that they'd reached a car park and the pair of them were looking relaxed and comfortable – somehow - perched on a big stone, waiting for me.

"You didn't tell me we could've taken the car up here." I

looked at Fiona, mock-accusingly, as I flopped down to join them, wiping my face with my sleeve. "We could've been up at the top by now – well, you two could, anyway."

"Now, now, remember that we need to maximise the exercise potential of these trips." Fiona had an infuriatingly superior look on her face.

"Hm. So, have you two caught up with work war stories? Anything a humble non-techy could understand?" I was genuinely interested in their careers, if not in the finer details of Ethernet cabling.

"Well, I was just telling Liksi that I'm not looking forward to my secondment finishing in August." Fiona moved over slightly to give me more room. "I've got used to a rather itinerant existence, and it's been great getting to all these former eastern bloc countries that I'd probably never have gone to otherwise."

"Yeah, very envious of that aspect." Liksi's job didn't really have any opportunities for travel.

"Me too." Although I had managed to get to a few interesting countries with the Travel and Tourism students' study visits.

"Right, come on, time to go." Fiona got to her feet – heavens above, I'd only just sat down. I sighed, and picked up my pack as I too stood up. We set off again, and I managed to keep up with them for a short while, even though it was a pretty steep climb. Not hard, just steep. We stopped briefly to look at a tall stone cross, which commemorated two shepherds and another family member. The shepherds were apparently known for breeding prize Herdwick sheep. I wondered idly what Herdwick sheep looked like, as we hadn't come across any sheep at all, and none were visible on the surrounding slopes and peaks.

"I wanted to tell you," said Fiona, as we left the monument, "that I've applied for a new job. It's in a University."

"Brilliant." Liksi was full of admiration. "Where, though? Didn't see one advertised in Manchester recently."

"That's because it's in London."

"London?" Liksi and I looked at each other in confusion. "*London*? How on earth will you get there?" Even my limited knowledge of English geography made me aware that a commute from Manchester to London would be practically impossible.

"Well, I've got to get the job first, so it might never happen. However, if it does I'll stay there during the week and come back at weekends. I might be able to negotiate a day working from home, too." She looked pretty happy at the thought.

"What about the kids? And Olly?" I was a bit taken aback - although Nathan and Jack were getting older now, they were going through GCSEs and 'A' levels, and I'd have thought they would still need quite a bit of support.

"It's OK, Olly and I've talked it through. His work is very flexible, and he can do most of it from home so would be there for the boys. I can afford to rent a studio flat or something in London."

This was interesting. Fiona'd said that they 'liked their space', whatever that meant, so was staying more at home just as acceptable to Olly as being able to nip up and down to London? I didn't feel I could ask her that, somehow.

"Hope you've got good take-away restaurants in the neighbourhood, or the boys'll starve." Liksi stated exactly what I'd been thinking. Olly's kitchen exploits were legendary - full of good intentions, he'd spend a morning using every utensil in the kitchen, but at the end of the exercise (according to his unimpressed wife) the floor would be carpeted in most of the ingredients, and the proffered dish was usually over- or underdone, or downright inedible.

I lost Fiona's reply as the wind had got up, and was competing with my own increasingly laboured breath as we climbed so it was difficult to hear any conversations ahead. It was time to concentrate on the terrain – although there was a well-defined path on the ridge on which we now found ourselves, it was compiled of loose stones which were a bit wearing on the feet. To take my mind off things I'd been keeping an eye on another collie – a big, stately animal who'd been following his owner closely all the way up. We'd passed each other a few times since leaving the car park but I hadn't seen them recently. As I climbed, I realised that Liksi and Fiona were out of sight, and it was pretty misty ahead. I sighed with exasperation, but at least there was a steady line of walkers, and a series of cairns – it was unlikely that I'd get lost.

By the time I could make out the shadowy outline of the trig point, the wind was fierce, and my concentration had turned to staying upright. As I struggled to reach the top, I could see Fiona and Liksi there waiting for me, balancing themselves against the gale. They were staring, as were other walkers, at the sight of the big collie posing at the trig point – his nose sniffing the air, and the wind racing through his white mane, while his owner took photos of him. It was almost as if the dog knew what was expected of a top-of-mountain souvenir photo.

"Great dog." I smiled at the man as I caught my breath. "Can I take a photo of both of you?"

He turned round and smiled. "That would be good, thanks. I've photos of Jack on top of scores of peaks, but very few of me. I'm sure people think he's got to the tops by himself." Jack obligingly pushed his nose into the man's hand as I snapped the pair of them, although it was hard to balance and I'm sure my hair would have been blown into the photo. In return we had a photo taken of the three of us, and then I made a fuss of the dog before they turned to go back down the slope.

"Wonderful animal," I sighed, looking after them. "Ah

Paths, Pals and Pints

well. How about lunch now?"

"Are you mad?" Fiona shook her head, laughing. "It's far too windy – we'd get chilled before we got a bite near our mouths. Come on, let's get down a bit first." Grudgingly, I had to admit she was right - it wouldn't have been pleasant to stay at the top for more than a few minutes and it was good to get on the move again. Once we got going, none of us really wanted to stop so Liksi and I just had a sandwich on the hoof. Fiona, who didn't seem to get hungry like normal mortals, didn't bother.

Much to her disgust, we went down the same way we'd come up. She hadn't planned an alternative route, and with the mist and wind it wasn't practical to get the map from my pack and try to work it out. The walking was easy, but as so often happens the way down seemed to take ages and was a bit of a slog. We were soon out of the mist, and the wind had dropped considerably, but walking was still tedious in bits. Until –

"What on *earth's* that?" Liksi was pointing to something down the grassy slope to our left. "Loose tarpaulin? Tent - making a bid for freedom?" We stopped to see what she was referring to, and then gaped at the strange sight of something white bobbing about in the distance.

"Bird? *Big* bird?" Fiona suggested dubiously. "Oh, it's gone – no, there it is again."

"It'd have to be a pterodactyl to be that size, and anyway what's it *doing*?" I'd never seen anything like it, and was totally at a loss to even hazard a guess. We watched in amazement as it floated from one hillock to another, then jerked down and disappeared for a while, only to re-appear gaily slightly further down.

"UFO." Liksi shook her head in surrender. "Weird, anyway. Come on, if we speed up we might catch up with it. Although, do we *want* to?"

With real curiosity, even I managed to step up the pace

and we gained ground slowly. Suddenly the object disappeared, and for quite a while we didn't see it. We'd almost given up when we rounded a corner, and there on a summit above a steep crag, was a person attached to, and fiddling with, what appeared to be a billowing white sheet. Next thing we knew he'd jumped off the crag and the white thing had unfurled into a smooth sail above him.

"A paraglider!" we shouted in unison, with some relief.

"God, that was surreal. Rather him than me." Liksi gaped in awe as the man descended, more smoothly this time. Laughing at our previous suggestions, we spent a few minutes watching him ride the thermals, then carried on down the hill, past the car park and eventually back round the leisure centre and into Keswick.

In spite of the alluring prospect of seeing Mark again, it was a unanimous decision to take our dusty, sweaty bodies into the George, as we all felt in need of a drink before even getting showered. A welcoming fire, a pint of Marston's Pedigree and I felt on top of the world again – aching feet temporarily forgotten, replaced by a warm sense of well-being. There hadn't been any significant rain all day, so the river level could only have gone down. I could relax now and not worry about the hostel getting flooded in the middle of the night. In fact, this hostelling business was much better than I'd expected.

"Not a bad day out at all." Fiona interrupted my thoughts as she reached for the crisps and tore the packet ready for sharing. "Here, help yourselves. Straightforward climb compared to Helvellyn, but that's us done two of the three tallest English peaks. Scafell Pike next time? What d'you call them again, Eilidh? Something Munros?"

"Furth Munros. Or Wainwrights, Marilyns, Birketts – OK, OK, I'll stop there, you Philistines. Here's to Scafell Pike." We raised our glasses and settled in for another well-earned evening of beer, food and chat.

Chapter 6 – Ben Lomond (June 2008) - Liksi

Ben Lomond, at 3,196 ft, is not one of the highest Munros. However, its proximity to Glasgow and the relatively easy climb to the summit make it one of Scotland's most-climbed mountains. The popular starting point is at the Rowardennan car park; descending by the Ptarmigan ridge makes it a little more challenging, and enables a 7.5-mile circular route with the final stretch being along Loch Lomond, on part of the West Highland Way.

Eilidh had said she'd been roped in as Alan's commis chef for the evening, so Fiona and I made our own way to Bearsden on the train. When we arrived, the house was warm with the smell of mysterious concoctions.

Alan, resplendent in a striped and splattered butcher's apron, emerged briefly from a steam-filled kitchen to welcome us – "What, you two here *again*? Anyone would think you lived here – HALLO there! Good to see you! Eilidh, I'll manage now – you can clear out." As he retreated into his steamy lair, Eilidh ushered us downstairs and out on to the patio.

"Glorious!" Fiona flopped down onto the nearest of the assorted deck chairs, whilst I chose one which was slightly in the shade. "Absolutely glorious – can't believe you're getting this weather here too."

"It's been like this for a couple of weeks." Eilidh was frowning with concentration as she poured out the Prosecco. "This OK for everyone? To celebrate the weather?"

"Thought we were supposed to celebrate *after* we completed a walk, not before." I stretched out luxuriously. "Not complaining," I added hastily, as Eilidh stretched over and threatened to remove my glass. "Could drink to a successful ascent of Ben Lomond tomorrow, instead."

"Seconded." We drank, savouring the fizz and enjoying the prospect it conjured up.

"Mind you, if it's like this tomorrow it'd be tempting to stay in the garden." Eilidh was looking lazily across the tops of her birch trees at the blue sky shot with rays of sunny gold. "I just *love* this weather!"

"This is wonderful, Eilidh – us relaxing in the garden while Alan does all the work. Olly'd probably be the same – the only difference being that it *wouldn't* be relaxing for me as I'd be worried about the end result, as well as the mess I'd have to clear up afterwards!" Fiona smiled wryly, but also affectionately, I noticed.

"You two don't know how lucky you are." I sighed with envy. "Pete can cook if he wants to, but he certainly *wouldn't* want to if it was just for us – only if he was trying to impress someone. I'd get shoved out of the way – but then I never did have any pretensions about cooking." I didn't add that they didn't know how lucky they were with their husbands *anyway*. I would save that conversation for a later date.

"So, how's Julie getting on with her dancing?" asked Eilidh. I looked at her sharply, wondering how much she'd guessed, and whether she was trying to change the subject for my sake. We chatted away about the kids, and their various sporting activities, and I was just about to ask about Nathan, but at that moment Alan came lumbering down the stairs saying, "Football? Did someone mention football?"

"Alan, you didn't come all the way down the stairs because you heard the hallowed word, did you? For heaven's sake!" Eilidh laughed and shook her head.

"Well, partly – but really to ask for assistance. Thought you were my commis chef, Eilidh?"

"Yes, but not your skivvy. OK, OK, I'll come up." I got up too to give her a hand, and before long we were all enjoying some kind of Persian chicken dish, in spite of the evening heat.

"No barbecue, Alan?" asked Fiona between mouthfuls. "I thought all you men could never resist the chance of a bit of pyromania?"

"Ah, well, I'm not like all men, y'know." Alan smiled smugly, as Eilidh raised her eyes heavenwards.

"Actually, barbecues are definitely *not* Alan's forte." She ignored his hurt look. "Luckily he'd rather give you something edible than something which is burnt to a crisp and would end up in the bin."

"That's a bit cruel, Eilidh. This is what happens when you three get together and Macbeth is re-enacted ..." He ducked to avoid being swiped with a napkin, then continued, "So it's the Ben tomorrow, is it? What happened to Scafell Pike? Thought you were going to finish your English Munros this time."

"Don't know really – it just seemed a good idea at the time." I guess we all felt the same – where we went was secondary to just being together. Anywhere.

"You lot do chop and change, don't you? Started the West Highland Way and dropped it, same with the English peaks – I can't keep up with your doings. Of course, I am a mere man so how could I ..."

"We've not dropped *anything*. We're choosing locations most suited to our current circumstances." Eilidh's mock pomposity made us all laugh. Oh, I just loved this easy company – Alan, though he could be a bit rowdy sometimes, was a hoot – a typical Glaswegian with a bit of Billy Connelly in him. I couldn't help comparing him with Pete – who wasn't easy, rowdy or comic in any way. Ever. I eased the sudden lump in my throat with a large gulp of wine.

We stayed out in the garden long after the meal had finished, enjoying the mellow heat and watching the sun slowly moving round the rooftops till it finally set in reddish golden stripes behind the distant Campsies. Even then, we were reluctant to go in until the evening insects decided to make themselves known, and we were getting a bit shivery anyway.

I spent the night on Eilidh's long and very comfortable couch again. I'd a great sleep and was only woken by the insistent sunshine forcing its way through every available chink in the curtains. I lumbered up and drew them back – glorious! This was going to be a great day for views, although possibly a bit *too* hot for comfort. I pulled on a T-shirt and shorts and went through to the kitchen.

"So you've finally deigned to join us, then?" Alan had latched on to my reputation for being a late riser. Justified, I had to admit – everyone else was gathered round the breakfast table.

"Toast OK, Liksi?" Eilidh asked. "Help yourself – there's cereal there too if you want it."

"Remind me." Alan reached over for the marmalade. "I've been told but I've forgotten – *why* are you called Liksi again? Anything repeatable?"

I sighed with resignation, having doled out this explanation many, many times over the years. "Lauren - Isabel - Katherine - Simpson – L-I-K-Si. Dad's favourite actress, Mum's name, Gran's name." I looked at him with amusement as he worked his way through this. "Some handle, eh? And I'm just *not* a Lauren. Isabel's too old-fashioned and if I called myself Katherine it would upset my mother. My brother called me Liksi early on, and it just stuck."

"Good God. Thankfully you can't do much with Alan John Robertson."

"Want a bet?" I grinned at him. "I'm sure I could work something out ..."

"Toast!" Eilidh timeously plonked a slice down on my plate.

We got going fairly quickly after this – Eilidh had decided

to take the car this time. She was well used to the drive, but after Balmaha where the road narrowed we'd to slow right down and sometimes even reverse to allow for traffic coming towards us. Unlike the other side of the loch, this road was not built with tourists in mind. When we finally reached Rowardennan, Eilidh managed to find a parking space with some difficulty. On a day like this it was inevitable that Ben Lomond would be swarming with walkers, and there would be other family outings along the shores of the Loch too, which meant cheek by jowl parking in amongst the trees.

"Back at Rowardennan – bit of déjà vu here." Fiona looked round before getting out of the car. "At least there's no midges this time."

"They'd fry in this. Anyone want sun-cream?" She rubbed some vigorously on her arms and neck, and I took the tube from her. It was a pleasant change to be putting on sun-cream rather than Skin-So-Soft or some other anti-midge spray. I shoved my squishy hat on for some sun protection; Fiona and Eilidh had no such qualms and both were wearing vest tops. Eilidh was already stretching out her arms and basking in the heat, with her face up to the sun.

"What a day!" Fiona adjusted her snazzy sun visor. "It just couldn't be better."

"It's all right for you two – I'll probably bake before long. Let's hope it's a bit cooler nearer the top. How high's it anyway?" I peered through the trees to try to get a glimpse of our destination, but the foliage was too dense.

"Oh, it's well over 3,000 ft – one of the highest ones, I think."

"It's not, actually," said Eilidh, and Fiona looked a bit put out. She always liked to be ahead of the game, but Eilidh had the local knowledge. She was also more aware of the Scottish hills than Fiona was – and as for me, well, it was *all* new to me. "It's only just under 3,200 ft, but because it's so near Glasgow it's one of the most climbed ones. The route's a bit like a motorway, I'm afraid."

"Good." It didn't actually to matter to me, but at least the height issue seemed settled. "Means there's no way we can get lost. Come on, you two – I'm assuming this is the way." I wanted to get moving in the hope that it would act as a breeze of sorts, so I threaded my way through the cars towards the sign at the far end of the car park.

Soon we were on our way, climbing up through the trees which Eilidh informed us were mainly oaks and birches. I was certainly learning a bit about nature on these walks – Eilidh had been brought up in the Highlands and was quite knowledgeable on this topic; Fiona's father had taken her hillwalking when she was small. My parents had hardly been out of Midlothian in their lives, and I'm sure the idea of 'going for a walk' had never occurred to them. Judging from the flimsy shoes some of the walkers we passed were wearing, I suspected they hadn't had much experience of this either. The good weather sure brought out all the amateurs (I felt absurd pride at considering myself above the amateur level, although I guess that was open to interpretation).

"Phew!" Eilidh gasped as we stopped at a break in the trees, where the path continued onto more open ground and we could get a view back over the loch. "It's *hot*! I've no more clothes to take off and I just hope I've got enough water with me."

"Look at that." I gazed in admiration at the expanse of water stretched out before us, glistening in the sun. The quality of the light was such that the trees and vegetation stood out in almost blinding greenery, and the mountains opposite were superbly clear against the cloudless azure background. Numerous small boats were dotted about the loch, weaving their way round the islands.

"Are any of these islands inhabited?" Fiona pushed up her visor to get a better view. "They look like great places for picnics."

"I think a few of them might be just now, though I don't think any of them are inhabited all year round." Eilidh screwed up her eyes to look over the water. "There's a mailboat that goes to them in the summer, and it takes tourists as well. It stops at Inchmurrin – it's over there, but you can't see it just now – there's a hotel on it, and you can have lunch there. It's a nice day out, actually."

"Could consider one of these trips when we're in our dotage and our walking days are over. Perish the thought!" I shuddered.

We continued along the path, which soon became less steep. In fact, it was only the cast of thousands making their way back down which gave any indication that this wasn't just any old hillside stroll. It felt as if the whole of Glasgow – and beyond – had decided to climb Ben Lomond today. They must have been up with the larks.

"Don't they have other things to do on sunny days?" I moved beside Eilidh to let a couple of fit-looking guys run past. "Like sunbathe in their gardens, for instance?"

"I know, it's quite amazing the number of people. That's why – well, one of the reasons why - a lot of the serious climbers are not so fond of it – it's just like a Sunday stroll for them."

"Look at the shoes on that one." Fiona was shaking her head in disbelief, after passing a willowy blonde picking her way fastidiously up the path. "Style first, always."

"I remember when I was at the Grand Canyon it was just the same." Eilidh and Alan had been over in the States a couple of years ago. "Girls in white high heels starting to walk down the stony path, with a sheer drop below. Our guide said that they only ever got a few yards down before realising that it was a non-starter. It's hard to believe that people can be so stupid."

"I'd like to know why so many people are coming *down*, already! I thought we'd made reasonable time this morning." This was becoming like the road from Balmaha, with passing places, I thought as I moved over yet again.

"Reasonable time for us." Fiona laughed. "We didn't dare try to get you up any earlier, Liksi!"

Ah well, I couldn't deny that I wouldn't have thanked them for it. Anyway, we'd the whole day, and it was June, so there was no rush in terms of daylight. The path was getting a bit steeper now, and zig-zaggy, but was still pretty straightforward. We managed to stay together all the way up to the summit trig point – easily discernible from the distance, due to the number of people there, posing in groups for the snaps for the family albums.

Enjoying the luxury of stretching out our weary limbs, we gazed around us, taking in the full splendour of a mountain-top view in the height of summer. Not only was the whole of Loch Lomond and its islands visible, but there were tons of other lochs and mountains.

"Come on, Eilidh, tell us what everything is?" I knew I'd only remember a fraction of it, but I had to start somewhere. Midlothian I could manage, but the rest of Scotland was a bit of a mystery to me. Ridiculous, really.

Eilidh swivelled round once she got her breath back. "Well, that's Loch Katrine over there, where Glasgow's water comes from. There's a steamer that goes up and down the loch – another trip for our dotage, girls."

She pointed to the hills beside the loch – "Those'll be the Trossachs; they don't have any Munros but they've got some lovely peaks – Ben A'an, Ben Venue and Ben Ledi. We can certainly do them some time." She turned again and continued, sweeping her arm round to indicate some mountains with rather jagged tops. "And those're affectionately known as the Arrochar Alps – the Cobbler's a great climb, so we can put that on the list too."

"And just look at Loch Lomond itself." Fiona waved her arm from one end of it to the other. "It's massive – and all those *islands*! Most of them seem to be concentrated in a line from side to side."

"Yes, that's the Highland Fault Line – remember, we saw it from Conic Hill? It separates the Highlands from the Lowlands. You know, there's a whisky made back there in Strathblane, called Glengoyne. It's made in the Highlands, and bottled across the road in the Lowlands. The only one which straddles the two areas – good marketing info. Actually, it's the distillery we were looking across at from the Beech Tree Inn."

"Not likely to forget that." Fiona grinned at Eilidh, who gave a dismissive wave.

"Beautiful." I gave a contented sigh. "Right, time for food before I keel over. How about down there, where it's a bit quieter?" We moved down to a flattish bit, and started to get ourselves settled. I noticed Eilidh seemed to have a natty wee mat to sit on. "What've you got there?" I was curious to see what this latest bit of hill-walking equipment was.

"Mm? Oh, this – och, it's just a mouse mat." She raised one buttock to show it off, laughing. "Someone told me they used one for sitting on in the hills, and I thought it was a great idea. It's all you need, unless your posterior is on the large side."

"Certainly is – I mean, a good idea," I added quickly. "Must see if I can find one for our next trip." In the meantime I made do with a piece of ground that had some stubbly grass on it, and we quietly ate our lunch looking down on the magnificent vista spread out before us. This was why we walked – to get away from cluttered workrooms, impatient staff, demanding students, exhausting children and difficult husbands. Well, mine anyway – although God knows what he got up to when I wasn't there. To be here by ourselves, in company that was becoming so comfortable it was like putting on an old glove. All over the summit area, little groups were doing the same thing. It was energising, but also humbling. I just felt so lucky to be here, and was sorry for all the people who didn't climb hills – they were missing so much. Most of the people I knew were very sporty, but I don't remember many of them talking about hills, or even just walking. Not for the first time, I felt very grateful that we had re-connected with each other again.

Fiona had been lying full length, glorying in the sun's rays, but now reluctantly stretched out and reached for the map. "I think you can take another route down." I couldn't help smiling at Eilidh's brief look of dismay. She'd done well so far today, but she'd be nervous about being too ambitious.

"Look, we can go down by the Ptarmigan ridge – it actually seems shorter than the way we've come up. Here, have a look." Fiona opened out the map properly and we leaned over to see. I wasn't a great map reader, but her suggestion seemed OK to me.

"Och, well, if it's shorter it should be OK." Eilidh looked relieved. "I'm all for that."

The descent proved to be a bit more demanding than I'd thought though – you'd to watch where you were putting your feet on the rocky ridge, and not be distracted by the still-glorious views. Once we got past that though, it was a steady trek down. Eilidh, however, was suffering again, and was starting to walk sideways. I stayed back till she caught up.

"OK, Eilidh?"

"Sorry, my knees are struggling, and my calves are so tight. I'll just have to take my time – don't worry about me."

I stayed with her for a while, but eventually found myself picking up speed and catching up with Fiona.

"She needs to get more exercise and cut down on the beer." Oh dear, no sympathy from Fiona here. "I just can't go at snail's pace – it's too difficult." Fiona was super-fit even by my standards, but she was also unwilling to compromise. We waited till Eilidh arrived, gave her a brief rest, then started again, and eventually all three of us reached the road, which followed the loch back round to Rowardennan. Knowing that Eilidh would get there eventually, Fiona and I went ahead until we got to a strange circular sculpture by the lochside.

"Maybe a war memorial?" I suggested, prompted by the very tattered wreath of artificial poppies beside it.

"Don't know, but it's good to have something to denote the end of the walk." Fiona walked round it again in case she'd missed something.

We waited there till Eilidh's limping form joined us, then walked along the remaining path together, till we got to the carpark. Eilidh threw herself down on the ground with relief. "Can't wait to get these things off!" She tugged at her laces. "Mind you, the way I'm feeling I'd be glad if I could remove my *legs*, and replace them with another pair."

"Poor you." I helped her remove her boots and set them on the ground beside her. "Never mind – did you say that there's somewhere we could eat on the way back?"

"Yes, the Oak Tree Inn at Balmaha. Remember? We had a drink there on our second West Highland Way leg. We could eat outside, if we can get a table. Sound OK?"

It wasn't long before we were doing just that, and congratulating ourselves on another day's successful climb – our first Munro together. Tiredness was forgotten, and only exhilaration and a sense of achievement was left. Our early outdoor dinner left us plenty of time for talk, both at Balmaha and later back at Eilidh's. For once, there was no sign of Alan so the chat gradually moved from varying opinions about Boris becoming the new London mayor, to Tory-bashing (from Eilidh; I kept quiet as she wasn't in the mood to be challenged on that topic), to sport, onto work and then degenerated into slurred comparisons of ideal and not-so-ideal males, and other girl-talk, before we finally called it a day.

Chapter 7 – The Cobbler (November 2008) - Fiona

Ben Arthur, more commonly known as the Cobbler, is one of the 'Arrochar Alps' and is noted for its distinctive shape. At 2,900 ft, it doesn't quite make a Munro like its two nearest neighbours, Ben Ime and Ben Narnain, yet it is probably the most climbed of the three. The start and finish point of this 6.5-mile walk is the Succoth car park opposite the village of Arrochar.

Hard to believe that we managed to get together for a third walk this year. The rest of the West Highland Way would have to wait though. It was getting too difficult to do a full day's walking whilst getting there and back the same day, so it made more sense to wait till we could all find time off work. So, this time the plan was to climb the Cobbler and again it was convenient for us all to meet up in Glasgow.

Well, convenient for us – poor Alan was landed with the three harpies again. I *think* he enjoyed us all being there, but with all his taunting I was never completely sure. However, arriving at Eilidh's from the train station on the Friday night, I was quite relieved this time to find that Alan was out, as I wasn't in the mood for rumbustious repartee.

Liksi had arrived before me, and carried my bag through to the spare room. The bedroom had become almost a second home for me over the years as I visited with various members of the family from time to time. Nathan and Jack – well, Jack anyway - had been more than happy to bed down on lilos in the lounge downstairs, although it was a good few years now since they'd been up.

"I'm looking forward to sleeping downstairs again – can watch TV till the early hours without being ridiculed for it." Liksi laughed as we made our way to the kitchen, but I wondered what was behind that comment. Pete had been pretty nasty to her when we'd been in Edinburgh, and since our last encounter I wouldn't put anything past him. How on earth could such a lovely person as Liksi have ended up with this boor? Oh well, we've all got our problems, one way or another, I reflected as we moved through to the lounge.

Eilidh had decided we'd have a take-away this time, and we settled down with a drink until the food arrived. "Hope you don't mind – we just ordered for the 3 of us, and Alan can eat any leftovers when he comes in."

"Not at all – good idea. What's Alan up to tonight, anyway?"

"Och, Friday night being boys' night has started up again. I used to resent it but now I rather like the space." Eilidh grinned at us. "Anyway, means we can have a decent talk without him butting in."

"Cheers to that." Liksi lifted her glass. "So, how's the new job going?" I'd started work in London in October, and was just getting used to being in the public sector, a very different environment from working for a corporation. It was also much more restrictive and a lot less fun than my EU secondment had been.

"It's different," I admitted. "I have to say, I'm missing all the travelling and if my secondment had been extended, I'd never have applied for this job."

"Big job – good for you getting it." Liksi made a wry face. "Rather you than me though." She'd always been very supportive of my ambitions, even if she didn't seem to have many of her own.

"How about the living away from home bit?" asked Eilidh. "Don't the kids miss you?"

"It's fine. I think Jack does, a bit, but I don't think Nathan'd notice whether I was there or not – or any of us, for that matter." I reflected rather sadly on the last weekend I'd been home. Nathan had barely made an appearance, and when he did deign to join us he'd spoken mainly in monosyllables.

"Maybe he's too taken up with his A-Levels? Joe's doing his Highers just now, and bites my head off at the slightest thing sometimes." Liksi shook her head, but her affection for that lovely boy of hers was still very evident.

"Oh, he's doing A-Levels all right, and did very well last year – but he seems to have no real *interest* in any of his subjects." We'd been aware of Nathan's high IQ for some time, and he'd had A's in every one of his exams so far. "I think he finds everything too easy and – and - beneath his notice somehow."

"Sounds good to me." Liksi laughed. "Wish I could say the same for Joe. Fingers crossed he'll get into Loughborough, but it's by no means guaranteed."

"Aw, he's a lovely lad, though." Eilidh smiled at her. "He'll do well whatever he ends up doing."

I noted wryly that she didn't voice the same thoughts about Nathan. People generally didn't these days – something I was painfully becoming aware of. Luckily, the doorbell rang at this point and we all homed in on the take-away, opening containers, heating plates and setting the table.

The conversation moved on, and I was relieved that there was no further reference to Nathan, although I did want to sound them out about him later, maybe tomorrow. Olly and I were both concerned about him, but were aware that we might just be over-anxious parents. Nathan *was* different in many ways – but then, aren't we all?

As usual, we left the table reluctantly – it was very tempting to just stay in that cosy dining room all night. After clearing up – which involved putting most of the leftovers onto one big plate for Alan - we had coffee and watched a bit of TV. The news channels were still full of Obama's victory. At least that was good news – global finance and UK politics was another story. As Gordon Brown's mournful face appeared on the screen I decided it was time to call it a day, and retired to bed. I don't think the others would've been far behind me.

Bright daylight shining through the curtains woke me up early the next morning. I looked out over the large unruly garden to the red roofs of the rows of bungalows inching their way up the hills. When Eilidh and Alan had moved here, they took a bit of ribbing about moving to an area with a high percentage of elderly inhabitants. "Ah, but we're not in a bungalow yet – that's the key thing!" Eilidh had said, with Alan muttering somewhat inappropriately, "Over my dead body!" However, it'd worked out well for them, and we all liked their roomy, spacious house and rambling garden.

Alan was uncharacteristically quiet that morning and didn't join us for breakfast, even though we weren't in any particular hurry ourselves for a change. "Don't ask," said Eilidh, rolling her eyes. "It must have been a 'dirty glass'! I think that curry is going to be staying in the fridge for a day or two, somehow."

"Oh well, as long as it was a good night. You get a great view from here." I was looking out the window. "What're those hills you can see in the distance?"

"That's the Campsies and Dumgoyne. Pimples compared with where we're going today. Ready?"

Eilidh was the driver again today, as we set off for Arrochar. It was one of these lovely pre-winter days – cold but still sunny, with the hills wearing their light dusting of snow proudly.

"I hope there's not too much snow on the Cobbler." Eilidh didn't sound worried, though. "It shouldn't be too bad on a day like this – and there's bound to be lots of people ahead of us, to trample it down."

"Is that it up there?" Liksi was pointing to a jagged peak ahead.

"Aye – looks nasty, doesn't it? And it's only a Corbett."

"A what?" Liksi frowned as she turned to Eilidh.

"A Corbett. A peak of between 2,500 and 3,000 ft. Ben Ime and Ben Narnain – you'll see them when we get nearer - are both Munros, but the Cobbler's a Corbett." Eilidh pointed out of her window, over to the other side of Loch Lomond. "Look, there's Ben Lomond over there."

"Quite a bit of snow on it now – bit different from June." It gave me a warm feeling, remembering. After all my years in England, it was good to connect with my homeland again, and its wonderful scenery. "So, why're we going up the Cobbler if the other two're higher?"

Eilidh looked at me in her mirror with a mixture of laughter and mock pity. "It's not *size* that matters, Fiona, don't you know that by now?" As I made a face at her, she continued, "You just *have* to do the Cobbler – it's a Glasgow favourite. Partly its distinctive shape, plus there's a nasty rock formation at the top; if you work your way through it and on to the *very* top, it's known as 'threading the Needle'. And no," she added hastily, "we're *not* going to try it."

"OK, OK." I held a hand up. "You're in charge today." Eilidh was a worrier, and I didn't want her distracted when she was behind the wheel. Anyway, I was happy at the prospect of an easier climb today as I wanted to talk through my concerns about Nathan later on, and didn't want everyone to be too worn out to listen. "A Corbett thingy's fine."

"Good enough for me." Liksi was peering at the map in the back seat. We'd turned off at Tarbet and the village of Arrochar was just coming into view, curving round the edge of the loch.

"And that's Loch Long." The arresting shape of the Cobbler was outlined against the blue sky, mirrored in the still water of the loch behind the village. "It's supposed to be a cobbler bending over his last," Eilidh added.

"Eh?" Liksi looked at her in the mirror with eyebrow

raised. "That takes some imagination."

I didn't get it either. "I guess its shape is partly why it's so popular though? After all, the other two beside it look very ordinary in comparison."

"They are. *That*'s why we're going up the Cobbler." Eilidh turned right at the junction, and we drove round the head of the loch, past all the hotels and guesthouses. As is so often the case in Scotland, some of them looked well past their best, although it was undoubtedly a picturesque location. Not long after, we turned left into Succoth car park. Once parked, we went through the usual rigmarole of lacing boots, putting on layers, hats and gloves, and buckling rucksacks.

"Ready. My God, you'd think we were going up the Eiger." I included myself as I took in all our padding, and the others' rather haphazard ensembles. Eilidh was sporting a lurid pinkish scarf, and Liksi's cream cords weren't exactly normal hiking gear. At least none of us were daft enough to wear jeans though, and we all had good walking boots. "OK, Eilidh – lead on."

We crossed the road to the start of the walk, and followed the substantial path up through the forest in easy zigzags. The branches were mostly bare, and the trunks fought for space between sad clumps of brown, withered bracken. When we reached a T-junction, at another wide path, there was a well-located bench, with clear views from there back down over the loch.

"Bags this for the way back." Eilidh stroked the top of the seat. "Note that I'm *not* suggesting we use it at the moment, though. By the way, I've been *running* for the last couple of months." There was an element of pride in her voice. "No records broken, but it's a different kind of exercise from the gym, and I feel good. So, maybe ..."

"Good for you." I was glad to hear it. "It'll get easier, honestly – just keep it up."

"Just look down there." Liksi was sweeping her arm expansively to take in the sight of Loch Long glistening below. "Guess that's Ben Lomond again." The snowy peak she was pointing to loomed higher than any of the others, but I couldn't really identify it from a different angle. I left that to Eilidh – but she was off again.

We followed her up, stopping occasionally to admire the views. The path opened up, winding its way along and over streams – or burns, I suppose I should call them - and round oddly shaped boulders, with the unmistakeable shape of the Cobbler looming closer.

"Those big boulders are called the Narnain Boulders." Eilidh was pointing out a couple of giants at the edge of the path. "Believe it or not, they used to be used as shelters by impoverished climbers." A quick glance at them made me thankful for Eilidh's hospitality – you couldn't really call the sheltered bit a 'cave'; it was more of a large overhang.

"Supposed to have fallen from Ben Narnain – that's that one up there."

The two peaks up to the right of the path were, as Eilidh had said, very ordinary-looking in comparison. I was glad I hadn't insisted on doing all three peaks - we'd left it a bit late anyway, and quite honestly I didn't have the energy today. Worry about Nathan was consuming me, and I just hoped that the others could put things into perspective. Eilidh didn't have kids, but she did have plenty of students so was maybe more in tune with teenagers and their issues. Liksi's kids seemed to be bright, happy individuals – but as a mother she could maybe understand my angst.

"I'm going to take you up the standard, slightly longer, route," said Eilidh as we stopped to inspect the last part of the climb. "We could scramble up the front – see, where those people are – but it's getting a bit icy underfoot. So, we go on a bit further and then you'll see some steps leading up the side."

We certainly had to watch our footing, and there weren't any opportunities for conversation as we concentrated on staying upright on our way to the top. The steps cut into the mountainside were pretty good though – useful, without being too much of a scar on the landscape. Well, from my point of view anyway – not sure what the purists would have thought of it. Liksi and I reached the top a few minutes before Eilidh, and waited for her at the foot of the tallest outcrop – the Needle. Liksi took a quick photo of me with her camera.

"Want me to take one of both of you?" asked a guy with a weather-beaten face and a black beanie hat pulled well down over his ears. It was bitingly cold at the top, and the slight breeze which had followed us all the way up had morphed into a wind with vicious gusts.

"Sure – but would you mind waiting a couple of minutes till our friend gets here?" asked Liksi, as he fought his way over.

"No worries. First time up Arthur?" There wasn't much of his lined and reddish face visible, between the hat and a well zipped up jacket, but he looked to be somewhere in his forties.

It took me a second to work out who/what 'Arthur' was, then I smiled and said, "Yes – though Eilidh there's been up a couple of times before. You?"

"My 51st," came the reply. "Why go up any of the others when you can get this view?" I looked at him sharply, then at Liksi. Did he mean this? Surely he was joking?

Eilidh had caught the end of the conversation as she drew level with us. "Did you say *51*? *51*?" She bent down to stretch her limbs and calm her breathing, then stood upright to draw in deep breaths of the cold, invigorating air. "I'd thought I was doing well, doing Dumgoyne 6 times – and that's just a pimple compared to this."

"Probably just a sign of madness on my part. If you move

over there with your pals I'll get you all in." He took a couple of photos with Liksi's camera before handing it back and moving off with a wave.

Liksi headed towards a patch of ground which had escaped the snow. "Seating." She pulled something out of her rucksack with a flourish. "On my luxurious, ultra-expensive portable seat."

"That looks suspiciously like a mouse mat." Eilidh sat down on the ground beside her. "I can't be bothered getting mine out - my waterproof breeks should keep out the worst of it. I hope."

"It *is* a mouse mat – you gave me the idea last time. Had a whole drawer of them – anyone want one for next time?"

"I wouldn't mind." I was making do with sitting on part of my rucksack. "A padded one, preferably."

The other two unwrapped their sandwiches, and I nibbled at the mixed seeds and dried fruits pack I'd brought.

"That looks *far* too healthy for me." Eilidh cast a disparaging look at my lunch. "I need comfort food. Want some coffee?" She poured out 2 cups of coffee, and Liksi took one of them. We ate quietly for a few minutes, then I got to my feet before the chill started to penetrate.

"Too cold to hang about, and my backside's nearer the ground than yours. We need to get down before the light starts to fade, anyway." I was starting to shiver, but the others got up almost immediately and we set off at speed.

The guy from the top must've started downhill not long after us as he soon caught up. He and Eilidh started an incomprehensible conversation about Munros, mountains in general and places in the Highlands. Much to our amusement, he kept in step with her almost the whole way down and they were soon well ahead.

"They seem to be getting on very well." I looked at Liksi with amusement. "That's one way to get Eilidh moving – pair her up with a mountain-mad male!"

"*Very* well. And there was me thinking she's no eyes for anyone but Alan." Liksi tut-tutted, laughing.

"She hasn't." Of that, I was absolutely certain.

When her new pal eventually forged ahead at the final bit of the descent to the main road, Eilidh waited for us on the bench she'd noted earlier in the day.

"Come on, you two – what's keeping you?" She laughed at the look on my face. "You have no *idea* how much I enjoyed asking you that."

"Well, imagine getting a lumber at your age." Liksi shook her head in mock wonder. "What on earth would Alan say?"

"What's a lumber?" I could kind of work it out, but I'd not heard the word before.

"It's a – a date, I s'pose. Or to get picked up. Something like that." Liksi frowned, trying to find a better translation.

"Ach, well, you're never too old, you know." Eilidh couldn't keep the smug look off her face. "You meet interesting people walking these hills. He said he'd started off intending to bag all the Munros, but got fed up driving miles from Glasgow for a day's walking. Now he sticks to Ben Lomond or the Cobbler – I think he's done the Ben about 50 times too."

"Well, I hope you don't want to follow his example." I sat down beside her. "I'm not coming all the way up here to do the same hill over and over again!"

"Nor me. Can't think of anything worse." Liksi made a face.

"I wouldn't *dare* expect you to." Eilidh was biting into an apple with enthusiasm. "However, he did have another suggestion that you might be more interested in – the Village Inn in Arrochar for a drink. Fancy it? It's right across the water there, near the end of the village."

I couldn't make out exactly what she was pointing at, but took her word for it. "Are you sure you haven't made a date with him?"

"Come on - what do *you* think? I'm a bit long in the tooth for all that now."

"You've just said that you're never too old. Make up your mind." I was delighted to see that Eilidh had gone a bit pink – or maybe it was just the exertion. "However, if he can lead us to good pubs, I guess that's a redeeming feature – what d'you think, Liksi? Should we risk it?"

"If we must," said Liksi. "We'll just need to keep a very tight rein on our walk leader though, and not let her out of our sight."

It was a good decision. The Village Inn was a warm, cosy place, with a wooden floor and a roaring fire. The barman was welcoming and recommended the guest beer, after the usual discussion between him and Eilidh. I spotted her new friend on a stool at the bar, looking very much like part of the furniture, and he waved to acknowledge our presence but seemed happy to stay where he was.

We dragged some chairs over to a table by the fire, and had a couple of drinks before moving across the hall to the restaurant. During our meal, the conversation got round to what our kids might do when they left school, and this gave me the opening I'd been waiting for.

"Nathan says he's applied to University in London – one of the new ones, I think – but he's not given us any details, just that it's a Business degree. I can't even remember the name."

"That's not like you, Fiona." Eilidh looked at me with a frown.

"Well, he said he's told us what he intends to do, and that he doesn't need any more prying into his affairs." I was rather ashamed to admit this, but I just had to talk it through with someone. Nathan was becoming like a big leaden cloud which was threatening to engulf me.

"Oh, no." Liksi looked shocked. "That's hard."

"'Prying'? You're his *mother*." Eilidh was quite

indignant.

"Well, you wouldn't think so these days." I took a big gulp of my beer. "He's been hiding in his room for most of this year, and doesn't seem to want to be anywhere near us. Or Jack, or his friends, if he still has any." This was a very inadequate description of the awful scenes we'd had with Nathan recently, and the hugely upsetting comments he'd hurled at Olly and me.

"Maybe he just feels that he needs to get away from home to be himself – like, to kind of *find* himself." I looked at Eilidh with gratitude, feeling pathetic. "I've had students tell me that they felt suffocated at home and just had to get away – although I'm sure that's not the case with him, Fiona," she added hastily. "He probably just needs to get out into the world and spread his wings."

"But why does he have to be like *this*? We're not *stopping* him doing anything." I was genuinely bewildered, especially at the contrast between Nathan and Jack, who was a happy child with loads of friends. "Joe doesn't seem to have any hang-ups about home, Liksi, so what're we doing wrong?"

"Doubt if you're doing much *wrong*, Fiona." Liksi looked thoughtful. "Sometimes kids just lash out because we're *there*. They feel there's an injustice somewhere and parents are an easy target to vent their frustration on."

"Could he be getting bullied?" Eilidh's suggestion was unlikely, as Nathan had never suffered fools gladly.

"I doubt it. He's not the type."

"You never know, though. All you can really do is keep a close eye on him, but from a distance - don't let him know you're doing it. You could maybe ask the school to do the same? We get quite a few requests of that sort from parents, even in college."

"Well, Olly'll have to do most of the observing as I'm in London a lot of the time – and I guess I do feel a bit guilty about that." I smiled at them both a bit weakly.

"Well, you can't be Superwoman at work and at home *all* the time. I guess all these poor London colleagues're wondering what's hit them!"

Eilidh's teasing led the way back to a more general conversation, for which I was grateful. The realities of middle age ... and the worries. I shook off my gloom and made as much of the rest of the weekend as I could. Nathan's cloud would make itself visible again only too soon.

Chapter 8 – West Highland Way 3 (April 2009) - Eilidh

This 14-mile stretch from Rowardennan to Inverarnan is often considered the hardest. The path along Loch Lomond is rough and uneven, full of large boulders and tree roots which require careful negotiation. There is also an unexpectedly long stretch after the head of the loch, through more gentle terrain before turning into Inverarnan.

Well, this was it – no going back now. Alan had dropped our bags off with Travel-Lite, and us at Rowardennan. It'd been 4 years since we'd done the second leg of the walk, and it was only now that the opportunity for the 3 of us to get together for 4 consecutive days had come at last.

You'd think that with our academic or reasonably flexible holiday entitlements, it wouldn't have been all that difficult. However, what with children's holidays and sport-related activities, husbands' input, looking after increasingly fragile parents, and professional commitments, it had seemed impossible at times. Inevitably, it was Fiona who eventually corralled us into agreeing a time period, and this was it. It wasn't without difficulties – Alan was a bit miffed I'd abandoned him for a few days of our Easter holiday, Pete'd had a furious row with Liksi about spending money on a holiday which didn't include him, and Fiona was almost crippled with anxiety about Nathan – but we'd set all that aside and were now really looking forward to the whole thing.

"Omens are good," Liksi remarked as we set off along the track along the loch. "No midges, anyway." There were still no midges as we passed the memorial sculpture which we'd noticed on our walk back from Ben Lomond. I'd since discovered that it was for members of the armed forces –

might have been useful if there'd been an inscription somewhere.

"The book says that this bit's the hardest of the whole Way." Because the official start was on my home territory, I kind of felt responsible for the trip. "I've done most of it before though, and it didn't seem that bad to me."

"It can't be as bad as the Devil's Staircase," said Fiona. "It won't be named that for nothing. Anyway, today's walk's along the lochside so it's flat."

"Just telling you what I've read." Sometimes I wondered why I bothered. Ach well, they'd find out for themselves.

The very first bit was actually a doddle though, along a wide forest track which passed the youth hostel, and Ptarmigan Lodge. This was plain sailing, till we got to a bit where a trail in front of us veered off to the left of the main track.

"The bottom bit's the original official path, but apparently it's now quite eroded." I wasn't sure if this was a good idea, but felt it was probably part of the deal. "Want to try it, to get down to the loch?" Unsurprisingly, everyone did – when you expect a walk to be along a loch, you don't want to head away from it unless there's a very good reason. There's something magnetic about water, whether it's the crashing waves of the sea, the rush or gurgle of a river, or the glassy calmness of a loch. Walking along the shoreline, riverbank or lochside all seem more appealing than being shrouded in dense vegetation, or tramping through bleak moorland with limited or dull views.

We were soon picking our way through woods and over rough steps – which had seen better days – to the water's edge, but stopped a while to admire the ripples on the otherwise calm water, and the outlook across to the other side. A lone mallard interrupted her serene sailing to move closer, hoping for something interesting to come her way. After that, the going definitely got tougher. Large boulders which seemed to have been flung with malice back in the mists of time, were firmly lodged in the middle of the path, with no easy way round them. We'd try to find footholds to hoist ourselves up and over, or hug the stone as we took tiny side steps to get round a skliff of path, ducking to avoid brambles or branches as we squeezed through. All this scrambling whilst trying not to trip over the myriad of thick tangled roots was exhausting - everything seemed deliberately placed to cause as much havoc as possible.

"Wouldn't take much to trip and go headfirst down into that." Liksi looked down at the dark water as she clutched a branch to steady herself. Even a show of primroses on a grassy patch at the edge didn't really take away from the sentiment.

"Aye, poor Rob Roy didn't have it easy along here." I eyed the rocky cliffs, partly obscured by the undergrowth back from the path. "One of these crags is supposed to have been his prison, and there's a cave of his further along somewhere."

"He seems to have caves all over central Scotland – or is that Robert the Bruce?"

"I don't know, Liksi – you're the historian, not me. I just point out the landmarks – ow! This bloody thing's attacking me!" I'd walked right into a jaggy branch and just missed getting my eyes poked out. "Watch out, you two."

As the path veered inland slightly Fiona pointed out a low stone cottage partly hidden in the bracken. "Could that be a bothy, d'you think? It's pretty run down – but maybe we should consider staying in one next time, maybe – to give Alan a break?"

"Huh. Don't worry about Alan – he loves pretending we're too much for him. As if. Aye, it's Rowchoish Bothy, I think."

"No chance anyway. Need my luxury on these trips." Liksi was looking dismissively at the rather sad-looking place. It certainly didn't look too appealing, and I'm sure it would have been pretty basic inside.

"Really?" I was slightly surprised by her reaction – I'd have expected that from Fiona more than Liksi, but then Fiona's the one who goes youth hostelling regularly. Ach well, there's nowt so queer as folk, as they say. *Even* pals you've known forever.

"Luxury?" Fiona turned round in mock surprise. "I doubt you'd call the Drovers 'luxury' exactly, from what I can make out." The Drovers Inn at Inverarnan was where we were headed that night.

"I mean, essentials like a BED and a SHOWER. We *are* going to get them tonight - Eilidh?" Ah – *that* kind of luxury.

"Yes, yes, don't worry. I wouldn't *dare* have you slum it, Liksi." As I laughed with them, I did have a moment's doubt when I thought of the last time I'd been in the Drovers Inn, but staying there overnight was something I'd always wanted to do. I just hoped the others would appreciate it; anyway with a bit of luck we'd be so exhausted that the finer points of the accommodation would be overlooked.

The track re-joined the main path not long after the bothy, but it didn't get any easier and it was hard going concentrating on every step. Most of the leaves were out now, and the density of the oaks meant that we couldn't always see the loch. However, when we did, there were loads of opportunities for photos framed by trees, often with the jagged outline of the Cobbler featuring in the background. Fiona wondered aloud how many times my 'friend' from last time would have climbed it by now. At Inversnaid, we stopped on the wooden bridge to admire the Arklet Falls, cascading down in foaming layers to the loch – another example of the lure of water – before finding ourselves in an open area in front of a large hotel[1]. After my faux pas over

---

[1] This hotel has been significantly upgraded since our visit.

the Beech Tree Inn, I'd made sure in advance that this place would be open, and the plan was to have lunch here.

"It'll make a change not to have a picnic this time." I started to loosen my rucksack straps with relief as we approached the front entrance – only to be met by a sign asking all walkers to leave boots and rucksacks outside. "Eh? What's this? *Boots?*"

"No chance." Fiona, borrowing Liksi's phrase, looked far from pleased. "Is this the local version of 'Walkers Welcome'? Well, stuff that." She marched straight in, and somewhat more apprehensively, Liksi and I looked at each other before following, rucksacks and boots still firmly in place. Stepping over a frayed tartan carpet, we found ourselves in the hallway of what must once have been a very grand building, but was showing severe signs of neglect. Unaccountably, I shivered, and not just from the change in temperature. The large bar was just off the hallway; a couple of customers raised their heads to stare at us, then went back to gazing into their drinks. The barmaid looked as if she was putting all her grudges of the day into pulling that pint.

"Do you have a bar menu?" Fiona's perfectly polite question was answered by a finger pointing to a chiller cabinet. "Lovely. Thank you *so* much," she said sweetly, and received a scowl in return. Inside the cabinet were a few plastic white bread sandwiches which had seen better days, and a very limited selection of soft drinks. We settled for coffee instead, which amazingly came with some shortbread, albeit the pre-packed stuff, and found an alcove as far away from the bar as possible.

"Don't have much luck with your lunchtime suggestions, do you, Eilidh?" Liksi handed me a cup, and looked suspiciously at the liquid that came out of the cafetière as she poured. I shook my head, feeling guilty again.

Recent reviews have been favourable

"It's like 'The Shining' in here." Fiona shivered. "I'm just waiting for Jack Nicholson to appear."

Although we all started giggling rather uncontrollably, she was absolutely right and we didn't waste much time over the coffee. I noted that in spite of her scowl, the barmaid hadn't dared to tick us off for bringing in both rucksacks *and* boots. Probably too scared of Fiona – most people were, in my experience.

"My God." I opened the front door and breathed in the fresh wholesome air again. "Highland hospitality at its best. Sorry about that."

"Highland?" Liksi looked puzzled. "Surely we're well south of the Highlands?"

"Depends on your viewpoint." I had had so many arguments about this over the years. "We're north of the Highland Fault Line – remember, we saw the islands from Conic Hill? Though personally I always feel that the Highlands don't really start till Perth. Anyway, come on, I don't care *where* we are, as long as we're out of that awful place. Oh my God, what's *that*?" I jumped, clutching Liksi, who happened to be nearest, as a blast of earsplitting noise came out of nowhere.

Looking round, we identified the source as a cruise boat, whose loudspeaker was blaring out recorded information about the loch and hotel. The deck was packed with tourists, waving inanely in our direction, and seemingly unperturbed by, and even enjoying, the racket.

"What a travesty, spoiling a lovely spot like this! Well, hotel excepted." Fiona was covering her ears while screwing up her face with disgust. "That volume *must* be illegal."

"It's a disgrace." I was glaring, futilely, at the offending vessel. "You wouldn't get tourist nonsense like that in the 'real' Highlands – from the point of view of a completely non-biased Highlander, of course."

"We'd better get a move on – looks like it's heading in this direction. They're in for a big disappointment if they're going into that hotel though." Liksi hastily finished tying her bootlaces.

Reeling from the assault on our eardrums, we set off again along the lochside as quickly as possible, trying to blot out the racket until at last it receded into the distance, and tranquillity was restored. The roots and boulders quickly reappeared, but somehow we were ready for them this time. Momentary glimpses through the dense undergrowth unveiled huge crags or clefts in the rocks, any one of which could have been Rob Roy's Cave, but we didn't stop to investigate. Tree roots, branches, boulders and bracken encased the uneven stone steps which climbed steeply upwards, before dropping down again. Their mossy surfaces made them slippy in places, and it took all our concentration to navigate them without incident. It was getting increasingly warm, and the sweat dripping down my face started to sting my eyes. I stopped for a slug from my water bottle, and took the opportunity to unzip the bottoms of my trouser legs, and remove them. Fiona'd already changed into her shorts in the hotel – I'm sure the barmaid would have loved that, if she'd spotted her.

"Shorts in April, in Scotland." I breathed a sigh of relief as I felt the air on my legs. "Who needs Benidorm? Good God, *look* at that!" I gazed in disbelief at the sight of a young lad coming up behind us on the path, wheeling a mountain bike laden with gear. His face was even redder than Liksi's, and was shiny with sweat, but he managed to gasp out a brief acknowledgement as he manoeuvred the bike past us.

"Don't envy him." Liksi was looking after him with a frown. "Imagine pushing that over all those boulders and things. Well, maybe not *over* exactly, but … why?"

"Nuts." I shook my head, watching as he bumped the bike over the rough gravel, swerving to avoid the larger stones. "Bikes shouldn't be allowed on long distance walking trails anyway."

"Why not?" Liksi looked curious.

"Well, mountains and lochsides weren't designed to be cycle tracks, and bikes disrupt the flow of walkers. Why should *we* have to stop and move aside to let them pass?"

Too late, I remembered that Liksi's son did quite a lot of mountain biking – but maybe only on bike trails. They let me have my rant anyway, and we carried on, trying to ignore the combination of heat and sore legs. Another steep climb, this time involving a set of wooden steps, and not long after that the view opened out and we could see the head of the loch at last. Walking down the slope we passed another stone bothy. It was more or less the same shape as the previous one, but as it was practically on the path we decided to have a nosey and slipped in through the open door.

"This confirms my thoughts." Liksi was looking round at the stone floor, and two stone raised platforms, which were presumably where you were supposed to put your sleeping mats. There was a graffiti-covered fireplace, which looked as if it was still in occasional use, a plastic chair and a sweeping brush, and that was it.

"Don't you *dare* suggest we use one of these next time." Her glare was followed by one of her big gutsy laughs. She knew us too well.

Not long afterwards, we reached the turnoff for the wee ferry at Ardleish Pier. It was tempting to hail it and pop over to the hotel at Ardlui for a pint, but I managed to put that alluring proposition aside this time, with regret.

Loch Lomond finally came to an end and we picked up speed, thinking we must be nearing our destination for today's stretch. The obstacle-strewn route gave way to a gentler path through fields, and though there were a couple of hilly bits, it was much easier walking and made a pleasant change. However, we were under the usual end-of-walk illusion – there were still a good couple of miles to go, and each step seemed one too many. We passed our cyclist again; this time he was flat out in the heather with the bike beside him – his face was still bright red and his eyes were closed as we passed.

"He *is* breathing, isn't he?" I asked, partly joking – but was relieved to see his chest rising and falling.

"Better not sleep for long or he'll have terrible sunburn." Liksi looked concerned, but we didn't want to disturb him and decided to leave him in peace. Shortly afterwards, we turned left off the main WHW path and walked past the rather inviting facilities at Beinglas Farm – pub, café and toilets. We crossed the small bridge over the river, and walked – or trudged – back along the busy main road to the Drovers. This historic inn looked as intriguing as ever; broken windows and peeling paint seemed at odds with the walkers and bikers enjoying their drinks at tables outside.

"Doesn't look like *this* is the kind of place to worry about boots and rucksacks." Fiona was dead right, and that was one of the reasons I'd wanted to stay here. The other was in evidence as soon as we walked into the reception area. The building had been operating as an inn from the early 1700s, and was magnificently still reminiscent of those days – not least via the ferocious but rather mangy stuffed bear, and the suit of armour which seemed to be doubling as the Leaning Tower of Pisa. Other very dead exhibits filled the hall, along with large framed pictures depicting what I guessed were Highland scenes. However, a reassuringly contemporary young guy sporting a ponytail and kilt checked us in and gave us the key to our room.

"Your bags should be over there." He indicated a heap of kitbags and larger rucksacks over in the corner of the hall, with tags saying 'Travel-Lite'.

"I'd forgotten all about them – but good to know the system works." Fiona bent down to retrieve her one.

"Thank God – would've been murder carrying this as

well." I couldn't have agreed more with Liksi, as I fished mine out – probably one of the largest there. Some poor sods would've had camping gear with them on the trail too – but not us.

We climbed the uneven wooden stairs, and made our way along creaky corridors with uneven floors and threadbare carpets to our room.

"Well, the room looks OK, Eilidh." Fiona, sounding a bit surprised, was first in and quickly claimed her bed in the corner.

"It does indeed." I looked around approvingly and with some relief at the very clean room with 3 beds covered in crisp white linen, and a sink in the corner. Even the tartan (ish) carpet looked clean and new. We discovered a large bathroom at the end of the corridor which was more in keeping with a previous period of history – the bath was large, cracked and stained, and on experimenting with the taps a stream of brownish water gushed out. The window was also cracked and patched up with peeling parcel tape, and the sill and other paintwork didn't look as if they had been cleaned since Rob Roy was roaming the area.

"I don't care – at least it should be *clean* brown water, and I'm not going to bed without a bath." Brown water didn't actually bother me, having been used to the occasional peaty colouring in various households in the highlands. "First, I need a drink – coming?"

We managed to squeeze round a table in the crowded, cheerful bar. All the staff wore kilts and black T-shirts, and seemed about half our age.

"It must be a fun place to work." I couldn't help feeling rather envious. "There's often live music in the evenings. A good array of pumps, too – what are y'all having?"

"Whatever you're having, Eilidh," said Fiona. "As usual – but a half, not a pint, remember."

"So good to sit down – and tell me, is this nectar?" Liksi

sighed happily with her first mouthful of lager shandy. "Don't think I ever want to move from here again."

In spite of that we took turns to go up for a bath. Fiona braved it first, and came down soon after looking a bit unnerved.

"Well, it works." She paused. "The water becomes only a *pale* brown eventually. But someone kept turning the doorhandle and trying to get in. It was rattling so much I was expecting them to burst in at any minute."

"Oh, I forgot to tell you." I'd been waiting for this moment with glee. "This place is supposed to be one of the most haunted pubs in Scotland. That must have been Angus the drover ..."

"Ha ha. God, I need another drink after that."

"*Now* she tells us." Liksi put her glass down slowly. "Who was Angus anyway?"

"Oh, it's a long story, to do with clan rivalries, cattle thieves, and a few murders – including Angus's. His ghost is seeking revenge."

"*You* should go next, Eilidh, and chase Angus away before it's my turn."

"With pleasure – but it's still daylight so I doubt there'll be any real ghostly happenings till later on." Unsurprisingly, Angus didn't disturb my bath slot, or Liksi's, and we went on to eat far too much in the dining room, overlooked by a row of stags' heads, before going to bed.

The problem with drinking beer though, is that you need to visit the facilities in the middle of the night. The walk along the dimly lit corridor, trying not to be spooked by the flickering shadows, rustles and creaks, was not for the faint hearted, and it was a great relief each time to return to the room and the comforting presence of my gently snoring friends.

Chapter 9 – West Highland Way 4 (April 2009) - Liksi

This 21-mile stretch from Inverarnan to Bridge of Orchy has no major obstacles or hills, but it is an ambitious distance to tackle in one day. The route starts back at Beinglas Farm and follows the River Falloch, passing by Crianlarich and crossing into Tyndrum, before moving along the glen to Glen Orchy.

I'd been pretty whacked by the time we got in last night. Hockey training didn't cover stepping over tree roots and dodging round boulders, and although yesterday'd been a bit challenging, overall it'd been less arduous than I'd expected. I woke up feeling rested and ready to go again, although I was a bit anxious about the distance. Twenty-one miles in one day was something I'd never even thought of doing before, and I did wonder if we'd been over-optimistic. However, I'd left the stage planning to the others, so I'd only myself to blame if it turned out to be too much. Anyway, the thought of three more days with these two – and, let's face it, without Pete – was wonderful. Not only that, but the weather was still good – not as hot, but still warm and dry. I'd been expecting it to be cold and rainy – after all, it was the Highlands – but this was a real bonus.

Leaving the Drovers with some regret, we went back along the road and across the bridge to Beinglas Farm, picking up the track again to the left of the farm. It wound its way through thick bracken on both sides, with woodland behind it. We'd noticed a trio of guys coming up behind us, and as they were about to pass I cottoned on to their accent.

"G'day, folks!" They greeted us cheerily, and a T-shirt advertising Fosters beer confirmed their origin.

"Hi there. You're a long way from home." I could never pass up the chance of speaking to Australians.

"Sure are. But this is my ancestral home – has to be, with a name like Macleod!" The speaker turned to one of his mates. "And he's a MacDonald. That cobber there's just a standard Pom, he don't count!"

"I'll give you Pom." The blond one aimed a blow designed to miss. "Just repeat that when your feet're rooted and you expect me to wait for you. S'truth – what I've got to put up with!"

"We've got a MacDonald here too." Laughing, I pointed to Eilidh. "Are you doing the whole Way?"

"Yup, the whole darned Way. Five days – then we're off to Skye."

"Well, you'll certainly be able to locate some MacDonalds and Macleods there." Eilidh moved to the side to let them pass.

"So we've been told. Well, so long – maybe see you in Fort William." And they were off – sadly.

"What's 'rooted'?" asked Fiona. "Knackered?"

"Yeah, more or less. Good luck to them doing this in 5 days." What we were doing was hard enough; I certainly wouldn't want to up the daily mileage. Fiona and I got engrossed in a discussion about the intricacies of Cisco networking, while Eilidh was busy examining leaves and bending down to look at plants. Luckily, I looked up in time to see the Aussie group disappearing in one direction, just as we'd carried on in the other.

"Hey, look, they're going the wrong way!" I turned to Fiona. "We'd better shout to them."

"Yip – oh, hold on a minute. Look back there – there's a sign we missed." Fiona ran back to have a look, then rejoined us looking rather shame-faced. "It's a sad day when the foreigners know our country better than we do ourselves."

We had a good laugh about it, as we turned back then followed the group up the path.

"Cisco must be such an engrossing subject – yes, I heard you two chuntering on." Eilidh was looking smug. "At least I was engrossed in the local flora – a much better excuse."

The dull roar of traffic on the A82, which was running more or less parallel to the Way at this stage, was a bit disconcerting – it felt like an intrusion in what was otherwise full countryside. However, this was forgotten when a rush of water alerted us to the River Falloch flowing below us, tumbling over rocks and splashing into small pools. Eilidh couldn't quite identify the Falls of Falloch specifically, but there were plenty of attractive small waterfalls with their mini-glades and overhanging foliage.

"What's that smell?" I stopped suddenly, sniffing the air. "It's rank!"

"God, it's strong, whatever it is." Fiona was holding her nose, and Eilidh was looking around, perplexed.

There was something musky, certainly – then I spotted the dark shapes through the foliage. "What's that – look – there."

"Ah, wild goats. I'd hoped to see them somewhere along here." Eilidh moved closer. "There's masses of them."

"My God, they're BIG." Fiona had stepped back, looking slightly unnerved. "Look at those horns." The latter were certainly impressive but the shaggy black animals ignored us, carrying on with the serious business of nibbling at the ground or on the leaves of the trees. They were actually rather attractive beasts, and I left them to it reluctantly, although I wasn't sorry when the smell faded away.

The walking was all very pleasant and straightforward, even the 'sheep creep', a very low tunnel under the railway; we had to crouch right down to pass through. Shortly after that, there was another tunnel to get us under the A82. As we climbed the hill on the other side, the views opened out across from Crianlarich, taking in some impressive mountains. Sheep grazed peacefully below us, and agricultural smells assailed our nostrils.

"Look – buzzard." We followed Eilidh's finger to watch the big bird drifting in the thermals, so near that we could see some of the markings on the underside of his black-tipped wings as he swerved overhead. "Maybe looking out for sickly lambs."

"Apparently this is about the half-way point of the whole route." Eilidh offered this with an air of relief, which Fiona immediately dashed by saying:

"Half-way from Milngavie to Fort William, I guess, not half-way on our current four-day jaunt?"

"OK, OK, I know that, but you might just let me enjoy the moment. Yes, from Milngavie to here is about forty-eight miles. Only another forty-eight to go."

"And we've got fifteen of them ahead of us today, so we'd better press on."

"You sure know how to motivate people, Fiona. When's lunch, by the way?" I looked at Eilidh sharply, but thankfully she was laughing.

"You're in charge." Fiona shrugged her shoulders. "You're the nearest we have to a native on this trip."

I left them to work it out. Apparently going downhill into Crianlarich itself would've been a bit of a detour, so they decided to keep going till Tyndrum, although it'd be well past lunchtime by then. I didn't really mind – I was happy to keep going, to get as far on as possible before fatigue set in. If not mine, probably Eilidh's.

As the scenery became more agricultural, we passed the moss-covered ruins of St Fillan's Priory and a very old graveyard, which Eilidh (with reference to her guidebook) informed us was 12th century. Both places did have an aura of peace somehow, particularly the Priory. It was a restful spot, looking back over the fields, and surrounded by woodland. St Fillan was the patron saint of insanity, apparently, and had something to do with Robert the Bruce.

Eilidh teases me about being a historian, but it's much more recent history that I'm interested in. 12th century just doesn't do it for me. Not for the first time, I wondered what on earth made me study Computing at Uni. Oh, well. At least I should probably always be in work, although I don't suppose that was a ringing endorsement of what I did for a living.

"How about those, then Liksi – would they be luxurious enough for you?" I was startled out of my reverie by Fiona, and peered ahead to see what she was pointing at. The woodland had been cleared to form a kind of park, with wooden huts dotted about – oh, Strathfillan Wigwams, according to the sign.

"They look quite cosy." I looked doubtfully at the well-constructed and shapely structures, with painted doors or French windows fronting them. "But do they have a toilet in them? If not – no way. I'm too old to grope my way outside in the dark in the middle of the night."

"Oh, Liksi, honestly!" Eilidh was shaking her head at me, laughing. "No sense of adventure."

"Just tell me one good reason WHY I should pay money to be uncomfortable? Mm?" I pretended to ignore the rest of their comments. Seriously, if I'd to share one of these things with these two I'm sure it'd be OK. If I'd to share one with Pete for any length of time, we'd drive each other insane and have urgent need of St Fillan's care.

Just before Strathfillan, the route had crossed the A82, and not long afterwards it crossed back again, which was a bit confusing. Eventually, it crossed over for the third time as we entered Tyndrum, and Eilidh, limping slightly by now, led us straight to a great big place called the Green Welly Stop. The car park seemed pretty full, and there were people milling about everywhere – bikers, walkers, families, older couples.

"'Stop', not 'Shop'". Eilidh couldn't resist correcting

Fiona. "It's got a bit of everything here. Including FOOD." I suddenly began to feel very hungry – and weary – and hoped for a reasonable length of stay here. But -

"We'd better not spend too long here." Fiona joined us as we squeezed into the padded bench seating in the spacious cafeteria. "There's still another seven miles to go. How're your feet, Eilidh?"

"Och, you've noticed – so much for me trying to walk normally." She grinned at us. "OK-ish, but probably blistered." Fiona'd been setting a cracking pace, right enough, but we'd all been keeping together so far. Looking at Eilidh now, I'd a feeling that might change soon. She refused offers of plasters though, saying that the last thing she wanted to do was take her boots off, only to put them back on again.

"Are you still running? You've been doing well today." I felt that a bit of encouragement might help, and she looked at me gratefully.

"Aye, I go out with some others a couple of times a week, and it's good fun. We're hoping to do the Women's 10K in May – I can't actually believe it. I'm definitely getting fitter – but being fitter doesn't stop blisters."

"Does Alan run?" asked Fiona.

"Ha! Alan? Only if there's a ball to chase, and they put him in goals these days anyway." Alan still played 5-a-side football every week, although according to Eilidh he and his team-mates resembled something out of The Mummy Returns, with the number of bandages they put on before playing. "What about Pete?"

"Pete – oh, he chases balls too. Little white ones. Goes to the gym a lot." Oh, he sure does – and admires himself in the mirror for hours afterwards. I forced a smile. What was the point in talking about Pete? I come away on these weekends to forget about him. If it wasn't for the children, I honestly don't know where we'd be now. Anyway.

"Anyone got the time?" asked Fiona suddenly. "We should get going." It turned out to be after 4 o'clock, so with some reluctance we got to our feet again and followed her out of the restaurant and back to the path.

Once we were clear of the village, the route was pretty flat, but there was a rather forbidding conical mountain ahead of us.

"God, that's a bit scary - glad we're not going up there." I pointed to its steep, dark slopes.

"Beinn Dorain," said Eilidh. "Apparently it's not quite so difficult to get to the top as it looks – the usual route is round the side there."

Before we reached it, a wide glen opened out to our right, and a grey stone viaduct could be seen in the distance. Not quite the Glenfinnan one of Harry Potter fame, but still pretty impressive. This whole walk was just so picturesque – so many of Scotland's loveliest locations were on show, and we still had most of the distance to go. Why had I never done any hill-walking before? The answer seemed obvious. Pete. He wasn't interested, so I hadn't even tried. Although that was a bit unfair, I suppose – I'd never really thought about it before.

It was easy walking, but it wasn't long before Eilidh started lagging behind. Pity; she'd been doing well today.

"There's only six or so miles to go." Fiona's tone was almost accusing, as Eilidh slowly caught up with us.

"I'm sorry, but I really don't understand why my feet're so sore." She leaned against a post to take the weight off each foot in turn. "I've done much, much more difficult trails than this."

"Mine are getting pretty tired now, too." I tried to encourage her. They were – I suppose 'weary' was the best way to describe them – but they weren't sore, and I wasn't struggling at all. "Come on, I'll stay with you."

"Sorry, Liksi, I just can't go at that pace," she said soon

after Fiona'd left us well behind again. The pace was fine for me – bit on the slow side, in fact – but I couldn't let her trail behind on her own. She was trying her very best.

"You'd think she'd slow down a bit." Eilidh sounded rather plaintive, as Fiona's pink jacket disappeared round a distant bend.

"Think she just finds it difficult to go slowly – some people are like that." I knew some of my sporting pals were a bit like Fiona, but personally I thought she could've tried a bit harder.

"Mm, not convinced. Look, there she is – what on earth is she doing?" We watched as the pink blob seemed to be performing a war dance, then dived off to the side of the track and up the hillside. "The track goes the other way. There she is again – she seems to be running."

"Well, if she's doing extra bits it'll give us time to catch up." I was right – we kept to the path and after a while came across Fiona sitting on a rock waiting for us.

"What happened?" asked Eilidh as she sat down beside her to take the weight off her feet. "You looked like a whirling dervish at one point."

"Wildlife." She batted away some flies and muttered, "See, they're after me again. I just kept running into hordes of them, and they're horrible."

"But why did you run up the hill and away from the path? Surely they weren't that bad?" Eilidh obviously couldn't think of any good reason to cover more mileage than necessary.

"Er, cows." Fiona screwed up her face.

"Cows?" I repeated stupidly. "You mean the ones in the field back there?"

"They weren't all in the field, and some of them were coming straight at me along the path. They looked a bit menacing and I wasn't taking any chances." There was a defensive note in her reply - it was unlike Fiona to admit to being afraid of anything, and I must admit I was rather amused at the thought of her being afraid of a few cows.

"Well you obviously cowed - ha! - them into submission. They were very well behaved when we passed them." Eilidh sounded smug.

"Didn't even notice them." I hadn't, not at all. "Glad you scared them off for us, anyway. There's advantages to having you go off in front."

This was the last episode of note before we continued with the long, final stretch, with Beinn Dorain still glowering down at us from the right. Eilidh lagged further and further behind as Fiona quickly disappeared from view again, and I ended up somewhere in between, stopping every so often for Eilidh to keep up, but trying to keep Fiona in my sights too. Eventually I gave up, and just stayed in step with Eilidh. It was a good, even path, more or less flat and with a pleasant open outlook on all sides. However, by this stage in the day it was also an endless, slow trudge, and Eilidh was so uncomfortable she wasn't in the mood for much chat. I did try, though, and eventually brought the subject round to something I'd been wondering about.

"How well do you know Nathan, Eilidh?"

She looked at me in surprise. "I've seen him a few times over the years, but not recently. Why?"

"Just wondered. Fiona seems very worried about him. Not too sure what the problem is, though."

"I – I shouldn't really say this, but I don't care for him much." I wasn't surprised at this response, as it confirmed my own feelings. "He's just sort of dour. The last couple of times they stayed in our place he hardly spoke. He seemed to be making it quite clear that he was only there on sufferance."

"Typical teenage growing pains?" I suggested. "Joe's not always an angel these days."

"Well, it could be, but I don't think so somehow – it's a bit extreme for that. He was doing really well in school at one point, but Fiona doesn't even talk about that now, though she's always happy to talk about Jack. No wonder."

"Yes, Jack's a good kid. Bright, too."

"Och well, I guess she'll tell us about him in her own time. Sometimes I wonder if she likes stomping ahead on her own, to think things through. You've no worries about your two though, have you?"

No, I didn't. I wasn't one of these boastful mothers, but I was proud of my two kids and enjoyed talking about them. Joe'd got an unconditional acceptance for Loughborough in October, and Julie – was just Julie. She was a very sociable kid, and schoolwork wasn't high on the priority list, but she was doing OK.

I think both of us were very relieved when the village of Bridge of Orchy came into view. It was little more than a railway station and a hotel, which also had a bunkhouse. We found Fiona there, already checked in – she'd made up all the beds, booked dinner and was curled up on her own bed reading a book, looking as if she'd just been out for a stroll in the park. Finding everything so organised, I think Eilidh almost forgave her for leaving us behind. Almost.

Chapter 10 – West Highland Way 5 (June 2009) - Fiona

The 21-mile stretch between Bridge of Orchy and Kinlochleven moves into more challenging territory. Starting at the eponymous bridge just behind the village, the path climbs up through woodland, then descends into the hamlet of Inveroran. From there it follows the old military road across Rannoch Moor, down past the Glencoe Ski area to the Kingshouse Hotel, up the zigzag of the Devil's Staircase to the highest point of the walk, and then down into the village of Kinlochleven.

Dinner at the Bridge of Orchy hotel had been hearty but of a surprisingly high standard, and breakfast wasn't bad either. I felt surprisingly good, but for the first time on the WHW my body knew it'd been working hard. My legs were pretty stiff, but I was looking forward to moving into a more rugged landscape today. Having said that, two consecutive days of 20-odd miles was bound to be a bit wearing.

"Good job you got us up early." Liksi was jamming things into her rucksack. "Going to be another long day."

"Aye, but at least we shouldn't be as late getting in tonight." Eilidh buckled up her pack, having somehow managed to jam everything in. "It's just a pity we couldn't have squeezed in another day somehow, to split these two long days."

"I know, sorry, but couldn't have taken any more time off work just now." Liksi's college was in the process of upgrading some of its networking.

"Och, it's not really a problem Liksi – working out accommodation would have been tricky anyway. Although I'd have loved to have stayed at the Kingshouse one night." Eilidh knew the area quite well, having lived there when she was very young. Apparently the Kingshouse Hotel was a well-known institution for walkers in the Glencoe area, but we were going to be bypassing it today.

It was still unseasonably warm for April, and everything seems possible when the weather's better than expected. Just behind the hotel, we stopped at the *actual* Bridge of Orchy to admire its attractive arched stone span over the narrow flowing river, before the path started to climb almost immediately afterwards. At the top, we stopped to take in the views. It felt good to stretch my legs again and breathe the fresh forest smells deep into my lungs. I wondered idly how Olly was getting on, then found myself hoping for the hundredth time that he'd be able to get through to Nathan. Somehow. I just couldn't do anything with him these days, and his aggressive reactions were wearing me down. He was due to go to University later in the year, but he kept avoiding discussions of what subjects he would do, where he would stay etc. There was something going on, and I just couldn't put my finger on it. Not for the first time recently, I pushed these thoughts away, and concentrated on enjoying the moment.

The path down took us through more open moorland to the bottom of the hill, where it turned onto a minor road, flanked by the Inveroran Hotel. This old coaching inn looked an inviting spot – small but well-maintained, with pots of yellow, white and violet pansies brightening up the gravelled and drystone-walled area at the front. The creamy white walls contrasted with the painted window frames topped by their triangular dormer roofs. It was tempting to join the other walkers sitting outside with their coffees, faces lifted to absorb the sun's warming rays. However, it was a bit early in the day for us to stop - maybe these people were intending to tackle a shorter stretch than we were today – and we had to make sure that we didn't lose time. I wanted us to enjoy our evening at leisure tonight. Reluctantly, we continued, walking past a stretch of pines which filled the air with their familiar sharp scent.

"How good's this - short sleeves in April?" I breathed in deeply again, drawing in as much of the bracing air as I could. "Who needs Majorca?"

"Yeah, none of that lying on the beach stuff for us." Liksi was at long last taking off a sweatshirt. She didn't seem to feel extremes of temperature, but just put on her normal 3 layers whatever the weather. She was such a petite little thing, but her habit of bundling up made her look like a mini Michelin man on these walks of ours. Eilidh, like me, had stripped to a T-shirt and was wearing her fleece round her waist.

After a while, we came across a lively group of guys sitting with bare feet in a burn, eating their sandwiches, and we stopped for a water break.

"Lunch already?" Liksi teased them.

"Aye – but bet we were up earlier than you guys." This was from a very tanned individual with a snake tattoo curling down his arm.

"Probably." If I had my way we'd be getting up an hour or so earlier, but I hadn't pushed it as it didn't really matter. "But we're not trying to win any awards in that respect. Liksi wouldn't be here if we were – would you?" Liksi shuddered, to a chorus of laughs. I watched the boys splashing their feet about in the mildly burbling water enviously; plunging my tired feet into cold water was always a treat for me, but again I just felt we couldn't afford the time today.

The terrain had changed not long after we left the hotel, with the ground now consisting of small hard-packed stones – unremitting, and relentlessly sore on the feet. Eilidh was trying to walk on the grassier verge where possible, but this was often more tiring and required greater concentration so I didn't bother. In any case, every so often the verge ran out and there was no choice but to get back on the path. And yet again, she was starting to fall behind – and we'd only done about five miles.

"Aren't you two finding this hard on the feet?" She'd an accusatory note in her voice as she caught up, joining us to lean against the wall of a small bridge. "I'm beginning to dislike this path intensely."

"Yip, hard going, but it's a pretty good path. I think it's an old military road." I looked at her with something between pity and exasperation.

"Well, it's certainly hard, and I'd prefer a grassy surface, but at least it's flat." Liksi thumped her foot down on the stony path a couple of times. "Blisters hurting?"

"Aye, but it's more than that – the soles of my feet're really sore. Like, *all* of the soles. I don't really understand it."

"Well, it's a lovely day, there's no hills to worry about, and lunch in the Kingshouse beckons. You said it was a good place, didn't you? You'll be fine." I knew I was doing my schoolmarm imitation, but thought that a no-nonsense approach might propel her on a bit. I pushed myself up from the wall, and we got moving again.

By the time we'd done about seven miles, ie about half the distance to the Kingshouse, Eilidh was completely out of sight, so we stopped for her again. As she limped up, misery etched on her face, my exasperation won through, although I didn't like myself for it.

"Eilidh, how about if we go ahead and meet you at the Kingshouse? You can just go at the pace that suits you, and we can have a longer lunch there and rest before tackling the last bit?" The weather was fine, the path was clear and very well defined, and there were loads of other walkers. She couldn't possibly have got lost or anything.

"Would you be all right on your own? It seems a pretty straightforward track, but ..." Liksi sounded doubtful, and would feel bad about this arrangement, but it was obvious that she was finding the pace slow too.

"Aye, it's OK, just go ahead and I'll get there eventually. I know exactly where we are, and where the Kingshouse is." Her mouth was set, but she had obviously decided to make the best of it. "Go on, off you go, I'll be fine." She took a swig of water and wiped her mouth, all the while shuffling her feet from one position to the other to relieve the pain. There was nothing we could do for her, so Liksi and I set off briskly, and as the gap between us widened I knew we wouldn't see her again for a good few miles.

After a while, we were overtaken by the group of paddlers. "Hallo again – great day for this, innit?" The snake tattooed guy was obviously enjoying himself, his brown face full of joie de vivre.

"Just passed your pal there – she says to tell you to get a beer in for her." This from a red-faced guy with a mop of curly black hair.

"That sounds like Eilidh. She doing OK?" Liksi asked anxiously.

"Aye, she's ace. Just taking her time."

"See you in the Kingshouse." With a backward wave, they were off at a cracking pace.

Liksi was a good walker and our speed was now much more comfortable. Still on the hard path, but now striding across Rannoch Moor, I felt lucky to be alive. Sun glinted on all the wee lochans, reflecting the deep blues of the sky. Occasional sturdy trees, forced into formidable twisted shapes by winter gales, stood guard over their territory. Larks and pipits soared and called out their shrill warnings. Shiehallion's[2] unmistakeable domed peak loomed in the distance and yet more mountains framed the horizon, some with the occasional patch of snow still holding out against

---

[2] 3,553 ft

the spring sun. Rannoch Moor had the reputation of being bleak, and although it must often be like that – in the dusk in driving rain, with leaden clouds and swirling wind – today it looked magical.

The path eventually led downhill and joined the road which led up to the ski tow. There would be no ski-ing now, but the road up was still quite busy, with loads of parked cars glinting in the sunlight. This whole area must be one of the most popular ones in Scotland, with so many wonderful mountains to choose from. I looked longingly at the mountain ahead of us.

"D'you think that might be the Buachaille?" I asked Liksi, stopping to get a better look.

"Oh, heavens, don't ask me. I need people to tell me what everything is, sorry. Here, have a dekko." She passed the map to me and once I'd unfolded it, I could see that I was right.

"Buachaille Etive Mor – 3,350 ft. I think this is one of the most climbed Munros." I gazed across at its hazy slopes. "Maybe we could do that one day?"

"Yeah, that'd be good. Wonderful scenery, isn't it?"

"Terrific. Lucky Eilidh, growing up here." Looking down towards the road, I pointed to the long white building across on the other side. "That should be the Kingshouse, there."

"OK – my round when we get there. No sign of Eilidh, but – "

I'd set off again, keen to cover the last few hundred yards to get to the hotel. It was an attractive if rambling building, made even more appealing by the number of deer clustered on the front lawn. Chewing the coarse grass placidly, mothers stayed close to the young and more skittish ones, only lifting their heads and fixing their eyes on us in the passing. After all, we were the interlopers, not them. Although the hotel had been a refuge for hikers since the 1750s, the place was obviously in a different category from the Drovers, being warm and welcoming without the spooky bits.[3] Pushing open the door of the pub, we walked past the group of guys we'd met earlier who were even more cheerful than before, and settled down at a table near the bar.

"Staying here the night?" asked one of them, a burly redhead with an infectious grin.

"No, heading on to Kinlochleven." I smiled at the questioner, then turned and winked at Liksi. "Although the thought of staying is very tempting. Looks a good place, this."

"It is that. Good craic every night – but specially tonight, eh lads?" He waved his pint glass at his friends and they lifted theirs too. It looked as if they'd had a few already, but they couldn't have been long in before us. We chatted to them for a while, while we ordered and waited for our food to arrive. They were from Inverness, and had set off from Milngavie five days ago, doing exactly the same stages as we'd done, but had decided to have an easier day of it today and call a halt earlier. It sounded as if every night had been a party night – they must have sound constitutions.

"Hey! Here she is!"

I looked up from my soup to see Eilidh peering tentatively round the door.

"Well done!"

"You made it – they're over there!" A tattooed arm was waved in our direction.

She was taken aback by all the cheers, expressions of welcome and beaming faces; even the bar staff seemed to have been expecting her. With a reddening but still smiling face, she made her way over to us and flopped down on the bench.

---

[3] Since writing, the Kingshouse has been extensively re-built, but the bar still welcomes WHW walkers

"Sit here and I'll get you a drink." Liksi was on her feet again.

"Oh my God, this is embarrassing." Eilidh acknowledged all the reactions wryly – now that she was here and able to sit down in comfort, any embarrassment soon began to dissipate. "Thanks, Liksi – this'll be the most wonderful beer I've ever had in my entire life. I mean it this time. How long've you been here?"

"About 40 minutes."

"Sorry to have kept you waiting." She sunk back in her seat and took a deep breath. "Thought I'd never get here. Are they still doing lunch?"

"Yip, they serve food all day." Just as well, as it was about 3 o'clock now. I passed over the menu. She ordered quickly, then turned back to us purposefully.

"Right, guys. I've come to a decision – I'm NOT going to walk on to Kinlochleven today. I just could not physically do another seven miles even if it was dead flat – far less over the Devil's Staircase." This particular bit was famous for being a severely zigzag stretch leading uphill, not long after the Kingshouse.

"Oh no, are you sure?" Liksi looked worried, and a bit puzzled. "What'll you do?"

"You two go on; I'll get a taxi to Kinlochleven. I'll go straight to the bunkhouse and meet you there – I can make up the beds this time."

"You absolutely sure? We could always try going really slowly." Liksi's a kind soul, but it was all I could do not to protest. At this stage in the day, I just wanted to get going again as it was likely that the hardest bit was yet to come, and I didn't want to be walking into the evening.

"No, I don't want to hold you back any more today. If I stop now, I might just be able to do tomorrow – though the way my feet feel now even that's in doubt. I'll be fine – in fact, just head off when you're ready. You two look as fresh and comfortable as if you'd just started out - don't know how you do it."

Decision taken – thank God. She was obviously sincere – she'd made her mind up and probably felt relieved that her walking was over for the day. We left soon afterwards, leaving her chatting happily to the guys, and accepting another drink from them.

"Don't think we need to worry about her too much." Liksi laughed, as we picked up the trail at the back of the hotel, passing a couple of hinds who lifted their heads briefly then resumed grazing. "As long as she remembers to *come* to Kinlochleven, and not stay drinking here all night. That guy with the red beard seemed to be *very* solicitous! Mind you, maybe she's the sensible one – she's not the only one with sore feet."

The path picked up the old military road again, which followed the busy A82 for a surprisingly long time, before at last turning to the right and climbing up through the heather. It wasn't long before we were negotiating the Devil's Staircase, a series of zigzags which took us to the highest point of the whole Way. Stopping to get our bearings, we looked back over the Buachaille and the other Glencoe mountains.

"Wasn't too bad, was it?" Liksi sounded almost disappointed. "Not very devilish after all."

"Nope, and it should be fairly straightforward now." I remembered that when we started walking from Rowardennan, I'd been sure that the Devil's Staircase would be the hardest bit. Oh well. Further afield, in the other direction there were more hills – in fact, there were hills everywhere. Layer upon layer, from green to dark grey, then purple, then hazy lilac as they melted into the distance. What a landscape – it would be *so* good to spend more time here, getting to the top of some of these peaks. "Downhill all the way to Kinlochleven."

Well, I sure got that bit wrong too. It was fine for a while – moorland and views – and it wasn't long before we passed the Blackwater Reservoir and thought we could see Kinlochleven at the head of the loch. Not long now. Well – it *was* Kinlochleven, but my God, those last few miles were torture. The moorland gave way to woodland, but the hill path suddenly veered downhill and became a wide, steep track composed of loose grey stones. They moved, they were sharp, and they were absolutely exhausting to walk on. Our conversation dwindled in the face of the deep concentration required to stay upright without twisting knees or injuring some other part of our anatomy. It felt as if we were slithering down an endless river of these stones, carried along by an irresistible force – it was such a huge relief when the path eventually levelled out and we found ourselves beside the old powerhouse. This forbidding building used to supply power to the aluminium smelter here, which closed in 2000. A familiar figure sitting against a heavy metal gate at the end of the track waved, and I knew we'd come to the end of the day's walking.

"Well done, guys. How was the Devil's Staircase?" Eilidh's bright welcome jarred, as all I could think of was getting this sweaty, strained body into a shower. "Bed's all made up; your servant's been busy."

"Thank the Lord!" Liksi threw her pack down as she flopped on the ground beside her. "Wish I'd had the sense to stop when you did – don't think I'll ever be able to walk again."

"Bad? What did I miss?"

"Nothing. Absolutely nothing." Liksi'd taken off her buff and was wiping her streaming face with it. "That's the longest seven miles ever – can see Kinlochleven miles before you get here, so you think it's round the corner from away back. SO discouraging."

"And it's the worst bit yet. Horrible winding paths with loose stones so you've to watch what you're doing all the time ... You did the right thing, Eilidh." I wasn't meaning to be condescending – she'd never have made it, today anyway.

"Looks like it." She looked at us sympathetically. "The lady at reception said that too – she said so many people have to get carried down that bit, with their knees completely gone, or their feet in shreds." She got up slowly. "I'll do that missing stretch with my friend Melissa one day – she's missed a bit of the West Highland Way too, so we'll fill in the gaps."

"Did you've to wait long for a taxi?" asked Liksi.

"Aye, a couple of hours as all the taxis were on the school run, apparently – but those guys at the Kingshouse kept me company. In fact, I had a *very* enjoyable afternoon ..." The story kept us going as all three of us limped along to the bunkhouse. Before going in, I stopped to admire its location, framed by the hillside with the roar of the dark peaty river in the background, and the old powerhouse looming over the whole site. In spite of my aching legs, and worries about Nathan, life was still good.

It turned out to be our most luxurious hostel/bunkhouse accommodation yet – with an en suite, which we made full use of, slowly.

"Don't know about you, but not sure I'll be able to carry on tomorrow." Liksi was examining her feet ruefully as she waited her turn for the shower, and they certainly didn't look too healthy, with raw angry blisters on a heel and couple of her toes. I looked at her in surprise though. For heaven's sake, was I going to be the only one walking tomorrow?

"I don't know." Eilidh'd put plasters on after her shower, and was quite concerned. "It's the *soles* of my feet – they've got huge water blisters covering most of the pads. It's not just tiny blisters that a normal blister plaster would sort."

She was looking a bit miserable again, and I'm sure she was dreading the thought of having to give up.

"Well, let's wait and see how you both feel tomorrow." I got up and reached for my jacket. "Think you can manage out to the pub? There's one across the road."

"Oh, God, for the first time in my life I don't know if I can make it to the pub. It'd better *be* just across the road." Eilidh groaned.

"Eilidh, if you can't manage the pub I'll be phoning the hospital to get you in. Just think about the beer – it's ideal for sore feet." I was already out the door, and of course the other two followed. We made our way slowly and painfully along to the main road, over the bridge and into the Tailrace Inn. It was full of people who looked as if they'd been spending the day in the same way we had; some of them looked pretty done in too. I wondered idly what bit they'd all found most difficult – Rannoch Moor, the Devil's Staircase or the slithery descent into Kinlochleven. We exchanged war stories with one couple, and heard about other people who'd had to give up for more serious reasons than a few blisters. And, of course, some others could've been climbing Munros rather than doing the walk – there was just so much scope round here.

However, nothing like a few beers to revitalise tired walkers – or to top up the alcohol level – and the short walk home felt much easier than the painful one there. Only one more day.

It was only as I burrowed gratefully under the duvet that I realised I'd forgotten to phone Olly.

Chapter 11 – West Highland Way 6 (April 2009) - Eilidh

The last 14 miles start from the outskirts of the village of Kinlochleven, with a steep climb through woodland. At the top, with mountains all around, the path takes up the old military road again, through the Lairigmor (the big pass), before passing Ben Nevis on the right and winding its way down through forestry to the outskirts of Fort William. (This walk was undertaken before the Way was extended to finish in the town centre.)

"There's no skin left!" Liksi's wail finally jolted me out of my half slumber – the type where you really, really don't want to wake up and face reality. Somehow finding the strength to prop myself up on one elbow, I stared muzzily across at the unedifying sight of Liksi examining her feet.

"Look at this – ever seen such a *mess*?" Liksi's question didn't really merit an answer, except offering the equally delightful sight of one of mine, which I stuck out of bed for comparison. About a third of the sole was one giant water blister, and the second foot wasn't much better.

"Yeuch! What a pair." Fiona was sitting on her bed fully dressed, with her boots on and laced up. She'd obviously no qualms herself – as usual.

"There's no turning back on this section." I sat upright slowly and stiffly, as the realisation of today's planned journey dawned. I so much wanted to do this last bit, and I knew I'd feel awful if I'd to just get a bus to Fort William and hang around waiting for the others to get there. "There's nowhere to turn off and get a bus, taxi or anything. If we start, we have to finish. We need to be sure we can make it."

Liksi looked slowly again at her feet, my feet, and then up at my face. "Think we can do this, Eilidh. If we plaster every possible dodgy bit of our feet, and you use the gel pads you said you'd brought too, we'll manage. We'll do this together, and don't worry, there's no way I'll be making any speed today."

At that moment, I loved Liksi and could've hugged her. If she'd that much faith in me, I wasn't going to wimp out, not now. Stripping the paper off the largest Compeed plaster I could find, I started the process of protecting my poor feet for the final onslaught, and Liksi did the same. By the end of it, we each had a pair of feet that wouldn't have looked out of place on Frankenstein. Fiona decided that we needed further fortification in the form of bacon rolls in the Highland Getaway; after that the decision was made – we were going for it.

Back on the trail again, we walked past the Tailrace Inn and headed out of the village along the main road. The Compeed seemed to be doing its job – my feet, though tender, were cushioned and I could manage a reasonable semblance of a normal gait. So far. The weather was on our side – once again it was a glorious April morning. The long sliver of Loch Leven sparkled through the gaps between the houses, often framed by delicate birch leaves which had not long unfurled from their early spring tightness. Everything was crisp, and bright, and *alive* and the heat seemed to bring out the rich and varied greenery around us. I breathed deeply, taking in the fresh scents from all the mixed foliage, basking in the fact that I'd made it this far (well, almost), and that I was still fit enough to attempt the last section of this magnificent trail. No, not attempt – I had to finish it; giving up was no longer an option.

The route soon took a right turn, off the road and into the woods – and upwards. The stone steps at the beginning were helpful, and after a while we reached a gap in the trees where we stopped for a breather.

"Mm." Liksi was gazing about her with awe. "Just look at that."

Kinlochleven lay below to our left, and Loch Leven stretched out languidly behind it. Peaks and ridges were layered before us in hues of grey and lilac – the iconic Glencoe mountains to the left, and the mighty Mamores round about us and leading up to the north. All of them alluring, and most of them challenging. I'd seen so many photos of Glencoe and its mountains, but being here, at this spot, looking round at all those glorious hills – it was breathtaking. In spite of having only lived in Glencoe for my first five years, I felt a real connection here. And yet, I'd lived in a city now for most of my working life. Part of me felt cheated, but I had to make myself remember that I'd actually had a pretty good life overall, and working in a city had given me many opportunities which I wouldn't otherwise have had.

"Most of these are Munros." I forced my thoughts back to the present. "We must come back here one day and do a bit of climbing."

"Yip, we were just saying that yesterday. OK so far?" Fiona'd been practically skipping up the hill today, but at least she'd stopped to let us catch up. Liksi had kept right at my side.

"Aye, think so. Coming up the hill was fine, as the surface was varied and the steps helped. At least it's not that awful Rannoch Moor-type hard-packed stone surface. You OK, Liksi?"

"Yeah, think so. Early days, but fine just now."

We'd a look at the map to see how far we'd got to on the trail. Apparently we were on the old military road again, which seemed pretty straightforward for the next stretch.

"What's this 'Lairigmor' mean, d'you know? I presume it's Gaelic?" Fiona frowned at the map. "I went on the Lairig Ghru walk with my father years ago, and I remember it being pretty horrendous. Mind you, I was pretty young, and going on a long walk with my father anywhere probably wasn't my idea of fun." Lucky Fiona - I'd always wanted to tackle the

Lairig Ghru, a notoriously gruelling 27-mile walk through the Cairngorms, between Aviemore and Braemar. Mind you, at this precise moment it didn't seem quite so enticing ...

"Yes, it's Gaelic. I believe 'Lairig' means 'hill pass' and 'mor' means 'big'." I looked over her shoulder to check the map. "I guess that's an accurate description in this case. There's plenty of hills to pass between, anyway." I looked in the direction we were going. "'Between' being the operative word, thankfully."

"Thought you said you didn't know any Gaelic?" Fiona turned to me. "What does 'ghru' mean then? Short for 'gruesome'?" I made a face – it would be useful if Gaelic was so easily translatable. Sadly not.

"I *don't* know Gaelic. I can manage a few 'I am' phrases – tired, hungry, cold and other essentials – and tell dogs to behave themselves in different ways, but that's the lot. No idea what 'ghru' means, but Rannoch Moor was pretty 'ghru' yesterday, I'm sure."

"Didn't your father teach you Gaelic?" asked Liksi. "Thought you said it was his first language?"

"It was, but he didn't. My mother didn't have Gaelic and when we were wee, she was the one we were with all day. Also, remember at that time people believed that bringing up a child to be bilingual would be confusing for them – changed days now, thankfully."

"Indeed. Nowadays you'd have been at a Gaelic medium school and totally immersed in it. In fact, I might've been too." Fiona's father had come from the west coast somewhere.

"Aye, it's a big regret of mine. Would be handy for map reading – even to know what all the mountain names mean. Let alone ask for 'Two beers please' which I can just about manage in most European languages!"

After that pleasant thought, we put dreams of cold beers behind us as we set off along the 'lairig'. The path had opened out as we'd emerged from the woodlands, and the glorious views extended in every direction. Sweatshirts were stripped off to make way for T-shirts, and it was too bright and fresh for flies to risk coming out. Just unbelievably good weather – and although I could increasingly feel my feet, the pain was bearable and it was just *so* good to be here. There were several inviting spots beside tumbling burns, and on a different occasion I would've wanted to just sit there, maybe with feet cooling in the water, taking in the peace of the hillside, at one with nature. I loved the sound of water in the hills – the freshness and purity, along with a kind of burbling joy. I hugged these thoughts to myself, wondering if the others felt anything like this – difficult to tell on today's route march.

"Look, there's a loch down there. And a road." Fiona pointed down to the left, to a small narrow patch of water next to a couple of small cottages and outhouses, spaced out at the end of a winding single-track road. Clumps of pines stood guard on the steep slope across from the buildings, whilst smaller deciduous trees were dotted along the nearside. I could just make out white blobs of sheep, spaced out along the greener areas. What a beautiful, if lonely, spot – I wondered what it would be like to live there, as opposed to staying there for a week's holiday. As we watched, a red van wound its way towards the road end.

"Post van." I recognised it suddenly. "I've had many a lift in one of these when we lived up north. A lifeline sometimes." With nostalgia, I remembered once undertaking a solo bike run to see a friend on the north coast, and being very grateful when the local postie'd offered me (and my bike) a lift halfway home the next day.

"And there's an actual *car park* here." Liksi was looking with some disbelief at this sign of civilisation just down from our path. Well, it looked like a rough car park, although unsurprisingly there were no cars there.

"Never mind that, there's a bench – the map says this is roughly the half-way mark, so how about lunch?" Without waiting for an answer, I was already getting my sandwiches out of my pack before I even sat down. It was actually an ideal spot – a motivating half-way marker, and a great view of the loch where we could watch the comings and goings of post vans and any other activity.

I was pleasantly surprised that I hadn't found the going more difficult. However, I dug out my book to find out what horrors still lay ahead. "Right, let's see where exactly we are. That is Lochan Lunn Da-Bhra down there, and the road the van came on is a shortcut to Fort William apparently." I was consulting my book. "It's four miles, as opposed to about seven on the main route." Liksi looked at me with concern. "No, it's OK, I'm not suggesting it, not now. I just didn't realise there was *any* way out."

"It would be four miles on tarmac too – very wearing." Fiona was peering over at the book too.

"We've got this far – there's no way I'm not going to finish it now." I was determined to do it and Liksi seemed to be doing fine too. I could manage another seven miles, I knew I could.

The next part proved to be very varied, and if I hadn't been so tired I would've wanted to look for the vitrified fort of Dun Deardail, which was supposed to be somewhere just off the track. It was an Iron Age fort, built from rocks and stones which fused together in a horrific fire. I didn't spot any turn-off to it anyway, which was maybe just as well. We soon found ourselves back in the woods, then up a steep hill which led to an open stretch with Ben Nevis looming majestically in the distance.

"Why didn't we do Ben Nevis instead – would've been much easier than this!" Liksi asked with a laugh.

"Next time, maybe. We can add it to our list." We couldn't avoid stopping for a few minutes though, to take in the grandeur of Scotland's highest mountain. Even with a shroud of mist obscuring the top, and large patches of snow hanging on in spite of the change of season, the craggy purple slopes still looked dramatic and alluring. From this viewpoint, it didn't look too daunting, but we must've been quite high up anyway, maybe 1,000 ft or so.

The path became more undulating as the scenery changed again. A set of steps led down to a lovely spot with a small bridge over a gorge, and we stopped for a minute to watch the foaming water cascade down, swirling at the bottom before continuing its journey. Of course, after that there was the inevitable climb back up again. By this stage it didn't really matter if we were going up or down – I've always been slow going uphill, but now my knees were struggling a bit with the descents, and the soles of my feet were starting to burn again. Liksi's knees were giving her bother too, and she stayed firmly with me. Fiona meanwhile scampered along in her usual mountain-goat style, getting so far ahead sometimes that we'd come across her sitting on a rock checking her phone while she waited for us. Infuriating.

The last two stages proved to be absolute torture. Our spirits had lifted when we first saw Fort William in the distance, but getting there was another matter. Plunging back down into the dense forest, the path started to run in wide zig zags – through cleared spaces where logs were piled up alongside, then back into the pines again. With exhaustion beginning to set in, the zigzags didn't always make much sense, and seemed to be extending the route out of sheer badness.

"Y'know, going *up* the Devil's Staircase was nothing to this." Liksi grimaced as we made yet another incredibly angled turn leading *away* from Fort William. "And that bit before Kinlochleven wasn't quite as bad either."

"What masochist thought that this would be a suitable ending to the trail?" I had to force the words out – it took too much effort.

"Are you two all right?" Fiona had stopped again till we caught up. "This is horrible."

"Sore." I was becoming incapable of speech and all I could think of was getting to the end and being able to sit down.

"Me too. Knees playing up." Liksi grimaced as she rubbed one of them.

"How about if I just go on ahead then? If I get us checked in and have a shower or bath or whatever, then it'll be free for you two when you get there." Fiona was just itching to race ahead, and now that I knew Liksi would be staying with me, I didn't care.

"Yes, go on. We'll be fine." I wasn't sure if 'fine' was the appropriate word, but we watched Fiona disappear into the distance almost instantly, and started dragging ourselves down over the remaining zigzags. They were interminable, and as we ploughed on with gritted teeth, Liksi too didn't seem to have any extra energy for conversation.

"Here's the road, with a pavement." Liksi gave me a weary smile as at long last the track came to an end.

"Civilisation. Won't be long now."

How wrong can you be? There was another one and a half or so miles of 'civilisation' before the end of the Way. I dragged my feet along in sheer misery, wincing as I placed one sole after the other on the tarmac. Plod, plod, plod. A hard surface, after these tortuous zigzags, was just too much. Who designed this bloody path anyway? Couldn't they have worked out a more appealing finish? I was too exhausted to voice any of this, and we completed the last bit in near silence. With relief, we passed the obelisk marking the end of the Way[4], without having the energy to take a photo – as

Liksi suggested, we could do that the next day – and turned right when we reached the main road. Fiona had phoned to tell us exactly where the B&B was, so finding it was straightforward.

As we clumped up to the front door, we exchanged exhausted but triumphant smiles.

"We've done it – and luxury awaits. Aren't you glad I booked a B&B instead of a hostel?" I started to unlace my boots before going inside.

"And we deserve every bit of it," said Liksi with feeling, as she unslung her rucksack and stood up to stretch out her back. "That bath awaits ..."

That night in the Ben Nevis Inn, with a hearty steak pie in front of me and a whisky in hand, it seemed to me as if life could not get better. I felt encased in a warm, sleepy glow – which had little to do with the heat inside the inn or the dull burn of my feet; here in this lively hospitable place, surrounded by walkers and climbers and my two wonderful friends, I was glad to be alive and the pain of the journey was already behind me. Proud of us, proud of Scotland. And so, so glad that we had walked the entire distance of the West Highland Way. Well, in my case, almost.

---

[4] The official finish has now been extended by a mile, to take walkers through to the other end of the village.

Chapter 12 – Loch Katrine (September 2010) - Liksi

Loch Katrine lies in the Loch Lomond and the Trossachs National Park, and has been the main source of Glasgow's water since Victorian times. A tarmac path runs for 13 miles from the Trossachs Pier at the east end, along the north shore to the head of the loch, then round the south shore to the pier at Stronachlachar. This walk takes in the first few miles of the path only.

I stretched lazily as I slowly came to on Eilidh's sofa. This privacy was luxury compared to bunk beds in a hostel, although I was getting better at coping with that. As the brightness of the day filtered through the curtains, along with the sounds of the morning waking up – the dull roar of traffic, planes overhead, the occasional train, car doors slamming and children spilling out into gardens – I recollected some of last night's conversation and wondered uneasily how today's walking would go. This was not going to be like our recent walks.

We hadn't even decided where we'd walk this time. Eilidh'd set the tone for the weekend when we last proposed a date – she'd said point blank that she wasn't going to do another Munro or long walk if we were going to walk ahead and leave her.

"I thought the whole point of these walks was to enjoy each other's company," she'd said over the phone. "How's that possible if I'm left tagging along at the rear? I walk as fast as I can – it's not that I'm *trying* to be difficult." She'd paused before adding, "I know you try, Liksi, and I appreciate it, but I'm just not as fit as you, so maybe you two should do the walking and I'll join you afterwards."

Talking to Fiona afterwards, I was relieved when she too dismissed this suggestion immediately. We both loved Eilidh to bits, and although it was a shame she wasn't as fit as Fiona and me, she wasn't *un*fit and she possibly loved walking and the outdoors more than any of us. I *had* to be fit – having done hockey and athletics training for decades, and spending most Sundays competing or coaching, it was hardly surprising. Fiona did quite a bit of hillwalking anyway now, along with swimming and regular fitness classes. Eilidh just couldn't compete, though she did at least go to the gym sometimes.

I felt really bad about the whole thing, actually. Eilidh was absolutely right – when hill walking, you should walk at the pace of the slowest. What if something happened to her and we were miles ahead? Or if Fiona dived off into the blue yonder and took a wrong path and we didn't see her go? It wasn't just a case of leaving Eilidh bereft of our company - it could be dangerous. I'd tried to talk to Fiona about it, but she just kept saying she found it impossible to walk slowly. I knew what she meant, as I felt rather the same, but I also knew it wasn't fair to Eilidh. The whole thing was difficult, and I felt torn in two.

We'd at least agreed to meet up again, in Glasgow so that we could do a relatively local walk. Last night we'd discussed a few possibilities rather half-heartedly. Somewhere called the 'Whangie' was suggested, or an 8-mile loop round Milngavie, or a walk along the canal taking in Kirkintilloch or Bishopbriggs.

"Well, I've only brought my trainers with me so it'll have to be relatively good ground." Fiona carried on eating after delivering this bombshell, and didn't see us looking at her in amazement.

"Trainers? No boots? Why not?" Eilidh asked, unable to hide the shock on her face.

"Well, I didn't think we were going to do much of a walk, and I was travelling light anyway."

"Light?" repeated Eilidh slowly. "Well, that certainly restricts our options, doesn't it? That's the Whangie out, and the Milngavie loop out ... not sure about the canal. Or anywhere really."

The subject was dropped for the rest of the evening, but I could see that Eilidh was quite perturbed, and I didn't really know what Fiona was thinking of either. Was this her way of saying that if we couldn't walk at her pace, she wasn't wanting to play? It certainly seemed that way. Oh well, as the clattering from the kitchen and the sound of Alan's cheery voice brought me to full consciousness, I hoped they'd sort it out quickly. I loved these weekends – apart from anything else, they got me away from Pete – and I'd be very sorry indeed if they had to stop.

In the kitchen, Alan was busy at the kettle and the grill, but greeted me in his usual inimitable fashion. "Well *hallo* there! Wondered when you were going to grace us with your presence – or even if you were *here*? Only kidding – bacon roll?"

"Sorry, y'know how I like to make sure everyone gets a chance at the bathroom before I take it over. To get the slap on, and my hair just right? Yeah, please, so long as you burn the bacon." I slid into the bench at the table.

"So, where're we going then?" asked Fiona, buttering her toast.

"Loch Katrine." Eilidh was surprisingly firm. "It gives us options."

"Loch Katrine?" Alan looked up from pouring my coffee. "The tarmac path? That's a bit of a come-down after the West Highland Way. All worn out, are we?"

Eilidh gave him a warning look. "We don't have much choice. Fiona's not got her boots."

"Eh? No boots?" Alan looked genuinely puzzled, but Eilidh's expression cautioned him against further comment, and Fiona was pretending to read the paper. "Oh, OK. Taking the car?"

"Aye – you won't be needing it today."

So, Loch Katrine it was. It was a drippy kind of day, which matched the mood – I didn't know anything about Loch Katrine, but from Alan's comment it didn't sound as if we were about to have a memorable walk. I just hoped Fiona and Eilidh would settle down without any fuss. Eilidh drove up through Aberfoyle's bustling main street, then over a very twisty road which she told us was the Duke's Pass. As we snaked round the bends, the rich autumn colours vied for place in the surrounding woodlands, although the persistent drizzle spoiled any distant views.

"Is that the loch there?" I was referring to the grey sheet of water lapping almost up to the road on the right-hand side.

"No, that's Loch Achray. Lovely, isn't it?" It was, framed with russet and gold trees under the lowering sky. One thing about Scotland – it didn't really matter what the weather was like, the scenery was great anyway. Not that something like that would ever occur to Pete. He'd never dream of having a holiday in Scotland, not even a long weekend unless it involved a group of males, probably golf, and definitely copious amounts of alcohol. And no wife.

"Loch Katrine's at the end of this road." Eilidh had turned off to the left.

"Thank God. That was some road."

"You OK?" I asked with concern. Fiona'd been very quiet on the trip and as I glanced round at her she did look a bit green.

"Will be. Should've sat in the front." As soon as we parked in the large car park she got out of the car and stood there taking deep breaths. I was quite surprised. She'd not shown any signs of being a bad traveller before, but I guess most of the time we'd been on windy roads she'd been the one driving. So, the super-charged Fiona had a weakness after all.

While Fiona recovered, Eilidh and I changed into our boots.

"As it happens, we don't need boots for this if we're just going to stay on the track. I'd hoped to go off it a bit though, and up Primrose Hill or somewhere, but there's no point if Fiona can't go off-piste." Eilidh gave her lace a hard tug.

"Maybe she really was just trying to travel light." I didn't think so, but didn't want to inflame the situation.

"She *always* travels light and still manages boots. No, she's trying to make a point in return for me not wanting to do any more big walks just now."

"Don't worry, it's good to get out anyway - see some more of Scotland. Won't do us any harm to have an easy stroll for a change. Seems to be quite a lot going on round here anyway?" I looked around as more cars pulled up around us, disgorging families, dogs, walkers and bikes.

"It's usually quite busy here at weekends. People cycle round the loch – well, not round it as the path only goes to Stronachlachar so you've to come back the same way. It's about 13 miles away, I think."

"Guess we're not going to Stronach-whatsit, then?" After all the trauma of Fiona's boots, or lack of them, I didn't think a 26-mile walk of any sort was on the cards today.

"Stronachlachar. No, we'll just have to walk along the path till we get fed up, then come back."

Fiona joined us then, looking a more normal colour, and we headed towards the start of the loch, where there was a boat pulling out – the *Lady of the Lake*.

"Could we walk to Stronachlachar and get the boat back?" I thought this might be a good alternative.

"Nice idea, but the timetable wouldn't work out." Eilidh shook her head. "I'd a quick look on the Internet last night."

So we started out along the path, mingling with the cyclists and strolling families. It was pretty busy, although after a short while it thinned out – what was a very low-key walk for us was possibly a major undertaking for some. I guess some visitors just had a quick stroll then went back to the car. There was a heavy railing between the path and the water, which afforded the opportunity to stop and gaze down at the depths or across at the other side which was heavily wooded. Near the path the water was clear, and you could see the stones at the bottom, but as you looked further away the depths seemed dark and forbidding – or maybe it was just the weather. I thought I'd read somewhere that it was a very deep loch. As we watched, another boat – a bigger one – came into view, heading for the pier.

"That's the steamer, the *Sir Walter Scott*." Eilidh took off her hat and shook out her curls.

"Of *course*!" It'd just dawned on me. "Scott country. He wrote 'Rob Roy' as well – saw something about him on a sign back there."

"Huh, *Scott*!" Eilidh made a face. "I forced my way through 'Waverley' once and swore I'd never read another of his, ever. Made 'War and Peace' seem a doddle."

"Really? I try to read a Scott novel every year. Not easy, mind." I liked a book to be a challenging read, and not just yet another piece of run-of-the-mill crime fiction.

"I *am* impressed." Eilidh was an avid reader herself, but she seemed amazed at the idea that one of us could read – and enjoy – Scott.

"You're both mad." This from Fiona, who had recovered enough to re-join the conversation. "I read to escape – there's enough challenges and problems at work. So, enjoy your Scott background then, Liksi. I'll content myself with just looking at his boat."

After a while, we peeled ourselves off the railings and carried on, admiring the small waterfalls that tumbled down on the right-hand side of the road. The scenery was certainly attractive; just a pity for us it was a tarred road – I wasn't quite sure if my West Highland Way-scarred feet had fully recovered.

"Where's Fiona?" I said suddenly. Eilidh and I'd been walking along together, engrossed in conversation about various classical novelists and had lost track of what Fiona was up to. We stopped to look round, and it was Eilidh who spotted her:

"Good God, she's *behind* us, not in front. What on earth is she doing?"

Fiona seemed to be making quick forays into the bushes at the side of the path, disappearing momentarily then continuing for a few steps before repeating the process. I couldn't understand it – Eilidh yes, as she was quite a wildflower enthusiast, but Fiona? We waited till she caught up with us – holding up a plastic bag and looking rather pleased with herself.

"Brambles." She waved the bag in explanation. "There's loads – I can make jam when I get home. Good job I had this bag in my pocket."

Eilidh and I looked at each other, shaking our heads.

"You never fail to amaze, Fiona." Eilidh's voice had a hint of exasperation. "Don't you get brambles in Manchester?"

"Yip, we do – they call them blackberries there – but there's not always the opportunity to pick them. Look, here's some more." She crossed over to the side of the road again and stretched across the ditch to grab another handful, popping one into her mouth before scrabbling about for more. There were certainly plenty of berries about – their thorny stems and delicate pink flowers were choking all the other grasses and wildflowers.

"OK, you can catch up with *us* this time," Eilidh said rather tersely as we got going again. I guess the point wasn't lost on her that this was Fiona *choosing* to lag behind, as opposed to when Eilidh had no choice. In fact, knowing

Fiona this was probably exactly the point she wanted to get across – but hey, I wasn't going to add fuel to the fire.

It was a pleasant, if uninspiring walk and we kept going for about a couple of hours, stopping every so often to admire aspects of the loch or distant mountains, or to wait for Fiona. She was definitely in strange form today, only joining in the conversation sporadically. Unusual, when she was the one who often took control. When conversations ran out, she'd be the one who'd ask a leading question and off we'd go again – but not today. After a while, we agreed that we'd had enough and should head back for the sake of our feet.

Retracing our steps, we noticed a tree-covered island which we'd missed on the way out. Eilidh stopped to chat to a couple who were consulting a map, and discovered that it was called Ellen's Isle, although its original name was Eilean Molach. In the dull light of a typical September afternoon, the island looked sombre and rather mystical. Maybe Scott had managed to get that into his novel too – I made a vague note to check it out some time.

Arriving back at the pierside, and after she'd patted a few dogs in the passing, Eilidh led us up the steps to the café, and we settled in for a very belated lunch.

"At least you got the café right this time, Eilidh. Bit worried when you said we wouldn't need sandwiches because we could eat at the café – think we've heard that one before?" I was relieved to see Fiona smiling too.

"Ha ha. Am I ever going to be allowed to forget that?" She shuddered. "Ugh – I can still taste that disgusting Kendal Mint Cake." Eilidh seemed to be making up for it now - having finished her soup and sandwich, she was now tucking into a ginormous piece of carrot cake.

"This is my last indulgence," she added apologetically as she caught me eyeing her plate. "I'm going to a hypnotherapist next week to try to kick-start a real diet. I'm a bit sceptical, but I've had rave reports from a couple of colleagues, and I have to try something."

"Really? Good for you," I was rather surprised at the matter-of-fact Eilidh even thinking of anything like this. "I'd be sceptical too, but it does work for some people and there's no harm in trying."

"Well, I've got to get fitter somehow. Today's shown me that this kind of walking's not for any of us. Anyway, we'll see how things are next time we meet up. So, to change the subject – how're all the weans getting on?"

I launched into a brief summary of my kids' progress. Julie was plodding along at school and about to go into 6th year. Joe had thrown himself into student life in Loughborough with a vengeance.

"I worry sometimes that his social life might get in the way of both his studies *and* his rowing – did I tell you he'd taken that up? - but hey, isn't that all part of a healthy university existence?"

"Well, my university life consisted almost entirely of social life." Eilidh gave a rueful laugh. "I'm sure he'll have more sense than I had."

"I was so amazed to have got into University at all that I worked really hard at it," I said. "In fact, the only one who wasn't surprised was my gran. No-one from our family had ever gone to Uni, and my mother wanted me to go out and get a job after school. Luckily, I adored my gran and always heeded her advice."

"Luckily indeed, or the three of us wouldn't be here now." Eilidh smiled and turned to Fiona. "And what about Nathan? He must be finished his second year by now?"

There was a long pause, and I looked at Fiona, surprised – and then shocked as she swallowed several times before her eyes filled up.

"Oh, Fiona, what's happened?" Christ, it must be serious – don't think I'd ever seen Fiona cry before.

"It's Nathan – he's – he's – I think he's dropped out. We – we don't know." Fiona dashed angrily at her eyes and took a gulp of tea. Eilidh and I looked at each other in concern.

"Oh no – I thought he was doing really well." Eilidh looked puzzled.

"Oh, he passed all his exams last year – just. He hardly bothered to come home in the summer, and when he finally made an appearance he said he'd decided to drop out. That Uni was just a waste of time and full of Hooray Henrys poncing about." She paused to blow her nose. "We had a terrible time with him, and he ended up storming out of the house. He – he – didn't come back, and we didn't know where he'd gone."

"Oh, Fiona, how awful." Nathan had always been difficult, and on the rare occasions I'd met him even when he was younger, he'd not displayed any endearing characteristics. But this – dreadful. I'd never had any relationship problems with Joe and Julie, and at this moment I realised how lucky I was with them.

"It seems he did go back to Uni after all, for a while, but he came home before Christmas and we couldn't get anything out of him. He stayed in his room all day, and would go out at night to God knows where till all the hours. Eventually he asked us for a very large sum of money – said he'd fallen behind with the rent." She paused to collect herself, twisting a sodden tissue round her fingers.

"He got angry when we asked for details, and Olly got equally angry when he wouldn't give a reason. Eventually we said we'd give him half of what he asked for, and more if he could show us evidence of what the problem was." She paused again to sip her tea, and I could see how difficult this was for her. I was beginning to have my own suspicions, but didn't want to halt Fiona's disclosures.

"He – he – oh, it was just awful – he – Nathan – was absolutely enraged, like – convulsed with anger. I don't know how else to describe it. But he took the money, then called us everything under the sun for withholding the rest. And that, really, is all I can tell you."

There was silence at our end of the table. I was shocked at her having such an unbearable gash in her otherwise successful life. I dared voice what I'm sure Eilidh was thinking too:

"Is it drugs, d'you think?" I'll never forget the look Fiona gave me – of complete anguish.

"We – don't – know," she said dully. "We think it must be, but keep hoping it isn't."

"Have you seen him since Christmas?" Eilidh asked.

"No. He phoned a couple of times since then to ask if he could get the rest of the money, and Olly said he'd be very welcome to come home and talk it all over. Nathan hung up on him. He won't answer his mobile, or any texts, and there isn't a landline in the flat he lives in. If he's still there, that is." Fiona looked up for a minute with a look of utter hopelessness.

"We even went down to London to try to see him. We got to the flat and a skinny greasy-haired woman answered the door but wouldn't let us in. She said Nathan wasn't at home, didn't know where he was just now but she'd tell him we'd called. She couldn't, or wouldn't, tell us the names of any of his friends, and he'd never mentioned any specific names to us either. At least it seems he's still alive."

After a pause, I asked, "What about Jack? Has he any insight into it all?"

"No. Nathan's always treated Jack like a house fly, swatting him away any time he tries to get close. Jack's confused, but doesn't like his brother enough to worry too much about him. He's getting on with his own life, and enjoying it. Thank God."

"Remind me – what's Jack doing?" asked Eilidh. I suspected that like me, she didn't really know what else to say about Nathan.

"Jack? Oh, he's doing Business at MMU and is totally into it. He's a pet, really – sorry, sorry, didn't mean to do this ..." Fiona was suddenly in floods of tears, and we all rooted about for tissues for her. How awful. I couldn't begin to imagine what I'd feel like if Joe or Julie got into drugs.

The only comfort we could give her was the level of our concern. No wonder she'd indulged in a cover activity of brambling – it'd kept her out of any conversation until she was ready for it. Fiona, who was always on top of everything, the one with the most impressive career – with an estranged and possibly drug-addict son. Life sucks.

We made a sombre trio as some time later we went into the Eat Mhor Fish restaurant in Callander, to give Eilidh or Alan a rest from cooking. None of us really felt like eating so soon after the sandwiches, but the fish was as good as Eilidh had promised, and eating out rounded off the day. What a strange weekend it'd been. I just wanted to get back home to hear Joe's cheerful voice on the phone, and give Julie a smothering hug.

Chapter 13 – Water of Leith (March 2011) - Fiona

The 12-mile Water of Leith Walkway starts at Balerno, on the outskirts of Edinburgh, and meanders its way through suburbs and the city to Leith. It has a very slight downwards incline, but is otherwise flat. In spite of its urban location, much of it passes through woodland as it follows the stream, and it is a pleasant escape from the buzz of the city.

I'd really intended to do some work on the train to Edinburgh, but found myself mostly looking out the window, my mind either muzzily blank or going round in eternal circles. As the lights of the city approached, I put down my report on advances in Cisco networking configurations, and drew a deep sigh. Not long to go now. What to tell them this time? What had changed since we met last year? An excruciatingly awful Christmas, still trying to accept the fact that our high-achieving son had dropped out of University and wouldn't be completing his degree any time in the near future, if at all. Although that was the least of our concerns.

Anyway, back to the present. We were still on the low-key walks till Eilidh decided she was ready to tackle more demanding ones again. Not that she'd said anything more about it, but we'd a kind of unspoken consensus to play safe. When Liksi suggested we joined her in Edinburgh to do a local walk, everyone seemed happy.

Getting off the train at Waverley, I spotted Eilidh at the barrier doing a mad pantomime dance to attract my attention, and hurried to meet her. She enfolded me in her usual, all-encompassing Eilidh-hug, then released me apologetically. "We need to go – Liksi's hovering on Market Street and I don't know how long she can park there. She's in a bus bit or taxi bit or something." She led me up an escalator and then a set of stairs to emerge into the malty night air on Market Street. Liksi had the engine of their elderly Capri running and as soon as we squeezed in she took off, with her parking slot immediately taken by another driver.

"Just going to go back to mine to collapse – OK?" Liksi looked at me in the mirror to check, as she drove up South Clerk Street, passing landmarks that were SO familiar from University days. The Minto Hotel – how many 18ths or 21sts had we celebrated there?

"Very OK." I was happy to relinquish all responsibility for further decisions for the evening. Although – "Pete in?" I forced myself to ask brightly.

"No, he's out somewhere – think he'll be staying with Dave to save the taxi home." I snatched a quick look at Liksi as she drew up outside their house. Thank God, and I knew that Pete wasn't high on Eilidh's list of preferred companions either. I did often wonder how two such diametrically opposed characters as Liksi and Pete could have got together in the first place, but then we're all different. Thankfully.

We got settled in quickly and ordered from a Chinese takeaway menu that Liksi thrust at us. We knew never to expect a home-cooked meal here. Liksi'd given up all attempts at real cooking years ago – she'd never been interested. Pete might've obliged in the early days in order to impress, but we were old hat now. Anyway, I hoped that his pathetic attempt to make a pass at me made it quite clear that it wasn't going to get the result he'd intended.

With heaped plates and full glasses in front of us, I asked Liksi what the plan was for tomorrow.

"Well, I wondered about the Water of Leith Walkway? Could get the bus to Balerno and walk back; it's about 12 miles." She moved a few dishes aside and spread out a map on the table.

"Is it mostly through the town?" I didn't want to be walking on tarmac all the time, especially after our last walk at Loch Katrine – though if I was forced to admit it, I suppose I was largely to blame for that.

"Well, kind of – but it doesn't use the main streets or anything. It's a path or walkway rather than a road. Just follows the river; the first half feels pretty rural really."

I wondered how long it'd be before Eilidh got over her strop about being left behind, and we could do decent walks again. Maybe that was a bit unkind of me, but - I looked at her a bit more closely.

"Eilidh! Have you been losing weight?"

"Aye, can you tell? 'Bout half a stone." She was looking unusually smug.

"You look great." Liksi smiled at her as she put the chutney back on the table. "Did you go to that hypnotherapist you were talking about?"

"Uh-huh. Went well - amazing, really. Never thought it would work." The smug look was still there – but rightly so; I was pleased for her. "So, salad instead of carbs. Should cut out wine too, but I need *something* to look forward to!" She held her wine glass up and laughed.

"OK, so Water of Leith it is tomorrow." Liksi folded up the map and took it through to the kitchen to put it beside her boots. "Can get back to the great expeditions when Eilidh reaches her fighting weight – maybe next time, at this rate."

"Right, well, I'm off to get my beauty sleep." I was shattered, and if I got to sleep before Eilidh came to bed, it'd avoid any opportunity for talking about Nathan till tomorrow. I was vaguely aware of Eilidh coming into the room not long afterwards, but must've gone back to sleep pretty quickly. The next I knew the birds were making a racket outside and it was time to get up.

Apparently we needed two buses to get to Balerno. As always Liksi, like most Edinburgh people, knew the numbers and timetables of most of the buses, and our one didn't take long to arrive. We got Eilidh organised with her fare and ticket – as she laughingly explained, "I don't do buses in Glasgow" – and piled upstairs like teenagers to get a seat at the front, for the views and memories of our old University city.

"Maybe we'll be able to take the tram next time." Liksi was watching us with some amusement as we peered out the windows.

"What? No way – I'll be walking. Vanity project, if ever there was one!" Eilidh's reaction took me aback, although I was aware that the trams were controversial.

"It's OK, they'll probably still not be ready anyway." Liksi shook her head. "Have to say, they *are* a bit of an embarrassment though, to say the least. All the shops, and taxi drivers, are up in arms."

"I should think so. Dreadful." One look at Eilidh's face made it clear that she wasn't joking.

"Why're you so against them?" I asked. "I thought you'd have appreciated their green credentials?" Of the three of us, Eilidh was usually the most environmentally conscious.

"'Cos the money going into the trams should've been spent on making the A9 fully dual carriageway!" she said, as I slowly worked out the connection. Her parents had moved to Inverness a few years ago, and as they fell prey to the usual ailments which come with longevity, she was up and down the A9 regularly, so I guess she'd a vested interest.

"People get killed on that road almost every month. Drivers've been petitioning to get it dualled for years." Her voice was getting louder. "Have there been any deaths on Edinburgh streets which could've been prevented by having trams? Of course not. They have no *shame*, these politicians – Edinburgh has the castle, the parliament and now it has to have trams. I get so ANGRY!!!"

I looked at Liksi, who was nodding slowly as she took in this new line of thought.

"Sorry about the rant." Eilidh took a deep breath to calm herself down. "I just feel very strongly about the whole thing. Even my students know about it now – I use the Edinburgh Tram Project as a very *bad* example of project management. At least they now know what and where the A9 is!"

"I hope you're not bringing your politics into your teaching, now, Eilidh." I teased her gently, although I could imagine her firing up her students and making them think outside the box.

"Well, I try not to, but if I'm given an opening I'll turn it into a discussion. Trams indeed ..." An expletive was lost in the roar of the traffic as we got off the first bus to wait for the next.

Some time later, we found ourselves in Balerno.

"Nice wee place." Eilidh, looked round appreciatively. "I like all these stone buildings, and it's got a proper village feel to it."

"Yeah; expensive though – prime commuter territory." Liksi pointed out a large house with a huge garden lined with deep pink rhododendron bushes. "Used to be a railway here – that's largely what we'll be walking along, the old railway line."

"Probably the demise of the line saved the soul of the village. Otherwise it would be fully swallowed up by Edinburgh now." Eilidh was fairly in crusader mode today.

We got off the bus in the centre of the village, and had to walk back towards Edinburgh to pick up the start of the walk, just by the school. I was glad to see it was indeed a path and not a road; though a bit muddy in places, I'd trade tarmac for mud any day. The 'Water' soon appeared – something of a cross between river and burn, rippling gently along on its way to the sea. Mallards waggled their rears in the air as they stuck their heads underwater in search of tasty morsels, while a pair of swans floated serenely past, swivelling their regal heads as they surveyed the scene. Dippers flitted about alongside and foraged on the banks, and the occasional heron surveyed the scene lopsidedly from a one-legged pose. I wished I could balance as well as that in my yoga class.

We walked through pleasant and leafy surroundings, with the few houses visible mainly large, modern and sporting well-maintained gardens sloping down to the river. Well before we saw them, we could smell the clumps of wild garlic which thrived by the wayside, their delicate white flowers and long leaves overshadowing shy wood sorrel and bright celandine. However, it didn't take long before there were signs that the city wasn't far away. The path led us, over a variety of small stone or wooden bridges, back and fore across the water a few times, and at one point we crossed right under the city bypass. Even if we'd somehow managed to miss the fact we were underneath a massive concrete structure, the increasingly loud hum of the traffic would have alerted us. Then there was the inevitable new housing development by the water – developers didn't miss an opportunity these days, turning a blind eye to minor inconveniences like space, privacy, or the possibility of flooding.

At Slateford, we crossed the busy main road and went into the Water of Leith Visitor Centre. The stone-built building still resembled the schoolhouse which it had originally been, with its slate-tiled roof and tall, multi-paned casement windows. It was pleasant enough, but felt half-finished somehow, and the "café" section was very basic – there was coffee, but out of a machine and watery, some wrapped chocolate biscuits and a dish of some healthier cereal bars and suchlike.

"Not quite what I'd had in mind for lunch." Liksi looked at us apologetically.

"Don't worry, Liksi, it'll help my diet." Eilidh limited herself to a cup of coffee and an oaty biscuit, and Liksi and I'd much the same.

"It's good to stop for a break regardless." I had downed my coffee and poured myself a second one. "Coffee's my essential fuel injection. Nice walk, Liksi – amazing that it's practically in the city, but feels quite rural most of the time."

"Yeah, and it's going to go right through the city proper now. You'll be going past places you know but might not've seen from this angle before."

We didn't linger over our meagre fare and soon set off again, passing beneath a couple of structures, one of which was the impressive 8-arched aqueduct for the Union Canal. It was strange to think we were actually walking underneath a substantial body of water – it just looked like a sort of bridge. Being a canal rather than a river, there was no rush of water to identify it. After that, the route became less wooded and more wasteland in parts, but busier. People passed by in noisy groups, and some looked as if they'd been enjoying a much more liquid lunch than we'd had.

"Are we missing something?" I turned to Liksi with a frown.

"Sure are. Murrayfield's over there - Scotland's playing Italy today."

"Of course." Eilidh looked over towards the complex metal structure of the famous stand. "Alan said he'd be watching the rugby, I'd forgotten. I used to be really into the whole Five Nations thing when I was a student, but I've got a bit lazy about it now."

"Did you go to the matches?" I asked.

"Yes, all of them. My flat was in the West End. A big crowd of us would meet there and then traipse out to the games. Usually quite tanked up." As a student, Eilidh'd shared a flat with five others, and had often regaled us with stories of some of her wilder exploits.

"We used to go armed with a carry-out." She was off again - "You could in those days. The empty beer cans came in handy for standing on if you were wee like me – I remember being propped up on them with a guy on either side to grab hold of. Those were the days ..."

"Are you into rugby then?" I was quite impressed. "I like it, but I haven't got a clue what's going on most of the time."

"Into it - are you kidding? I'd the stupidity on one occasion to ask – at the top of my voice, of course - what colour the All Blacks were playing in! You can imagine how that went down, specially with the Kiwis in the crowd."

It took a few seconds for this to register with me, but Liksi let out one of her belly-laughs almost immediately. She probably knew more about rugby than either of us, due to her sporty background. Most of my limited knowledge was through osmosis, if I was honest. Olly was more into rugby league, but he kept an eye on rugby union too, or at least on the internationals.

"Nice one! Bet you kept a low profile for the rest of the game." Liksi wiped her eyes.

"I don't think I knew *how* to keep a low profile in those days. No shame. Oh well."

"Maybe we'll be able to catch a bit of the game in a pub later?" It would be good to take in the atmosphere.

"Can make sure we do that – no bother." Liksi stepped up the pace and we carried on making our way past the rugby fans.

The path became quite leafy again for a while in spite of the encroaching city, leading us into the wonderfully atmospheric Dean Village, one of my favourite places in Edinburgh. In fact, if I ever ended up here again, this is where I'd want to live – if I won the lottery. The majority of the Victorian buildings were privately owned houses and flats, some with amazing high turrets, others with attractive stone walls sometimes topped by decorative wrought iron railings. The bottom layer nearest the water had some painted properties, whereas the higher layers followed the contours of the hill and sported the grey sandstone for which Edinburgh was famous. Almost all must've had a great view of the river – gentle, but lightly burbling and at one point tumbling over a weir of stones spaced out in an arc. Lots of greenery featured on the banks, alder and birch trees reached down towards the water, and there were some lovely gardens - not easy to achieve in a crowded residential city centre. Even this early in the year, some of the windows had colourful flowers cascading down from baskets or boxes.

"Expensive, I guess?" I asked Liksi wistfully.

"Excruciatingly so. Quite exclusive down here, as you can imagine."

"It's one of these places I never really got to know when I was a student here. I didn't even know there was a walkway." Eilidh looked around with appreciation.

"Too far from the pubs, Eilidh?" I couldn't resist teasing her.

"Huh. You're a fine one to talk. Don't tell me you didn't see the inside of some of Edinburgh's finest drinking dens in your time."

"You might be right. Just a few ..."

We wandered through Dean Village and under the Dean Bridge, passing a stately Roman folly with a domed top and a statue of a female inside.

"St Bernard's Well." Liksi stopped briefly to make sure we took it in. "That's supposed to be the goddess of health, Hygeia – but don't be fooled; the water's not fit for drinking now." The path continued alongside the popular district of Stockbridge. Suddenly, without saying anything, Liksi led us off the route and up to the street. Before we knew what was happening we'd followed her straight into the Bailie Bar. Raised voices, shouts and cheers led us to one of the big screens, where over a couple of drinks we watched Scotland see Italy off in a 21-8 victory.

"No wooden spoon for us this year." Liksi drained her glass in celebration.

"Sad when you feel that's a real achievement, though, isn't it?" Eilidh looked resigned. "Wonder if we'll ever see another David Sole leading out the team to win the Grand Slam. What a moment that was. Oh my God, it was 21 years ago!"

"We're getting old, Eilidh, that's the sad truth." I didn't find the prospect of getting older much fun. Life was difficult enough as it was. "50 I was able to cope with, just – but 60?"

"Och, Fiona, how many 50-somethings d'you know who would be able to do what we're doing? Or who could've managed the West Highland Way?" Eilidh protested. "We must be doing something right."

"Sure are. Right, come on – last lap then I'll take you to the Raj if you're good." Liksi was still in Edinburgh tour guide mode.

With reluctance, we left the Bailie and retraced our steps to re-join the Walkway. Passing alongside the Stockbridge Colonies, the terrace of houses formerly inhabited by local craftsmen, we moved through the neighbouring district of Canonmills and then past increasingly semi-derelict or industrial areas with large sheds or warehouses, eventually arriving at Leith. The official end of the Walkway was at Victoria Bridge, which marked the beginning of Leith Docks and its reincarnation as an area of bars, restaurants and new-build, or re-developed flats. It'd been one of our least taxing walks, but very pleasant for all that, and not having had any lunch, we headed straight for the Raj which wasn't far away. The restaurant had been a favourite when we'd been students, and it was good to know it was still doing well.

"So, Fiona, is now an OK time to ask you about Nathan?" Once we'd ordered food and drinks, Eilidh asked the dreaded question.

"Oh God, I guess so." I looked at their concerned faces and almost backed out. "I've been kind of putting it off, but am also a bit desperate to talk about it, if you know what I mean."

"You said something on the phone about Christmas having been awful," Eilidh prompted me.

"Yes, well – y'know we'd tried to get hold of him for weeks before then? Kept leaving messages, no luck. Eventually Jack – bless him – offered to go to London himself to try to persuade him to come home. We thought he might be more likely to confide in Jack if we weren't there." I looked into my glass of Cobra as I swirled the beer round, searching for the right words.

"So, he got to the flat, and was told Nathan had moved out weeks ago. The guy he spoke to was very reluctant to give anything away and said he'd try to contact him to see if he wanted to speak to Jack or not. The shits - his own brother!" I could feel the rage starting up again, but waited till I calmed down before continuing.

"Jack went back the next morning, and was told that Nathan would meet him at Tottenham Court Road tube station some time between 2 and 3. So poor Jack had to hang around the agreed exit for almost an hour, not knowing if he'd turn up or not."

The food arrived at this point, but it was clear that the others were happy to leave it till I'd got it all out. Probably just as well, or I might have bottled it. I rushed on.

"Jack said he almost didn't recognise him. Dirty, long straggly hair, skeletal. Anyway, told him we all wanted him home for Christmas, we were worried sick and would do whatever we could to help him. Nathan didn't refuse, so

Jack basically frog-marched him to Euston, bought tickets for both of them and got him home. Oh, God, it was awful!"

I looked down at the table and held my head in my hands. He'd been filthy, smelt to high heaven and hadn't made much sense, but I didn't want to go into all that. I couldn't bear re-living it, let alone sharing the absolute horror of it all.

"To cut to the chase, Nathan's on heroin. He'd been living partly on the streets, and when his money ran out we think he'd been begging – or worse. He asked us for money again; we refused but said he could stay with us as long as he wanted to. Christmas was a total disaster – don't want to talk about it – and well, you'll have read about this kind of thing. Stealing, lying, rages, disappearing out of the house for hours on end, promises not kept."

I paused for breath, working out how to condense the horrors of the last few months. Liksi ordered another beer for me, and Eilidh gave me a hug.

"Take your time, and just tell us what you're comfortable with." I smiled at Liksi gratefully, before continuing.

"Thanks. He's currently on methadone, and trying to hold down a job in a local supermarket. We've no idea how this'll go; he's recently been seeing a girl who's been on methadone for some time so we can only hope that they'll help each other – although it could just as easily go the other way."

"At least he's had the sense to know he's got a problem." Eilidh sounded thoughtful. "If he's on a methadone programme, I mean. That can only be a good sign?"

"Maybe." In theory, yes. I knew I should try to hold on to that thought, but it was hard. There was nothing much either of them could say, and we finished the meal in near silence, apart from both of them saying that they'd always be there for me, at the end of the phone or in person.

"Thanks, much appreciated," I managed to say. "You've no idea how good it is to get it off my chest, though I can't bear telling you all of it, not yet anyway. No-one at work knows, and only a couple of close friends have worked out what's going on. Anyway, that's it; no more – don't want to spoil the weekend."

They took me at my word, and managed largely inconsequential chit-chat as we made our way back to Liksi's by bus. Eilidh remembered that The Killing was on TV that night, and ruefully suggested that we could watch that to cheer ourselves up. It was a relief to lose myself in the latest episode of dark and sombre – but brilliant – Scandinavian escapism.

Chapter 14 – Ambleside and Wansfell Pike (September 2011) - Eilidh

This is an attractive 6.6-mile circular walk in the Lake District. It starts in the village of Troutbeck and follows an old drovers' road to the top of Wansfell Pike (1,581 ft), then heads down into Ambleside. From there, via Skelghyll Wood and the viewpoint of Jenkin Crag, it loops round to re-join the drovers' road back into Troutbeck.

We'd chosen the Lake District this time for Fiona's sake; she deserved a break from the journeys to Scotland. She picked Liksi and I up at Oxenholme station and drove us to the Windermere Youth Hostel, skirting Kendal, dipping into Windermere, then climbing up a narrow road towards Troutbeck. We turned left before the village into a narrow drive and before long were parked up in front of an imposing yet slightly formidable rectangular cream building. It was composed of 4 vertical blocks – the outside ones higher than the inner ones, which were joined by a central, wider block. Each was topped with a flat roof. To my uneducated (architecturally) eye, it reminded me of all those austere buildings of 1940s Germany. The large windows with their long vertical bars added to the stern and rather official appearance of the hostel.

However, once inside there was more of a casual ambiance and the room was spotless. After claiming our bunks and dumping our packs, we headed straight back out and into the fresh air.

In front of the hotel again, Windermere was glistening in the distance, framed by distant hills and nearer woods. The late afternoon sun threw a golden haze over the scene, and I already felt warm, mellow and far from the bustle of settling in new students, interviewing late entrants, worrying if we'd have enough numbers to run classes – the usual beginning-of-term madness.

"Isn't this lovely?" I sighed as we set off towards Troutbeck. "All these stone cottages and houses. Just look at those flowers." Most of the buildings had colourful displays of petunias or lobelia tumbling over small walls or jostling for space in pleasantly crowded gardens.

"Such a change from all the nasty harling[5] that you get all over Scotland." I was in envy mode. "Supposed to help weather-proof the brick – but surely they get bad weather down here as well?"

"They do, and you'd be a bit stuck out here in the winter. No cinemas, theatres, gigs ..." Fiona needed her regular culture injections, as well as her busy social life.

"Pete would go spare down here. He needs all the big town attractions. Mind you, maybe *I* could move down here ..." We laughed with Liksi, but privately I thought that leaving Pete wouldn't be the worst idea she'd ever had.

"Oh, look - *how* good is that?" I indicated the large white hotel with a sign proclaiming it to be the Mortal Man, which had appeared on the right. The three-storey building with its multiple dormer windows looked well maintained; through the trees we could see tables and benches on the sloping garden, claimed by a variety of occupants. Children were running around with dogs in tow, while more elderly canines were stretched out luxuriously, flexing their ageing joints in the warmth. "There's nothing like an *English* country pub. Coming?"

We grabbed a table which a couple had just vacated and I headed into the shady interior to get the drinks. We just didn't have pubs like this in Scotland, or at least not many of them – and certainly not with wonderful beer gardens *and* the weather to enjoy them. There was even an affable, chatty

---

[5] rough cast wall covering

type behind the bar, who was happy to let me taste a few of his ales, and talk me through them.

"Loweswater Gold," I announced as I set the glasses down outside. "Even yours, Liksi, in the shandy. Cheers."

The talk turned to the usual unintelligible world of networking. A curly haired mutt with a bent ear seemed to have taken a liking to me, so I was happy to fondle his ears and scratch his back whilst vaguely listening to groans about new systems and procurement problems. The dog plonked himself down on my foot and promptly went to sleep; the extra warmth he gave me was welcome in spite of the evening sun. The growing dusk settled and wrapped round us. Idly, I wondered how Alan was doing – and then moved back to the present. Alan would be fine – he always was. I loved him to bits but I liked my space too – independence was still important.

Ordering, eating and drinking more Loweswater kept us occupied for a while, and by the time we were ready to leave it was completely dark outside, apart from any street or building lights. As soon as we left the houses – and the lights – behind, we realised we were in a bit of bother.

"Er, anyone got a torch?" asked Fiona.

"No – got a phone, though not much battery left." Liksi fished her phone out of her bag and turned on the torch facility. It was faint, but better than nothing. I didn't even know you could get a torch on a phone.

"What idiots we are – real amateurs." I laughed as we started walking three abreast along the road, following the thin wavering light. "What gear d'you normally carry with you, you two?"

"A torch!" Fiona grabbed hold of me to move closer into the beam. "Don't know what happened this time though – brain fog or something. Plasters and paracetamols. Not much, really."

"Just plasters normally. Compeed. Tissues." This was Liksi's contribution.

"Ach, well, just as well you've got me." I sounded smug. "Small first aid kit with wipes, plasters, scissors, bandage, antihistamine, midge stuff. Oh, and a survival blanket." My superiority was dented somewhat as I stumbled into a pothole. "Oops - might need to use some of it at this rate."

"Well, you can add a torch to the list next time." Fiona was understandably not impressed – on this occasion anyway.

We squeezed right into the side of the road as a car passed, wishing we'd had the sense to put on brighter clothing. Momentarily blinded, we tried to get back on track, following the road as it swerved round to the left.

"Ow! Watch out – OW! Oh my God, I think we're in someone's rose garden – careful! For fuck's sake, the battery's gone ..." Liksi was jabbing at her phone as she grabbed at her arm.

I started giggling as we huddled together while Fiona and I tried to unearth our phones. "Just hope there's no searchlights, or guard dogs ... shouldn't laugh – here it is ..." and suddenly we had light again from my phone. "Right, how do I get the torch bit?" I was scrolling up and down, without a clue about what I was trying to do. "I usually rely on students to help me find anything other than the basics."

"Mine's a Samsung too – let me see it." Liksi took over the technicalities, and suddenly we were in business again, with a reasonable beam.

"Thanks. Come on, let's get out of here. We must've gone up someone's drive instead of the road." I led the way for what seemed to be an endless walk back to the hostel, occasionally hopping into the ditch at the side of the road to avoid any cars. Luckily, the weather had been very dry recently so the ditches were too, otherwise we'd have been filthy. We turned wearily into the hostel lane at last. At least

I'd learned how to turn a phone into a torch – if I could remember in a week's time. We went straight to bed when we got in, although the hysteria started again as Liksi removed a murderous-looking thorn from her sweatshirt, and we all had a headful of white fluffy stuff which must've come off some bush or other.

"Forgot to say," came a sleepy voice from the top bunk, once we'd got settled at last. "Wansfell Pike and Ambleside tomorrow? Circular walk?"

"Perfect," I mumbled as I turned over to go to sleep. Said it all - we'd enjoyed the evening so much that the purpose of the trip had gone right out of my head. Liksi and I never questioned Fiona's suggestions for the Lake District anyway, as we barely knew it; a circular walk sounded just fine. I was still a bit wary of long walks or climbs; although I'd managed to shed almost a couple of stones I wanted to test the effect before tackling anything major.

The next day, the weather was just as hot again, and after a hearty hostel breakfast we set off - by retracing our steps to the Mortal Man, and re-living every twist of the road.

"Look, must be the drive we went up." Liksi pointed to an imposing house on the right, at a bend in the road. It was some garden – beautifully laid out – and I just hoped we hadn't damaged anything. Mind you, there were so many bushes and plants that any damage would probably go unnoticed. I hoped. The giggling started again – honestly, no-one watching or listening to us would believe that we were respectable ladies of a certain age – and was compounded when the Mortal Man came into sight.

"Maybe if I asked them, they'd put beer into my water bottle ..." I thought this was a very good idea – after all, we'd hip flasks in Scotland for whisky, so why not beer bottles in England? Sadly, I was pulled away down a track at a sign proclaiming it to be Nanny Lane, and the walk started in earnest. There was a clear, wide path and only a gentle incline. In spite of that, it didn't take long before all the sweatshirts were off and draped round our waists, and we had to stop to put on suntan lotion.

"I never expected it to be quite as hot as this at this time of year." I slathered the stuff over my arms and face. "But I just love this heat. An added bonus."

"Mm." Liksi took the tube from me and followed suit. "A little *too* hot for me for walking, but am absolutely not complaining."

It didn't take us long to get to the top of Wansfell Pike, as it was just a small hill and an easy climb. "A Birkett, I believe, ie a Lakeland fell of 1,000 ft or more." I imparted this knowledge to raised eyebrows and rolling eyes. Yes, everything had a category in hill terms.

We sat there for some time taking in the views over Windermere and beyond, and luxuriating in the afternoon heat. Grasmere, which I'd always thought of as Windermere's smaller and prettier sister, peeped out from behind, and the Langdale Pikes loomed beyond that again.

"Wansfell is up there," Fiona pointed up to the right in the direction we'd been walking. "It's very slightly higher, but you're not really going to see much that you can't see from here." That was unlike Fiona, but suited me fine. In some ways, it was a pity we didn't have sandwiches with us so that we could've prolonged our stay right here. It was one of these rare days when even at height the sun was still strong enough for us sun-starved Scots to sit there in T-shirts and enjoy it. However, we eventually managed to peel ourselves off the ground, or in my case off my mouse mat, and headed down towards Ambleside, whose numerous pubs were beckoning. It was quite a steep descent, but the close-packed stone path made it easy to navigate, and further down it followed the course of a pretty burn.

"Beck." Fiona corrected me as I voiced this thought. "You're not in Scotland now, you're in the civilised south, which has lakes, becks and fells – not lochs, burns and hills."

"I stand corrected." I laughed. "Glad we've got a Sassenach with us to make sure we don't disgrace ourselves –" I dodged a blow, which made me lose my balance and I landed in a heap in a pile of bracken. Or should it be 'ferns'?

"No sympathy, serves you right for cheeking the walk leader." Fiona hauled me up unceremoniously and I dusted myself off. "You can buy me a drink in Ambleside to soothe my hurt feelings."

"Done."

The path joined a small road, and we made our way down, past the ubiquitous grey Lakeland stone walls and into the village. The small town was, as usual, heaving with tourists but it was still lovely. We slowed our pace, enjoying the transition from walker to tourist as we looked around for a likely pitstop that wasn't too crowded.

"Here? The Priest Hole? Looks perfect." Liksi was already winding her way towards the only empty table on a busy terrace outside an attractive looking establishment.

"Don't think it's a pub, though," I warned, with my dreams of foaming Lakeside ales dashed as I read 'Restaurant and Tea Rooms' on the side of the building.

"Well, we'll be having lunch and they'll maybe have a licence anyway." Fiona plonked herself down beside Liksi and I didn't have the heart to force them to move. It *was* a nice place – and, as I soon discovered when I picked up the menu, it had bottled beer so all was well. Once the paninis and something with grains and seeds for Fiona arrived, along with the drinks, we were happy to sit and chat for a while. Mind you, when were we *not* ...

"So, Fiona, now that the SNP have taken over Holyrood, you'll need to watch in case they'll only let you back over the border with a passport soon." I threw the opening ball to see where it would land. We were reasonably low-key in our political discussions; although I regularly teased Fiona about her "Englishness", she never read any paper but the Guardian and I was reasonably sure of her political sympathies. Liksi wasn't always as easy to read, but ...

"That MAN!" she spat out. "His ego'll swallow him up one of these days. Can't stand him."

"My goodness, Liksi, that's not like you. I take it you're referring to our very own Mr Salmond?" I asked sweetly. "Not a fan?"

"Absolutely not. SO full of himself."

"I'm with you there." Fiona was fanning herself with the menu.

"But you have to admit he's sharp." Although I hadn't been a fan of Alex Salmond originally, I'd come to respect his political acumen in the last couple of years. "In fact, I don't think there's a politician north of the border to match him."

"Well, that doesn't say much – they're a pretty poor lot these days." Liksi's expression matched her grumpy tone.

"True, but he's *very* clever. He can hold his own with the best of them – and that includes the ones down south." No-one disagreed with me on that score. We exchanged a few more disparaging comments about politics in general, and Scottish politicians in particular, and found we were *almost* in agreement, without the others nailing their colours too much to the mast. Probably best – we all valued our little triumvirate too much to jeopardise it through getting too het up about politics.

"OK, Fiona, so can we ask you about Nathan now?" Liksi changed the subject suddenly.

"Oh – well, still much the same, really, but thank God no worse." Fiona sighed sadly. "He's still on methadone, as far as we can tell, and he's still got some hours in the supermarket. Although, I honestly don't know if that's a good thing or not."

"What d'you mean?" asked Liksi.

"Well, should we just be glad he's holding down a job – *any* job – or wishing he'd gone back to Uni?" She looked down at the table. "He's moved in with the girl. They turn up on a Sunday every few weeks for half an hour or so, so at least the contact is there and we know he's alive."

Poor Fiona. As I asked for the bill, I reflected on the fact that Nathan was probably never far from her thoughts.

The walk back to Troutbeck seemed quite quick – but then the whole walk was only about 6½ miles in total. Very short for us. Having said that, once we got out of Ambleside there was a steep climb through the woods to the viewpoint at Jenkin Crag. The path was uneven at times and we'd to keep a sharp lookout for signposts as they were sometimes hidden in the foliage. Felled trunks lay scattered about, rolled in moss blankets as if they were sleeping in the warm sun, and they sometimes blocked the path. It was certainly a good way to work off the paninis – *and*, I was relieved to note, I did still seem to be keeping pace with the others, more or less. Gasping our (my) way to the top, we stopped at the viewpoint to look down over the tops of the sturdy oaks and more delicate birches to the huge expanse of water that was Windermere, which was now a glistening dark blue. Over to one side there was a small marina, and white dots of sails peppered the water. It'd be lovely to be out in a boat on a day like this, although there wouldn't be much wind for the sails. However, I was more than happy getting my quota of fresh air through walking, and wouldn't have it any other way.

Walking through High Skelghyll farm, the route eventually became the varied path called Robin Lane. We made our way past more grey drystone dykes, the stones of which became threaded with flowering climbers the nearer we got to Troutbeck.

"Anyone know what these are called?" I asked. "I keep looking for ideas for our garden."

"Nope, sorry." This was Fiona's contribution.

"The yellow ones might be campanula, but I'm not sure." Liksi was examining the leaves.

"I can only do wildflowers, and I think these must be domesticated," I said by way of apology. "Maybe another thing to get into once I retire."

"For heaven's sake, Eilidh, you're years away from that yet." Fiona turned to me in surprise.

"Not so many – I'm stopping as soon as I'm 60," I said firmly. "Nothing like forward planning."

"Don't even want to think about retiring." Liksi looked horrified at the thought. "They keep moving the goalposts anyway so no point."

"Think we'll still be doing these walks when we do retire?" I asked.

"For God's sake, Eilidh – of course we will. Every week!" Fiona laughed at me. "Isn't that what retirement's for? But I'm with Liksi – long time to go yet."

"OK, OK, I'm just more practical than you two – oh, look, we're back in Troutbeck and isn't the Mortal Man just up there?" I didn't need an answer, and we headed back up to what was currently my favourite pub in the world, for a much-needed refreshment.

I took my first long draft of another Lakeside ale. "That was a really nice walk, Fiona. Well done. Just goes to show we don't need to embark on a marathon each time to enjoy ourselves."

"Nope, but it's good to have a challenge. Particularly as we get older – since you brought up the topic. Glad you enjoyed it."

Talk of getting older made me think about my parents – they'd moved to Inverness to be nearer to family and hospitals.

"Liksi, how're your parents these days?" I asked suddenly, with a slight feeling of guilt that I hadn't asked her before now. Fiona'd lost both parents while she was at University; the loss of her father in her final year had almost derailed her completely, but somehow she'd struggled through to get a 2:2.

"Oh, limping along." Liksi looked down at her drink. "Their lives revolve round the TV, and our visits. They seem happy enough, but need a *lot* of persuasion to go out of the house."

"I guess they'll miss Joe now that he's at Loughborough?" Fiona asked.

"Yeah, absolutely – he was very good with them and they miss his banter. Julie's happy to visit, but she doesn't quite have the same empathy with them. Pete has no interest in them whatsoever." There was a bitter note in Liksi's voice, which was unusual.

"That's hard for you." I sympathised with her. "My parents are at a similar stage, and you can just feel the relationship changing, and the parent becoming the child. It's very sad."

"Right, you two, food." Fiona butted in. "No more melancholy. Anyone hungry, or is it just me?" She was ready to eat so we all had to jump. Oh, that was unkind – I was suddenly starving too. We finished our drinks, and headed back to the hostel.

"Oh my God, the rugby – I forgot." The sickly strains of 'Swing Low, Sweet Chariot' drifted over as we got in the door. It was the Rugby World Cup, and Scotland had been playing England today. In all the enjoyment of the day, I'd completely forgotten. Heading quickly in the direction of the noise, we found ourselves in the common room, where a group of young-ish guys were lounging in front of a screen.

"Oh, no." I couldn't help letting out a semi-wail as I saw the inevitable result on the screen – England had beaten us 16-12. "Not again."

"Scottish, eh? Bad luck. You played very well." An unmistakeably antipodean accent confirmed this, with little comfort. A few heads turned in our direction, with sympathetic smiles, and we watched the replays on the screen. With reluctance, the offer of a drink with the Kiwis was declined. We were too grubby and hungry to settle down just yet, and after gratefully accepting their commiserations, we headed upstairs to address the first of these impediments, before heading down again for dinner and maybe a couple of beers in the hostel. After our escapade last night, and our walk today, it was unlikely we'd be able to summon the energy to visit the Mortal Man again tonight. Sadly.

Chapter 15 – Pentlands (May 2012) - Liksi

The 12-mile walk starts at the village of West Linton (15 miles south-west of Edinburgh) and follows a minor road north. This becomes a path, which turns right into the old Roman road leading to Carlops, before turning back up to cross over the Pentland Hills. It skirts the North Esk Reservoir, going straight on to the flank of King's Hill, then descends to follow the north side of Threipmuir Reservoir and Bavelaw Marsh, finishing in Balerno.

"At last!"

Although Eilidh voiced the thought, we probably all felt the same. First Eilidh and then Fiona'd had to cancel trips for different reasons. On both occasions, there'd been a mutual agreement not to proceed without the full team being present. With three of us, the chemistry was just right, and it wouldn't have felt the same with just two.

Fiona'd got the airport bus into town and we'd met her at Haymarket, which is why we were now perched on stools in a corner of the very crowded Le Di-Vin wine bar.

"Cheers! Nice place this." Fiona was looking round appreciatively. I was glad she liked it – it was a favourite of mine with the high ceiling, the wooden walls and furniture, and the long bar with the wine bottles stacked up behind it in a high wooden boxed arrangement.

After a couple of glasses, I took them to another favourite – the Edinburgh Rendezvous. The good thing about these two is that they were prepared to eat anything, unlike me. Even Eilidh, who'd said that Chinese wasn't her favourite type of food generally, was perfectly happy to try a 'good' restaurant. This one had been around for over fifty years, so I hoped it would meet with her approval.

"Pete swears by the aromatic duck if that's any help." I passed the menus round. "I'll be having the chicken chow mein." I always did.

"So, what's the plan this time, Liksi?" As soon as we'd ordered, Fiona didn't waste any time in making sure things were organised.

"Well, Julie's staying the night with a friend, so you've got a room each again. Whoever stays in Julie's room'll have to put up with the colour scheme – she's going through a sort of Goth phase."

"What's that mean?" Eilidh helped herself to another spoonful of rice. "I'm not up on all these trends."

"You're lucky. Black and purple, basically, and dreadful clothes. However, could be worse - thank the Lord she's avoided the tattoos and piercings – so far." I grimaced at the thought.

"And Pete?" Fiona sat back while she had a sip of wine. "What's he up to tonight?"

"Oh, he's out somewhere." I took a deep breath and decided to go for it. They had to know some time. "In fact, he's not been home for a couple of weeks."

"Weeks?" The puzzlement on Eilidh's face immediately gave way to concern. "Is he working away?"

"No, he's shacked up with some 30-year-old with long blond hair and a large chest. Couldn't be more pathetically typical." There, I'd said it. No sugar coating. There was a stunned silence for a few seconds.

"*What?*" Fiona's utterance accompanied her shocked expression, while Eilidh's jaw couldn't have dropped further if she'd tried.

"Oh, no – Liksi, how awful!" Eilidh was so stunned she hardly acknowledged the food being brought to the table.

"Sorry, hadn't meant to let you know quite like this – hoped to lead up to it a bit more gently."

"But that's *terrible*! How *could* he?" Poor Eilidh was horrified. "Liksi, you ..."

"It's OK, honestly." I looked at them both rather sadly. "It's been brewing for months, and I'm pretty sure he's had other affairs over the years. It's actually a relief to have it out in the open like this. Go on – eat." I took a mouthful of chicken.

"But you've never *said* anything." Eilidh was looking distressed, and was struggling to get to grips with it all. Her eyes filled with tears, and she was suddenly hugging me tightly. "Oh, Liksi, how *awful*."

I swallowed the lump in my throat as I disentangled her gently. "Eilidh, honestly, I'm all right. I've lived with this for years, and just got on with it for the usual reason – the children. Now, they're both adults, and Julie anyway has a good idea of what's going on."

"But you're so *calm*!" Poor Eilidh, I could see this situation was so far removed from anything she'd ever have experienced with Alan that she was having difficulty taking it in.

"I'm *fine*. Honestly."

"So what'll you do?" Fiona asked. "Kick him out?"

"Yeah, I'm working towards it. Should've done it years ago probably. Just – I just need time. Come on, eat, and then let's go home and check out the maps. We can talk about it tomorrow." I knew they were still in shock, but I was tired and it was getting late. I really, really, didn't want this to cast a pall – these weekends were so often what'd kept me sane over the years, and had stopped me dwelling on an increasing awareness of the sorry state of my marriage.

Later, at home, I opened up the maps, and laid them out on the table.

"OK, here's the plan." We pored over the rather scruffy specimens I'd managed to find. "Thought we could do a walk in the Pentlands – bus to West Linton to the start, then bus home from Balerno. About 12 miles, I think. Sound OK?"

"Absolutely." Good old Eilidh – everything was always fine for her.

"The path doesn't seem all that well defined, but I guess you've got a good idea of where we go?" Fiona folded the map so that the proposed route was uppermost.

"Er, kind of. The general area, anyway, though I've not done this particular walk before."

"Well, we're in your hands." Fiona stifled a yawn. "Now, if you don't mind I need to get to bed – seeing I'm first, I'll have the non-Goth room if you don't mind." Before Eilidh could even *think* of objecting, Fiona was away up the stairs. Eilidh looked at me in amusement.

"I wish I was even *half* that assertive. Now, Liksi, are you sure you're OK?"

"Yeah, really - don't worry. Looking forward to a better future – honestly, believe me. Now get to bed." I shooed her up the stairs, and breathed a sigh of relief once she'd disappeared into the purple and black cave. They knew. At last.

The next morning, we'd our usual muddle of breakfast – porridge for Fiona, Coco-pops for me, and toast for Eilidh. I made real coffee for Fiona, as she was a bit sniffy about instant – Pete usually made the real coffee in this house, so I guess I needed the practice from now on. Strange, I didn't even feel sad – just relieved that it was out in the open, and knowing that things could never go back to the way they'd been.

We got buses to West Linton quite quickly, and I made a reasonable job of putting up a cheerful front on the 45-minute journey. I'd always liked West Linton – it was one of these friendly small towns, where everybody seemed to know everyone else. Houses and cottages were right on the main street, with only a narrow pavement separating their front windows from the road. Shops were mainly local and independent, and therefore interesting. Today, the village was bustling and there was obviously a market or something similar going on. People were staggering about with arms filled with crates or trays of drinks, baking, fruit and veg, and a hotch-potch of other items.

"Village fete or something?" Fiona suggested. "It's obviously not started yet, so no point in hanging around."

"Agree. Pity though, it's a pretty wee place." Eilidh was looking round appreciatively, probably sussing out future drinking possibilities.

We left the village behind regretfully, heading north, and turned right on to an old Roman road (they *did* get around, those Romans) which gave us an easy walk into Carlops, which was only about 3 miles from West Linton along the main road. This was a smaller village, and seemed to consist mainly of a row of houses on each side of the main road. However, it too was lively, with loads of people going in or out of what appeared to be a village hall. Fiona and I were keen to have a look, and Eilidh, who always proclaimed she was not a 'shopper', reluctantly followed us inside. It was the usual mix of craft and food stalls, so we bought a few things to nibble at, and surprisingly it was Eilidh who bought a piece of jewellery.

"Och I know, I know, I *don't* like shopping – but I *do* like jewellery, and when it's right in front of me like this I can't just walk away." She had a sheepish look on her face as she put her purchase carefully in her rucksack.

"It's OK, you don't have to justify your shopping habits, it's just nice to know that you're human like the rest of us!" Fiona was laughing as we came out into the fresh air again.

"Right, no more distractions." She zipped up her jacket and looked round. "Where to now?"

I got the map out again. "Up here to North Esk Reservoir, then straight on to King's Hill, on a bit and turn right there, head down to that bit of water – think it's Threipmuir Reservoir, skirt the north side and then head into Balerno."

"OK. No real hills today?" Eilidh was adjusting her poles as a precaution. She'd mentioned on the phone that she'd got a set, and that she hoped it would make a difference to her knees and walking generally. I had one pole – a cast-off of Pete's but rarely used it, and I think Fiona was the same.

"No – well, it's all kinds of hills really, but not what *you'd* call real ones. Just up and down stuff."

Actually, I was sounding more confident than I felt. I didn't know the Pentlands well, and had only ever done a couple of short walks there – and that was some time ago. However, I was pretty sure we couldn't get properly lost, and it wasn't exactly wild or remote countryside. I'd made an attempt to read the map properly rather than leave it to Fiona, but there was no point in getting Eilidh to do the same. Increasingly over the last couple of years she couldn't read without her glasses, but she never took them with her on our walks.

The walking was easy, if unexciting, to begin with, mainly along farm tracks and we got to North Esk Reservoir without incident. The views over the farmland and hills were a bit disappointing; I'd hoped to be able to see right over the Forth, but maybe that would come later on. Although the sun was still out and there was no hint of rain, we'd had a few wet days previously so it was quite boggy underfoot and we'd to navigate round the dryer bits.

"Oh, no – look at that!" This came from Fiona, pointing ahead to a group of brown and black-and-white cows, well spread out and bang in the direction we were aiming for. They all seemed to be female though, and even with my limited agricultural knowledge I didn't think there were any bulls in their midst. However, Fiona wasn't convinced. "We'll have to go round the long way. They look a bit menacing."

"It's OK, there's no calves. No horns either, not like the last time. Look, they're just chewing, minding their own business – they'll ignore us." Eilidh was always quite authoritative with her rural knowledge; I just hoped she was right this time too. However, Fiona as always had decided we'd do things her way and was heading for the incline on the right, trying to get as far away from the animals as possible. That might've been a reasonable idea, but we soon found ourselves right in the heart of the bog, and before long our boots were covered with oozing, sticky and very smelly muck – it was only too obvious that the cows had been here before us. It crossed my mind that if the cows did decide to go for us, we'd have had it – there was no way we could run; it was taking all our strength to haul each foot out of the squelchy mess.

"Bugger!" This was Eilidh, as she staggered to regain her balance after hauling her pole out of the depths and then examined the tip. "Bugger – the thingy at the end's come off. God, I hate this glaur[6]!"

"It's a bit firmer here." Fiona was prodding the earth with her foot. "We could head over towards that stone and then go round."

I didn't even check, just followed her blindly. When we eventually found ourselves clear of both cows and mud, and stopped to draw breath, I wasn't exactly sure where we were.

"Why don't we just follow that wall?" I suggested, trying to sound as if I knew what I was talking about. A well-built, drystone wall extended up on our right and off into the distance. "It must lead somewhere, and it gives us a line rather than trying to work out a path from the map."

Well, I doubt that that was my best idea of the day though no-one, not even Fiona, came up with an alternative. It was a very, very *long* wall, and our walk rapidly became a

---

[6] soft, sticky mud

miserable trudge. It was the usual story – though normally applied to a series of falsely imagined summits – at every rise, we thought we'd see the end of the wall, or it taking a turn, or leading downhill, or opening up with a gate, or *something*. When, after what seemed an eternity, all these things suddenly came at once, Fiona flung herself down on a tuft of heather at the corner and slung her rucksack on the ground.

"Right, I don't care if there's a view, or what's over the other side, I've had it. Lunch!"

"Best suggestion I've heard yet." Eilidh joined her immediately and dug out her sandwiches as quickly as possible. "I'm starving, but even if I wasn't I've had enough of all this having to watch every step. I'm *knackered*. Amazing no-one's lost a boot, or gone over an ankle. We must be made of strong stuff." She tucked into the sandwich with relish, and leaned back against the offending wall with a sigh of relief.

I went over to check the view, as no-one else was going to and I felt responsible. A gap in the wall, with the rusted remains of a gate, led to another walled area but this time I could see the sprawl of Edinburgh, and over the Forth to the Fife hills and beyond. What was much more important though, was that in the near distance I could also make out the grey houses of Balerno, at the end of a trail of small towns that were really now just suburbs leading into Edinburgh. Unfortunately, it was still further away than I'd have hoped. At least we could now see where we were aiming for.

"Sorry, guys – must be the worst walk we've had yet." Trust it to be my choice. "But the views are here."

"Not to worry – good for the moral fibre." Eilidh was always supportive. "Exercise, lots of fresh – if sometimes smelly – air, and I take your word about the views. I'm not going to move till I've recovered. That was hard going – and for once NOT because of my lack of fitness."

"How've you been finding the poles? Legs any better?" I felt that the poles were probably a good idea for her – they should take the pressure off her legs and feet, anyway.

"Aye, I think so, but it's hard to tell with all that mud. *And* I lost that thing at the end."

"Ferrule. Anyway, I'm pooped too."

"That an English expression, Fiona?" I laughed as I joined them on the ground.

"Or Enid Blyton's? Famous Five stuff." This was Eilidh's suggestion, through a mouthful of something.

"Nope. Only three of us anyway. Need to think of another name. And I'll ignore the bit about being English."

"Alan thinks we're like the three witches from Macbeth." Eilidh stirred an imaginary cauldron vigorously. "Maybe we should just call ourselves 'We Three'. As in, 'When shall we three meet again?' And this is certainly a blasted heath."

"Not very catchy, but at least it's got a literary bent, to match the high joint IQ of the group." Well, we were all graduates, although the two things didn't always seem to go hand-in-hand.

"Not high enough to think of a better name, unfortunately." Fiona grinned. "'We Three Trudge the Pentlands' displayed in Waterstone's window isn't really going to cut it."

"Well, no-one would read it except us, so we could call ourselves anything we want. It'd be a chapter, not a title, anyway. Could try a bit of alliteration to make it catchier – how 'bout 'We Three Battle on to Balerno'?" I hoisted my pack and got ready to move off, ignoring the snorts of derision beside me.

When the other two struggled to their feet reluctantly, even they were a bit cheered by the view and the sight of Balerno. The sandwiches'd probably helped a bit too.

"Right, before moving off look out for cows, walls, bogs, or any other potential obstacles – I'm suggesting we aim for that track over there. Takes us down to Threipmuir Reservoir; if we go round the top edge we can join the path there – might even be a road, not sure – then even we can't miss Balerno. OK?" I looked at Fiona for confirmation, knowing that Eilidh was likely to go along with most suggestions.

Amazingly, this idea worked and there were no more mishaps. The scenery even got a bit more interesting beside the reservoir – patches of tall trees rose above smaller shrubby ones, and long pale rushes grew in large clumps in the water. We crossed over onto the other side, into the trees, and Eilidh went off to check an information board. She informed us that there was a wildlife reserve here too, called Bavelaw Marsh, with lots of birds – mainly ducks. The sun even came out again, and we followed the path round to the right along the water, before taking the first opportunity to cut across to the main road. By the time we were walking into Balerno the misery of cows and mud – or 'glaur' as Eilidh called it - was well behind us. However, I was slightly concerned there might be one last problem ahead ...

"Is this *it?*" Fiona could be very scathing about what she saw as the parochial aspects of Scotland, but even I had to agree with her on this one. Balerno's high street wasn't exactly inspiring. Unlike the lively villages we'd been in earlier, this place seemed pretty dead. Very few people walking about, hardly any shops or facilities, and a lot of the grey concrete buildings and walls that Scotland did only too well. I scouted about, and finally stood outside the Grey Horse and announced that it was the only place within obvious reach of the bus stop. It was at the bottom of a pedestrianised slope leading up to the post office, and a quick glance inside didn't enthral. However, needs must and we traipsed in.

It turned out to be a cosy enough little bar after all; reminiscent of the spit-and-sawdust mainly male pubs that so dominated Scotland for years. We were viewed with a certain amusement by the two or three customers already there. You'd think they'd be used to walkers here, but maybe not – I suppose most walkers headed straight back to the city. But then not all walkers were caked in dried mud up to their knees, with wild tangled hair and a general wind-beaten look. I couldn't help sharing the thought with the others once we'd settled down at a table with drinks.

"I *beg* your pardon!" Eilidh bristled with mock indignation. "Are you suggesting that other people would manage to do that walk *without* getting clarted in mud? And what d'you mean about our hair? I got mine cut the other day – thought it looked *very* stylish."

"Other people wouldn't be so daft as to do that walk," I felt bound to admit. "Or if they did, they'd take a different route. And your hair's lovely, Eilidh – or at least it was when we set out this morning."

As the gentle banter continued, and we settled down with our drinks, I realised something with a jolt.

"You know, have hardly thought about Pete at all today. Can't quite believe it." I paused for breath, looking for the right words as I wasn't trying to elicit sympathy, at all. I didn't want Eilidh in tears again.

"I mean, it's not that it hasn't crossed my mind – but it almost seems an irrelevance, if you know what I mean? Do you?" I looked anxiously at them.

"Well, I'm glad you brought the topic up again, as I wasn't quite sure if you'd want us to." Fiona looked at me closely. "You tend to keep a lot to yourself, I think – and I can understand that."

"Really?" I was surprised at this. "It's not a conscious decision – and today, honestly, I was more concerned with mud, cows and soggy feet than normal life. Although, what *is* normal in our house these days?" Mm, the bitterness *was* still there. Maybe I did need to unload.

"Am I right in thinking that things haven't been right for a while?" asked Eilidh.

"Well, they haven't been great." I thought for a bit as I sipped my wine. "You know, think I'm just glad that he's actually gone, which'll make it easier to have a clean break. No more snide remarks, no more put-downs, no more having to second guess what he's up to and hoping the kids aren't aware."

"And are they?" Fiona wore a slightly sceptical expression.

"Yes and no. Joe … is such a happy-go-lucky individual, and so into his sport. Not sure he realises that there's a real world out there – or even in our own home. But Julie can't help but be aware now, as he's moved out. She's started to ask questions but I wasn't quite ready for them."

"D'you think he's going to stay with this person?" asked Eilidh.

"Doubt it. She'll see through Pete pretty quickly, and financially he's no great catch. We've got to see the kids through Uni or college, and there's still a mortgage on the house to pay off."

"Well, I probably shouldn't say this, but I'm glad it's come to a head. He's treated you like shit for years – not just with women, but in the house, taking you for granted with the kids and things. You're going to be much better off without him." Fiona was quite worked up, which surprised me. Had it been that obvious? I wondered suddenly if he'd ever made a pass at her. She might tell me in time.

"Interestingly, he's always admired *you*, Fiona." I couldn't help enjoying the thought of Pete lusting after someone who probably despised him – although she hadn't gone as far as to say that. Yet.

"Liksi, it might sound a bit premature, but – if you are serious about splitting up, you might want to get hold of a good lawyer as soon as you can." Fiona was looking concerned. "You don't want him to get the upper hand."

"I know, but - I just need to see him first and have a conversation. We *have* been together now for about 23 years, and I feel I owe him that."

"You don't owe him *anything*! Don't start feeling sorry for him, or going soft – he's been a bastard and deserves everything he gets!" Fiona's sudden outburst was rather shocking, and as I caught her gaze and held it, I'd the feeling that my supposition had some truth in it after all. She looked away, and after a second or two said quietly, "Sorry. It's not fair of me to say that."

"It's OK, Fiona. It's not a problem. I know you're trying to help – both of you've helped immensely today just by being there. Taking me away from the whole thing for a while. You're the first people I've told, and I'm so glad." I meant it – with these two there was absolutely no embarrassment. We didn't meet up often, but they could read between the lines and we knew each other so well from all our conversations over the years that I knew I'd get their full support.

As we headed for the bus and home, I was once again so grateful for our friendship, and slightly overwhelmed by the realisation of how much it meant to me.

Chapter 16 – Scafell Pike (September 2012) - Fiona

Scafell Pike at 3,208 feet is the highest mountain in England, and is situated in the Borrowdale area of the Lake District. There are various routes up; this one was convenient for Borrowdale Youth Hostel. From there, it goes through Seathwaite, over Stockley Bridge, past Styhead Tarn and up through the pass into the Corridor Route. Passing the slope of Lingmell on the right, a steep climb leads to the summit. The total return distance from Borrowdale Youth Hostel is around 10 miles.

Driving up the M6, I reflected bitterly on Wednesday's news. I'd never forget that moment in the consultant's room when Olly's diagnosis was finally confirmed. We knew anyway – at least, we'd got it down to one of three conditions – but there was always that tiny hope that we'd be proved wrong, that all those hours of amateur research on the Internet would result in only a false alarm.

Parkinson's. My husband of 24 years had Parkinson's. Olly – who shared my passion for keeping fit, spent hours at the gym and used to love fell running – had Parkinson's.

I shouldn't even be coming up here, I should be with him. He'd persuaded me that staying at home this weekend wouldn't change the diagnosis, wouldn't make the illness better or make it go away. So here I was, turning into the car park at Penrith railway station to meet the others. How was I going to tell them? I'd been moaning for the last couple of years about Olly's increasing irritability and reluctance to socialise outside the house. Middle-aged laziness, I'd called it. OMG.

And there they were, at the entrance, waiting to start another healthy, chatty weekend, oblivious to the bombshell that had just changed my life forever. Angrily, I swiped at the moistness forming round my eyes and switched into work mode – functional, smiling, all evidence of personal turmoil packed well behind that shield I could so easily erect. I swerved in, wound the window down and shouted:

"Hi there, just throw your bags in the boot and we'll head straight there."

"Much appreciated." Liksi climbed in easily in after Eilidh.

After a bit of the usual chit-chat, I managed to head off any further talk for the time being and concentrated on driving, but I knew I'd have to tell them about Olly over the weekend. Not yet, though. Not quite yet.

Our destination today was Borrowdale Youth Hostel, near Rosthwaite. Snatches of distant, mauve-coloured hills were just visible through the late afternoon cloud, and farmland with grazing sheep and healthy-looking cows flanked the road. Navigating Keswick's busy streets was tricky as always, and I was glad to come out the other end alongside Derwentwater. The lake glimmered in patches through the tangled trees and shrubs, which had almost transformed themselves fully into their autumn colours. With Eilidh keeping an eye open for any likely-looking pubs in sleepy Rosthwaite, we arrived at the Youth Hostel after taking a right turn at the crossroads.

It was a long, low wooden building, mainly on one level, although the bedrooms were on the upper floor. Inside, the predominant material was wood, in keeping with the environment. As usual, we wasted no time in going back out again. The hostel was tucked away in a peaceful spot by the River Derwent, and it was a pleasant stroll along the lane, crossing the road and continuing on to the Langstrath Country Inn. The bar was just as you'd expect – well set up to cope with walkers with an interesting row of beers and hearty menu options, but also smart enough to appeal to less active customers. It wasn't long before Eilidh was ingratiating herself with the barman, sampling a few ales before announcing that the Westmoreland was terrific and coming back to the table with beer, merlot and crisps.

"This is the bit of our walks I always like best." Liksi pulled her jumper over her head and then stretched luxuriously. "Eilidh waiting on us, Fiona not driving any more, unwinding totally – the weekend starts here!"

"Mm, nice beer." Eilidh had already made considerable inroads into her pint as she set her glass down. "How are things at home now, Liksi?"

"Good, thanks." Liksi sounded so much happier. "Calm. Stress free. Once Julie got over the shock of realising what a bastard her father is, we've settled into really good girl time together."

"Did I tell you I got made up to Curriculum Manager last year?" Eilidh said suddenly.

"Think you said something about the post coming up. Well done – how's it going?" Liksi's memory must be better than mine – but then I hadn't been concentrating on anything much recently.

"Well, I've got a team of around 15 to look after. They're a good bunch, but there's the odd one that still terrifies me." She reached out for the bag of crisps. "You know, I really wanted this job, but sometimes I wonder if I actually merit it. Maybe I'm just not cut out for promotion."

"I'm sure you're more than deserving of it." From what I'd been able to make out, she should have been given that job years ago. "For heaven's sake, you've worked your butt off in that place for years – you deserve recognition."

"Sure, from that point of view – but I hate confrontation, and it's looming."

"Who does? You'll get used to it." I ignored Eilidh's sceptical look. I knew I didn't suffer fools gladly, and sometimes even I felt sorry for my staff, especially recently. "I've got plenty of weirdos in my team – it *is* IT, after all. There's always some crisis or another – my staff just seem to *exist* on problems – but hey ho, that's the way it goes."

"Mm. Och well, I wanted the promotion, so now I'll just have to get on with it."

"You'll be great at it – good for you anyway. Here's to mastery of your team!" I raised my glass and managed a smile which I hoped was encouraging. I wondered what Olly was doing, if he was managing to hold it together or if he'd told anyone yet. He'd know that I'd tell the girls this weekend, but I doubted that he'd talk about it with any of his own mates just yet. We'd agreed not to tell the boys till we could see them face-to-face, and they'd promised to come home next weekend anyway for Olly's birthday. Although God knows, it was hit and miss with Nathan. As if we didn't have enough to contend with. Oh, I should've postponed this trip ...

"Fiona! You're miles away – anyone home?" Eilidh waved her hands in front of my face.

"Eh, sorry – can you say that again?" I swallowed the lump in my throat that was threatening to take over, and made an effort to join in the conversation, ignoring Eilidh's slightly puzzled look.

Somehow, while the other two proffered the usual work or family news, I made it through to closing time. I guess all these years of keeping my personal life completely separate from my working life helped. We emerged into the velvety black of the night sky, denser somehow than that of the city. The journey back along the pitted road and uneven path needed a bit of concentration, so there was less opportunity for difficult conversations. Back at the hostel, we went to bed soon afterwards. With my face to the wall, I let the silent tears fall at last.

Next morning, the weather was not too promising. It wasn't exactly raining, but it felt dank, and the surrounding hills were covered in mist. The odd grey top broke cover from time to time as the wind blew the thick blanket away, only for it to reform quickly as a new swathe was swept in. However, after breakfast we bundled up in layers and assembled outside. In spite of the elements, I could still appreciate that it was a lovely spot. The wooden building blended in well with the landscape, and it was far enough away from any main road, so no traffic noise disturbed the peace. The isolated bleat of a sheep reminded us that we were surrounded by farmland, and the sound of the Derwent burbling along nearby raised even my low spirits slightly.

"I'm looking forward to doing a climb again." Eilidh was testing out the height of her poles. "Shedding two stones and using these things should make a big difference. I hope."

"You'll be fine," said Liksi. "Don't worry about it – you look great, anyway." She did, actually.

Eilidh tried to brush the compliment away but only succeeded in beaming. "Thanks. Which way, Fiona?" Honestly, she seemed to have no sense of direction outside Scotland. However, I was grateful to have a leading role in today's walk, to keep my mind focused as much as possible, so pointed in the direction of the road south.

"We head for Seathwaite first, so back to the road for a bit, then we branch off to the right and walk along a track parallel to it."

The mist seemed to get closer as we turned off the road and onto the track. The peaks were still doing their now-you-see-them, now-you-don't act, and the cold dreich atmosphere made us move as quickly as we could to keep warm. In spite of the weather there were quite a few walkers around, which was encouraging, and when we stopped to adjust our clothing and have a drink we got into conversation with one of them who seemed to know the hills well.

"Yup, I'm going up the Pike as well." His leathery, rosy face indicated a life spent outdoors, as did his worn waxed jacket and mud-caked boots. No tourist, this one – he seemed very much at home with his surroundings. "Which route you girls taking?"

"We've not made up our minds yet. Just looking at the weather." Actually, I hadn't given the route proper thought, I realised with a start.

"Mist only going to get worse." He offered this information with some relish. "Wouldn't advise going up the corridor route unless you've been up that way before. It's a bit tricky, specially the gully."

"Which way are you going?" I asked.

"Corridor route." With a cheery wave, he was off, striding confidently up the path. Obviously not one to be put off by the weather – and neither would we be. It wasn't as if we couldn't see *anything* – the valleys and tarns were visible, and we could see right down to Wast Water, framed by its forbidding grey scree slopes. Looking up towards Scafell Pike, the immediate trail over the moorland and rocks didn't look particularly daunting, although it was steep.

"OK, girls, corridor route it is. Don't see the point in going all the way round and up the back and prolonging the exercise." I could see Eilidh's face, alarm showing clearly at the thought of going against local advice, but having begun to say something, she changed her mind and reluctantly fell into step behind me.

There were a couple of gullies to negotiate, and a bit of scree, but nothing that we weren't used to. Visibility got worse as we climbed, and conversation dwindled as we concentrated our efforts on keeping sight of the path. Eilidh did really well – she was still on the slow side, but she kept going steadily and was right behind us all the way up. Thank God for those poles of hers. In spite of her doubts and the weather, we made it to the top without any real problem. Jackets were zipped back up again against the cold for the usual group photo which was taken by another willing walker, and we managed to have a quick and damp lunch in the lee of the stone shelter.

"Well, we're obviously not here for the view." Liksi huddled down into her jacket and turned round to make sure she hadn't missed anything. By this time we were right up in the mist, and could only see shadowy outlines of the boulders and cairns surrounding us at the top, and leading away in several different directions. "Can't say these cairns are of much help. Can't see past the first couple so don't know where any of them lead to, and they all look the same. Anyone know where we should go down?"

"That's the way we came." Eilidh was pointing back into the mist. "If we're going back the same way, that is?"

"Yes, we are." Unfortunately, it just wouldn't be practical to try to do a circular trip this time. "But it must be that way – look, where all those people are heading." I pointed out a steady trickle of climbers making their way towards one of the cairns, then disappearing shortly afterwards.

"Well, if you say so." Eilidh looked doubtful. "But I'm sure that one there is the cairn we passed on the way up – I can tell by the shape."

I wasn't going to start relying on Eilidh's poor navigational skills at this stage, so before she could put up any more resistance, I started off down to join the trickle and the other two followed me anyway. The mist got even more dense, and we soon found ourselves scrambling down a really nasty steep gully. It was hard work and took a lot of concentration to get down without losing our footing on the sharp scree, and there were yells and expletives accompanying skinned knuckles and ankle knocks all the way down. I waited for the others as they slid and zigzagged their way to the bottom, and looked anxiously back at the way we'd come. This was *definitely* not the same path we'd taken to get to the summit.

"Well one thing's for sure." Eilidh was dusting herself off vigorously. "We didn't go UP that last bit or we'd have known about it. Look down there – that's not the valley we came up, is it?"

Moving round, I could see that she was absolutely right – we'd come the wrong way completely, and probably *should* have gone down the way she'd suggested in the first place. We'd left the worst of the mist behind, and the few farms and houses we could see dotted about in the distance were certainly not those we'd seen at Seathwaite. Christ, how could I have been so stupid?

"And another thing's for certain." Liksi was unusually firm. "I'm damn sure I'm not going back up there again. God, that was hard going - knees'll take weeks to recover."

"OK, nothing for it." I was furious with myself, but could only manage a grudging admission; I just couldn't take much more. "We'll have to go all the way round the bottom now, but we'll need to head to the right unless you want a climb."

"No more climbing." Eilidh had also found her assertive streak. "I'll go for distance rather than height."

"Well, if that's what you want we'd better get going." I knew I was being surly, but I hate it when I've been shown up and can never handle it properly. I was also on the verge of tears – they'd never been far away in the last few days – and didn't want to prolong the discussion. I turned and led the way round the side of the slope we'd just come down, which was OK, but then we had to pass through an unavoidable boulder field. Eilidh landed on her rear end on a jagged spur as her pole caught between two rocks while her legs tried to move forward, but she picked herself up and carried on gamely. At least she was keeping up with Liksi no bother – that weight loss had definitely paid off. The boulders were interminable - different shapes and sizes over treacherous gaps. Some were loose, and others were covered with wet moss. We'd to concentrate on every single step, testing each stone out before putting weight on it. When I turned round later after hearing shouts, I found Eilidh still rubbing her buttocks ruefully and Liksi up to her knees in a peat bog, and – of course – she was wearing her cream cords. Why on earth would anyone – except Liksi - wear cords that colour on a walk anyway?

"Oh, my God, it's absolutely FREEZING. And look at the MUD! I'll *never* be able to wear these again!" Liksi looked at us helplessly and with absolutely no sign of any criticism, started laughing uncontrollably. I loved her for it – I don't think I could've done that. She managed to kind of wade her way out of it, and we ploughed on, eventually ending up back on the path to Seathwaite and familiar territory. By then we'd done about an extra 3 miles and the light was failing, but we managed to make it back to the hostel without having to use Eilidh's torch – just.

Absolutely exhausted, we collapsed inside the entrance. It went without saying that none of us wanted to – or were fit to – walk one more step more than necessary for the rest of the evening, and specially not all the way to the Langstrath again. Thankfully, we were able to book a meal in the hostel before we stumbled our way upstairs to get changed. Our boots were soaking, inside and out, and covered in mud – as were both of Liksi's legs by this time. After showers, Eilidh and I went to claim a table in the dining room, and Liksi took all our boots to the drying room. We'd just been having a look at the menu when she joined us, choking with laughter.

"What's happened?" I asked.

"Oh, it was priceless – I'd put your boots out on the rack. Then I had another look at mine and decided that they *and* my cords were beyond saving." She was still laughing as she sat down. "So I chucked them with some ceremony in the bin. This guy must've been watching me and came over looking really worried, saying, 'Oh, don't give up! It can't have been that bad – you'll need them again some time.' Oh, you should've seen his face ...!" and she was off again, and within minutes we were all laughing helplessly with her. I was happy to let the tears run down my face too, and then I blurted out:

"I'm sorry to do this – I've got something to tell you and I've got to do it quickly or I'll chicken out again."

There was instant silence, as two tear-streaked faces turned to me with their whole attention, and I delivered the momentous words: "Olly has Parkinson's."

Chapter 17 – West Island Way, north loop (June 2013) - Eilidh

The West Island Way covers about 28 miles of the isle of Bute. This section of approximately 18 miles starts in the main town of Rothesay, crossing the island towards Ettrick Bay. The path then heads up towards the most northerly point, before skirting round the coast to Rhubodach. Leading back up the hillside, it moves south before going through Port Bannatyne on the way back to Rothesay.

I was quite excited about this one – train, ferry, island and another recognised distance walk, not to mention an extra day off work. Besides, I'd only been to Rothesay a couple of times before, but really liked it and was looking forward to showing it off to the others.

After Fiona's bombshell about Olly when we last met, I'd wondered if she'd be able to make it up north again. I didn't really know much about Parkinsons, but I did know it was not something he would ever recover from. However, she was as keen as ever to meet up, and when I met her at Glasgow Central station on the Thursday, she seemed very matter of fact.

"We're fine, Eilidh, really – we just have to get on with it. It was such a blow when we heard, and we've had to make a few adjustments, but life just has to go on. What's the alternative?"

I looked at her as she spoke – Fiona was rarely one to admit defeat in anything – but she did look OK. I gave her a hug anyway. "That's for Olly as well. Come on, train's this way."

When we got off the train at Wemyss Bay, we found Liksi wandering about the lovely old station. With her short hair glinting in the sun shining through the windows, and her bright green jacket, she looked like a wee pixie.

"Fantastic." She waved her arm to indicate the high ceiling with its magnificent glass and steel curves. "Had a good time already – took the bus and got here a couple of hours ago. Just been reading in a café and walking about."

"I couldn't quite get why you took the bus and not the train?" asked Fiona. "You'd have got here in half the time."

"Just like buses. Much cheaper and you get more of a chance to see places properly. Anyway, I'm from Edinburgh, remember – we *do* buses!"

"You do indeed – at the moment." I noted Liksi's puzzled look. "How're those trams coming along, by the way? They should never've ..."

"Come on, never mind trams, here's the ferry." Fiona was already heading down to the pier, and once the foot passengers disembarked, we got on board. I did like these CalMac ferries – the company got bad press sometimes, and it might be different if you relied on one of them to get you to and from somewhere on a regular basis, but I just loved the sheer romanticism of a ferry taking me over an expanse of water to an island. It conjured up childhood holidays in Lewis and Harris, where the ferries were often full of people known to my father, if not myself.

"Mm, this is good." I sniffed the seaweedy air appreciatively, as we hung on to the rails on the deck. "This definitely feels like a holiday, not just a weekend. I'm sure just *breathing* the sea air is good for our health. Pity it's only a 35-minute crossing."

"Don't think I've been on a Scottish ferry before." Liksi was obviously enjoying the experience too. "Disgrace, really. Where's that place up there?"

"That's Dunoon. You get such great views from here – if you look in the other direction, out to sea, you'll see a wee island. That's Millport. Good for another trip some day."

"How're things with you anyway, Liksi?" Fiona turned round, brushing the hair out of her eyes. "It must be nearly a year now since Pete moved out."

"Yeah, and it's *great*." She beamed at us, and I couldn't help laughing. "I *love* it – know this sounds a bit extreme, but I feel as if I've been released from prison or something. I feel so *free*! You've no idea how wearing it was, and how – belittling." I was really pleased for her – it was so obvious that she was enjoying life to the full again.

"Come on, up to the front and we can see Rothesay as we head in." The town stretched out along the curve of the bay, with the houses gradually petering out at each end. Near the centre was the ferry terminal, and along to the right the pavilion and genteel esplanade with a well-manicured garden area. Some very large houses were spread out up the hill – there must have been money here at some stage. I pointed out the famous Victorian toilets near the pier – B-listed, with marble fittings and mosaic floors, they were probably the best preserved of their type in the UK. "They're male only, but with original tiling and everything. Apparently females can go in and see them if they're unoccupied."

"It's OK, thanks, Eilidh, I think I'll give that one a miss." Fiona looked at me rather pityingly. "What happened to the female ones?"

"Och, the males had a more pressing need, apparently. They used to get drunk on the paddle steamers – yes, that's where the word "steaming" comes from – and there weren't sufficient facilities on board. You've just no sense of adventure." I teased her, but didn't press the point. I could see them another time. Once on dry land, we headed off to the right along the main street to look for our hostel. Although we passed a lot of imposing houses, many of them looked as if they'd seen better times, and the shop fronts looked tired and neglected.

"It's not exactly pretty, once you see it properly, is it?" Fiona echoed my thoughts. "Kind of faded grandeur."

"Aye, it used to be buzzing, and hugely popular – one of the steamer stops 'Doon the Watter' from Glasgow in post-war times. I guess people go to Spain instead now. It's still a lovely island though – believe me."

The hostel turned out to be a rambling affair of three adjoining houses. After wandering around the extensive public areas, we finally realised that the rather kitsch eastern ornament sitting on a dresser was in fact a bell. When Liksi shook it experimentally, it was hardly surprising that its grating tones produced someone almost immediately, and we were directed upstairs to our room. Fiona went in search of the shower-rooms and toilets and came back shaking her head with an even worse grimace, if that was possible.

"I'd try not to spend much time in there, if I were you. Bins are overflowing, sinks don't seem to have been cleaned and you stick to the floor."

"Well, we won't be indoors much anyway." Liksi at least didn't seem too bothered. "Too much island to cover. Don't worry, Eilidh, it'll be fine."

I knew they'd make the best of it, but it was a disappointment after the excellent hostels we'd stayed at in England. This'd been the only hostel I could find in Rothesay, so I just hoped it wouldn't let me down too badly.

We walked back along the front to check out the restaurant scene, and ended up at the Waterfront Bistro. Thankfully it was lively and bright, with an interesting menu and a chatty waitress. Things were looking up.

We survived our first night in the hostel, and the next morning avoided the showers in the hope that they'd be cleaned by the time we got back. The sun was shining, the water was sparkling, and we were in high spirits as we left our accommodation. Breakfast in a small café, followed by a visit to the tourist information centre to pick up a street map of Rothesay, and we were ready to go.

"If we'd more time here, we could have a proper look at

the castle." I looked at it regretfully as I led them past it. "I remember wandering around there when Alan and I were over a couple of years ago. We hadn't realised in advance that it was the Rothesay Highland Games that weekend, and the place was heaving. Prince Charles was around somewhere, but we managed to avoid him."

"Probably just as well for Alan's blood pressure." Liksi laughed. "Wouldn't have thought meeting the Duke of Rothesay in full Highland dress would be his idea of a day out."

"No, indeed – nor mine. Duke of Rothesay, indeed. Huh." There was a chorus of snorts in agreement.

"My God, what on earth d'you make of that?" Liksi was gazing at a very long, rectangular, modernist building that we were passing on our right. It was perched on the hillside, jutting out towards the sea with great views back across to the mainland – but what a depressing sight. Flat roofed, windows boarded up or broken, weeds peering through wherever they could get a hold.

"It's the old Rothesay Academy – and believe it or not, it's listed so it can't be demolished." I was quite chuffed that I'd read about this on the train into Central Station.

"Listed?" Liksi was incredulous. "But it's grotesque – what an eyesore."

"Yes, it had to be council buildings or a school, didn't it?" Fiona studied it briefly, before continuing, "Come on, let's get moving and away from the town – it's depressing me."

I thought that was a bit harsh – after all, it was just one building, however ugly – but I was keen to get out into the country too, so we upped the pace and soon left the roads for woodlands and then a golf course. From there we could look down onto Kames Bay with its small marina and Port Bannatyne, which really just seemed like an extension of Rothesay, and across the water to the Cowal peninsula. We'd to go back onto a tarmac road again for a short while, but soon afterwards the route led onto a very flat track through farmland which cut right across to the east of the island to Ettrick Bay.

"I remember down there being a nice spot." I pointed to the sandy strip, with a seaweed-strewn shore. "There's a café there if you want a short detour."

"Too early for detours," Fiona announced, and she was probably right as we'd quite a long day ahead of us. In any case, although I really liked Bute – as I did any Scottish island I'd been to – I found its gritty grey beaches disappointing, and couldn't help comparing them with all the wonderful stretches of white sand dotted further up the west coast mainland, as well as on the islands. I was happy just to follow the track instead, and turned north, heading for the hillier part of the island.

"I feel we're not on a proper walk unless there are hills and views." Fiona fell into step behind. "All these straight paths or tarmac roads feel like cheating, somehow."

"Agree. Beaches, cliffs, mountains and lochs are the best." Not for the first time, I regretted that my choice of job had led to me settling in a city. "But this'll do me very well today – the highest point must be one of those hills over there, and it's not even 1,000 ft."

"There seem to be lots of abandoned townships around here. Guess there must've been a lot more people living here previously, like so much of the Highlands." Fiona was pointing to another information board, this time for Balnakailly Loop. "What do you want to do here? Official route or scenic and historical one?" The board indicated that the Loop led to another ruined village and a woodland walk which would take us nearer the north of the island.

"How about doing the Loop – it sounds interesting – and having lunch at the top, looking over to Colintraive? Or Colintrive, however you pronounce it. One way's posh and the other isn't." I could never remember which was which.

"And," I remembered suddenly, "there's a pub up there, at Rhubodach. If we go the direct route we might miss it." Decision made – a no-brainer, as they say.

The diversion was worth it – more woodland, with the sad remains of houses struggling to be seen above the encroaching cow parsley and nettles, then emerging onto another bay, this time pebbled. We'd our lunch sitting there looking over at the tiny islands, and the smattering of dwellings that make up Colintraive on the mainland, across the kyle.

"Look, there's the ferry leaving Rhubodach. It's tiny – but it goes every half hour." I pointed out the ferry as it disgorged its occupants on the other side minutes after it'd left Bute. "It must be one of the shortest Calmac crossings, if not *the* shortest one."

"They must've been over here for the pub." Fiona laughed. "Hope they've left us some beer."

We walked round the corner of the bay towards where we'd seen the ferry depart. "Next ferry in half an hour – guess that one'll be back soon then." Liksi was reading the sign beside the slipway. "Where's this pub, Eilidh?"

I looked around, trying to remember its exact whereabouts – it'd been a few years since I'd been here. Unfortunately there was nothing remotely resembling a pub that I could see. "I'm not sure - must be on a bit." We carried on a few yards, but it was pretty obvious that there were only a couple of private houses soon after the ferry, and with a sudden sinking feeling I realised why.

"Oh, no, you're going to shoot me. I've just remembered – the pub is at the *other* side, in Colintraive! I'm sorry, sorry, I just got it mixed up – it's been a while." I looked at them shamefacedly, but also with genuine dismay as I'd been looking forward to relaxing in what I remembered as a very convivial small pub.

"Oh, Eilidh, you dangle pubs as carrots to keep us going,

then they're either closed or at the other side of a ferry crossing!" Liksi, along with Fiona, was doubled up with laughter. Thankfully. "Remember the Beech Tree Inn? Nearly put me off doing the rest of the West Highland Way altogether."

"Ha ha." But I was relieved they were taking it so well. "Apologies again, but we really need to get going now. There's about six miles to go yet and look up there." We turned from the bright and sunny vistas looking back towards the ferry, and up at the hillside we were about to head for. The sky had darkened, the mist was coming down, and the tops were starting to disappear.

"Oh dear." Liksi was peering into the distance.

"Oh dear indeed. Come on then." And Fiona was off, with Liksi and I close behind – to start with, anyway. It wasn't long before Fiona was up to her old tricks and disappeared into the mist. However, before I could get annoyed she'd reappeared in the distance, pointing up to the right where we could just make out a signpost – we'd have missed it otherwise. It was an arduous few miles – not particularly steep, but boggy, sloped and with no clear path. However, our Sherpa didn't let us down and eventually we worked our way through it, emerging suddenly at the top of a hill with a clear view down to Port Bannatyne.

It was an easy walk from there onwards down to the village, but we were all tired as we must've been walking for about eighteen miles or so, although I'd lost count by then.

"Right, we're stopping at the first pub we find." Liksi was unusually authoritative. "I'm done in and need a reward for my efforts. Any ideas, Eilidh?"

"I'm surprised you'd even ask me." I grinned at her. "No, I don't know any other ones on Bute. The first one will do fine."

We were walking along the road which followed the coast by this stage, and the first contender we came across was the

Port Royal Hotel[7]. It looked a bit unusual but we couldn't put a finger on it, so we walked straight in – to an incredibly warm reception from a small individual whose beaming face was largely hidden under a Russian fur hat.

"Come in, come in – ladeez, come in! Eat? Drink? Yes? Well, well, sit and we'll see!" He – I thought it was a he - practically danced to a table by the window and offered it to us with a flourish. Looking at each other in mild alarm crossed with amusement, we flopped down and turned back to our host with interest.

"Walking? Many miles? Feet is tired? Vodka – vodka for tired feet. LUDMILA! LUDMILA!" This last was delivered at the threshold of pain, and a large lady with rosy cheeks and a big flowery pinny appeared through a door at the side. "Tree vodka! Tree!" I was about to object on the grounds that I hadn't had a vodka which was not part of a cocktail since I left my teens, but was lulled into submission through sheer shock. In any case, three small but full glasses were almost immediately placed in front of us by Ludmila, along with a smile radiating such kindliness that we just couldn't refuse. Especially as both individuals were hovering expectantly. We looked at each other and took a wary sip.

"Wow!" from Fiona, with her eyes watering.

"Mmm!" I managed, trying hard to look delighted whilst my head felt about to blow up. I didn't dare look at Liksi.

"Good, good?!" Not sure if this was a question or a statement, we all nodded madly and Fiona had the presence of mind to say, "Lovely! Best vodka I've tasted," whilst turning on the full force of a charming smile.

The couple nodded happily at each other, then the man looked at us again. "Now eat?"

"Er no thanks." Liksi got this in quickly, and we shook our

---

[7] Apologies to previous owners for a certain amount of artistic licence

heads to show our agreement. "We - we haven't got much time." The pair looked crestfallen.

"Just a beer, please," I asked timidly. "A pint of beer – er, Heineken?" I didn't usually drink this but I could see that it was available on tap and I didn't want to risk any other surprises.

"Me too – a half." Fiona must have needed something to wash down the vodka.

"And a half Heineken shandy for me please," Liksi added quickly.

The smiles returned, and Ludmila disappeared back through the door she'd come in. Our host went behind the bar to pour our drinks.

"Oh my God, that was *fierce*." I whispered.

"But wonderful." Fiona agreed, with a spaced-out smile on her face and I realised she'd finished her glass.

"Here, have mine." Liksi pushed her glass quickly towards her. "Just pretended to sip it – I couldn't have put it past my lips. Go on, take it."

Fiona picked it up, swirled it round and took a gulp. "I really, really like this."

"Well, you can have mine too when you're finished – just swap glasses so he doesn't realise." I'd never taken to vodka.

"D'you realise this place is also called The Russian Tavern?" Liksi'd picked up a leaflet from the sideboard.

"That explains it." I stopped speaking as our second lot of drinks appeared in front of us. I looked up anxiously in case there was anything else with them, but apart from delivering another of his beaming smiles, our host seemed to think he'd done his bit and left us to it.

"Look at all the paintings and china and things." Fiona was gazing round the room. "They all seem to have a Russian theme." It really was an amazing place – maybe not so amazing if that was what you were expecting to find, but going into somewhere called the Port Royal Hotel, on Bute, did not prepare us for an experience like this. We downed our beers with relief, but not before Fiona had knocked back her third vodka, and was wearing a rather glazed smile.

"Come on, you – home! If you can call the hostel home – if you don't move now who knows what'll happen." I held out a hand to haul her up, and after paying at the bar, we left without further incident.

"Mm, besht vodkas ever. Ouch – how'd that get there?" Fiona's indignation was lost as she missed the pavement, and Liksi grabbed her before she fell.

"Come on, Fiona, not far to go." I looked at Fiona with amusement as she tried to pretend there was nothing amiss. "I think we'd better just stick to the road now."

By the time we got to the hostel, we each had one of her arms to keep her walking in a straight line, but she was sober enough to insist on a shower straight away. It seemed to do the trick and she was a bit more with it when she emerged – without even mentioning the cleanliness – or otherwise – of the shower. It was early evening by then, so after Liksi and I followed her example we went off in search of sustenance.

The mist we'd encountered earlier had now come down to street level, along with a heavy drizzle. Nowhere's at its best in that kind of weather, least of all Rothesay, and the murky atmosphere didn't endear Fiona and Liksi to the island, sadly. However, we eventually found a Chinese restaurant which was perfectly OK. Liksi as usual couldn't eat all of her chow mein; Fiona polished it off along with her own chilli chicken. I don't think I'd ever seen her eat as much – but it certainly helped her recover from her visit to the Russian Tavern.

Afterwards, as we huddled down in our jackets to avoid the worst of the rain for the short walk back to the hostel, I feared the worst for walking conditions the next day.

Chapter 18 – West Island Way, south loop (June 2013) - Liksi

The second section of the WIW starts in Rothesay, moving south down the middle of the island to cross Loch Fad before continuing down through farmland to Stravanan Bay. From there it leads east to Kilchattan Bay. The final part hugs the east coast till it reaches the bottom of the island, then heads back up inland via St Blane's chapel, to finish back at Kilchattan Bay. (This walk was cut short so was only about 8 miles.)

"Come on, you two. Up you get. Breakfast calls!" Fiona could be *so* irritating – she'd missed her calling as a mistress in a girl's public school.

"It's bucketing out there." I could hear the rain hammering against the window, without even emerging from the duvet to look outside.

"Well, it might improve; either way we've got about another 18 miles or something to do so we need to get going." Fiona was unrelenting – but probably right, I thought grumpily. Sighing, I poked my head up to find Eilidh on her way to the shower.

"You're mad - you'll get soaked the minute you step outside. I'll have mine afterwards." Why on earth would anyone have a shower *before* a day's sweaty walking?

"You're absolutely right, but I'm not able to function in the mornings unless I have a shower. See you shortly." Eilidh disappeared out the door and there was no option really but for me to get up. Slowly. Fiona was lying on her bunk, dressed, and reading her Kindle.

I peered out the window, more in hope than anything else, but the sky was an unremitting grey, reflected in the sea with no clear delineation between them. The mainland wasn't visible, and I could hardly see as far as the pier - 'dreich' didn't even begin to describe it. I wondered idly if the Scots had as many words for 'rain' as the Eskimos purportedly had for 'snow'.

"D'you think we should be attempting a long walk in this?" I pulled on my clothes rather half-heartedly.

"Well, we're here. What else would we do in this place?" I could see that Fiona wasn't exactly taken with Bute, and I had to agree with her. It'd seemed dull and gloomy even when the weather was better, and Rothesay itself was disappointing. I hadn't been to many Scottish islands before – in fact, one, Skye, for the day - and had a vague notion that they should all be picture postcardy – although why, when rain featured so heavily on the west coast, I really don't know.

Eilidh came back in, showered and cheerful in spite of the weather. "Maybe it'll get brighter later on. Can we go back to that café for breakfast?"

"What was the shower like?" I asked, remembering last night's rather unpleasant experience. "Don't suppose anyone's used a bottle of Flash or anything in there since yesterday?"

"No change – oh, the bin's been emptied. Guess that's something." Eilidh was busy pulling her waterproof trousers back out of her rucksack. "Might as well put these on straight away."

Looked like there was no getting away from it – we were set for a wet walk. I rolled out of bed at last and joined them in their preparations. Idly, I wondered what Pete would've thought of all this – that we were all mad, and that I didn't have enough spine to stand up against them, etc etc. He could never see why we bothered with the walking bit when all we wanted to do was spend the day wittering, as he called it. Oh, it was so good not to have to listen to all that any more ...

Over breakfast in the café, Eilidh asked me how things were going since we'd last met up.

"Well, if you mean Pete, don't often think about him. I mean, I do in terms of what's going to happen long-term, but not much otherwise. Can't believe we've been married for all these years and I don't miss him at all."

"What about the kids? How do they deal with it?" Fiona was toying with her scrambled egg as we spoke.

"Well, he was never all that interested in Julie and I think she feels that. She doesn't often talk about him, although she'll meet up with him sometimes. Joe was the 'son and heir' so to that extent Pete has bonded a bit more with him, but now that he's in Loughborough there aren't many opportunities to meet up."

"Sad though. Do you think you'll get divorced eventually, or not bother?" asked Eilidh.

"Don't know. At this stage, I don't really care and I'm enjoying so much being on my own. He's still with Jayne – God knows how she puts up with him. I just hope he stays there."

"Well, let's hope he doesn't come back with his tail between his legs." Fiona looked scornful. "Have you had the locks changed?"

"Oh, I'm sure it won't come to that." I was quite shocked at the thought. In any case, I didn't feel we needed to go down the divorce route right now. They couldn't possibly understand – how *good* it felt to be free, and I really couldn't face all the paperwork, lawyers and unpleasantness that was bound to arise if we made the split final. Maybe some day.

By the time we'd finished breakfast, the rain had settled to a heavy 'mizzle'; not exactly unpleasant to be out in but with next to no visibility. We set off anyway for the south section – at least there didn't appear to be any more of the misty moorland to cope with. We went back out the main road which led to the west of the island, then cut off down a minor road. This soon became a well-defined path, which skirted the top of a long expanse of water Eilidh said was Loch Fad.

"I guess this would be quite attractive if you could see it properly." Fiona made a game attempt to compliment her surroundings. "It's a bigger stretch of water than you'd expect."

"It must be lovely in the summer." Eilidh's glass was still half full.

"This IS the summer." Fiona hunkered further down into her hood. "Summer in Scotland. Wonderful."

Poor Eilidh. I could see her taking a deep breath with pursed lips – she hated anyone decrying Scotland, and she'd been very keen to do this walk. However, we did our best and marched on. The rain became progressively heavier, and our banter got correspondingly less. We were concentrating fully on keeping as dry as possible – one foot was wringing; should have worn my boots, not these trail shoes – and also, frankly, just getting to the end as soon as possible. This was *not* fun.

The walking was certainly very easy, and a big contrast to yesterday's up-and-down, barely visible moorland. Most of the landscape was farmland, and the trail used well-defined paths lined with drystone dykes or low-level natural hedges. Good chatting country, if things had been otherwise. Sometimes it was good to have a walk which didn't involve any brain power; you could just put one foot in front of the other knowing you weren't going to fall through a gap in the heather, or turn your ankle on a cobbly stone. On the other hand, the monotony of this terrain seemed to emphasise the 'what on *earth* am I doing here?' factor. At some stage we came across a viewpoint, and stopped to get our bearings. We looked at each other, and couldn't help laughing.

"Some viewpoint." I couldn't even speak without rain getting into my mouth. "The only things I can see are your two faces – tiny ovals with your elasticated hoods drawn up round them! Look – can *you* see anything?" I waved around in all directions, taking in the wall of mist that had enfolded us, with heavy rain forming a double layer of moisture. Our faces were wet, and I could feel a drop of rain dripping from my eyelashes and into my eye.

"Eilidh." Fiona had had enough. "Is it possible to cut this short? I don't know about you two, but I really don't want to do this for another 4 hours or whatever."

"Glad you said that." I backed her up immediately, but Eilidh's stricken expression made me wish I hadn't been quite so direct.

"Well, if you *really* want to –."

"I do."

"I *suppose* we could cut it off at Kilchattan Bay. That'd mean we'd miss the last 5-mile loop round by St Blane's Chapel." There was a hopeful tone in Eilidh's voice here, but -

"That's fine." Fiona'd obviously decided that enough was enough, and I heartily agreed with her although I didn't like hurting Eilidh's feelings.

"St Blane's Chapel is a really special place. It'd be a shame to miss it." Eilidh tried valiantly one last time.

"What's special about it?" I asked.

"It's just such a wonderful, peaceful spot. If I wasn't an atheist, I'd say it was almost spiritual." Eilidh looked somewhat apologetic; she knew that this would sound a bit strange with her antipathy towards all things religious. "It's like – a bit like the island of Iona. You just *feel* something, though don't ask me what."

"Well, being realistic, how much of it could we see in this? I don't think I'm in the mood for a spiritual experience just now." Fiona'd made up her mind, and Eilidh did what I knew I'd do too in similar circumstances – gave in.

"OK, agreed, guess I'm outnumbered. Maybe I could persuade the two of you to come back another time. Or not –

" she added hastily, as she saw the expressions on our faces. "Right, I get it. Look, if we can get to Kilchattan we can get a bus back to Rothesay."

We'd a look at the map, and came to an agreement – we'd continue on towards Stravanan Bay, in the vague hope we'd see *some* scenery, or that the weather would change, and from there follow the route to Kilchattan Bay but no further. It might've been *slightly* quicker following the actual road to Kilchattan Bay instead, but we were all reluctant to walk on tarmac if there was a softer alternative.

When we got to Stravanan Bay the mist had lifted slightly, and we were able to see the curve of the small sandy stretch, before turning up through the golf course. We plodded our way through the woodlands – for once, even Eilidh didn't seem interested in a second glance at leaves, stones or birds - and finally emerged onto a street of solid sandstone houses overlooking the grey water of Kilchattan Bay.

By this time I was completely drenched – both feet were soaked, and my trousers were twice as heavy as they'd been when I started. Why did I never bother to bring waterproof trousers? Eilidh was complaining that she didn't know what was sweat and what was water inside her jacket, and Fiona was threatening to take *her* jacket back to Tiso's as her zip had let in water down the front.

We found the bus stop and discovered we'd to wait 20 minutes for the next bus.

"It would've been too much good luck to get one immediately." Fiona had a rueful smile on her face. "Hope we don't start chittering by the time it comes."

We were all quite warm from our exertions, but it didn't take long before the chill set in. Standing for any length of time whilst soaking wet is not a pleasant experience. We walked across the street and back a few times, but eventually found it best just to huddle down together on a nearby wall.

"What a sight we must be," I couldn't help saying. "Bet any locals're having a good laugh at us. They'd know *much* better than to go walking on a day like this."

"Bus!" Eilidh was on her feet, but then we were horrified when the bus just carried on past.

"No-o ... ," wailed Fiona.

"It's OK, it's going to turn." Re-assurance was required here. "It'll come back – Kilchattan's the end of the road according to the map." Much to our relief, this was confirmed by an elderly man in a cap who'd joined us, and as a few other people started to materialise, we began to relax – just as the bus did indeed return. We hauled our dripping selves inside and collapsed in relief, trying not to shiver too much during the 30-minute trip back. When the route started to hug the coast again, Eilidh tried to revive our interest in Bute by saying you could usually see seals on this stretch, but (a) there weren't any and (b) all I could think about was getting a hot shower and putting on dry clothes.

Back at the hostel, we made full use of the boot rack in the porch, and squelched upstairs in our sodden socks. There didn't seem to be a drying room in the building, so we had to drape everything over every bit of bed, chair, hook or door handle that we could find, and then took turns to shower – Eilidh for the second time that day.

"You know, we were only walking for about 4 hours." Fiona was raking about in her pack for a clean – and dry – pair of socks. "That must be our shortest walk ever."

"Oh well, at least we can say we've *almost* done the West Island Way – just missed out the last five miles. Not bad really." I pulled on a second jumper, desperate to get properly warm.

"We could come back some time to do that last loop. Really, that bit round St Blane's Chapel is worth seeing." Eilidh just didn't give up.

"Thanks but no thanks," said Fiona firmly. "I for one will not be coming back to Bute in a hurry."

"Don't think it would be a first choice for me, either." Even I'd been put off by the cheerless main town and the weather.

"That's a shame. You've not seen the place at its best, honestly. It really *is* a nice island – several of my colleagues've come here to retire."

"That's exactly the problem – it's full of retired, sleepy people." Fiona laughed.

"Och well, if Alan and I decide to retire here I guess we'll just have to come to the mainland to see you." Eilidh gave in gracefully, and I went off to make us coffee in the rather unhygienic kitchen. Finding myself sticking to the floor with each step, I took it through to the lounge and we had it there, then decided to read for a while. At least the lounge was comfortable – and clean.

"What're you reading this time?" asked Eilidh, from the depths of a cavernous armchair.

"Something about Berlin." I looked up from the pages. "Going there for a conference soon, and might take a few extra days to wander round on my own."

"Good for you." Fiona was always encouraging about anything job-related.

"Yes, strange feeling but I'm actually looking forward to doing something *I* want to do, and on my own. What're you both reading?"

"Just a Ruth Rendell." This from Fiona, as she pulled her cardigan more tightly round her. "I'm *still* cold."

"You know, Fiona, it was you who got me into reading decent books, away back." Eilidh stuck her finger in her own book to keep her place.

"Really?"

"Aye, remember when I was going off on holiday somewhere, you presented me with a pile of books you considered suitable – Jane Austen, Daphne du Maurier, etc – can't remember the rest. I've never looked back."

"Oh. Well, I'm glad I got something right. But you were always a reader, weren't you?"

"Yes, but two years of English Lit at Uni dampened my enthusiasm for anything decent for a while. I didn't appreciate picking everything to bits and analysing every last sentence. Thank God I can just enjoy the books without thinking about that now."

I was always slightly envious of Eilidh and Fiona having shared a flat in London, and gone through lots of experiences together which I was still hearing about. Mind you, I suspect that Eilidh was envious of me from time to time, having spent much longer in Australia than she did. I guess we've all had different highlights in our lives. As for Fiona, I couldn't imagine her being envious of anyone.

A couple of hours spent reading, or talking about books, whilst listening to the rain lashing against the windows – the wind had got up now – was very pleasant. For the hundredth time, I thanked my lucky stars that reading was so important to me. I never went anywhere without a book – in fact, I think the other two were the same. We might've carried on reading a bit longer, but then a couple of guys with guitars came in and started jamming; apparently they were tuning up for an informal session that evening. Pleasant as it might've been to stay and listen, hunger – and thirst – took over and we reluctantly donned still-damp waterproofs to head out in search of something to eat.

The Black Bull proved to be a lively and comfortable refuge, although Eilidh was not at all impressed by the range of beer. Over the meal, I asked Fiona how things were at home. She hadn't seemed to want to discuss the subject yesterday, but it wouldn't be right not to give her a chance to talk about things properly.

"Well." She ran her finger slowly round her glass, "We're coping. Kind of. Nathan is still with Sally, and may or may not still be on methadone. He's not in the supermarket any more – seems to be working now and again for a delivery company, and Sally works part-time for the council. He doesn't talk to us about his situation, and doesn't ask us for money, which we take to be a good sign."

"Sounds about as good as you could hope for, really." I was quite surprised though. I'd always thought that it was very difficult for a heroin addict to hold down any kind of job. Maybe the methadone made the difference – but I really didn't know about these things. Thankfully.

"And Olly?" Eilidh asked.

"Olly – well, I have to say I'm very proud of him." Fiona's voice cracked slightly, and she looked away. "He seems to be doing everything he can to stay as healthy as possible – keeping up his gym sessions, though he has to be careful with weights in case he has a tremor. He also cycles as much as he can, which seems to work well for him."

"Didn't you say you were thinking of leaving London? Can he cope on his own in the house?" I thought I could detect a slight criticism in Eilidh's tone, but Fiona seemed to take the questions at face value.

"I'm keeping an eye out for a job nearer Manchester, but there's not many at the level I want. Olly doesn't have any problems with meals and things, and anything more complex can wait till I'm home at the weekends."

I did wonder how hard Fiona was trying to find a job, and what Olly really thought about her staying down there, but knew better than to comment. Poor things – they were living with a time bomb.

"Mm, that wasn't bad." Eilidh had cleaned her plate as usual, and sat back happily, rubbing her full stomach. "I don't mind eating a lot on these weekends – feel I've deserved it."

"So endeth our weekend in sunny Bute." Fiona was clearly grateful for a change of subject. "Sorry, Eilidh, but I won't be putting it on my holiday list."

"Nor me - but it was a great weekend," I added quickly. "Well done for organising it, Eilidh."

"Yip, absolutely. *And*, don't forget - the best vodka I've ever tasted!" Fiona raised her glass of wine. "Here's to the next trip."

Chapter 19 – St Cuthbert's Way 1 (April 2014) – Fiona

St Cuthbert's Way runs for nearly 63 miles from Melrose, in the Borders, to the island of Lindisfarne, off the Northumberland coast. It follows the working life of St Cuthbert, from monk at Melrose Abbey to the Abbot of Lindisfarne. This first stage covers the 15 miles from Melrose to Harestones, with a slight extension to Jedfoot Bridge. It starts with a climb up to the Eildon Hills, passes through farmland, follows the River Tweed then the Roman road Dere Street, before going through more woodland to arrive at the bridge.

It'd been harder to leave Olly this time, very hard. He was still working, though from home now, but tired easily and wasn't able to focus so much in the afternoons. His tremors had been confined to his left side so far, so he was still able to write without difficulty. Barring something unexpected, he could manage reasonably well on his own. He'd encouraged me to go and re-assured me he'd be perfectly OK. That was good, but it didn't stop me from being consumed by guilt at leaving him. What if he fell? What if he got suddenly worse? Would he be able to carry his meal from the kitchen to the living room without spilling and possibly burning himself? It was an inescapable fact that he'd become more and more dependent on me, and I wanted to enjoy "my" time while I could. But, I'd be away for three days this time …

Anyway, back to the present. We'd all been keen to do this walk. The St Cuthbert's Way was our first long-distance trail since the West Highland Way, and we were all up for it. Eilidh'd lived in the Borders for a couple of years, and Liksi had relatives there. I knew nothing about the area, so was keen to change that. On paper it seemed like a gentle, flowing stroll with nothing in the way of significant hills, going through some lovely pastoral scenery. Good for the soul – I hoped. It should take me away from constantly imagining Olly's every move, and worrying about the future.

Last night Pete, of all people, had given us a lift down to Melrose. He and Liksi still met up occasionally, mainly to do with the house or the children, and apparently when he heard that our next walk was in the Borders, he had very uncharacteristically offered to give us a lift. I'd long been of the opinion that Pete didn't do anything unless there was something in it for him, and as we waited on Waverley Bridge for him to pick us up, I wondered what it'd be this time. Liksi too had seemed bemused by this burst of generosity, and had only accepted the offer to avoid the long bus journey.

All was revealed when a long green car screeched to a halt beside us, with a grinning Pete at the wheel.

"Good God, it's an Aston Martin." I couldn't help admiring the sleek lines of the elderly model, and turned to Liksi, incredulous. "Liksi, when –" but Liksi's face was white, and she seemed just as shocked as we were.

"Where's our Golf, Pete?" she asked quietly. They'd changed their Capri for a Golf a few years ago, and on separating they'd agreed that Pete would keep the car as he needed it for his job, and Liksi rarely drove anywhere anyway. However, there was also an understanding that if she ever needed a car for anything important, she could have it. I'd thought at the time she'd been mad to trust Pete to stick to the arrangement.

"Gone to a new happy owner. See, travelling in style these days, Liksi. Don't know what you're missing!"

"Don't you think you should've discussed this with me first?"

"Ach, I knew you'd be happy for me. Here – that's the boot opened, just put your stuff in. There's the lever for the front seat – you slim things can fit in the back no bother." I exchanged a look with Eilidh – this was awkward, but we did as we were told. So too, did Liksi, but she was practically shaking with fury as she flung her rucksack in. The journey was extremely uncomfortable – not only because of Pete's inane commentary about the merits of the car and Liksi's frosty silence, but Eilidh and I were squashed into a back seat that wasn't designed for anyone other than a teenage gymnast. It was a relief when we reached Melrose, and managed to manoeuvre ourselves out opposite the B&B on Buccleuch Street.

"Thanks for the lift." I noticed Eilidh's appreciation was perfunctory, rather than delivered with her usual enthusiasm.

"Yip, thanks," I felt obliged to add. We got our bags and left Liksi with Pete while we checked into the attractive stone house. We'd booked a double and a single, and Eilidh and I settled into the double until Liksi turned up a while later. The set expression on her blotchy face said it all.

"Right." Eilidh got up from the bed and took Liksi's arm firmly. "Come on – we're going to get you a drink before we do anything else. The Kings Arms is just down the road on the next street."

The pair of us kept up some inane chatter till we got there. It was just after 5 pm, and the bar was empty, so I got served immediately and handed Liksi a large glass of Merlot.

"Bastard!" she managed to blurt out, after demolishing about half the glass. "Bastard! He *knows* I hate driving big cars. Been going on about an Aston Martin for years and now he's finally got one – where from, and what with, I dread to think. Wouldn't tell me. AND it's racing green!"

"Maybe the bidie-in[8] lent him the money." I wasn't quite sure what the significance of the colour was, though. "Talk about a mid-life crisis!"

---

[8] Slang for 'female he's living with'

"Bastard! All part of his grand plan to show me how much better off he is without me, and to make me suffer at the same time. He knows I won't drive that thing." She was still shaking with rage, and I suspected she was spot on in her analysis; I was only surprised that this most recent piece of nonsense had upset her so much.

"Liksi." I turned to her when Eilidh went up to the bar for refills. "I take it the car was in *his* name, with you as a named driver?"

"Yeah. Well, the Golf was. Says this is the same, but don't know if I believe him."

"Don't you think it's time to see a lawyer? Even to draw up a separation agreement? You won't have a leg to stand on otherwise, and who knows what he'll try next." I was glad to see she was calming down a little; she'd been gripping her glass so tightly I worried it would break.

She looked at me miserably. "Just couldn't face all that. Why can't he just behave like a decent, normal human being?"

"Because he isn't," I said bluntly. "Sorry, but you know it, and I know it. What about bills, the kids' Uni fees – OK, I know you don't pay fees up here, but they still need money, don't they?"

"Well, Joe's finished now, but he'd a student loan and Julie has one now. They've both got part-time jobs but I give them extra every so often."

"Does Pete give them anything?"

"Not much. Promises them the earth but doesn't deliver." She looked down at her hands, which she was twisting together. Honestly, she was far too soft. Pete had probably been playing the field for years, let alone spending the larger part of their income.

"Oh, Liksi, I know you don't want to get lawyers involved, but he's walking all over you. You *must* do something about it. Promise me you will."

"Fiona's right. Seriously, Liksi, you need to think of yourself for once." Eilidh put the drinks on the mats and thrust a bag of crisps at each of us.

"I'll think about it. Seriously. Thanks for – for putting up with all this. Sorry you had to get caught up in it all." She fished a large spotted handkerchief – a *handkerchief!* – out of her bag and blew her nose loudly. Poor soul – you just wanted to pick her up and cuddle her. She didn't deserve all this.

"Look on the positive side – seeing the effect he has on you at first hand has resulted in us giving you our expert, free advice." I smiled at her, trying to lighten the atmosphere. "Come on, drink up and we can go and get something to eat."

We continued helping Liksi drown her sorrows at the Station restaurant, after puffing our way up the hill to get there. Must've been the drinks we'd already had – you wouldn't have thought we were in any fit state to be setting out on a major walk the next day. It was an atmospheric place – great use of one of the Borders' disused stations – with very tasty food, and they were in no hurry to chase us out afterwards. By the end of the evening, Pete and all his stupidities seemed a million miles away, and even Liksi joined in, albeit slightly watery-eyed, with our often hysterical musings about life and the Universe.

The next day, as we gathered in the foyer to settle up with the delightful couple who ran the B&B, you wouldn't have guessed that any of us had a care in the world. Outside, Melrose's newly unfurled leafy streets glowed in bright sunlight, and I breathed in deeply, filling my lungs with the fresh, crisp air. This was why we were here, and the prospect of three days of gentle walking, well away from everyday cares, was just the best. I hoped Liksi felt the same. At that moment I felt sorry for all the millions of women who *didn't* walk.

"Right, selfie time. Here, in front of the door." I had my camera out, but Eilidh was pushing it aside.

"Let me. I've never taken a selfie before – you can show me what to do."

I took her phone from her and showed her how to put the camera in selfie mode, and she took the photo, grinning with satisfaction.

"Managed it without students to show me how to do it! Thanks, Fiona. Must practise a bit more – the square's round here." We followed her away from the doorway.

"Och, it's just SO good to be back here." She looked around the square we'd got to before leading us to a small shop where we went in to get some nibbles and things. "I'd forgotten how nice it is."

"Yeah, always loved visiting Jean and Douglas here." Liksi, I was glad to see, was looking a bit brighter. "Well, in Jedburgh – it's lovely too. They consider Melrose to be a bit up itself though – pretty, touristy and expensive."

"I lived in humble Galashiels when I was here – I don't think you'd call it lovely, exactly, but I really liked it. Anyway, it doesn't matter where you live in the Borders – everywhere's lovely."

"I don't think the Borderers would agree with that." Liksi laughed. "'A day oot a' Ha'ick's a day wasted.' Isn't that what they say?"

"Aye, in Hawick! Another one is, 'It's better to be a lamp-post in Ha'ick than the Toon Provost o' Gala'!" Eilidh spluttered. "Honestly! I actually heard someone say that in all seriousness."

"Mm, I can see why you had to leave eventually." I looked at her with amusement.

"No, not at all – I really liked it here. I'd probably never have left if it hadn't been for Alan. He used to say that it wasn't just 72 miles between Glasgow and Gala, it was a case of going back 72 years. Maybe I'd have become the Toon Provost if I'd stayed ..."

At that unimaginable prospect it was time to go. We retraced our steps from last night to walk up the steep hill that led from the square, and passed the turnoff to the Station restaurant. Not long afterwards, a signposted left turn took us almost immediately out of the village and into open countryside – and quite a steep climb.

"I thought you said this was a gentle walk?" Eilidh was making good use of her poles. Since she'd got them, she'd used them extensively and they seemed to make a big difference. "Unless I'm imagining things, this is a HILL – these are the Eildons, and a walk up here was considered to be very good exercise when I lived here."

"It *is* a gentle walk – once we get past the Eildons. And we're only skirting them, not going over them, so stop moaning." I looked up at the three gentle peaks, but they weren't very high anyway. "You should be savouring the history of this area to take away the pain. Didn't the Eildons have something to do with the Romans?" I'd read a bit about this on the train on the way up, but had already forgotten the details.

"And King Arthur's supposed to be buried under here somewhere," Liksi added. "Or so it says in one of the Scott novels, can't remember which. As well as in scores of other places – he does seem to get around, even in death."

"Mm. I believe you. Aye, the Romans built a fort down by Melrose, and called it Trimontium after these three peaks. They're lovely hills, and you do get a great view from the top. They make a great setting for the rugby ground, too. Over there." Eilidh had stopped and was pointing back towards Melrose.

"Yeah – The Greenyards, it's called." Liksi knew the Borders well too, particularly relating to rugby and relatives. "Did you go to the Sevens when you lived here?"

"Oh aye, both years. Loved it. They just eat and breathe rugby here, and you trip over Scottish internationalists wherever you go."

We stopped briefly to remove some clothing and admire the views. You could see for miles today – in one direction lay the Cheviots and England, and the nearer hills were the Lammermuirs. Below us the Tweed wound its way round a scattering of small villages, each with white dots of cottages and the ubiquitous stone church. Trees were everywhere, sharing their spring glory with the world.

"You can see the Forth Bridges from the top on a clear day." Eilidh turned round, smiling. "But I'm not doing any detours at this early stage."

"Wonderful country, Scotland." Liksi's eyes slowly swept round the 180-degree vista. "How 'bout the Referendum, then – you'll need to make sure your passport is up to date for your next visit, Fiona?"

"Ha ha. Not a chance – you're not going to get rid of me as easily as that. There's no way it'll come to anything – all a piece of posturing."

"Heaven help us if it's a Yes." Liksi scowled. "Becoming independent would be an absolute disaster. All our IT systems and procedures are linked inextricably to the whole of the UK."

"I guess so." I agreed with her, although I wasn't sure how I'd feel if I actually lived north of the border. "Are you still using Blackboard these days?"

"Well, yeah, though we're looking at Moodle seriously now. How did you find the open-source element?"

Ignoring Eilidh's pantomime raising of the eyebrows, we launched into a lengthy discussion of the comparative merits and demerits of the different learning platforms, as we set off again.

"Five minutes, I'm giving you," Eilidh announced. "Five minutes – no longer." She stepped up her pace and left us to it. I know she didn't *really* mind; in fact Eilidh quite often walked on her own and left the two of us to it – systems talk, or swapping tales of our kids' exploits. Of the three of us she was the quiet reflective one, Liksi told all the stories – about her family, sporting occasions, or anything else in her very sociable life – and I liked to think I was the one who asked the questions, to draw them out. OK, maybe I also liked to tell them about the more onerous details of managing a large team – but that was gone, for the time being at least. I'd left the job in London at the end of last year, as I felt it wasn't right to be so far away from Olly now. In fact, my new job wasn't even with a university any more – I was working with a very small team of consultants, who just so happened to have a vacancy for an IT specialist on their books at the time I applied. Private enterprise – a very different world and I was still getting used to it.

The route wound its way gracefully above, over and along the gently flowing River Tweed, flanked by golden celandines and pink cuckoo flowers, with clumps of wild garlic dotted about under the trees. It was a heart-warming kind of walk, somehow – not taxing in the least, just – lovely. It was almost disappointing when we reached the attractive village of St Boswells, where we stopped for lunch in the Buccleuch Arms. It was packed with families, and tables were set with mats so was obviously well used for lunch rather than just drinks.

"It's a rare treat to have a proper lunch in a pub. I mean, instead of a sandwich and drink of water, trying to get comfy perched on a mouse mat with a stone or plant digging into your rear end, and fending off flies or midges." Eilidh was certainly making the most of it, tucking into soup and an enormous baguette, washing it down with a pint of something.

"Glad you're enjoying it." I spread some Camembert on my oatcake.

"Shouldn't have *too* much just now," said Liksi somewhat belatedly. "We'll have Jean's farmers' portions to cope with tonight. Be prepared." We were going to be staying with Liksi's relatives Jean and Douglas just outside Jedburgh, so that would be another treat – no hostel or B&B tonight.

After a while we reluctantly hauled ourselves up and continued with the walk. Again, it was lovely restful scenery – easy walking on farm tracks or paths along the river, over streams and strips of boardwalks. Farms of all sizes were dotted about, and all the trees were in full leaf. Eilidh stopped us at one point to listen out for a woodpecker, who obliged by demonstrating his heavy drumming skills, whilst disappointingly keeping well out of sight. The track turned onto Dere Street – a Roman road which at one stage had extended all the way to York. It was typically straight, leading through farmland and woodland, and although easy going, by then we'd been walking for about twelve miles and it became a bit of a trudge. Eilidh's periods of not talking were getting longer, and I was feeling a bit weary myself. We walked past the sign to Harestanes Visitor Centre, which was the official end of today's stretch, and carried on through the trees and shrubs until we found ourselves climbing some winding steps which came out at a road bridge.

"This is it – Jedfoot Bridge. Hadn't realised it was quite so near or I'd have phoned Jean earlier." Liksi whipped her phone out and summoned her relative, and we sank down gratefully to wait.

"Your poor rellies." I stretched my weary legs out and flexed my feet. "Have they thought through the implications of having three very dirty, smelly, exhausted females landing on them? It's above and beyond ..."

"Speak for yourself! No, don't worry, nothing fazes them. They're amazing – even Pete loved coming down to see them – we could never eat for about a week afterwards."

Just then a very dirty 4x4 pulled up, and a chunky lady with unruly grey curls and dungarees tumbled out. "Liksi!" She opened her arms wide and enfolded Liksi in what must have been a numbing bearhug before holding her at arms' length and examining her closely. "OK?" she asked, peering into her eyes. I suddenly realised she'd probably not seen Liksi since Pete had left the scene, and I guess she was anxious to make sure she was coping.

"Very OK." Liksi laughed as she disentangled herself. "But very sweaty – as are these two – meet Fiona and Eilidh."

"Hi, thanks so much for picking us up." Eilidh got to her feet with some reluctance.

"Yes, it's very good of you." It was certainly a welcome change, and it was good to think that we'd probably be spoiled from now on.

"Och, not at all – pleased to meet you and delighted to have you here. Any friends of Liksi's are always welcome. Jump in, bags and all. Plenty room."

Jean drove us the few miles to their farm just outside Jedburgh. We were met at the door by Douglas, whose leathery smiling face spoke of a life lived outdoors. He too was in dungarees and gave us an effusive welcome – as did two prancing collies and two curious black and white cats. Eilidh was immediately in her element, exhaustion forgotten as she fussed over the dogs who were competing for her attention.

"That's Black and the other's White." Douglas was watching her with approval. "Down, White! Behave yourself! Cats are Nut and Bolt – can't remember which one's which; you'll have to ask Jean for that." But Jean was already shooing us into the hall and getting us organised.

"You c'n dump your boots here. Fiona – and Eilish, is it? Eilidh, sorry – you c'n take these rooms. Bathroom at the end there and if one of you comes with me I'll show you the shower room. Liksi, you know your way round – you're in Lucy's room and you c'n use our en-suite."

Jean had obviously decided that we all needed a good wash before going anywhere near the rest of the house, but as I apologised for the state we were in she boomed at us:

"This is a FARM! We're used to muck and glaur and worse besides! Away with you – take your time and come on through to the sitting room – that room yonder – when you're ready. White! Leave Eilish alone and get outside – go on!" She shoved the reluctant dog out the door, and the other one flopped down on the mat, his eyes following Eilidh as she went to her room.

Once I'd my shower and felt human again, I found everyone in the sitting room with brimming glasses. Black had his head on Eilidh's knee, gazing at her adoringly as she stroked his head and fondled his ears. It was impossible to tell which of them was happier. A cat launched itself from Douglas's knee, nearly knocking over his glass, and rubbed itself against my legs, miaowing loudly. It followed me to a chair and settled itself on my feet – but not for long as we were almost immediately summoned to the kitchen.

And *what* a kitchen. It was a huge L-shape, with the shorter part taken up by a couple of mis-shapen sofas full of newspapers, toys, clothes, towels, ropes and other unidentifiable things. Jean bundled them all up and dumped them in a laundry basket out of the way; they were swiftly replaced by the cats, with Black edging his way in surreptitiously, to lie on the floor below them. An Aga lined another wall, with pans bubbling and steaming on the top, and a wonderful looking pie cooling off on one side. As for the wooden table – it was probably the biggest I'd ever seen in a family house. Mats depicted cheerful farmyard scenes, condiments were in the form of a chicken and an egg, baskets were stacked with different kinds of bread and a cheeseboard with huge slabs of hard cheeses rested in the middle.

Steaming bowls of soup were placed on the mats, and we were instructed to 'Get stuck in – there's plenty more.'.

Some time later, I found myself in bed at last. I wasn't sure if it was the walk or the food that'd exhausted me, but I was so tired I could hardly think. The soup had been followed by wonderfully succulent pork chops, at least three veg and two different types of potatoes, apple sauce and chutneys. As if that hadn't been enough, the pie turned out to be apple and cinnamon, with the tastiest pastry ever, served with gallons of thick creamy custard. I really wasn't a big eater, and I was trying to go easy on meat these days - but oh, my goodness, what wonderful food. And that custard! No wonder Pete liked coming here. The nasty part of me revelled in the fact that he was unlikely to be invited again.

It didn't take long for me to fall asleep, aided by the wonderfully soothing sound of Nut or Bolt purring for Britain on top of my stomach. Sheer heaven ...

Chapter 20 – St Cuthbert's Way 2 (April 2014) - Eilidh

This 18-mile stretch starts back at Jedfoot Bridge, and follows the Teviot. Open land, farm tracks and minor roads, passing the castle at Cessford, lead into Morebattle. From there there's a climb up to Wideopen Hill with its stunning views, before crossing Crookedshaws Hill and moving down into the villages of Town Yetholm then Kirk Yetholm.

It was with great reluctance that I left that wonderful farmhouse. Jean and Douglas's hospitality, the animals, the lovely rural location ... Both dogs jumped in the car as Jean got ready to drive us back to Jedfoot Bridge, and when we climbed out Black did too, apparently determined to stay with us as we said goodbye to Jean. He sat on my foot and thumped his tail, looking hopefully between Jean and I, maybe thinking he could persuade her to let him go with us for a walk. White, maybe older and wiser, knew this was a no-no and viewed the proceedings more sedately from the back window.

"Come on, you, into the boot – get, now!" This time, there was no mistaking the command and good sheepdog that he was, Black reluctantly joined his team-mate. With more hugs and instructions to come back soon, Jean finally drove off and we started our walk to Kirk Yetholm.

"What lovely people, Liksi." I had thoroughly enjoyed our brief stay at the farm. "I missed the exact connection – is Jean your cousin?"

"Second cousin. Our mothers were cousins. They're pretty special – glad you liked them."

"They were terrific. Now, remind me, how many miles did we do yesterday?" I asked Fiona.

"About 15. Even more today – 17 or 18, I think."

"Oh, God ..." I couldn't help groaning. My feet'd been throbbing by the time we'd finished yesterday, and I hoped they wouldn't let me down today. I was also feeling pretty stuffed with all the food we'd consumed last night, so all in all I wasn't feeling at my most sprightly.

However, my grumps didn't last long. How could they? The weather had held – we seemed to be really lucky with spring walks. Trees proudly displayed their new leaves of different shades and shapes, and rays of sun peeked through the verdant canopy to light up the path, highlighting the pink, white and yellow carpet of woodland flowers. Breathing in all the fresh smells seemed to cleanse my system, and sore feet and a full stomach were quickly forgotten.

We stopped in the middle of a long suspension bridge over the Teviot, and looked down at the brown but transparent water as it burbled its way along over the stones.

"Did you play Pooh Sticks when you were wee?" Fiona threw a couple of twigs over one side and turned to watch them on their journey downriver.

"Can't really remember." That was a *long* time ago. "I did read the Winnie the Pooh books though. Happy days ..."

"Was that before you discovered Enid Blyton?" Liksi asked.

"Now you're talking." Fiona brightened. "Famous Five, Secret Seven – what else was there?"

"The Chalet School books." I sighed with nostalgia, remembering my addiction. "I loved them."

"Doesn't ring a bell. I went on to ponies – the Jill's Gymkhana series." Liksi had always been keen on horses.

"Well, we may laugh now," I said, "but see what our early reading habits have produced – two IT specialists and a lecturer, and we still love books."

"And not one of us has been corrupted by non-PC language, or sent our children to private school." Fiona was quick to point this out, and we basked in a bit of self-satisfaction for a few more minutes. It was so pleasant leaning on the rail, half-watching the water trickle by and reminiscing, each taking a turn of throwing a stick in and watching as it bobbed out the other side. Eventually we started off again, with the conversation moving on to Harry Potter, then Lord of the Rings, and the impact of both on children and adults. At the back, I couldn't always hear everything but I was perfectly happy walking along by the river, looking out for herons or trying to identify some of the wildflowers. I used to be good at flowers in particular, having had a brilliant primary teacher who took us out on nature walks – but that was becoming a *very* long time ago and I was getting rusty now.

"Look – this is part of the Borders Abbeys Way too." I had stopped at a signpost. We were always on the lookout for new walks.

"Continuing the religious theme." This from Liksi, with a smile. "You know, don't think we've even *discussed* that aspect yet. What does the book say about St Cuthbert?"

"He started off as a monk in Melrose, and ended up as Bishop of Lindisfarne," I said. "He was right into solitude, and when he knew he was dying even Lindisfarne wasn't small enough, so he went off to Inner Farne, a tiny island where he'd spent time before."

"Where's that?" asked Liksi.

"A bit further down the coast, kind of opposite Bamburgh."

"He was into nature and coastal scenery – a man after my own heart. Makes up for me being an atheist." I was generally happier admiring a church or cathedral from the *out*side. "What about you two? Can I assume that this isn't a religious pilgrimage for you either?" I was pretty sure of my ground here, but was interested in what they'd say.

"No, indeed – haven't gone to church since I was coerced into being a Sunday School teacher when I was about 16." Fiona held back an obtrusive hawthorn branch to let me pass.

"Nor me – without the Sunday School bit." Liksi moved past too, before I released it. "Weddings and funerals."

We left religion behind as we moved on, with the path opening up a little as it climbed slightly. The Eildons came into view behind us, before grassy tracks and minor roads led down again - through farmland, past the sturdy-looking Cessford Castle and into the little village of Morebattle, where we had another pub lunch. Two in a row – I liked St Cuthbert ... The Templehall Inn had a very informative barman – owner? – who answered all our questions about the local area. It was good to rest the old feet, but we were bearing up surprisingly well, so didn't spend too long over our soup and sandwiches.

Back on the trail again, we soon found ourselves climbing, and stopped a few times to get our bearings from the views that presented themselves. We followed a drystone dyke till it met another one with a stile, next to a sign indicating that Scotland was one way and England the other. A trio of young and fit-looking males – who turned out to be New Zealanders – asked us to take their photo there, and we chatted to them briefly, offering the standard tongue-in-cheek Scotland v England observations.

"Nice bit of eye candy there." As we left them rather reluctantly, Fiona put into words what I'm sure we were all thinking.

"Yes indeed. Bet they won't be thinking the same though." Liksi handed me back my pack when I got over the stile. "More like 'What are these old hags doing on a long-distance walk?'".

"Speak for yourself." Fiona wore her mock-affronted look. "How do you know they weren't full of admiration for our looks and stamina? You need to look on the positive side, Liksi. There's life after Pete."

"When we were their age, we were too busy juggling children and jobs to have time for outdoor pursuit." Liksi pointedly ignored the last comment. "And both those things haven't helped either looks *or* stamina much."

After a further gentle climb, it wasn't long before we reached the highest point of the whole Way, the summit of the wonderfully-named Wideopen Hill. The horizon was a bit hazy, but we could just about make out the sea away over to the east, although our final destination, Lindisfarne, wasn't visible.

"Doesn't look *too* far away, does it?" Liksi screwed up her eyes. "Pity we couldn't have done the whole walk in one trip." We were intending to get as far as Wooler tomorrow, but hadn't been able to take more time off.

"I guess one more day next time will do us?" asked Fiona. "Might be a long one, though."

"Well, it *might* be possible – but remember we've got to watch the tides in terms of getting over to Lindisfarne – and back." I was also keen to make the most of our time on the actual island. "It'd be a shame to go all the way there and have to race back almost immediately."

"And, after 18 miles or so, I don't think *any* of us would be fit to race back in any case." I tried to hide my relief - it wasn't often Fiona agreed with me about the return leg of a trip! "Anyway, if we don't get a move on we'll never get to Kirk Yetholm, let alone Lindisfarne."

The path took us down the hill onto a track, which increased in significance until it morphed into a busier road which led to the outskirts of Town Yetholm. We knew the two Yetholms were close together, but this was deceptive, and when the path turned off the road again and took us along the river, it seemed a very long way before we got to the bridge between the two villages, and dragged our weary feet down the lane to get to the hostel at Kirk Yetholm.

And a quirky place it was too. It wasn't part of the YHA, but was a "Friends of Nature House". We weren't too sure what this involved, but when we were greeted with a welcoming smile and a cup of tea, it didn't matter. We sat down on the steps to remove our boots, as steaming mugs were handed to us by someone who we assumed was the warden of the hostel.

"Oh, how good does that feel?" Fiona tugged off her second boot and wriggled her toes luxuriously. "You get to the stage that you feel your boots have melded into your ankles."

"Where did you come from today?" asked the man, who informed us he was called Simon.

"Jedfoot Bridge." Liksi put her empty mug down on the step. "Miles away. This is just the best cup of tea I've ever had – thank you."

"I suspect the seat on the cold stone step is the best seat you've had all day, too." Simon laughed as he collected our mugs.

"Definitely." Liksi stretched out to touch her toes. "So pardon our ignorance, but can you tell us more about the hostel? We know it's not YHA, but that's about it."

"Well, the building was originally the village school, but it's been used as a hostel for almost seventy years. The Friends of Nature group started in Austria, and their houses are for walkers and lovers of the countryside. There are a few in England, and only two in Scotland."

We chatted to Simon a bit more, discovering that he was a volunteer, not the warden. Eventually we summoned the energy to walk up the stairs to our room. None of us were able to move very quickly, and by the time all three of us were showered and vaguely presentable it was getting on for 8 pm.

The Border Hotel was right next to the hostel, and looked very trim and inviting, so we were looking forward to crashing out there over a pint and some pub food. However, it was very busy and they weren't able to take any more bookings. That was bad enough, but then we were informed that there wasn't anywhere else in Kirk Yetholm and we'd need to go back down to the Plough Hotel in Town Yetholm.

"Oh, God, I can't bear this." I really couldn't – I was absolutely exhausted, and the thought of going the half mile down the road and then back up again was too much. "We don't even know if they'll take us – we might be too late there as well."

"Well, we won't know unless we try, and I need food." Fiona started walking, and there was no choice but to do the same. Under other circumstances we'd have enjoyed the stroll back down to the river and over the bridge, but it was a bit painful. At last we piled gratefully into the Plough Inn, which was reasonably full and pretty lively. Edging our way to the bar, we caught the eye of the barmaid – in fact, it was hard to take our eyes off her, as she had two pigtails sticking out almost horizontally at the sides of her head, and large black "freckles" dotted all over her nose and cheeks.

"You want to eat? We've closed the restaurant part, but if you don't mind eating in the bar we could do something?" She looked at us doubtfully. "It's going to be a bit noisy later on – is that OK?"

I didn't know about the others, but I'd have agreed to *any* suggestion that involved eating and sitting down, regardless of location and noise. "Perfect!" I made my way to the table the barmaid was indicating. It was right in front of the bar, so we weren't going to be forgotten about. As we sat down, another barmaid appeared, with a *very* short black skirt, white blouse with tie, and hair in bunches.

"D'you think this is the local 'look'?" whispered Liksi. "Very fetching."

"She said it was going to get noisy later on – maybe it's a fancy dress thing." I couldn't think of any other reason – and it *was* a Saturday night.

"Oh well, we can just pretend to be down-and-outs or something." Fiona's matter-of-fact delivery had Liksi spluttering. She wasn't far wrong – although clean, we weren't exactly dressed for a night out. As the evening progressed and the bar got busier, we stood out even more as we were the only people eating – and possibly the only non-locals, judging from all the merriment and hugging going on. More bar staff trickled in, all dressed like schoolchildren, even the males. As more people came in, the original barmaid would greet them all with a rowdy telling-off, although we couldn't hear what she was saying. The odd few who came in fancy dress got a big cheer – although they weren't all in school outfits.

"What's the occasion?" I eventually managed to ask the guy who came to clear our plates - the others were too busy admiring his shorts and braces.

"Well, it's supposed to be a St Trinian's night." He paused in the act of balancing the stack of plates on one wrist. "Except, something's gone wrong with the advertising. Most people didn't know it was fancy dress at all, some thought it was *any* fancy dress, and it seems that it's mainly the bar staff who've got it right. Typical."

A big cheer went up as three young guys came in, each sporting a skirt of some sort and a long-haired pink wig.

"Watch – Tricia won't be giving these three a rollicking, that's for sure!" Tricia appeared to be the barmaid, who welcomed the three loudly but berated the lesser mortals behind them, who were in their civvies.

"Mm, I could enjoy myself here tonight." Fiona still had her eyes on our informant as he left us with a grin. "It's been a good day for eye candy."

"Come on, Fiona, enough of that." Liksi shook her head in mock despair. "What *would* Olly think?"

"I'm not sure." Fiona shook her hair back from her face as she reached for her glass. "He'd probably just think – correctly – that I was momentarily deranged, and should know better than to lust after someone half my age. One thing's for sure, he wouldn't be in the least bit worried."

The barman came back to clear the glasses at the table beside us, and we started giggling like teenagers.

"Anyway." Fiona leaned in as soon as he was out of hearing, "Liksi, it's you who should be keeping an open mind about these things. Nothing to stop *you* looking at the options!"

Liksi made a face. "I *could*, and in some ways I'd love to give Pete a shock to his smug, self-satisfied self, but I really, really, don't have the energy. Been there, done that - kind of thing."

"But that's the point, you *haven't*." Fiona wagged her finger at her. "It's time you did – we'll keep an eye out for you, won't we Eilidh?"

"Don't you *dare*. Anyway, I'm far too tired tonight to even consider anything like that. Oh, look, what's happening now?" We followed her gaze to a corner of the pub, where a couple of guys were setting up what appeared to be an old-fashioned disco system.

"Look, they're using *records*." I watched incredulously as they were being laid out and sorted. "My goodness, I thought they'd gone for good."

"Pay attention, Eilidh." Fiona tut-tutted. "They're making a big comeback – haven't you heard of 'vinyl'?"

"Er, uh-huh, as in flooring." I looked at her suspiciously. "Vinyl - why?"

"Records are being re-branded as 'vinyl' and becoming all the rage." Liksi was nodding agreement – why wasn't I aware of this?

"Eh? Records are *coming back*? I must be getting older than I thought." I gave a loud sigh. "I just don't get it – I remember Alan trying to persuade me all these years ago how superior CDs were to albums – and now we're going backwards?"

"Supposed to be more authentic." Fiona shrugged. "But I tend to agree with you - why should crackles make for a better experience?" However, as sounds of Cockney Rebel filled the air, followed by the Pretenders, the source of the music quickly became irrelevant.

"Oh God, *wonderful* – they don't make music like this anymore." I had to shout to make myself heard. "I don't care if there's crackles – this is *real* stuff. Takes me back – I saw the Pretenders in London. Brilliant."

"And Cockney Rebel – reminds me of Teviot Row union. Oh, the drunken nights we had in there ..." Liksi was away back in Uni days, as she swayed in time to the beat.

Vinyl or no vinyl, sore feet and scruffy clothes were forgotten, as we lost ourselves in the strains of Brown Sugar, Bohemian Rhapsody, Meat Loaf's gripping lyrics, and Black Sabbath's unforgettable beat. The pub got busier and louder, the wigs ended up at impossible angles and the stage freckles smudged on shiny faces. The locals got friendlier if less coherent, the music got louder and we stayed till the very end, loving every minute of it (and the beer wasn't bad either).

As we eventually staggered up the road, our feet reminding us that they'd been overused that day already, I don't think I'd enjoyed myself so much since my enthusiastic head-banging days as a carefree student.

"Those *were* the days ..." I sang for the hundredth time that night, stumbling into a pothole and grabbing hold of Liksi just in time to prevent further damage.

"... my friend, I thought they'd ne-ever end ..." Fiona's tone-deaf singing brought us back to the hostel. Following loud "Dah dah dah da, da, da's" and only slightly quieter "shushes" and giggles we attempted to get up the stairs to our room without waking anyone else, and in all probability failed spectacularly. We were three happy bunnies as we crashed into bed that night.

Chapter 21 – St Cuthbert's Way 3 (April 2014) - Liksi

Kirk Yetholm is also the north end of the 268-mile Pennine Way, and the first mile or so is shared by both routes. The 12-mile walk leads out of the village through farmland and up to moorland, then crosses into England before going through the hamlet of Hethpool. Skirting the Cheviots, it passes Yeavering Bell with its iron age fort, leads through a rather exposed and boggy stretch, then heads down through Wooler Common to the village of Wooler.

The next morning, with the music of my wilder days still lingering in my subconscious, I groggily came to. Against my better judgement my thoughts slowly turned to Pete. Last night, in spite of being slightly the worse for wear, I'd been relieved when the setting up of the disco distracted Fiona from suggesting it was time I looked elsewhere. She was always so *certain* of everything – whether it was something in her life, or anyone else's. Couldn't she understand that I was just happy to be free, and that was enough? If someone came along, fine, but I wouldn't be actively looking. No way.

Then, immediately, I felt bad. Fiona, for all her career successes, had been dealt the shittiest hand of all of us – a drug addict for a son, and a husband with Parkinson's. You couldn't get much worse than that, really. What was an errant husband, and parents with dementia, compared to that? These days everyone's parents seemed to develop dementia – Eilidh's too – so I wasn't unique. And my kids seemed to be doing OK – I doubted if either of them would ever set the heather on fire, but they were warm, decent human beings, and I was so proud of them.

"Liksi! Have you gone back to sleep? Are you still dreaming about that barman ...?" Eilidh's voice jolted me back to the present.

"Come on! Breakfast next door then off to Wooler. Chop chop!" I could see that Fiona was fully clothed and was even putting on her boots, so there was no point in trying to avoid the inevitable. I got up – slowly.

"Only 12 miles today." Fiona announced this brightly later, as we pored over the maps after a quick breakfast at the Border Hotel. At least there hadn't been any problem getting a table at this time of day.

"Nice place here." Eilidh looked round appreciatively. "But not the same standard of barman. Made the trek back to Town Yetholm almost worthwhile."

"Well, we'll just have to pin our hopes on Wooler today". Although I was quietly amused by the fact that I could even consider thinking about anyone again. "For you guys, anyway. *Only* 12 miles – that supposed to be motivational, Fiona?"

"Of course, of course – a doddle!" We smiled at Fiona, gearing us up for our last day's walk – on this trip, anyway. Apart from the beginning of St Cuthbert's Way, I'd been completely unfamiliar with the territory, and though I think Eilidh missed the more rugged scenery, this pastoral walk with its gentle hills was just right for me. We were all able to stay together as it wasn't too taxing, so conversation flowed, and it took my mind off Pete. I knew I'd have to do something about him eventually, but I didn't want him to spoil the day, even vicariously.

The signs for St Cuthbert's Way and the Pennine Way pointed in the same direction. "We're heading down to your country today," Eilidh couldn't resist saying to Fiona. "You'll be quite at home when we cross the Border."

"I'm quite at home now, thank you," came the retort.

"How long's the Pennine Way?" I asked. "Is that another one for us some time? Could walk all the way down to Fiona's."

"268 miles, I believe." Eilidh grinned. "I think we'll have to reserve that one for our retirement. Of course, as I'm the baby of this group, you two'll just have to wait till *I* retire, if you want the pleasure of my company."

"Only another 3 or 4 years to go then." Fiona steered us round a muddy bit on the road. "Nice thought."

"Speak for yourself." I shuddered theatrically. "Not intending to retire for a *long* time yet. Thought you weren't either?" Actually, I didn't want to make any decisions of this sort till I was completely free of Pete, because God knows how money would pan out. So, I suppose I really *should* try to move things on there. Maybe Fiona was right.

"I don't really know now. It depends on how Olly progresses. He's doing OK at the moment, just, but we're under no illusions that this'll last forever. At some stage he'll need much more care, and I guess that's going to be me."

"That's a hard thought, Fiona," said Eilidh. "My parents are needing much more care now and it's getting very difficult, but must be much worse when it's your *husband* that needs the care."

"Can't imagine you giving up work ever – you've always been driven." I looked at Fiona as we stopped for a breather.

"Well, I certainly *was*. Since I came back from London and got this job though, I'm not so sure. I still like the challenge of taking on new clients and sorting out their problems. There's a promotion to regional manager coming up soon – but I don't know." She looked down at her feet before continuing.

"I *have* to put Olly first. He doesn't deserve Parkinsons, and we'll have to work through this together. I can't just keep on chasing ambition – there's other priorities now." Wow. Never thought I'd hear Fiona say this. In fact, I'd always assumed that her move back to Manchester was just to give her breathing space till she and Olly came to terms with his diagnosis. Instead, she'd shot up the ranks of her new company, and was now area manager.

"It must be difficult – you have to think of the future, but you want to enjoy what you can while you can – both of you." Eilidh was extending her poles, ready for use.

"Too true. Come on, let's get going – next stop the Border, where no doubt you'll get a chance to tease me again ..." She headed off, and away from the subject, and we followed her down into the dip, then up to a gate in a wall with a double sign beside it. One part pointed the way we'd come, proclaiming 'Welcome to Scotland': no prizes for guessing what the other said. We stopped to take photos – first of all for ourselves, and then for a group of Polish girls who had materialised and were very taken with the sign. The usual conversation ensued –

"But Scotland is part of England, is it not?"

"No, absolutely not. Scotland and England are both *part* of the United Kingdom. Along with Wales and Northern Ireland." Eilidh was quick to put them right.

"But Scotland is ruled by England, isn't it? And it wants to become independent?"

"Well, mostly – and partly. We have a devolved Government which can make some decisions, but we're still under UK rule, which comes from London." Eilidh was doing her best to keep things simple, but the girls still looked puzzled.

"And not everyone in Scotland wants independence, not at all." I thought I'd better make this clear.

"No?" Confusion showed on their faces.

"No. We don't – well, *we* don't but this one's not sure." Fiona pointed at Eilidh, who shrugged her shoulders.

"It's complicated," was the best she could do eventually, without detaining them for a lecture on Scottish history and politics. They smiled anyway, expressing a love of all things Scottish, and set off the way we had come, pulling their jackets tighter. I wondered idly if they expected Scotland to be dramatically colder than England. Probably.

The peaceful and pastoral surroundings became a little more populated as the path sloped downhill, through fields bordered by dykes and hedgerows to the tiny settlement of Hethpool. Tiny but well-maintained, with some neat stone cottages and prosperous-looking farms with large fields of sheep, probably Cheviots. We stopped to admire the lambs in one of the fields beside the road.

"Look, that one might be about to give birth." Eilidh was pointing to a sheep near the wall.

"Certainly seems to be agitated about something." I felt sorry for the poor thing. The animal was half standing, and moving round with difficulty, making some distressed noises. "Wish we could help it – oh, it's on its side now."

"You should be an expert on sheep, Eilidh, coming from the Highlands." Fiona winked at me.

"Huh. The number of times that – or worse – has been said to me over the years. I've must have heard all the sheep jokes there are by now. My father could've told you about lambing - though he was famous in the family for not being at all interested in sheep. His sisters did all the sheep chores – he used fishing, or mending the boat, as an excuse to avoid them. However, he wasn't able to avoid the issue altogether."

"Sounds a sensible man to me." Fiona's tone indicated that she'd have done the same.

"He is. Was." Eilidh sighed heavily.

"How *are* your parents these days?" I looked at her sharply.

"Not good." Eilidh's face took on a more sombre appearance. "They're both failing quite rapidly now. Mum's stick thin and keeps falling. Dad's beside himself with worry most of the time."

"And how's his own health?" asked Fiona.

"I – I'm pretty sure he's suffering from some form of dementia now. He won't admit there's anything wrong, as all he wants to do is look after Mum. He doesn't realise that he needs as much looking after as she does."

"Oh, Eilidh, I'm sorry." I knew how close she was to her parents, and how bad she felt about living so far away from them. No wonder she went on about the A9 so much. My parents were deteriorating too, but they lived in Edinburgh and I was able to see them most days. Sure, it was a bind sometimes, but at least I could keep an eye on them.

"It's just the way it has to be, I guess." Eilidh shrugged, but her pain showed. "Sorry, this is so depressing – look, she's having her lamb now!"

With some relief on Eilidh's part, we stopped talking to watch the arrival of Hethpool's newest inhabitant sliding out onto the grass in a bloodied mucus. We were like anxious parents ourselves, not relaxing until the mother nuzzled and cleaned her bemused offspring then edged it, miraculously, to its wobbly feet. It looked around, unfocused, then let out a faint bleat as it struggled to stay upright.

"Amazing." I even felt slightly envious. "It's a lot easier for animals than humans. Julie and Joe took a lot more persuasion than that to stand up."

"Well, at least you didn't have to lick them," Fiona said with feeling.

As Eilidh had indicated this morning when she'd been reading up about today's walk, there didn't appear to be a shop or pub in Hethpool. Luckily we'd picked up a few things in the village shop before starting, which was just as well. We'd our lunch in an idyllic spot on the riverbank, and afterwards Fiona and I idly watched Eilidh as she wandered along the pebbly shore, overturning stones with her feet to have a closer look at things.

"Poor Eilidh, she's quite upset." Fiona was delicately picking at a crunch bar. "I think she feels very guilty that she can't do more for them."

"I guess so. Y'know, it's a bit like having kids." I'd been thinking this through recently, in relation to my own parents.

"What d'you mean?" asked Fiona.

"Well, you look after your kids for years, so you're used to it. Watching out for them, making sure they eat properly, getting medical assistance when required. There's no real difference with elderly parents."

"Except that they can be even less biddable, I'd imagine. Although I don't know ..." Fiona looked away, and I'm sure she was thinking about Nathan, whom she hardly mentioned at all now. It must be so sad, having a son that you rarely saw, and only ever if you forced the issue. "And then there's husbands ..."

"Oh, Fiona, you've got it hard. D'you see much of Jack? How's he coping with it all?"

"Jack's an absolute darling, and I don't know what I'd do without him." I looked at her, surprised, as she rarely talked about anyone in such an affectionate way.

"D'you see much of him?"

"Yes, he comes in every second day or so, even for a short time, and he eats with us at least once a week. It's good for me that he can see how Olly is, and understand how things are."

"I hate to ask, but - does he still see Nathan?"

"Very, very occasionally. He messages him, and sometimes gets a reply. At least Nathan'll communicate with him, if not with us." Fiona looked away, towards Eilidh who was standing at the water's edge looking rather blankly downriver. "We've all got our problems, haven't we? No-one's life is perfect."

"Right, I'm going to paddle!" she added suddenly, and before I realised what she was doing she'd her boots off and was up to her ankles in the water, standing on the pebbly bottom. "Wonderful – you should try it."

"You're mad – it must be freezing," I shouted at her. "*And* painful, to walk on all these stones."

"It is!"

"She's off her trolley," was Eilidh's assessment as she came back to join me. "Always thought there was something missing."

"Nonsense, you pair of wimps. Refreshes the feet ready for the next stage." Fiona was hopping back over the pebbles, boots in hand. She flopped down, dried her feet with a sweatshirt, and was soon ready to head off again. Shaking our heads, we got up to go too.

The next eight miles to Wooler were relatively unremarkable, but *long*. As Eilidh said, "Y'know how some walks seem much longer than others, even though they're not?" The walking was easy enough – an upward slope led into a forest, which in turn opened out onto moorland. Visibility was reasonable, but there was nothing notable in the vistas which opened out. The rough heath gave way to grassland eventually, as the path sloped downward again, and although Fiona was leading, our progress was quite slow.

"Not the most exciting part of the Way, is it?" I asked. "Hope Wooler's worth it."

"It'd better be." This rather curtly from Fiona, and I looked at Eilidh, who shrugged. I wondered if she was thinking of Nathan, or Olly – or if we'd somehow managed to say or do something to offend her. Not that that'd happened before on any of our walks – however different we were, we got on very well together and were generally respectful of each other's foibles. Or tried to be, anyway.

"We seem to be nearing civilisation now," said Eilidh, as we arrived at a car park where a sign informed us that we were at Wooler Common. We examined our map, which showed one path curving round a couple of ponds, and another continuing with the Way. Both led into the village, and I headed for the latter route.

"Sorry, guys, but I'm pooped." Fiona's voice stopped me in my tracks. This was *not* something we were used to hearing from her. "I'm cutting across by the ponds, which is the quickest way."

"But the route goes that way," Eilidh pointed out.

"Are you OK, Fiona?" I asked.

"Sore foot. Didn't say anything earlier – thought a bathe in the river might've helped, but it's on fire. Just want to stop walking as soon's I can – you two carry on and we can meet at the hostel." And she was off, before we even got a chance to find out exactly what the problem was. Eilidh and I decided just to follow her, for all the difference it would make.

Actually, it was rather pleasant walking round by the ponds, after all that heathland; at the end of it we came out on a village street lined with houses. Unfortunately, that also proved to be rather long, and we missed the hostel sign and had to double back. Finally we arrived somewhere that proclaimed itself to be 'Wooler Hostel and Shepherds' Huts'. An individual with long straggly hair was sitting outside the entrance, attempting to lounge on a stool that was far too small for him.

We were about to open the door and go inside, when he said, "Staying here, are ya?" As we mumbled assent he lumbered to his feet and went in before us. We looked at each other in amusement mingled with apprehension – if this was the warden, what would the facilities be like? He booked us in, and then we walked along a rather featureless corridor to our room, where a whiff of damp followed us inside. Other than that, however, the room was fine – more spacious than most, and with our own en-suite.

Fiona sank down gratefully on one of the bunks and immediately started tugging at her laces. When she removed her sock we could see that she had a shiny inflamed patch on her big toe joint.

"It's on the bone – started bothering me a few weeks ago after a weekend walking in the Lake District. I should've seen about it before now. Don't worry – we made it, and I'll be all right now, honestly." She shooed us away, and we got on with the usual rigmarole of peeling off socks, boots, sweaty clothes and taking turns in the shower.

Eating and drinking proved somewhat difficult, but then we're maybe a bit fussy in that respect. We went into, and speedily out of, a couple of pubs which were far too busy and "shouty", then finally managed a quick one in the Angel Inn. We didn't fancy eating in any of the pubs, so inevitably landed up in an Indian restaurant - The Spice – which was extremely good. We did over-indulge slightly (again), feeling that this was justified after three days of walking, and by the time we got back to the hostel we were all slightly hysterical (again).

"Well, thanks both – and thanks to St Cuthbert. In fact, we've got a lot to thank monks for – with the notable exception of Buckfast." Eilidh threw herself down on the bed, flinging her arms out and closing her eyes briefly. "Oh, it's great to relax though."

"Yeah, it's been good - though tonight wasn't the same without the music!" I'd already made a mental note to look out some of my old albums when I got back. Wonder if the record player still worked?

Fiona went off to the reception to see about booking a taxi to get us to Berwick on Tweed the next morning, and when she came back we looked at dates when we could complete the rest of the Way.

"Can we agree on two days to finish it off, not one?" Eilidh looked ready to put up a fight if Fiona protested. "I *really* want us to be able to enjoy Lindisfarne properly."

"Like we did Bute? Not sure about you and islands." I couldn't resist teasing her, I really couldn't.

"Ha ha. Philistines. You just don't appreciate beauty when you see it."

"There are times when it's *definitely* in the eye of the beholder, Eilidh." Fiona raised a playful eyebrow at me. "However, I agree with you – I don't fancy getting caught by the tide. But maybe we could go somewhere less taxing for the next walk, if that's OK, to give me time to sort this foot out?" Seemed a good idea to both of us.

This trip had given me a lot to think about. I was a bit embarrassed about how badly I'd reacted to Pete's stupid mid-life crisis purchase, but the thought of a complete and final split was beginning to take hold. Maybe he'd done me a favour after all, and Fiona was right? I'd been stupid to let him upset me so much – it was just a car, after all. I wondered how Joe and Julie would react to a divorce - or even if they'd care. Must start looking for a solicitor when I got back.

And then there was Olly's health, elderly parents and Eilidh maybe a Nationalist, and Fiona – *Fiona*? – with a sore foot ... we sure covered a lot in the three days ...

Chapter 22 – Ben A'an (June 2014) - Fiona

Ben A'an is the third highest mountain in the Trossachs. At 1,490 ft, it is comparably small in climbing terms, but it more than makes up for it in other ways. It is often said that it is a perfect Scottish peak, with varied terrain, an attractive shape and magnificent views. The climb starts and finishes at the official car park on the A821 – in this case with an extension round the side of the hill, to come back via Loch Katrine.

It'd been a last-minute decision to do this trip, but I was so glad to be here, and to see Eilidh's welcoming face as I got off the train in Milngavie. A weekend in Scotland was exactly what I needed – I just had to get away, and as Eilidh broke away from my tighter-than-usual embrace she looked at me closely.

"Journey OK?"

"Yip, fine – though ScotRail's First Class isn't quite the same as Virgin's."

"Ach well, it was ever thus. Come on – you must be thirsty." She marched me through the tunnel and up to the pleasant shopping precinct. Tubs of begonias took pride of place in the centre of the paving, and hanging baskets graced several windows above the shops. I followed Eilidh into a corner building which seemed to be a bar at that end, then a bakery, and then a restaurant as it retreated further up the side street. There was a cosy window table which I settled into, and Eilidh came back from the bar with two glasses of Caesar Augustus.

"Oh, this is good." I put my glass down half empty after a long sip. "Just what I need."

"Me too. So, great to see you – but what's up?" She looked at me with concern. "Or d'you want to wait till tomorrow so Liksi can hear too?"

"Oh, God, is it so obvious?" I put my head in my hands for a minute then looked up at Eilidh. "Am *I* so obvious? I've been trying to keep the worst of it from Olly; he's struggling a bit just now – and really, I probably shouldn't be away just now at all but I just had to ..." I took a deep breath and let it out –

"Nathan's been arrested. Possession – maybe worse." It was a relief to get it out. Apart from Olly and Jack, I hadn't told a soul – and Olly didn't know all the details.

"Oh, Fiona, no! I thought he'd been doing quite well recently?"

"So did we – or maybe we just wanted to think that. How could we *really* know when we never see him?"

"So – possession of what? And what d'you mean 'maybe worse'?"

"Cocaine. A lot. Which means he could get done for dealing, not just possession."

"Oh *no!* Fiona, I'm so sorry – that's just awful." Dismay was etched into every corner of Eilidh's expression, and I felt the tears prick as she leaned over and covered my hand with hers.

"He's out on bail just now, pending trial. Our solicitor thinks he can limit it to possession, playing on the fact that it's a first offence, but even so – oh, God, what if he gets jailed?"

"Let's hope that's the case – I mean possession. Can't they just fine him? Sorry, I know very little about drugs."

"You're lucky, keep it that way. I'm learning fast. Yes, he's bound to get a hefty fine, at the very least."

"But – I don't understand – if it's a first offence, then a heavy fine or something might put him off and it *could* be a one-off?" Eilidh was looking rather confused.

"Eilidh, we've been kidding ourselves for years. We saw what we wanted to see – him with part-time jobs, living with a girlfriend, wanting to lead his own kind of life, hoping his addiction had been cured. More fool us." I reflected bitterly on how naïve I'd been – we'd both been. Nathan had been so difficult during his university years that we were just relieved when he left home and seemed to be self-sufficient. It was painful – and exhausting – to think about it too deeply.

"Apparently Jack had an idea of how things were, but was torn between not wanting to destroy the tenuous link he still had with him, and not wanting to upset us. Oh, God, where's this going to end?" I looked at Eilidh bleakly.

She shook her head slowly. "And how's Olly – himself, I mean?"

"He's – he's still OK, but there are more and more symptoms becoming obvious now. He walks very slowly and carefully, and sometimes his right side will go rigid, and he stumbles. His grip on that side isn't so good either. He's becoming less inclined to go out of the house at all now – I think he's losing confidence in social situations."

"Oh, Fiona, I don't know what to say." Eilidh was almost in tears by now.

"There's nothing you can say, I've just got to get on with it. Just being able to let it all out's such a relief – honestly." I pulled myself together and started to collect my things. "Come on – time to go and see that husband of yours." Eilidh put her arm round me and squeezed my shoulders, then finished her drink and we set off walking the mile or so to her house.

We spent a quiet evening with Alan – who seemed to sense the mood and was more sombre than usual, though we didn't discuss Nathan in front of him. I knew Eilidh would tell him later anyway. He'd made a delicious seafood pasta, and after a couple of glasses of wine, Eilidh and I had an early night, leaving him to watch some spy film or other.

Liksi arrived by train the next morning, and after dumping her overnight bag in the house, we got in Eilidh's car and headed for Aberfoyle. Eilidh'd decided that we were going to climb one of the nearby Trossach hills.

"How's your foot, Fiona?" Liksi leaned forward from the back seat.

"Oh – it's OK, better I suppose in that it's not bothered me too much since Wooler. I did get it checked out, but apparently it's just really wear and tear on the bone. I *could* get an operation, but otherwise I just need to watch that I'm not doing too much walking at any one time." I'd almost forgotten about it, actually, but at least I could test it out today.

"This walk's a bonus." Liksi was looking out the window at the thick woodland and puffy clouds. "Thought we mightn't manage to meet up till September. Is this a practice run for the final assault on St Cuthbert?"

"Ha – I don't think so!" Eilidh glanced in her mirror to smile at her. "St Cuthbert's easy but long; Ben A'an's steep but it's not high."

"How high?" I hoped it was at least enough to give us a decent day out.

"Well, it's not a Munro. In fact, it's only about 1,500 ft – but it's a great wee mountain. This, by the way, is the Duke's Pass – it gets pretty dodgy in the winter."

"D'you think I don't remember it from before?" I'd made very sure I was sitting in the front this time when she'd told us where we were going. Each of these bends was ingrained in my memory from the last time, however lovely the wooded countryside surrounding them was. It seemed an interminable amount of time before the road straightened out a bit and a loch appeared on the right.

"Loch Achray," Eilidh reminded us. "Again, small but beautiful. Could be Scotland's motto. It's glorious in autumn, with the colours of the trees reflected in the water."

It looked pretty glorious in early summer too, surrounded by the rich greenery of birches, oaks and alders. A few mallards were taking their sedate morning swim, some with their brown-speckled ducklings in tow, each making their own rippling wake on the still water. A heron was picking its way daintily through the reeds near the roadside, turning its head from side to side and fixing its penetrating eyes on items of interest. I felt an element of calm settling on me – for a few hours at least, I could immerse myself in scenery and friendship and try to forget the misery waiting for me back home.

We drove past the turnoff for Loch Katrine - thankfully, as I didn't want to be reminded of the last time we'd been there, when I was not in a good place either. Nathan loomed once more - I hoped he wasn't going to spoil today for me as well. We rounded Loch Achray to park at the designated Ben A'an car park and got out to put on our boots – and in my case, to breath the fresh air with relief.

"Oh no, not again!" I let out a wail, choking as I breathed out. Almost immediately, this green paradise turned into a form of hell as a dense cloud of midges descended, all determined to get their breakfast at our expense. Jungle Juice, Deet and Skin So Soft were frantically located at the bottom of rucksacks, and slathered on richly but a tad too late. Our version of the arm-flapping Mad Midge Dance only ended after Eilidh pointed to a steep track across the road.

"Up there! If we get going we'll lose them as we gain height." This was a rather abrupt start to our day's climb, but we followed Eilidh's advice and charged up the track. It was quite steep, so as soon as we thought we'd lost our predators, we slowed down as we negotiated the rocks on the path, but we kept going till we reached a bridge, where we stopped to lean against the wooden rail and get our breath back.

"Oh, my God, that's not good for you!" Eilidh's rosy face was glowing, and she was well out of puff. Not that we were much better.

"Maybe not, but this is." Liksi waved her hand expansively over the glistening stretch of Loch Achray below us. Further away was a much larger expanse of water curving its way into the distance.

"That's Loch Venachar, with Callander at the far end." Eilidh was fanning herself with a map.

"Mm, good for the soul," I murmured. There was something about water sparkling in the sunlight. You couldn't help but feel lifted, somehow.

"I've done a few walks round here over the years, and there are some absolutely beautiful paths, before you even look at the hills." Eilidh, having caught her breath by now was happy to act as tour guide. "And they might not be Munros, but there are some crackers. Ben Venue and Ben Ledi are the highest in the Trossachs, but you can't see them from here. You should from the top."

"So why d'you pick Ben A'an?" I was genuinely curious, as I would normally go for the highest if there was a choice.

"I'm just a bit wary of leading people up a hill I've not been up myself." Eilidh looked a bit sheepish. "I know it's a bit ridiculous, but I'd hate it if I took you somewhere and we got lost, or we couldn't park there in the first place which would be even more embarrassing."

She caught my look. "Yes, I know, neither of these things would bother you but I'm more of a wimp than you."

"Not at all." But she was probably right. Eilidh always wanted to please people, to do the right thing, and I could imagine her beating herself up if something went wrong. I rather guiltily remembered our Scafell climb, when I led them down the wrong way. I suppose I was a bit embarrassed about that one, but there *were* extenuating circumstances.

We carried on through the trees – a gentle uphill with a slight breeze ensuring our midges didn't resume their pursuit. At the top of some stone steps, we came to a clearing where a young woman was sitting on a rock with a baby, bouncing the child up and down on her knee and chattering baby-talk to him.

"My goodness, he's a young climber!" Liksi went over to admire the youngster, who was delighted with his new audience, and showed his appreciation by blowing raspberries at us and treating us to a toothless smile.

"Yes, but this is high enough. His father's gone up, but I didn't want to risk the steep bit in case one of us slipped carrying him." The young mother looked pretty fit herself, but she was obviously completely wrapped up in her baby's welfare.

"Good decision." Eilidh held out a finger for the baby to grab. "My heart's always in my mouth when I see babies or toddlers on the back of bikes, too. And yet, wasn't there recently a photo of a one-year-old who's been at the top of ten Munros or something? Doesn't bear thinking about."

"Oh well, he's only four months so he's got a bit to go yet." She smiled up at us. "I suppose if you chose the Munros carefully, there might be some which aren't *obviously* dangerous. We'll see how this wee fellow gets on. It's actually rather pleasant just sitting here in the sun." She was the picture of contentment, watching her following her baby's every movement. With a lump in my throat, I remembered those days with Nathan. What had gone wrong since?

After we left them, the rocky path climbed steeply, to the right of the main peak. However, it wasn't too long and there were plenty of good footholds, and we soon emerged at the top of the cleft. A youngish guy was just about to make his way down – we guessed from the empty baby carrier on his back that he was the father. The path then led through moorland in a gentle sweep round the back of the hill, and a short rocky climb found us at the summit.

"Oh, my, *what* a view." Liksi voiced all our thoughts. For such a small hill, the views were magnificent, all the way round. The long expanse of Loch Katrine lay stretched out below, and we could see the white specks of a couple of cruise boats making their way to their destination at Stronachlachar. Peaks jutted out everywhere: Eilidh pointed out Ben Venue ahead of us, and when we turned round to see even more mountains, there was Ben Lomond, standing proudly apart from other lesser peaks. There was a real feeling of being on top of the world here – no wonder this was a favourite of many local climbers. The summit was full of clusters of people squeezed into small grassy clearings amongst the rocks, picnicking, pointing out the sights, or just generally sitting back and taking in the panorama before them. We did the same, and I just savoured this bit of time out, with Liksi's and Eilidh's conversation comfortably in the background. Up here, I felt wrapped in a protective layer of peace and beauty. I shut my eyes – if only this could last ...

"Come on, you! Time to go back down – or will we just leave you there?" Liksi's cheery voice reminded me that I'd have to tell her about Nathan – but not here. I got to my feet briskly and asked for the map.

"You don't really need it." Eilidh was about to put it back in her rucksack. "We just go back the same way."

"Oh, there must be another way down." I reached out my hand for it, and had a good look. "See, this way here ..."

"You can get down that way all right, but it's boggy and you end up back on the tarmac round Loch Katrine, which we've done already." Eilidh was obviously not keen, but I always tried to avoid going back the same way, and I needed new territory to keep me alert and divert my thoughts from home.

"Well, we can try it anyway." I started off on the path, ignoring Eilidh's pained look. I know, I know, I can be very bossy – but sometimes someone has to make these decisions in order to make life more interesting.

The path wasn't always obvious through the dense heather, but we picked our way down towards the loch, heading for the deer fence. It wasn't *hard*, as such, but you had to watch where you put your feet in case you went into a hole or tripped over a rock. At the bottom, the heather gave way to very wet and boggy grassland as it followed the fence to the left. We slithered our way over it, grabbing at the fence sometimes to avoid falling, but a loud yell from behind told us that the technique hadn't worked for everyone. We turned to see Eilidh lying full length in a particularly muddy patch but laughing hysterically, waving a strangely angled pole in the air.

"I told you we shouldn't go down this way! Sod's law it's me that had to fall, not you." She gave me a mock glare but then burst out laughing again. "Look at my *pole!*"

The pole was bent – the top half must have bent backwards with Eilidh when she went down, with the bottom half trying to stay put in the mud. We went back to help her get up, but all got the giggles as we saw the extent of the damage to her clothing and poles.

"Sorry for laughing," Liksi managed to blurt out, wiping her eyes, "but that was spectacular! Wish I could've seen it as it happened."

"Oh really? Well, maybe you could stop laughing at my expense and help me up? I could be badly injured lying here ..." It was obvious that she was perfectly OK, as we hauled her up, trying not to touch her filthy clothes. She was covered in very wet mud, and it had gone in over her boots too.

"What on earth happened to the pole?" I looked at the ruined item she was trying to clean. "Aren't those the ones you bought in Bulgaria last year?"

"Aye, and I thought they were great, too – but now I see why they were so cheap. I went one way and this one wanted to stay where it was – much good it is now. I have NO luck with poles."

"What happened to your old ones?" She'd had quite a good pair, I'd thought – Leki or something.

"Och, the screwing mechanism just seized up. I got them checked out, but they're done. That's partly why I got cheap ones this time – I don't trust the screwy bits. Ach well."

By this time she was tentatively using the operational pole and carrying the other one, so we re-commenced our precarious journey, keeping well away from Eilidh just in case. Thankfully, we soon reached firmer ground, taking us down through the trees and then onto the tarmac path by the loch. The rest of the route was straightforward – as Eilidh said, we'd done it before.

"Coffee in the café at the pier?" Liksi looked for confirmation as we arrived at the car park.

"Oh aye, as if I can go in there like this!" Eilidh displayed her muddy rear view in despair. "It's not a greasy spoon, you know – it's quite respectable."

"Look, why don't you take your boots off before you go in, and your jacket. We could leave them somewhere – why don't I go and ask that bicycle hire place if you could leave them there?" I shot off before she could refuse, and came back shortly with the expected affirmative answer.

"Nice lad – he even found a plastic bag for them. Come on – boots off." I bundled the items into the bag and headed back to the bicycle shed, whilst Liksi went inside with Eilidh, who hobbled up the steps in her socks.

"Not the first time you've ended a walk in your socks." I heard Liksi reminding her.

When I got up to the café, Eilidh had gone to the toilets to finish the job of making herself look presentable. Liksi and I had coffee, which gave me an opportunity to tell her about

Nathan – I just gave her a brief overview of the facts as I couldn't face going over it all again in detail, but she was every bit as sympathetic and supportive as Eilidh. What would I do without these two? I hadn't even told my friends at home.

Luckily, a transformed Eilidh quickly appeared, having divested herself of her trousers and replaced them with her waterproof ones which she'd had in her rucksack. She was still in her socks, but that didn't quite explain the rather stiff-legged way she walked over to join us. Turned out that in her haste to sort things out, she'd jammed the zip up one leg – it'd only got half-way up her calf and the rest was held in place by poppers which, as she said, could pop at any minute.

"Oh, Eilidh, you're a scream." I wiped my eyes as we dissolved into hysteria again. "You'd better not have one of these cakes then, or you *might* pop!"

In spite of this we all ended up having a slice of carrot cake, while we calmed down, before collecting the bag of dirty boots and jacket and heading home for baths, showers, and another of Alan's blistering curries. The evening had an exciting end with Alan, Liksi and I on their big lollopy couch, and Eilidh on the floor leaning against Alan's feet, watching Brazil beat Chile on penalties in the World Cup.

As Liksi said later on, it's not always the climb or walk we remember most, it's what happened during it, and the conversations we had in the process. And sometimes more importantly, remembering where we were when we disclosed some of the key moments of our lives to each other. The café at Loch Katrine was one of these places.

Chapter 23 – St Cuthbert's Way 4 - Eilidh

The stretch from Wooler to Fenwick is about 12 miles, with a 2–3-mile detour to accommodation in Beal. The gently undulating path leads across moorland, farmland and woodland. It includes a stretch of the Devil's Causeway, another Roman Road, and takes in the hamlets of Horton and Fenwick, and St Cuthbert's Cave.

"How d'you feel?"

"OK, I think. Better than yesterday." I stretched groggily as I tentatively replied to Fiona. My throat was still a bit sore, but it hadn't stopped me meeting Fiona in Berwick-on-Tweed as planned yesterday. By the time my train had arrived I was feeling rather sorry for myself, but a couple of drams in the Rob Roy Inn and a good chat helped things along.

"Maybe we managed to nip it in the bud – no pun intended." Fiona smiled. "I enjoyed sharing your medicine anyway – fierce stuff, Talisker."

"Well, we certainly tried." It was unlikely that I'd escape a lurking lurgy as easily as that, even with my favourite whisky, but I'd no intention of letting it put me off completing the St Cuthbert's Way over the next couple of days. "Hope you don't get it too, whatever it is."

If she did, she probably wouldn't be aware of it anyway – she was possibly the healthiest person I knew. She'd more than her share of life's problems though, and it was just as well that health wasn't one of them. Nathan had been found guilty of possession only, and had been given a substantial fine but avoided a jail sentence. I could guess who was going to pay the fine.

We walked up to the train station, crossing the Tweed via the rather quaint single-track bridge. Liksi's train arrived just after we got there, and we took a taxi to Wooler, to start the walk where we'd left off in April. It was a crisp bright autumn day, and the sun threw its warming rays over us as we started off. I pushed thoughts of sore throats and blocked noses out of the way – this was going to be fine.

We passed the school and followed the road uphill. It was a gentle incline, but even so, I let the others do most of the talking. I needed all my reserves today. The path left the road and headed up to the left, towards Weetwood Moor. Liksi was talking about her father; her parents' situation was not all that different from mine – sadly.

"What kind of 'losing the place'?" Fiona's question made me focus more on the conversation.

"Oh, anything, really. Never know what's going to happen next. Did I tell you about the car saga? No? Well – he can still drive well enough, but he gets into the car and forgets where he's supposed to be going. He can be away for hours, and Mum's sick with worry."

Funny, but also so, so sad. Liksi's jovial, fun-loving father.

"His other trick was forgetting where he'd parked the car. If it was one of these large supermarket carparks he'd often end up going up and down every lane methodically till he found it. *That* could take long enough – but if it was on-street parking he hadn't a chance. The last time it took Mum, my brother and I walking scores of streets on the South Side before we found it – how we didn't wear the key batteries out, I don't know."

"Oh, no – what was his reaction that time?" Fiona turned round.

"Totally mortified, and really upset at all the worry he'd caused us. Maybe it was a good thing though – he immediately agreed to give up his keys to my mother, and only to drive if there was someone else with him. So, we're going with that at the moment."

"What a shame, Liksi. At least you've bought some time with a compromise. It doesn't get easier." It was a significant milestone, though. I just hoped he'd stop completely when the time came, without drama.

"Sorry, forgot about *your* father's driving. How're things there?" Liksi had stopped to look back over the hills, towards the bare brown slopes of Wideopen Hill and the rolling farmland below.

"Oh, he's still very bitter about it. So are we, though very glad he's not still on the road." My father had never been a good driver, but had been completely oblivious to the fact. Tootling along country roads at a snail's pace, stopping every so often to look at the way the hay was baled, or to follow a hovering bird of prey, had been his preferred mode for as long as I could remember. Moving to Inverness had put paid to that, and for the first time in his life he was having to contend with roundabouts and traffic lights on a daily basis. On top of that, he was permanently worried about my mother and getting more and more stressed.

"Who was it that reported him again? A nurse?" Fiona re-tied her laces before setting off again.

"Not quite – some kind of social worker or counsellor, I think." Dad had offered to give her a lift home after she'd been in to see Mum, and she got such a fright when he wandered across lanes at a roundabout that she reported him to his doctor. The latter had called him in for an appointment on some pretext and dropped the bombshell that he was not to drive any more. My father was devastated; although horrified, I was also hugely relieved that he wouldn't be in charge of a car again so I didn't take it any further.

A series of gates, walls and stiles didn't give me any real bother, although it was quite an effort to lift my legs high enough to get over the stiles. I was convinced that all these high stiles were designed for long-legged farmers, not short-legged creatures like me. At least we were going slightly downhill now – always welcome.

"How're you feeling now?" Fiona looked at me doubtfully as we rested above the stone arch of the picturesque Weetwood Bridge, with its long smooth line flowing evenly away from us in both directions.

"OK so far." I pulled out the folding information sheet that went along with the map. "Bit tight-chested though, so taking it easy. By the way, did you know that we're leaning on a Grade I listed structure? It was built in the early 16th century, apparently."

"Listed *structure?*" Fiona raised her eyebrows as she leaned over to admire the stonework of the arch. "I thought you only got listed *buildings*."

"Me too. Well, that's our new fact for the day. Eilidh, why don't I take your pack for you?" Liksi indicated her almost empty one. "I could put mine into yours, easily."

"No, I'm fine thanks – honestly." I'd got into that frame of mind where I just wanted to keep things as they were. The comforting warm and familiar presence of my rucksack didn't seem to be doing me any harm, though I'm sure my refusing to relinquish it must've seemed a bit churlish – and I'd probably regret it later.

"Anyway, I've my new set of poles with me – haven't you noticed?" I waved one of them at them. "Lekis again, but with a clip extension mechanism this time, rather than a screw. Brilliant!"

"So, they're not going to give way on you, or get stuck on fully extended or fully retracted?" Fiona laughed as she took one to get a better look at it. "Nice."

"They'd better not – they cost me enough!" I did feel that I'd got a great set of poles this time though, and I certainly needed an extra pair of "limbs" to help me along today.

"Pity, we'd a good laugh last time." Liksi took the pole from Fiona, and tested out the clips.

"Ha ha. Warped sense of humour you've got. Not fair – remember, I'm an invalid today." I grabbed it back, and made a big play of leaning heavily on them, then raising one in admonition before stomping off across the bridge.

We carried on through West Horton, turning left onto the Devil's Causeway, another of these dead straight Roman Roads. However, we were only on it for a few hundred yards before the Way turned east at East Horton. We passed the tall stately farm buildings, with their buttery stone walls, tall sash windows and red-tiled roofs. Next was Old Hazelrigg; there was a cottage there but nothing else to indicate that it was formerly a medieval village. The surrounding landscape was all very open – flattish farmland mainly, until we hit a more wooded area with a slight incline.

"St Cuthbert's Cave's supposed to be up here." Fiona was looking at the track that led uphill, off the main path. "Coming to check it out?" Liksi was right behind her and nodding, but I decided to play safe.

"Go on up, you two. If I can get to Beal tonight I'll be doing well – if there's any detours I might never get there. I'll stay here and recharge the batteries." Pottering round caves or peculiar rocky outcrops was normally very much my thing, but I just didn't have the energy today. In fact, my chest was tightening up even more and my throat was starting to burn again. Just what I didn't want – and with another day to go tomorrow.

It was a nice spot to rest, though. The weather was warm without being hot, and bracken and soft grasses made a comfortable nest. I curled up and shut my eyes, listening to the animal rustles around me, and the bird calls above. It would've been easy to fall asleep here – and probably a lot better for me than continuing with a 12-mile walk – more, to get to the hotel at Beal. After a few minutes though, I felt hungry, and elbowed myself up to forage in my rucksack. Along with a sandwich, I took out the book I'd brought with me and started reading. I knew there was a good reason not to have handed my pack over to Liksi.

They re-appeared after ten minutes or so, apparently quite taken with the place.

"Nice spot. St Cuthbert chose well." Praise indeed from Fiona. "In fact, I don't know why he wanted to move from a nice warm cave like that to windy Lindisfarne."

"He *didn't* choose it." I laughed, my sense of humour triumphing over my ailments. "He was deid! The monks kept moving his body around and they stopped at the cave for a rest. They were trying to avoid marauding Vikings at the time."

"Oh. Oh well, the monks chose well then." She looked at me, by this time halfway through my sandwich. "Lunch? Guess that must be a good sign?" She sat down to join me.

"Not really. Just needed some fuel, and something to calm my throat. It's working, slightly, but I don't think I can manage the other half."

"You must be seriously ill, Eilidh, not being able to finish a sandwich." Liksi looked at me with something between concern and amusement. "Come on, now – give me that pack."

By this time I felt it might take up less energy to accept the offer; in any case the pack was already on the ground so I didn't even have to manoeuvre it off. Liksi carried very little with her, so she was able to put her whole pack into mine, and carry it easily.

"Thanks. Remind me to add Strepsils to the list of essential First Aid equipment next time."

"Here, why don't you take one of these?" Fiona thrust a handful of rather sticky wrapped toffees at me, and I put them in my pocket with a view to spacing them out over the next few miles.

"By the way, talking of essential equipment, found out I've been carrying a compass with me on the last few walks, without even knowing I had one." Liksi gave a slightly sheepish grin.

"How come? Did you find it at the bottom of your rucksack or something?" Fiona asked.

"No, it's much more interesting than that." Liksi picked up her pole and unscrewed the top – and proudly displayed a small built-in compass. "How's that for class?"

"Mm, smart." I was impressed – I'd never seen one embedded in a pole before. "D'you know how to use it?"

"What d'*you* think? Haven't a clue! Kids gave me these poles a couple of years ago, but I never thought of unscrewing the grips. Just happened to be fiddling with them the other day and made this wondrous discovery!"

"Come on, James Bond – you can practise using it by leading the way. To give you a hint, it's that way!" Fiona pointed to the only possible route, laughing as she set off.

I found it harder to get going again, and instead of the brief rest picking me up a bit, it seemed to make my limbs heavier, and my chest tighter. Everything was starting to prickle – eyes, nose, throat. I knew the signs well now – I was in for it. Fiona's cheerful comment that we were more than halfway now was meant to motivate, but all I could focus on was *sore*. I managed what was meant to be a brave smile but was probably more of a grimace.

However, on we went, on a path called Dolly Gibson's Lonnen – on another day I'd have wanted to know who Dolly Gibson was, but not today. In spite of the apparently flat landscape, there were still some ups and downs, and every so often we'd get a glimpse of our ultimate destination, Lindisfarne, with the castle as a blimp at the far end. I was beginning to think that it wouldn't matter if I didn't get there tomorrow after all – a day tucked up under a duvet seemed much more appealing. Rather pathetically, I started dreaming of quilts, pillows, cups of tea – and tripped over a tree root.

"Ow! No, I'm OK – really. I think." I winced as Fiona helped me to my feet. "Just throat sore – not foot." My throat was now so sore that I don't think I'd have noticed if I'd *broken* my foot.

"Be careful, now – we need to get you there in one piece. Oh, see that cottage over there?" Fiona stopped for a closer look, then consulted the map. "I thought so - 'Blawearie'. Isn't that the name of the place in 'Sunset Song'?"

"Yeah, Chris Guthrie's home – the farm. Don't think it's a real place, though." Liksi, like all of us, had probably read Sunset Song whilst still in school. "I think there's a Blawearie in the Borders somewhere too."

"But how strange, finding it down here." Fiona was frowning as she turned to the information sheet. "Look, apparently it means 'tired of the wind'. But surely that's in Scots, not in English?" Shrugging her shoulders, she put the map away and set off again. It was interesting, though. Something to check out later, when I'd the energy – if I ever had it again. Certainly, I could imagine this place being at one time pretty lonely, and subject to wind and weather, just like Chris Guthrie's home in Aberdeenshire.

We skirted a village that they told me was Fenwick, and headed towards Beal, where we'd a hotel room booked.

"The instructions say to take the minor road round the back of Beal, so we need to cross the A1, then head round to the left." Fiona'd taken over map-reading completely now; I didn't care. I was just numbly putting one foot in front of the other to do what I was told, and forcing myself on.

"Wouldn't it be quicker just to go up the A1?" asked Liksi tentatively. She didn't often question Fiona's decisions, but I think she was quite concerned for me.

"Maybe, but there's no pavement, and with all the fumes and Eilidh a bit staggery, I think it'd be safer to go the back road."

So we crossed the A1 – which wasn't easy or pleasant, with the fumes from the lorries and other vehicles thundering up and down – and started walking along a small tarmac road. I blanked other thoughts out, and kept focused on the thought that we'd stumble into Beal any minute now.

After a while, Liksi stopped with a frown. "Er, aren't we heading towards the sea? Should we be?" She stopped to look at the map with Fiona, while I just stood there uselessly – 'hinging', I think the word is.

"Oh dear, I think you might be right." My heart sank, as Fiona looked around and then announced, "We're going to have to cross the railway line then head left. Over there."

The railway line appeared to be almost as busy as the A1, and a large warning notice confirmed that we needed to take great care. We were instructed to use the special phone to check when the next train was due before crossing – and were told to wait seven minutes. I sank down to sit on a stone. At least it was a rest.

"Have we gone the wrong way then?" I managed to ask, swallowing with difficulty.

"Looks like it; we should've crossed further north. We're going to have to sweep round the back in a bit of loop. It's going to mean an extra mile or so." Fiona, typically, did not apologise and I felt too weak to protest. I just wanted to find myself in that hotel ...

"Up, Eilidh – train!" Liksi's warning was hardly needed – the oncoming roar was pretty loud, and by the time she'd helped me up the train was well past. We walked over the line as quickly as we could, and commenced the long drag round the lanes. I guess the little settlements, with sea views, would've looked very appealing normally, but I could hardly lift my head to look at them.

"Look, there's Beal over there. Only about four more fields, that's all. Nearly there." Liksi was trying hard, but by this time my poles seemed to be all that was holding me up, and I used them like mechanical limbs. My head was pounding, the soles of my feet were burning, my chest was hurting – in fact, *everything* was hurting. "One field gone, just three more ..."

"Here's another ... Oh, not *quite* at Beal, sorry Eilidh. Looks like we've got to go along this road first. Didn't spot that earlier." Liksi sounded almost upset. We'd been able to see the hotel we were aiming for, but as the crow flies, and unfortunately we weren't crows. Just as well I hadn't been relying too much on the number of fields – I was in robotic mode now.

"What the hell?" This was Liksi. "Another railway crossing? We must've gone round in a great big loop."

"We did. Anyway, the lights are flashing so it can't be long now." Fiona gave me a sympathetic look, and seconds afterwards, a south-bound train came roaring across the road and we were free to stumble on. At last, the most longed-for sight ever, right in front of us – the Lindisfarne Inn. A well-kept, white-walled traditional inn which would've been welcoming anyway, but today seemed like Valhalla.

"I'll run ahead and get us checked in." Fiona was off, and by the time Liksi and I got to the front door she was there with the key. "The room's the last on the left down there."

Liksi opened the room door and I flung my pack and jacket down on the floor before collapsing onto the nearest bed. "Headache pills," I mumbled. "Please." Two pills and a glass of water were quickly thrust at me and I forced myself upright again to take them, before throwing my head back down on the pillow. I was vaguely aware of someone unlacing my boots and taking them off.

"Eilidh, we're going to get something to eat – can we bring you anything back?" Liksi's voice was a faint blur.

"No - thanks. Sleep."

They did a quick turnaround and as they shut the door quietly behind them on their way out, the last thing I heard was, "Poor thing. She'll never make it to Lindisfarne tomorrow. And she was so looking forward to it."

I didn't care – I was warm and not walking any more, and cosy, and drowsy, and ...

Chapter 24 – St Cuthbert's Way 5 (September 2014) – Liksi

The distance from Beal to Lindisfarne village, along the north of the island, is about 7 miles, starting on the minor road on which Beal is situated. This route uses the causeway to get to the end of the island closest to the mainland, rather than the Pilgrims' Path which goes over the sands to the village. Access to the causeway depends on the tides.

Eilidh was still out cold. Fiona'd shaken me awake, and we were tiptoeing about the room trying not to wake our friend.

"D'you think we should bring her back a filled roll or something?" I whispered.

"Could do. Though not sure if she'll be able to eat it."

"Mm? Eat what?" Eilidh's tousled head appeared from under the duvet as she viewed us with suspicion. "You two aren't off already, are you?"

"Good God, you're awake! We thought you might've died!" I gaped at her in amazement. She was dressed in the T-shirt she usually sleeps in, and didn't look much different from normal.

"Oh really – is that why you were planning to bring me back a roll?" She grinned at us, rubbing her eyes, then ran her fingers through her hair and swung her legs over, ready to get up. "Wait a sec, I'm coming with you."

"Eilidh, take it easy – you were in a bad way last night." Fiona was looking at her, then me, in disbelief as we watched her throw on some clothes. "Mind you, you must've undressed at some stage because all we did was take your boots off, and you went straight under the duvet."

"Really? I don't remember a thing except the relief of getting into this room. Thanks for looking after me – I must've been a pain yesterday."

"Don't be daft – you'd do the same if it was one of us. Just glad you seem to be OK." I looked at her dubiously – how could she have recovered as much as that?

"I'm fine, honestly. Well, maybe not exactly fine – but VERY fine compared to yesterday. Head's a bit thick, but throat seems OK – not like swallowing glass any more. And I'm STARVING!"

We grinned at each other as we left the room together. If Eilidh was hungry again, then she was well on the way to recovery. We were met at the restaurant by the same Polish waiter as the night before, who looked at Eilidh with raised eyebrows.

"Three for breakfast? You feel better today?"

"Much better – and hungry!" Eilidh beamed at him, as she headed for a table. Fiona gave the waiter one of these shrugs that said, 'I don't believe it either, but there you are' and joined her. He'd heard all about our walk, and our sick friend, last night – now he was probably thinking we'd made it all up.

Breakfast arrived – porridge followed by scrambled eggs for Fiona, full English for Eilidh, and a piece of black pudding and a couple of rashers of bacon for me. I looked at the bacon sadly – I'd asked for it to be very well cooked, almost burnt, but it was nowhere near the crisped, blackened item I would have cooked myself. Still, looking at the speed with which Eilidh was devouring hers, I could always offer her seconds. I thought of the many times Pete had scorned my eating habits, and how good it was to be free of him. I also wondered if my solicitor had sent the letter to him yet. After the fiasco with the Aston Martin, I'd slowly come round to following Fiona's advice in terms of starting the divorce procedure. However, when I met him to discuss this, he'd just shrugged it off.

"What's the point?" That arrogant, 'I'll just do what I want anyway' look on his face was there in force. "Unless either of us wants to get married again, I can't see any advantage." No, he wouldn't, would he – when he can still manipulate things his way and avoid contributing anything to the children's welfare. He dismissed the idea scornfully, and refused to believe that I was serious. Hence the letter, confirming my intentions and asking him to find a solicitor himself.

I realised I was drifting, and came back to the present when Eilidh asked, "So did you work something out with the manager for tonight?" The hotel website had indicated that they had a service to get people to and from Lindisfarne.

"Sure did." I might have known that, as usual, Fiona would sort out the logistics. "Jamie's going to pick us up at 9 pm at the Marketplace. He's the one that checked us in last night – not that you'd remember. Brilliant service, I have to say."

"They couldn't be more helpful here." I was very impressed by the whole place – after all, it was just a small hotel. "Last night, they were all for making you up a doggy bag, but we weren't going to risk waking you up. Didn't dare, in fact!"

"Good decision – that sleep was *wonderful*, the best ever. That's great though – gives us the whole day in Lindisfarne without worrying about having to get back before the tide or anything."

"Remind me – when were you there last?" I thought she'd said something about a birthday.

"I spent my 30th birthday here with Dave – remember him? No big party for me."

"All loved up? How romantic! Does Alan know about this?" I was teasing her, but also couldn't help being envious once again of her and Alan's relationship.

"It was anything *but* romantic. Bit like flogging a dead horse, really. And yes, I told Alan ages ago, and true to form he found it highly amusing. Huh."

"So what d'you do for your 40th?" I was genuinely intrigued. I'd always had a big party on my big birthdays – any excuse to get a crowd together for a good time.

"Walked out to Sandwood Bay. I'd always wanted to go there – very remote, south of Cape Wrath, and you've got to walk 4 miles to get there. It was wonderful, and we stayed the night in a really nice wee guesthouse in Kinlochbervie. So before you ask, yes, that one was VERY romantic."

"Enough reminiscing, you two, or we'll never get out of here. Eilidh, are you absolutely sure you're up for this? We'll be stuck there till 9, which won't be much fun for you if you get a relapse."

"I'm fine, don't worry. Fighting fit." She did look remarkably well, I had to admit. Tough wee cookie, Eilidh. She rarely got a cold, and had laughingly put her good health down to her and Alan's refusal to adhere to use-by dates in their kitchen. She was convinced that this helped build up immunity which today's obsessives were missing out on. Maybe she was right, though I'd been relieved when she said that anything green and furry *did* go directly into the bin.

We set out shortly afterwards with renewed energy. I was so glad she was with us; we made such a good threesome that it wouldn't have been the same without her. It's also always a good feeling to be on the last leg of a long-distance walk – I remember how Eilidh and I felt on the last morning of the West Highland Way. We weren't convinced we'd make it, but our stubbornness in ignoring the pain paid off. Today, unless Eilidh was hiding anything from us, we were all positive and in good spirits. It was quite a short walk anyway, only about seven miles, which was part of the reason we decided to take the causeway rather than the shortcut of the Pilgrims' Path.

"Feel that we're cheating by not going across the sands like the pilgrims." I was watching a small group wading across the sands through ankle-deep water. "Mind you, it's not exactly a dry route."

"Well, we're definitely not pilgrims," Fiona said firmly, "and we'd just be trudging through wet grey sludge, so we're not missing much." That was me told – but I guess she was right. Anyway, the guidebook'd recommended wellies or bare feet for the Path; we didn't have wellies and I certainly didn't fancy walking in bare feet for that distance. There was also the fact that we'd be on Lindisfarne for hours – putting wet and sandy feet into boots didn't sound a good idea either.

We walked along the road to the start of the causeway, and took time to read all the signs dotted about – they were mostly warnings about the tides. I s'pose it was too much to hope for much sun at this time of year – yesterday's warmth had been a bonus – but there was something about all the greyness that increased the other-worldly appeal of the island. Unremitting grey sky – no clouds as such, and no patches of light, just different densities the nearer it got to the horizon. This gave the impression of brightness above, but melancholy all around. The sands themselves were a dirty, sloppy grey. The white central markings of the dark grey road, just emerging from the silvery waters rippling on each side, led rather eerily between two rows of posts to the main island, which seemed to consist of one low-lying grey-green mass with a small village at one end.

"You know, I'm even more convinced that St Cuthbert should've stayed in that nice warm cave." I shivered slightly. "Bit eerie here, to say the least."

"Aye, but that's what makes it. It's a bit like going to Venice in misty weather rather than baking sun – it's much more atmospheric. I love the mystery and – and – *aura* of the place." Eilidh had her arms wrapped round herself to keep warm, but she was looking really happy just to be here.

Paths, Pals and Pints

It was a bit tricky walking across – there was a fair trickle of cars going over, with the odd one returning to the mainland, and there was no pavement as such. The sides of the road were full of water-filled potholes, so you had to concentrate on what you were doing to get off the road. About half-way along there was a tall box thing on stilts, which apparently was a refuge for anyone caught out by the tide. Reassuring – or not? I shuddered as we passed it, glad we weren't in a situation where we'd to use it.

"Looks like one of the aliens from 'War of the Worlds'." Eilidh was also looking at the construction with apprehension. "I'd an album once with the music from that film, and loved it."

"Who wouldn't love Richard Burton's voice?" Fiona agreed. "No wonder Liz Taylor couldn't stop marrying him."

I snorted. Marrying once was bad enough in my case. "Maybe; at least he'd the sense not to try to sing. Unlike many others." My thoughts turned to past hits. "So, what would you guys have in your Top 10 then?"

There was silence for a minute, then suggestions came thick and fast.

"*Sultans of Spring* by Dire Straits. I saw them live at an open-air concert in Rockhampton in Queensland, during my backpacking stint." (Eilidh)

"*American Pie*. Takes me back to the hockey team singing along to the radio on the school minibus." (me)

"*Maggie May* – takes me back to my rebellious youth. Yip, I know, no surprises there." (Fiona)

"*Without You*. I'd just broken up with first boyfriend and I howled every time I heard it – for years." (Eilidh)

"On that note, think I should select *I Will Survive* – I *am* surviving!" (me, with fervour)

"You are indeed – very well." I felt ridiculously pleased by this, from Fiona. Usually she pulled me up for being too passive or something – certainly at least as far as Pete was concerned. "I love *Walking on Sunshine* by Katrina and the Waves – the kids used to sing it in the back of the car as we headed off on holiday."

"That was optimistic, in the British weather." Eilidh was still managing to rock herself to the beat in her head though.

"Well, we were usually going to Cornwall, so it was fine. If not sunshine, at least there were waves!"

"We should've chosen the theme music from Chariots of Fire and ploughed across the Pilgrims' Path humming it." My choices, inevitably, included a sporting theme.

"Just as well we didn't, if I'm as tone deaf as you tell me I am." Fiona most *definitely* was tone deaf. "We might've ended up in quicksand or something if I got the notes wrong."

That sobering thought found us at the end of the causeway, where it was a relief not to worry about getting soaked, falling into a pothole or getting run over. When a path appeared on the left indicating The Snook, we were all happy to turn off into the dull red sand dunes, pushing up through the spiky marram grass.

"The name – the Snook - reminds me of a character in the Moomins – er, I guess neither of you have read the Moomin books?" This from Eilidh, as we looked at her with pity as we shook our heads.

"They were brilliant – you've had deprived childhoods. Oh, wait a minute, I think it was the Snork, not the Snook. He was a goody, I think."

"Oh, well, I'm relieved about that." Fiona raised a conspiratorial eyebrow at me. "Maybe we'll come across a Snook/Snork then."

"Huh – uh oh, look at that – we might need a local of any sort to get us out of here." Eilidh was looking at the bottom of the slope; we were heading straight for a large marshy area, with a kind of overgrown pond in the middle. The path we'd been on had disappeared, and we were having to fight our way through tall grasses which hid what was underfoot. We headed round to the right of the pond, but it still wasn't easy – you either risked wet feet or got stabbed by those grasses. It was a relief when we emerged, not entirely unscathed, at the far side of the pond where there was a small cottage, and another small building with a rather incongruous tower at one end.

"Wonder what that was for?" Eilidh mused. "Spotting marauding Vikings?"

"Hardly." Fiona gave the tower a cursory glance. "It's not nearly old enough. Maybe marauding Snooks?"

Oh dear, we were all in silly mode today. Probably the relief of having Eilidh well again. We skirted the buildings and headed for the coast, having unanimously agreed to go right round the coast to the village, rather than going anywhere near the road again. The wind was bracing as we walked round Coves Haven and Keel Head, both sandy stretches, and then down the rockier part till we reached the castle.

"Pretty dramatic, isn't it?" I was looking at the small but attractive castle, perched at the top of a small rocky hillock. "Want to go in? It's bound to have a café or something."

"Great idea. I could do with getting warmed up." Eilidh started climbing the path and we followed her, looking forward to relaxing with a welcome cup of coffee and maybe something to eat. However, when we got to the wooden reception hut at the top, the National Trust person informed us that we'd only half an hour before the castle closed, and worse - there was no café.

"Isn't 4 o'clock rather early to close?" Eilidh asked.

"It's because of the tides. We have to make sure any staff can get off the island, so the opening times are slightly different every day."

"Oh, of course." Eilidh looked a bit crestfallen. "How stupid of me."

Her woebegone look must have struck a chord, as the official then suggested that we bought one ticket between the three of us as we'd only limited time. "It'll give you a flavour of it, and with a bit of luck you'll want to come back again, for longer." He smiled at us, and we couldn't refuse, although we didn't normally visit museums or castles etc during our walks. It took away from time in the fresh air.

However, once inside, I was pleasantly surprised. It was really a perfect small castle, and felt lived-in, which most other castles certainly didn't. When we learned that it had been restored by Lutyens in the early 1900s, and that it was hired out for weddings etc that helped to explain things. We whizzed round it, determined to see every room in the half hour, but decided to leave the Gertrude Jekyll Garden for another time. By this stage we were all desperate for a coffee, so we carried on down the coast to the village. The attractive small harbour was framed by the Castle at one end, and the village at the other, but there was no sign of any café.

"There's a mead distillery – or brewery – whatever you call a place that makes mead." Eilidh brightened. "Somewhere. It might have a café."

"A meadery?" This was Fiona's contribution, but whatever it was called, I didn't care as long as I could get a coffee there. We passed Pilgrims' Coffee House, which seemed an even better prospect as it came first – but it was closed.

"Aaargh! Closed too? Don't get this. Surely they still have loads of visitors at this time of year – it's not exactly the middle of winter." I wasn't at all impressed with this aspect of Lindisfarne, but then maybe I was too used to living in the city.

The mead place was closed too, as were a couple of other cafés we passed.

"It's Sunday – and this is Holy Island. Maybe we shouldn't be so surprised nowhere's open?" Fiona was the one to voice this unwelcome thought.

"Oh, God – don't tell me we're stranded here till 9 and everywhere's closed?" Eilidh's teeth were starting to chatter, although she still looked pretty healthy compared to last night. We tried a couple of pubs but found them closed too and were beginning to get seriously worried – then at last found sanctuary in the Manor House Hotel, which had a functioning bar serving coffee. For once, not one of us ordered an alcoholic drink, and we huddled gratefully in comfy chairs, hands firmly clasped round large cups of steaming coffee.

"Well, if we haven't already caught your lurgy, Eilidh, we'll all have caught *something* by the end of today. Look at Fiona's nose – it's almost as red as yours." I couldn't help laughing as they turned to look at each other.

"This is England's payback for us giving them a fright last week." We looked at Eilidh. What was she going on about now? "The Referendum. IndyRef. Don't tell me you've forgotten about it already?"

"Well, actually, I had – temporarily," I admitted. "Too busy concentrating on our usual highbrow discussions. Like - Top Ten hits, or Snooks and Snorks – you know the sort of thing."

Eilidh snorted. "I must confess, I'd actually forgotten about it too till just now, though I'd a much better excuse – the state of my health. Anyway, I'm relieved about the result, but at the same time I'm kind of disappointed. Alan and I wavered right up till the day itself."

"Seriously?" I was genuinely quite surprised – these two always seemed to have very definite political opinions.

"Well, yes. The economic argument was really the only reason we didn't take the plunge. I just feel, somehow, that we've missed the boat. Imagine being free of all those Tory plonkers in Westminster once and for all – how wonderful would that be?"

"But there's not much quality in Scottish politics either, whatever the party, is there?" Fiona can usually be relied on to say something disparaging about Scotland, but in this case I tended to agree with her.

"I'm just thankful that it was No," I said. "Those smug b......s in the SNP would've been unbearable if they'd won."

"I'm in the huff with them anyway – I wasn't allowed to vote, as I don't live there. Absolute nonsense – I was *born* there, for God's sake. That should be enough." Fiona was not amused.

"You and Sean Connery both." Eilidh grinned at her. "Except I can't imagine you're in the tax exile category, unless there's something you're not telling us."

We spent about an hour there, but there was a limit to how much coffee we could consume so we went outside and had a rather aimless wander around, then sat on a bench overlooking the Priory ruins for a while. Fiona was dispatched to find out if there was anywhere we could eat in the evening, and came back with the rather dispiriting news that the Manor House and the Crown and Anchor were fully booked. The only other possibility was the Ship Inn, which didn't open till 6.

"Three reasonably intelligent people – why did none of us think that this might be a problem?" Fiona looked at us in mock despair.

"I don't think I want to answer that. I don't know about you lot, but I'm going to wait outside the Ship Inn and be first over the door when it opens." Eilidh got up and, for lack of any other suggestions, we followed her. It was just after 5.30 when we got there, and the door was very firmly closed. We looked at each other rather foolishly.

"I don't think I've ever queued outside a pub to get in, even in my wildest student days." Eilidh was shaking her head. "This is ridiculous." She looked at us and I got the giggles, then Fiona started too.

"Just look at us! Three old bats, standing outside waiting for opening time. On a Sunday too – how desperate is that? If my colleagues could see me now ..." Actually, I doubted if the other technicians would believe their eyes; I was pretty sure they saw me as the sane and sensible member of the team. Mind you, that was maybe because most of their ribald jokes fell on my deaf ears ...

Somehow, we managed to pass the next half hour through a combination of political observations and daft chatter which made us increasingly hysterical, so that when the heavy door was finally unbolted from the inside, the barman must've thought he'd three madwomen to contend with. However, having confirmed that the bar was not only open for meals, but that it would be possible to order straight away, we thanked him effusively and tried to persuade him that we didn't normally make a habit of queuing outside pubs.

He looked at us with amusement as he led us to a table and handed out menus. "Really? Isn't that what you Jocks do all the time? Only joking – always pleased to see any of you down here. Now, are you drowning your sorrows or celebrating?" We looked at him in confusion.

"Yes or No?"

Light dawned. "We all voted No." I spoke for all of us.

"That's the stuff. We didn't want you to leave us – did we, Janey?" The barmaid elbowed her hair out of her eyes as she looked up from pulling pints.

"No, no, joined at the hip we are. It's OK – just sit there and I'll bring you your drinks." By this time there were a few others sitting round the bar, listening with interest.

"You had us worried, though." A woman with arresting auburn curls turned round to focus on us properly. "*Almost* half voted for independence – it's not going to go away."

"Well, it should do," said another, grumpily. "Once in a generation, according to Alex Salmond." There were a few snorts at the mention of his name, but by and large all the comments sent our way were very positive. This enclave of England very obviously wanted us to remain, which was rather comforting. Our new friends were then curious about why we'd come to this part of the world in the first place. As we told them about doing the St Cuthbert's Way, it occurred to me that it'd been a strange coincidence, deciding to undertake a walk from Scotland into England, during the year of the Independence Referendum.

When we settled up at the end, the barman insisted that the first round of drinks was on the house, 'to celebrate the Union', and we left the pub to a chorus of good wishes and 'come back soon's'. Jamie from the hotel picked us up at the Marketplace at the agreed time, and as I sank into bed not long after, I reflected yet again that I'd voted the right way. These decent people were no different from most Scots, and the ties that bound us were far more important than any misguided notions of doing our own thing.

Mind you, in the taxi to Berwick the next morning, the driver told us how the place was being overrun with immigrants, and that it was all due to the last Labour government, and it was time the government clamped down - and I almost had second thoughts ...

Chapter 25 – John Muir Way 1 (February 2015) - Fiona

The John Muir Way runs across central Scotland for 134 miles from Helensburgh on the west coast, to John Muir's birthplace in Dunbar, on the east coast. This 15-mile section starts in the attractive town of North Berwick, then leads inland to the village of East Linton before heading back to the coast, the extensive sands of Belhaven Bay and the town of Dunbar.

We'd started the John Muir Way in November, having unexpectedly managed to fit in another walk before the end of the year. Due to the unpredictability of Scottish weather, we'd only attempted nine miles – Helensburgh to Balloch – and we seem to have spent most of that day drinking copious amounts of tea in the Kilted Skirlie at Lomond Shores, overlooking the Loch. The Way appealed because the route was never far from either Eilidh's home or Liksi's, the terrain was pretty straightforward, and it seemed a good idea for less dramatic walks in winter months. This time, we'd agreed to do the last part.

Memories of life in Edinburgh came flooding back as I went up the steps to the side exit from Waverley Station, emerging in the gloom of Market Street. After crossing the road I paused at the entrance to the steep steps of Fleshmarket Close, breathing in the familiar malty smell of the city. Walking up the steps, whiffs of weed mixed with less salubrious odours were added to the miasma, yet even then it didn't seem unpleasant, only nostalgic. My thoughts moved to Nathan, then quickly swerved away again. My juvenile sorties into experimenting with hash weren't worth mentioning in comparison, but anyway, I didn't want to think about him tonight.

Throwing open the door of the Half-Way House, I was pleased to see that it hadn't changed much – or at least, not that I could remember. Tardis-like, at first sight it was jam-packed inside, but after I forced my way through the throng at the door the rest of the tiny but long pub was quite quiet. Liksi and Eilidh were comfortably settled at a corner table, with plenty of room for me to join them. I hugged each in turn and flopped down with relief.

"Oh, it's good to get here and relax – what a day." I took a grateful gulp from the large glass of red wine handed to me.

"See you've dressed down for the occasion." Liksi pointed with a grin at my business suit. "Hope you're not planning to wear those shoes tomorrow?"

"Ha ha. Cheers." I raised my glass, then turned to Liksi. "So, what's the plan for tomorrow?"

"Well, I'm thinking bus then train to North Berwick, walk to Dunbar then do train and bus back. About 15 miles. Sound OK?"

"Great. – I need a good long stretch for my legs. So, we've done the beginning of the John Muir Way, and now we're about to do the end?"

"Bet Alan had a good laugh about that?" asked Liksi.

"And how." Eilidh made a face. "Says it's only women who could start the West Highland Way by going backwards - twice, then pick another long-distance walk and do one end, then the other, and plan to eventually end up somewhere in the middle!"

"S'pose he's got a point." Liksi laughed. "It does sound mad when you put it like that. Anyway, why be the same as everyone else? Oh, whose mobile's that?" We all automatically scrabbled about to locate our own. "Oh, sorry, it's mine!"

I looked up to find she'd shoved her phone back in her bag, but had turned rather pink and wasn't meeting anyone's eye.

"Liksi! What're you up to? Who was that?" I'd rarely seen anyone out of their teens look as shifty as she did at that moment. "Have you got a new man or something? *Liksi*! You have!" The expression on her face said it all.

"A man? Well go on, *answer it* for heaven's sake!" Eilidh's reaction was the same as mine. "Phone him back – now!" With a further guilty look, Liksi grabbed her phone and rushed out the door, leaving Eilidh and I gaping at each other.

"How *exciting*! If anyone deserves a bit of romance, it's her. She's had years of Pete running her down and her self-esteem's at rock bottom." Eilidh looked thoughtfully in the direction of the door. "I just hope she knows what she's doing though."

"Well, we've both just forced her outside to chase after him, so she didn't have much choice. Good for her." I was stunned though – somehow I'd never expected Liksi to meet someone else, and she'd only recently started divorce proceedings. I went up to get another round and when I returned with the drinks, Liksi came back in and flung herself down beside Eilidh, breathlessly.

"Here, you'll need this." I put the glass in front of her. "So, you *are* a dark horse – should we be celebrating?"

"Would've told you, honestly, was waiting for the right time – just got a surprise when he phoned and – d'you think I'm *mad*?" Her cheeks were still pink but those hazel eyes of hers were sparkling. Well!

"Mad? *Bad* – for not telling us. Liksi, that's brilliant that you've met someone – but come on, *tell all*!" Eilidh pushed the glass into her hand. "Here, drink – then start at the beginning. Don't leave *anything* out."

Obediently, she did. After a large gulp of wine, she told us. Alex Crossland – she'd met him in the Café Royale, where her hockey club had been celebrating one of their recent wins. He was the brother-in-law of one of the girls. Accountant by day, keen amateur footballer by night.

"Been out together a few times, but just want to keep it low profile. No intentions of getting out of the frying pan into the fire. So keep it down, OK?"

"Oh no you don't – if you're going to become a WAG we need to know ALL the details!" We all laughed at this – anyone less like a stereotypical WAG than Liksi was hard to imagine. For a start, she was tiny, and had probably never worn a pair of stiletto heels in her life. I tried again. "Age? From? Inside leg measurement?"

"Year younger than me. Divorced. From Edinburgh, lives in the New Town." Although still rosy-cheeked, she was absolutely glowing, although she tried to hide it. "Now that's quite enough just now, so you'll just have to wait. Come on – drink up, then bus."

Back in Liksi's cluttered sitting room, she filled in the details. I just hoped it would work out for her. For all her laid-back exterior, she'd had a hard time and didn't deserve any more man-problems.

Next morning, there were no blue patches in the pale grey canopy above, but no dark clouds either. Though cold, it wasn't biting, and seemed quite promising for this usually cold and dank time of year. At my insistence, we sat up on the top of the bus so that I could see as much of Edinburgh as possible while I had the chance – the architecture still took my breath away sometimes. We passed the Scotsman building on the left, went over the North Bridge, and turned the corner with the iconic Balmoral Hotel leading into Princes Street. As we got off the bus I glanced briefly down the long sweep of the street, past the nearby Scott Monument, backed by the mighty castle towering over everything. Superb. At Waverley we didn't have to wait long for a train to North Berwick, and by 11 o'clock we were at the start of the day's walk.

We strolled through the streets, following the signs to Berwick Law, and for once I reluctantly went along with the general consensus and bypassed the climb to its summit. I don't like avoiding challenges, however small, and although I could probably have raced up and down and caught up with the others pretty quickly, I didn't think that plan would've found favour. If it'd been later in the walk I'd probably have done it. Pity – I'm sure the views would've been good.

The route was straightforward, although it was disappointing that so much of it led inland. Somehow, I felt that a walk from North Berwick to Dunbar should've been entirely along the coast, and it looked, on paper at least, as if that should have been possible. However, maybe sand, marshes and inlets would have made a direct route tricky – this was all pretty flat, going through fields and farmland mainly, with the odd bit of woodland.

"I guess it's lunch in East Linton, Liksi?" I should've checked earlier to make sure that lunch was definitely on the agenda, somewhere.

"East Linton's about halfway, and it's a reasonable size of village so we should find somewhere." Liksi's laid-back answer confirmed my thoughts. I really should pay more attention to the organisation of *every* walk, not just the English ones.

However, when we arrived at East Linton we found the Crown and Kitchen pub easily, although it did seem to be the *only* place around. We piled in through the entrance, to be met by the alarming sound of breaking glass. A cheerful if sheepish barman was gingerly dusting himself down as he stood next to a small pile of glass shards. He grinned at us with only slight embarrassment as he ushered us in, saying, "It's OK, just watch this bit here – come round this way. Don't let this put you off – it's not a regular event or anything. Just don't think that I've had a different kind of accident, will you?" I couldn't help smiling as he indicated the location of a spillage on his person, while theatrically grabbing an apron to hide the damage.

"Well," I said, "We don't usually have *quite* that effect on people. But as long as you've got other glasses and more beer, there's no problem." Leaving Eilidh at the bar to inspect the choice of beer on offer, Liksi and I sat down and admired the pub. It looked as if it had been recently refurbished – the wooden flooring, crisp fresh paintwork and clean lines were a good contrast to some open brickwork. When the barman came over with Liksi and our drinks, he confirmed this.

"The building's been a pub for decades, but was lying empty when it was bought by the current owners in 2013. They practically gutted it, and it looks totally different now."

"They've made a good job of it." Eilidh was looking round with approval as she sat down. "The style works really well. Oh, *and* you've got some decent beers, which helps."

"When it's not spilt on the floor. Can I get you something to eat?" We each ordered the usual combination of soup and/or sandwiches.

"So, Eilidh, how're your parents coping these days?" asked Liksi. "Sorry, should've asked you earlier but was somewhat distracted by last night's conversation."

"You weren't the only one." Eilidh laughed, but then her expression clouded over and her eyes filled up. She swallowed hard and continued. "They're living on the edge – one bad fall by Mum, or one really daft action on Dad's part, and there'd be a crisis."

"Oh, Eilidh, that's awful." Liksi put down her glass as she looked at Eilidh with concern.

"I know. I'm going up again next weekend for a meeting with someone from social services, so maybe we can sort something out. Or not."

"What about your parents, Liksi?" I asked, after a pause.

"Oh, managing pretty well really, now that Dad doesn't drive. In fact, think he likes being chauffeured about – makes it a lot easier for all of us – *and* the public is safer.

Mum's still as healthy as a horse, touch wood, and though Dad's losing the place, he's happily acquiescent – know what I mean?"

"God, I really feel for you both. I wonder, is it worse to see your parents deteriorating gradually but significantly, or to lose them suddenly, without having time to prepare for being without them?" I thought back to that awful time when I had lost both parents within the space of a few months.

"I know, I shouldn't complain. I've been lucky to have them so long." Eilidh smiled rather sadly, stood up and reached for her jacket. "Thanks for listening – now, time we were off. Come on, guys, we need to get back to Edinburgh by closing time."

I was more concerned about the remaining hours of daylight, and the distance we had to walk. Inevitably, at this time of year, it seemed much colder and duller than it had when we went into the pub – the afternoons were definitely getting shorter. As we started off again I tried to set a brisk pace, but that didn't last long. Liksi was in story-telling mode, which meant that every so often she felt obliged to stand still to emphasise the point she was making – which I'd lost long before – and as for Eilidh, as soon as she discovered the area was famous for birds, she was stopping at every information board, trying to identify the birds wading in the distance. I recognised the curlews, with their distinctive curved beaks poking about in the sand, but I hadn't known what a redshank was before. Mind you, they were well named so I had a vague chance of remembering them in future.

"What d'you think this was for?" asked Liksi, as we walked along a path above a raised embankment. We'd reached the coast, but the tide was out and we were a long way from the sea. The extensive mudflats were perfect for Eilidh's birds, I suppose.

"Looks like they built this up to reclaim some of the land from the estuary." I thought I'd read something about this in the book, but it was in my pack and I didn't want to stop to hold things up. Shortly afterwards we found ourselves in the John Muir Country Park, with the East Links Family Park attraction on the right.

"For one of these, that's quite attractive." Eilidh turned round as we passed an upmarket-looking climbing frame and play area. "I suppose that's a bit snotty of me – never having had kids, I always see these places as blots on the landscape."

"It *is* snotty, Eilidh!" Liksi's smile belied her indignant tone. "This is a great place – used to take the kids here often. Even Pete liked coming – there's so many different things to do. There's a miniature train, golf, climbing walls, animals – in fact, even you'd like it, I'm sure."

"S'pose so. I'd like the animals, certainly – I've often felt like borrowing a child or two so that I could go to one of these children's farms."

"Yes, kids can be useful sometimes! You could've borrowed mine any time you wanted – but we weren't seeing much of each other in those days."

"I know – wasted years, eh? Right, what do we do now, Fiona?"

I was amused that Eilidh asked *me* this, rather than Liksi, the local. We'd come to a point where the official path led away from the expanse of Belhaven Bay, but the town of Dunbar and our end point was directly across the sand. There was a board which indicated that there was a footbridge across the sand, although it was not always available due to the tides. I looked anxiously at my watch, then the fading light and the way ahead.

"I think we should just go straight over the sand. We're running out of daylight, and if we want to finish the walk before dark we need to get a move on. It looks pretty solid ahead, and you can see the bridge over there." Eilidh had that dubious look on her face, but we pressed ahead. The path was an obvious one, though longer than it'd first appeared, and the others were tiring – after all, we must've done about twelve miles by now. However, when we got to the sand there was still a long way to the bridge. It seemed solid enough, with its long metal curve and stone steps at each end, but it was standing in an expanse of seawater and looked rather eerie. We stopped again.

"I don't think this is a good idea." Eilidh zipped her fleece up to her chin and pushed her shoulders up to warm her neck. "I'm sure that's what they call the 'Bridge to Nowhere', for obvious reasons. Look – there's water all round it and if we can see it from here it's probably quite deep."

"There's no-one crossing over the sands or the bridge, and the official path's been quite busy so far." This was Liksi's contribution.

"We could take off our boots and wade across." I was still a bit reluctant to give up.

"No," said Eilidh, firmly. "It's going to be too deep by the time we get there, and if the light fades and we've got to come back, I don't fancy being in the sea in the dark. I'm heading back now."

"OK. It's a much longer route, but if that's what you want." I knew she was right, but it still irked, as I turned round and started to retrace our steps. It seemed even longer on the way back, and we had to go away upstream to cross via another footbridge, then along a walled embankment. By then dusk had really fallen, and not for the first time, I wished we'd got up earlier this morning.

"My God, will you just look at *that*!" Liksi had turned and was looking back the way we'd come.

"Oh, boy. *What* a sky!"

"Stunning." After that, the three of us just gawped. It was one of the most incredible sunsets we'd ever seen. Fiery skeins of crimson, scarlet, ochre and amber streamed across the darkening sky, reflected in the still waters below. The black, winged silhouette of a solitary gull made its way slowly and majestically across the bay in front of the flaming embers of the dying sun. In the distance the smoky outline of Berwick Law stood out from its bloodshot background. There was a surreal quietness, as if all of nature was holding its breath to maintain the almost supernatural spectacle for as long as possible.

"I wouldn't have missed that for anything." Eilidh was practically whispering. "I don't care if it's dark now – that is just, just –"

"Awesome." I agreed wholeheartedly. Eventually we tore ourselves away and started walking again, with countless glances backwards. The path led us onto a road, following the river back down towards the coast.

"What's going on?" I looked at a car seemingly abandoned in the middle of the road. Then another, and another –

"Look." Liksi pointed at one of them. "Everyone's getting out of their cars to take photos." And so they were – and not just with mobiles, there were tripods set up too.

"It's not just us who find it amazing." Eilidh was staring at all the enthusiasts. "This must be a truly exceptional sunset."

The feeling of having been witness to an extremely rare natural phenomenon kept us going as we faced the disappointment of not being able to complete the very end of the Way, which had promised to be the most dramatic part. We'd been looking forward to getting to the coast, which at least we'd managed to see in daylight, but the rocky clifftops round Dunbar would have been a fitting end to the day. Instead, we walked along the edge of Winterfield Golf Course as the rosy glow faded into darkness, and the decision to cut the walk short was unanimous, if regretful. The prospect of our tired legs attempting the wooden steps to get to the clifftop by torchlight was foolhardy, even for me.

"You'll just have to come back another time." Liksi gave the coast a final glance before heading inland. "We can do the steps, the clifftop, and John Muir's Birthplace."

"And browse round the shops in North Berwick." I'd vaguely hoped we would've managed to fit that in too today, but hey ho. Liksi led us up through the side streets to Dunbar's centre to look for a bus. By now we were cold, tired and anxious to get back to Edinburgh as quickly as possible.

Shivering our way on and off buses and trains all the way back to Waverley, we didn't waste time finding a suitable pub to warm up in. Settling into the Mitre on the Royal Mile, by the time we were on our second drink, the warmth of the company, and memories of the day's highlights were all that was needed for a full revival.

Chapter 26 – Ben Lawers and Beinn Ghlas (July 2015) - Eilidh

Ben Lawers, at 3,983 ft, is Scotland's 10th highest Munro. However, as is the case here, it is usually climbed from the carpark signposted uphill from the A827, on the north side of Loch Tay. The carpark itself is around 1,400 ft which gives a good head start. The route to the summit includes the summit of Beinn Ghlas at 3,619 ft, so this is a "two for the price of one" hill walk. The walk down takes the same route.

"Bloody road!" I reined in my impatience to sit it out in the slow-moving line of traffic somewhere north of Dunkeld. "Bloody government, bloody trams, bloody EDINBURGH ..." The trams had finally started running last year, and now – *only* now – the preliminary stage of making the A9 dual carriageway was about to start. Both projects were inextricably linked as far as I was concerned – money for Edinburgh came before saving lives in the Highlands - and as I'd been driving up and down to Inverness almost every second weekend for months now, I felt as if I knew every inch of that treacherous road.

I tried to calm down as I could feel my stress level rising. After all, this was a weekend for me, not my family. In May, after many fraught weeks of hospital visits, meetings with social workers/occupational therapists/financial advisors to name but a few, I'd managed to get Mum and Dad installed in a care home in Inverness. However, I was still going up every other weekend, so that they didn't feel that they'd just been abandoned there.

With a start I remembered that it wasn't only me who'd had a hard time. Also in May, Liksi's Dad had died suddenly, from a heart attack. This would be the first time I'd seen her since then.

Anyway, here I was – after weeks of worry, stress and time off work, I don't think I'd ever looked forward to a walking weekend so much. I'd decided to drive to Pitlochry early so that I'd have a couple of hours to myself before meeting the others – and in spite of the traffic, that's what happened.

Things looked promising from the start – Fiona'd booked our accommodation via an exceptionally good deal. Wellwood House was a lovely Victorian manor house, which proved to be really cosy and comfortable in spite of its imposing appearance and setting. After checking in, I reluctantly turned my back on its charms and headed for the main street, wandering in and out of the shops (SO unlike me!) until it was time to meet the others outside Fisher's Hotel. Fiona'd been up in Edinburgh for a conference and had stayed with Liksi last night, and the pair of them had elected to come to Pitlochry today by bus. Or, strictly speaking, Liksi'd persuaded Fiona to come up by bus.

"Oh, God, that must be the most uncomfortable journey I've had in a long time." Fiona stumbled down the bus steps. She grabbed hold of me and added, "Never, and I mean *never* - let me agree to go on a bus again. Eilidh – good to see you – would you mind getting my bag for me *please*, I need to stretch." My anxious look dissipated as I saw Liksi making pantomime eye and hand movements in the background.

"She's OK, just not used to roughing it," she whispered with a laugh as we collected their bags from the luggage compartment while Fiona did some rather showy stretches before collapsing onto a nearby bench. "The journey was fine."

By the time we got up to Wellwood House, then back down again to the Old Mill Inn for a drink, Fiona was practically her normal self again.

"I think we should eat in Fern Cottage," she announced. "Drink up. They mightn't have a table if we leave it much longer." Mm, I preferred her when she was weak and jittery ... However, we'd a very good meal in Fern Cottage, and over coffee we brought the conversation round to Liksi's Dad.

"Was Pete at the funeral?" Fiona put down her cup. "I just wondered if it'd been awkward for you."

"Oh yes, Pete was there. Playing the full bereaved son-in-law role, as you can imagine. Oh God, that's awful of me – at least he *came*. I should be grateful."

"And Alex?"

"He was there too." There were no rosy blushes on Liksi's face this time. She'd incorporated Alex into her normal no-nonsense life quite quickly, and I was really glad for her. "He kept in the background, but was really supportive."

"I'm glad that's going well." I was also glad not to have to watch Pete making her miserable any more. "I'd a good chat with him at the funeral, by the way – don't know if he said - and he seems a really nice guy. Good choice, Liksi!" She looked at me gratefully. No matter how old you are, it's always important to have the new man in your life approved of by your friends.

Shortly afterwards Fiona decided she'd had enough and wanted her bed, and for once even Liksi was happy to acquiesce. She and I were emotionally exhausted, and Fiona was still suffering from the trauma of the bus journey.

The next day it was blowing a hoolie[9]. I looked doubtfully out of the window at the swiftly moving grey clouds, chasing each other across the pale sky.

"The forecast doesn't indicate much in the way of rain, just very strong winds. Apparently there's likely to be gusts of 45 mph or so – not sure how bad that is." I glanced up from my Metcheck app.

---

[9] gale (Scots)

"No worries, I'm sure we'll be fine." Liksi was always the optimist. To be fair, I was only slightly concerned – I was in the frame of mind this weekend to tackle anything. Bracing fresh air, countryside, exercise – boy, how I needed them. After picking up sandwiches in Pitlochry's Co-op, we set off south in my car. Turning west off the A9, we passed through Grandtully then Aberfeldy to reach the attractive spot of Kenmore at the top of Loch Tay. As I drove, I regaled them with snippets as memories came back to me ...

"Grandtully! That's where I canoe'd all the way down with a left-handed paddle - fuddled brain due to hangover - only fell in at the falls at the end ..."

"Kenmore – friends have a timeshare there and they go for the opening of the fishing ..."

"Spent a couple of weekends in Edinburgh University's outdoor centre somewhere around here – can't remember what it's called, though. Firbush, maybe?"

"Yeah, think so. Eilidh, did you ever do any actual work at University?" Liksi butted into my ramblings.

"Well, not a lot, I have to confess – but I did make a lot of lifelong friends. What's more important? Anyway, I wouldn't have known you two if it hadn't been for our links with Edinburgh Uni."

There was no answer to that, and I concentrated on driving over Kenmore's attractive humped stone bridge, through the small village enlarged by timeshare and holiday lodges, and alongside the expanse of Loch Tay. The wind had whipped up the uninviting brown water to foaming peaks, unlike the calm blue it'd been the last time I remembered seeing it. We followed the loch for about 12 miles before I spotted the turnoff to the Ben Lawers carpark on the right.

"OK, now, I'm not sure if you've done your homework, you two. This is actually a bit of a cheat," I said as I turned off the engine about a mile later.

"Oh?" Fiona halted in her tracks as she was about to open the door.

"Well, Ben Lawers is almost 4,000 ft – it's the 10th highest Munro."

"Good stuff." Yes, I thought Fiona would approve of that bit. "And?"

"This car park's over 1,000 ft, so we're cutting out a good bit of the climb." I watched Fiona's face fall slightly. "However, the good news is that we take in Beinn Ghlas as well, so we're getting two Munros for the price of one." I didn't dare tell her that there were two other well-established hillwalks – the Ben Lawers Five, and the Ben Lawers Seven. Two peaks were quite enough for one day.

"An added bonus." Good old Liksi. A reluctant grunt of assent from Fiona followed as we got out of the car.

"I didn't mention anything earlier in case Fiona decided we should start from ground zero somewhere in the middle of nowhere." I was only partly joking, but Liksi gave me a sympathetic smile as she looked up from lacing her boots.

"I'm not *that* bad. You make me out to be an ogre." Fiona brandished her pole threateningly.

"Methinks thou doth protest too much," I misquoted, ducking to avoid being walloped.

"Macbeth?"

"Hamlet. Who was the one who didn't work hard at University?"

"OK, OK, I give up. Get At Fiona Day. Come on, let's get going in case the wind gets worse." She set off at a cracking pace but I was pleased that I was now more or less keeping pace with Liksi. The views back over Loch Tay would've been striking in decent weather, but the cloud cover was low and there wasn't much to see except the water and immediate surroundings. Ahead, we could make out a peak but I suspected it wasn't a summit – it never is. In fact, the path got steeper and rockier along a long shoulder, before the top came into view and we made the final ascent up Beinn Ghlas where it flattened out a bit. By then the wind had picked up and the mist was swirling, and even I wasn't interested in staying there for long.

We pressed on, descending slightly then following an up and down route to the next summit. I'd known from reading about the path in advance that it didn't have any particular dangers, but it was still a challenge to walk uphill in these conditions. We found ourselves slowing down considerably as it became necessary to bend forwards to stabilise against the wind. Although we could still see where we were going, just, visibility was increasingly poor and it was all we could do to keep from getting blown backwards. Sheer determination kept us moving forward, and I kept well into the side of the mountain. I might have more ballast than the other two, but I was aware of my tendency to clumsiness, and I wasn't taking any chances.

When we finally arrived at the summit, it was more a case of us suddenly realising with relief that we were hugging something that turned out to be the trig point, after following a yell from Fiona which led us there.

"Thank God!" Liksi shouted above the gale. "If these are your 45-mile gusts, I don't like them!"

"Me neither," I called back. "Guess we'll have to leave lunch till later!" It would've been almost impossible to open a rucksack to get any food out, let alone try to eat it. What's more, it was getting cold and my woolly gloves were pretty mist-sodden.

"No summit photies either today," shouted Fiona. "OK – ready to go?"

She turned and headed back down, Liksi and I moving as quickly as we could after her, but suddenly there was a yelp ahead and we realised Fiona'd fallen down the slope, away from the path.

"You OK?" called Liksi, as she started down to get her, but Fiona was up and moving slowly on all fours back up the rocky slope towards the path, gasping but laughing at the same time.

"I got blown over! I'm fine, just a bit stunned. I'll need to hug the rocks till we get down a bit." She moved close to the hillside, and started to walk at a much slower pace, making each step hit home before starting another. For once, I was almost grateful for my more substantial frame. We continued down, pressed into the rock with our arms spread out to keep our balance, looking as if we were all auditioning for Spiderman. Once back on the shoulder between the two peaks though, the wind lessened, and the low cloud was rising, revealing a bright strip hiding a watery sun.

"Lunch?" I said this more in hope than anything else – it seemed a long time since breakfast.

"Probably better to wait till we're further down – it should get warmer by then." That was fairly obvious even to me, but I was sure also that if Fiona wasn't ready for lunch yet, we wouldn't be having it till she was.

A small group of fell runners passed us on their way up, making us feel like amateurs. They waved cheerily as they sped past, picking their way daintily round boulders and heather clumps as if this was a natural, everyday activity. They seemed happy enough, but I did wonder how much of the scenery they could take in, going at that pace.

"Come on, you two, keep going and then we can have lunch." Fiona was off, and hunger drove me to follow her. She didn't seem to be any the worse for her tumble, and by the time we caught up with her she was sitting with her boots off and her feet in a burn – with the sun finally winning its battle to break through the clouds.

"You're mad!" Liksi shuddered as she sat down beside her on a grassy knoll. "It must be freezing!"

"It is." Fiona sighed happily. "Wonderful." She waggled her toes about in the clear flowing water and somehow managed to hug her knees at the same time.

It was incredible how different the weather was now. It wasn't exactly warm, but it was getting there and we were quite sheltered in this part – the birch trees that we'd gone through earlier weren't far away and were probably helping to absorb the wind, which was now little more than a gentle breeze. It was still Scotland in July though – we were wearing fleeces, and I for one had no intention of taking mine off today.

"How's your mum?" I asked Liksi as I poured her a coffee from my flask.

"Amazing, really. They were very close, and it was very sudden. She's been very practical about everything so far, but there've been times when I've gone round and I'm sure she's just been crying. I think about how much I miss him, then I think how awful it must be for her."

"It's hard though, isn't it?" I watched Fiona putting her socks back on. Parents do so much for us over the years, and in the end there's very little we can do to ease their last days.

"You're very pensive, Eilidh." Fiona's voice broke into my thoughts after a while. "Life, death and the universe?"

"Aye, pretty much." I roused myself with difficulty, and looked for a brighter topic.

"Any news of Nathan?" Liksi got there before me. We usually left it to Fiona to talk about him if she wanted to, but she hadn't mentioned him for some time. "Does Jack still see him?"

"He's been trying to for months now, but nothing doing." Fiona looked down at her re-laced boots. "It's so, so hard. Olly doesn't really talk about him now. It must hurt him that Nathan's shown no interest whatsoever in Olly's health. Jack texted to let him know when he got diagnosed, but he's never once phoned or come to see him."

"Oh, Fiona, I'm sorry." I would've given her a hug but she'd got up suddenly and turned to face the direction we were going. Poor Fiona, she tried so hard not to show her emotions, even with us. Liksi and I fell into step behind her as she strode off.

"Don't know how she copes with everything." Liksi watched her as she built up speed. "Did you know she's just doing three days a week now?"

"Heavens, no – that's hard to imagine for Fiona, but it makes sense. Because of Olly?"

"Uh-huh. He's pretty well house-bound now unless she takes him out. He's lost confidence in leaving the house with anyone else."

"That's sad. Such a strain on her." It was a shock to think of Fiona giving up on her career, but in spite of the sometimes hard exterior, she was devoted to Olly. No wonder she was a bit brittle at times though.

Back at the car, it was still only mid-afternoon and I suggested a drive to Killin at the other end of the loch to see the Falls of Dochart. We were all a bit subdued on the way there, but the first glimpse of the Falls banished all gloom and we took countless photos of the tumbling, churning waters. They weren't particularly high, but they made up a spectacularly wide expanse - so much *water*, it was absolutely breath-taking. It wasn't just one stream of water – there were so many different parts of the rapids, where the water raced down or swirled round the rocks, whipping up foaming tops, coming together then dividing again.

"Fabulous place." Thankfully, Fiona seemed to have cast aside family problems for the time being, and was mesmerised by the spectacle before her.

"Guess you didn't canoe down *these* rapids, Eilidh?" Liksi turned to me for confirmation as we stood on the bridge to get a panoramic view. "You couldn't – could you?"

"Well, you *can* – they're not always as impressive as this. Remember we've had a lot of rain recently. These're Grade IV or V rapids, which really means you should be at Expert level to tackle them." I'd only joined the University Canoe Club because the students advertising it at Freshers' Week had made such a good job of it. "I doubt if I attempted these, but I did canoe somewhere near Killin. I remember being told to lean over to avoid getting poked by branches at the side of the river. So, what did Muggins do? Leant *backwards* and promptly fell in!"

I was glad to see Fiona laughing along with Liksi. "Was it difficult to get you out again?" Liksi asked.

"Er, not exactly – when I surfaced, I scraped my bum on the rocks and realised that the water there was only about waist deep. Not my finest hour."

"Didn't you keep it up?" asked Fiona.

"No, I guess life just got in the way. The last time I was in a canoe was when Liksi and I, Tom, Trevor, Catherine and Elanne took a cottage in Wales for a week."

"Oh, boy, do I remember that! Didn't Catherine and Tom ...?"

"Yes, they certainly did! Enough said. Remember the canoeing?"

"Sure do. You were the only one who didn't just go round in circles!"

I grinned, happy to have my comparative 'expertise' acknowledged. "Well, if you've both had enough of the view I'm getting cold again. Fancy a drink?"

The Falls of Dochart Inn looked inviting but wasn't open, so we retraced the route to the other end of the village and had coffee in the Killin Hotel. After a brief stop there, we drove back to Pitlochry and enjoyed the home comforts of

Wellwood House for an hour or two. By the time we went out to eat, we were pretty worn out so opted for nearby Mackays, which advertised hearty pub food and was well positioned in the main street.

"Apparently there's live music on tonight." Fiona sounded a bit doubtful.

"As long as it's not karaoke." I found watching – or listening – to this excruciating. "I wouldn't want to risk hearing you sing along – ow!"

"Nothing wrong with my singing. So what if I'm tone deaf?" Fiona almost looked as if she was proud of this defect, and marched into the pub defiantly.

In fact, the music was great though sadly we didn't catch the name of the group. Folky/ Scottishy – just my thing. We stayed on for a couple of drinks after the meal, just to listen (and sing), but decided to make a quick exit when the volume got turned up and the music got more, well, *young*.

As we walked back up the road to Wellwood House, I reflected on how much good this weekend had done all of us. We'd all had a difficult time recently, and though for Liksi and I life had got somewhat easier, if sadder, Fiona's situation was likely to get worse. I hoped that in some way we, and these weekends, helped to keep her on track.

Chapter 27 – Glentress and Peebles (October 2015) - Liksi

Glentress Forest is situated on the north side of the A72, between Innerleithen and Peebles. Although good for walking and wildlife, it is best known for its network of cycling trails. Facilities include a bike hire and clothing shop, and a café, as well as nearby accommodation of various types. The route undertaken, by bike, was from Glentress, crossing the A72 and cycling along parts of the river Tweed to Traquair House, then Innerleithen, on to Peebles and back to Glentress – approximately 12 miles.

"Thanks, I needed that." Eilidh sipped the coffee I'd just made for her appreciatively, sneaking a glance at Alex as she did so. It was the first time they'd met, and so far so good. Alex'd been intrigued to hear of our walking exploits; unlike Pete he'd never tried to downplay or make fun of them, so I felt it was time for him to be brought into the picture. Eilidh'd just driven over from Glasgow, with the intention of picking me up and driving to Glentress. Alex had elected to stay until we left, which was fine by me, although I'd been ridiculously nervous. I so much wanted them to approve of each other.

Mind you, it wasn't a walk that we were undertaking this time. We'd agreed to try a cycling weekend for a change. Fiona and I cycled regularly – me around the city, and Fiona'd gone on cycling weekends with friends since her kids were small. However, it would be totally new for Eilidh. She was a good sport though, and had agreed to give it a go – with the proviso that we didn't aim for anything too ambitious. The plan was for Fiona and me to use our own bikes, and Eilidh to hire one.

However, the most awful thing had happened since we last met - Nathan had died. Suddenly, and shockingly. A monosyllabic Fiona had phoned me with the awful news.

She hadn't wanted to go into details, and just said that it'd been an overdose. By the end of the short call she was so distressed that I offered to phone Eilidh for her, to save her another miserable conversation. The inquest took three weeks and afterwards there was a completely private funeral. Eilidh and I were wondering what to do when Fiona phoned to say that the best thing we could do for her was to agree to another walk, and soon. Except, could it be a cycling weekend instead as she'd bought a new bike and wanted to try it out. In the midst of all her grief, she could still surprise us.

"I'm rather apprehensive about this trip, I have to say." Eilidh's admission was slightly apologetic.

"They've got good bikes at the centre. I'm sure you'll easily find one that suits." said Alex. We (he and I) had been up there recently, just to double-check the location before settling on it for this trip. However, the Glentress cycle shop and trails had been regular haunts of ours for years, as Joe'd been a keen cyclist at one stage.

"Well, I'm glad you think so – but that's not what I meant." She grinned at Alex, then turned to me. "Fiona. How on earth will she be? How can anyone go through what she has, and with Olly the way he is too, and survive? I mean, I know she'll *survive*, but oh my God – how?"

"Sounds as if she wants to handle the grieving process her own way." I stuffed an extra T-shirt into my rucksack before leaving it at the back door. "No fuss, leave her alone to get over the initial shock, and now she's maybe ready to talk about it."

"Aye, I kind of worked that out too. I did wonder about her having the motivation to buy a new bike, but apparently it's for a holiday she'd booked for the end of this month, ages ago."

"Yeah, she'd mentioned that her old one was getting problematic. Awful though, just awful."

"Anyway, better get going. Don't want to get there too late." I stood up reluctantly. "Alex, would you mind helping me get my bike into Eilidh's car?"

Eilidh had an Audi hatchback; after putting the back seats down we managed to fit my bike in without taking too much of it to bits. I wasn't confident I'd be able to put a dissembled bike together again. Eilidh discreetly slipped into the car, whilst I said goodbye to Alex.

"Take care," he said softly into my ear as I hugged him, nuzzling into his neck to breathe him in. "I've only just found you – I don't want you capsizing on kamikaze downhill trails."

"Don't worry. Will be sticking to completely flat, mainly tarmac routes – Eilidh'd kill us otherwise." I looked up into those glorious brown eyes of his, which were now crinkling at me with mischief. "Anyway, this is too good to give up." With one last squeeze, he let me go and I got into the passenger seat.

"Mmm, good choice, Liksi," was Eilidh's contribution as we set off. "You keep hold of that one. I'm now trying to work out if that look on your face is smug or coy?"

"Probably a bit of both. Happy anyway." Oh, boy, I was – *so* happy.

We kept the conversation light till we got down to the Borders. Eilidh used to live in the area, but wasn't so familiar with the A703 which ran through Penicuik and Leadburn. At least I was able to offer the information that Penicuik had strong links with Robert Louis Stevenson's novels *Kidnapped* and *Catriona*. Once we got to Peebles though, Eilidh was on familiar territory, and we turned left at the junction heading for Innerleithen, till we reached the sign for the Glentress Hotel, which was a boxy-concrete building just off the main road.

"Is this it?" Eilidh seemed a bit disappointed. "Aren't we staying in a pod?"

"No, pods're over there, up that track. We're in the hotel."

"Oh. I must've got that wrong then. Pity. I've always wanted to stay in a pod. But the hotel's fine," she added hastily. "Luxury compared to our usual hostels."

As it happened, it certainly *wasn't* luxury. A basic and rather cold room with three beds, but at least it had an en-suite. We'd not been there long when Fiona knocked on the door and came in.

"Fiona!" Eilidh jumped up to give her a hug, and I did the same. "We thought you might be a while yet."

"Oh, I've been here for a couple of hours, but decided to go for a cycle before checking in. Which bed's mine?" She headed for the one that was pointed out, while Eilidh and I exchanged rather nervous glances. Trust Fiona – even in her current circumstances, she was still one step ahead of everyone else. She looked pale and drawn though, and her smile seemed forced.

"How's the new bike?" I asked as she got her things sorted out. I knew that Eilidh, like me, would let her come round to talking about Nathan in her own good time.

"Pretty good. It's a bit overly responsive sometimes though, so I've to watch. I'm not used to *instant* braking – had to pull on the brakes yards before I actually needed to with the last one."

There wasn't a lot of space so we soon decamped to the bar, which, unlike the room, proved to be warm and friendly. 'Bony's Steakhouse' wasn't the type of eating place I'd normally frequent – in fact I'd probably throw up if someone presented me with an actual steak. However, the vibes were *very* acceptable, from the chatty barman with the glorious silky locks who directed us to a comfy sitting area, to the lovely rich Merlot and the very acceptable burger I ended up with.

"This is almost *too* cosy." A hearty meal, and several glasses of wine later, Eilidh stretched luxuriously. "I could stay here for ever ..."

"None of that, now. Early start tomorrow." As Eilidh and I groaned, Fiona stood up – and promptly sat down again. "Oh." The look of surprise on her face would've been funny, if she hadn't re-focused on our concerned faces and crumpled. "S-sorry, so stupid, did-didn't want to do that – can we go to bed? I – oh, I needed to see you. Shouldn't have had that last glass. Can we ..." but she'd lost it, and she bent down and hid her face in her hands while her shoulders shook. Tears leaked out through her fingers, and Eilidh, who was beside her, put her arms round her and held her tight.

"Coffee," she mouthed to me. There was no need to ask what was wrong. "I'll have the same."

I scuttled up to the bar, and re-assured the barman that our friend was just upset, not ill. He helped me take the coffees to the table, where Fiona was now making distressing mewling sounds.

"Here, get some of this down you." I held out her cup.

"And don't worry – if you can't break down in front of us, then where *could* you do it?" Eilidh released her slightly and fished in her bag for some tissues, thrusting some into Fiona's other hand. "It's OK, just cry – as much as you want to."

And she did. Poor, poor Fiona. In between gulps of coffee, nose-blowing and eventually hiccups, she cried and cried. All we could do was hold her, mop her up and refill her coffee – she wasn't fit to speak coherently. Eventually, when she'd calmed down enough to move, we got her upstairs and helped her into bed. I found a glass, filled it with water and put it on the floor beside her.

"I wonder if she's allowed herself to let go like that at all, or if this's the first time." Eilidh whispered as we got into bed ourselves.

"Don't know, but she had to let that out. Poor thing – hope she'll be OK tomorrow." I turned out the light, and in spite of the hard and slightly knobbly mattress, I was soon out for the count.

The next morning, Fiona was up and dressed before we'd fully wakened up.

"Come on, you two. Up. It's OK – *I'm* OK. Really. Thank you so much for last night. I was dreading telling you all the sordid details, but I wanted to as well."

"You didn't tell us *any* – you were too far gone. But don't worry, we've got all weekend." Eilidh smiled reassuringly at her as she headed for the en-suite.

"Absolutely. Take your time." It was a relief to see her in control again.

We got ourselves ready without further reference to Nathan, though we couldn't resist teasing Fiona – gently - about her hangover. We decided to forego breakfast, and have something up at the bike centre instead. Fiona and I got our bikes out of the cars, and wheeled them up the hill. It was a pleasant short walk through the trees, but the weather was drizzly and not very promising.

"It's quite a place, this." Eilidh was having a good look around as she walked along beside us. There were signposts for trails everywhere, and loads of cyclists passed us, most in full protective gear. Joe'd been keen on the blue routes, but thankfully he hadn't shown any desire to move on to the tougher ones – football had usually won out anyway. We stopped at the bike hire shop.

"I'm in your hands." Eilidh smiled at us. "Just get me something simple that I won't fall off." We did our best and with the help of the shop assistant, selected a sturdy hybrid. She managed a wobbly but triumphant loop round the outside of the shop.

"What's all this for?" she asked as she came to a halt, pointing to part of the bike.

"Gears, Eilidh, gears." Fiona was running her hands over the seat. "There's twenty-one – that's about average."

"What?" Eilidh looked shocked, and not a little alarmed. "Last time I was on a bike I think it had three, and that was quite enough. How on earth do I work them?"

Not an auspicious start, but I think she was hamming it a bit and with a bit of help she soon got the hang of the basics at least. We waited out a shower in the Peel Café, part of the bike centre complex, then set off at last, cycling back down to the main road. We crossed over onto a track which led quickly down to the river, and then continuing along beside it.

"It's good to see the Tweed again." Eilidh shouted out as she rode along. "Almost makes this expedition worthwhile. Just think, we could've *walked* here, without all the kerfuffle of bringing or hiring bikes."

"You're managing fine." It was true. "Stop moaning and enjoy it." The path was flat, with a good surface, and by and large followed the curves of the river. There were several other cyclists about – mostly families – and the inevitable dog walkers, trying to calm their barking charges as we sped past.

The weather soon cleared up and we got Eilidh as far as Traquair House, which involved climbing a small hill where she was able to practise using her gears – with limited success – and then cycling in through the imposing tree-lined driveway. At least, there were trees along the left-hand side, tall mature ones which were beginning to change colour and shed their leaves, leaving a patchy blanket on the ground. We cycled past the ticket kiosk which appeared to be unmanned, and then turned left at the tearoom, which also looked closed - but it was still quite early in the day.

"There's a brewery in here." Eilidh looked at us hopefully as we stopped in the grounds to take stock. "It's nice beer too – strong." Mm, if Eilidh got into a brewery we'd never get her back on the bike again. "They have it in the Traquair Arms in Innerleithen too, though – if you think it's still a bit too early to start drinking?"

"Hmph." Fiona was looking around appreciatively. "Nice place. Didn't I read somewhere that there was a maze, and peacocks?"

"Yeah. I guess we'd need a ticket to see the maze though. Another time?"

Regretfully, we decided that our priority at this time of the day was exercise, so we got back onto the bikes again and found our way out of that lovely place and back onto the road we'd come in on.

It didn't take us long to get to Innerleithen, but at least it was *practically* lunchtime by then, and going into a pub felt a bit more respectable. In fact, respectable was the operative word as we entered the traditional bar with the ubiquitous mock-tartan carpet and rectangular mahogany-stained tables and chairs. There were even three men in plus fours and tweed jackets at the bar, and the accents which drifted across were certainly not from these parts.

"God Almighty, I didn't think people still dressed like that." I kept my voice low as we took our seats. "Do they not realise how *daft* they look?"

"Now, now, it takes all sorts," said Eilidh. "And don't be decrying their dress sense – Alan's got a bonnet like that. Sorry, a *'bunnet'*. He thinks it's the height of fashion." She made a face as Fiona started to giggle.

"Alan's a fine one to speak, laughing at my jim-jams that time." I was relieved to see Fiona seemed to be enjoying herself, though she'd been much quieter than usual. She opted for a mineral water when I went up to the bar. Eilidh was delighted to get her Traquair ale, and I played safe with a lager shandy.

"Right, I want to tell you what happened." Fiona put her glass down suddenly. "I just couldn't face it earlier, and I've hardly discussed it with anyone outside the family – or what's left of it. No, it's OK, Eilidh – I want to tell you. I need to." She took a sip of water, as Eilidh and I looked at each other apprehensively.

"To get the worst out first – Nathan's body was found by a dog being walked down by the canal. There was so much rubbish around – bits of cardboard, tarpaulin etc – that no-one had noticed. The area's notorious for shooting-up. And yip, it was an overdose, but he was in such a frail state that he – he just - well anyway, that's what happened."

I closed my eyes to take this in. What could possibly be more awful than your child ending his days like this? Ending his life before you *at all*, but this ...

"It took a day or so before the police were able to identify him – they tried the methadone clinics, but he hadn't been attending regularly and it was hard for staff to be sure, as they see so many. Anyway, they worked it out eventually. Apparently when he enrolled originally, Nathan had given Jack as his next of kin, so poor Jack got the call before we did." She hid her face in her hands.

"Oh, Fiona, don't! You *can't* blame yourself –" Eilidh's eyes were brimming as she gently brushed Fiona's arm.

"But I *do*! We both do – we were more involved in our careers than our children's welfare. Otherwise how could it ever have *started*, let alone ..."

"But look at Jack - he's a great kid – and *he*'s never blamed you for Nathan's addiction, has he?" I had a soft spot for Jack – he was between Joe and Julie age-wise, and had got on well with both of them on the few occasions they'd met.

"Oh, I don't know, we must've just not been there when he needed us. Maybe because he was the oldest child, and then when Jack arrived we focused on him, and Nathan felt rejected -"

"But you don't *know* this, do you?" Eilidh broke in gently. "Nathan always seemed to want to go his own way, even when he was a child."

"Yes, but *why*? Why did he reject us? Why?" The look she gave us was tormented, but we couldn't offer anything other than platitudes. Why do any children turn out the way they do? Why can two children in one family turn out so differently?

"What about his girlfriend?" asked Eilidh. "Was she still in the picture?"

"I don't think so, but we don't know. We'll never know now. The funeral was just so, so awful – only the three of us, with the minimum number of officials. And my boy in that box ... can I have a whisky after all please?"

After knocking back the whisky I brought back for her, she told us the rest of the sorry story – she and Olly identifying Nathan's body together, the painful process of informing relatives and barring them from the funeral, holing herself up in the room that had once been his and crying until there were no tears left. Days off work, then going back to work against advice, but as she said, it was the only way she could cope – though it left Olly on his own with his grief, and no work to occupy his thoughts.

It was a sobering conversation, but Fiona – typically – seemed to draw herself together suddenly and announce that we'd better get on with the cycling. So we did. We headed back towards Peebles, with Eilidh leading the way and shouting out that this cycling thing was easy – what had she been worried about? I didn't like to put her off by reminding her that our route today was pretty flat, and therefore a bit artificial. When we got to Peebles we decided it'd be daft not to at least have a daunder round the town, so we tied the bikes up on the purpose-built bars and indulged in a bit of window-shopping. The main street seemed designed with tourists in mind, with an abundance of gift shops selling very twee crafty things. There was a wonderful shoe shop though which I just couldn't resist. There's something about the smell of leather, and oh, those *boots* …

Fiona seemed happy enough browsing inside too, but Eilidh was hilarious, as usual. She walked round quickly, examined a pair of boots without comment, and then hovered around watching us, fidgeting and generally looking uncomfortable.

"Enjoying yourself, Eilidh?" I couldn't resist teasing her.

"Ha. Just humouring you two. Why on earth would anyone in their right mind want to wander round a shop if they'd no intention of buying anything?"

"But I can *wish* – aren't these lovely?" Wistfully, I stroked the embroidered fabric which made up the shin part of a pair of boots.

"They're OK, I guess. Why don't you try them on if you like them so much?"

"Have you seen the price tag? They're almost £200 – and can you imagine walking about in *these* in our weather? Anyway, they'll never have them in my size."

"I rest my case." She shook her head in mock despair.

"OK, I know the signs, Eilidh's hungry." Fiona joined the conversation.

"No, I'm not – but now you mention it, there're some rather nice coffee shops in Peebles – come on." She expertly managed to steer us away from leather goods and along the main street till we found a cosy little cafe set back from the road, with an eye-watering display of what looked like home baking inside.

"Mm, I could get used to the idea of nice ambling cycle rides, with all the stops for sustenance." Eilidh looked up from buttering her scone. "Pity I couldn't pretend to be a novice at walking too, with the same result."

"Don't even think about it." Fiona passed me over half of the carrot cake we'd agreed to share. "We need a challenging walk next time – or cycle?"

"Walk. Don't get me wrong, I'm enjoying this wee escapade – but I would still rather walk."

"Would you *go* on another cycling weekend?" I asked with interest.

"Mm-hmm, in the right circumstances I s'pose – but I much prefer walking. Same amount of exercise maybe, but you can't appreciate the scenery, or the – the *outdoors* as much when you're not walking *in* it. If you know what I mean."

"I do. It's called 'bias'." Fiona's response was somewhat hampered by a mouthful of cake, but it was good to see her attempting some humour.

"Oh, that was good - I need energy for the rest of the trip." Eilidh was conveniently ignoring the fact that we were less than 10 minutes away from our hotel. "Hadn't we better get going? It looks as if it might bucket any minute."

The sky had darkened, and had a foreboding yellowish tint, so we paid up and decided to cycle back to the hotel along the main road, ie the quickest route, which followed the river. Just as we were putting the bikes in the hotel's shed, the first heavy drops started falling.

We'd booked dinner in the Tontine Hotel for later on, so had time on our hands which was quite welcome. Fiona went off to the lounge to check her emails, Eilidh lay down on her bed with a book, and I found a chair in the corridor overlooking the road, and picked up the newspaper beside it. A bit of 'time out' was essential occasionally. I wondered idly what Alex was doing just now. I was SO looking forward to seeing him again tomorrow – what a change from before, when going back to Pete brought me home with such jarring reality.

The deluge ran its course, and after a while we walked back into Peebles along the main road. The Tontine proved to be a warm, comfortable old hotel in the middle of the main street. The food was more refined than I'd expected, ie not at all 'pub grub' – we were certainly eating well on this trip. We tried to keep the conversation general, but near the end of the meal Nathan's name came up again – it was difficult to avoid the elephant in the room – but Fiona was more in control now.

"I just want to say, that I have never needed you so much as I did this weekend." She looked at us both in turn, eyes conveying her feelings as much as her words did. "You were wonderful – I feel I've unlocked something that I couldn't release earlier. I'm sorry for making it heavy weather for you though."

I felt a lump in my throat as we tried to re-assure her. "You two saw me through all the horrible times with Pete too." They'd been great – even if I'd not always wanted to hear what they were trying to tell me. "Not that he's in the same category."

"Still. So much appreciated. Right – it's raining again – we're going to get a taxi and I'm paying for it." Ignoring our protests, she got up and went to the Reception desk to arrange it.

In the taxi, Eilidh launched into a discussion with the driver about the newly re-opened Borders railway – but wasn't quite prepared for the reaction.

"Better for Peebles? *Better?!* Doesn't go anywhere near Peebles – been left out of it completely, as usual! All the money goes to Gala – we don't exist. It's rubbish anyway – not enough carriages, overcrowded, cancellations – they're welcome to it ..."

As we got out with some relief, after learning more about Borders rivalries than trains, I reflected that it had been one of our more interesting – albeit heartbreakingly sad - trips.

Chapter 28 – John Muir Way 2 (January 2016) - Fiona

This is a 9-mile stretch of the John Muir Way, starting in the town of North Berwick and heading west alongside the golf links. It moves inland, along pavement then fields, past the Yellow Craigs plantation, through the villages of Dirleton and Gullane then on to Aberlady. It is a very flat walk, with a sizeable portion of the walk along the busy A198.

TransPennine's First Class alcoholic enticements had been very acceptable, but the grey, featureless expanse of the Solway Firth mudflats did nothing further to lift my spirits. Grey, grey, grey – I stared out blankly, the motion of the train lulling my mind into shut-down mode. Even then, I couldn't shut it *all* out – as evidenced by the now-familiar hard knot in my chest, the prickling behind my eyes, the lurking pain at the back of my head. I couldn't help feeling that somehow it was all my fault. Maybe if I'd focused more on Olly and the kids rather than my career, maybe if I hadn't moved to London, maybe if I'd just been –

Maybe. What a word that is, to beat yourself up with. What if ...? If only ...

Next thing I knew, it was dark and the train was pulling into Waverley Station. The gin had done its work after all and I must've dropped off. Blearily, I got my things together and stumbled out onto the platform, and made my way out of the station to Market Street, then up Fleshmarket Close.

The rush of warmth and humanity that emanated as I pulled open the door of the Halfway House gave me a comforting sense of déjà vu – it was less than a year since we'd met here. It wasn't hard to spot Eilidh and Liksi, cheerfully chattering in a corner, with the usual pint and glass of red wine in front of them. What *was* different this time was that Alex was there – my God, he was quite something. Good for Liksi.

"Hi there, *great* to see you – you too, Alex. No, no, I'll get one myself – you sit." I threw my bag down and ordered a mineral water at the bar before joining them.

"Been on the First Class gins again?" Liksi pointed to my glass.

"Not at – well *yes*, actually. Don't worry though, this is just a temporary pause to recuperate from the journey – and maybe from the gins too. Travelling makes me thirsty." As I took a long gulp, I thought I'd need to go easy on the alcohol in case it brought on the tears again – although they'd probably all gone by now and I'd dried up, in more ways than one. Anyway.

"I was just reminding Liksi that the last time we were here together was the first we heard of Alex." Eilidh was eyeing Alex with amusement.

"Indeed; little did I know what I was in for then." He grinned cheekily at Liksi and squeezed her hand, before turning back to us and holding up his hands. "It's OK, I know my place. I've been allowed to join you tonight on the condition I make breakfast tomorrow and don't put in any further appearances till after you've gone. It's a hard life."

"Er, Alex – remember what's happening tomorrow night?" Liksi looked worried. "Haven't told them yet." This was intriguing.

"Yes, sure. I have a BIG confession to make. Really, really sorry, but friends of mine invited us to dinner tomorrow, and I said yes before I remembered you two would be here. Liksi hasn't really forgiven me yet."

"Would you mind *very* much looking after yourselves tomorrow night?" Poor Liksi looked quite put out.

"Er, no, not at all." Eilidh and I exchanged part-amused, part-puzzled looks. "This man of yours has to come first."

"Don't say that, makes me feel worse. Stop sniggering! Anyway, you can eat in the pub across the road or get a takeaway, and just make yourselves at home."

"No worries. Anyway, breakfast sounds good, Alex – that means Liksi'll get her long lie." By the look on Liksi's face, that was *exactly* what she was planning.

"Anyway, how're *you* doing, Fiona?" Eilidh looked at me anxiously. She was a good soul.

"Oh, hanging in there. Trying to get my head back into work – I'm OK when I'm there, mainly because I get out and about to other organisations. It's good to be with people who don't know anything about me." I was anxious to get off the topic, as I didn't want to dampen the otherwise happy Friday night mood. "How's work with *you* these days?"

"Och, you know. Same old, same old, I s'pose. Another restructure."

"Not again! Will it affect you?" Eilidh's college seemed to have a restructure every few years.

"Probably – by making life more difficult, I should think. They always do. However, my position isn't going to change as such – there's no way I'm going for any promotions again." She smiled. "Only two years to go, and I don't want to increase the stress levels. Not good for someone my age – you two should remember that – being *older* than me." The smile morphed into a smug grin.

"Still don't envy you, though." Liksi shuddered. "Can't imagine being retired – don't know what I'd do instead."

"Will you keep going till you get your state pension?" I directed this at Liksi, but from the look on Eilidh's face, this prospect was not one she was prepared to countenance.

"Probably. Unless the job changes significantly." Liksi looked resigned to this, but I knew she enjoyed work.

"I know, I feel a bit guilty at work." Eilidh's smile faltered slightly. "I'm lucky enough to be able to afford it, but I've got lots of colleagues who can't. At least you don't want to stop working yet, so it's not quite so bad." She turned to me. "Fiona, what about you?"

"Oh, I don't know. Haven't thought about it yet. Depends on Olly, I suppose." I really hadn't thought that far ahead – life was too complicated as it was.

"Don't worry, I'll still be working to keep you public sector workers in funds," said Alex – then added quickly, as he saw Eilidh's face, "Willingly. Well, if not willingly exactly –"

"Mm." Liksi frowned at him. "Have you any idea how long it's taken me to get to this level of salary, how many extra hours I've worked, without ANY perks –" I was happy to let them bicker away gently. Maybe Alex wasn't perfect after all ...

When we came downstairs the next morning to an exquisite breakfast of smoked salmon and scrambled eggs, fresh coffee and croissants, I forgave him any dodgy political leanings. He and Liksi were all over each other, so all was well. As for me, my mood was already lighter.

"So, it's North Berwick to Aberlady today, I believe." Alex held out his hand to refill my mug.

"Yes, another opportunity for Alan to mock." Eilidh proffered hers too. "Thanks, Alex."

"Why mock?" he asked.

"Because we always do long-distance walks in non-consistent directions. Last time it was North Berwick to Dunbar, this time we're starting in North Berwick again but walking in the other direction."

"OK – er, why?"

"Transport – makes it quicker to get back to Edinburgh at the end of the walk. *Does* make sense, honestly." It should be a pretty easy day – flat, coastal, do-able even if the weather did turn. It was January, after all. Too easy really, but I guess I'd just lost my appetite for dictating what we did recently. It didn't matter any more, as long as I got away.

North Berwick's a pretty little place, full of cosy tearooms and independent shops. I remember thinking last year that it'd be nice to spend some time browsing around, but that was not going to happen this time either. Maybe when I did retire, I could come back to Scotland and live somewhere like this ... Reluctantly ignoring the shops, we headed down to where the John Muir Way met the town. Turning left, we started off along by the golf course, and past the large and imposing red sandstone Macdonald Marine Hotel.

"Good to get some sea air again." I sniffed the slightly tangy air appreciatively.

"Enjoy it while it lasts." Liksi was looking regretfully in the direction of the coast. "'Fraid we'll be heading inland after a bit."

"Thought the east coast part of the trail was *all* coastal?" I *had* taken my eye off the ball.

"Not exactly, unfortunately. We *could* go round the coast." Liksi looked doubtful. "It would take much longer and the path wouldn't be so good."

"It's OK, we'll be going through Dirleton and there's a good place for lunch there." Typical Eilidh on two fronts – food, but sticking to the official trail too. She's a great follower of rules, Eilidh.

"Look – there's the Bass Rock." Eilidh pointed it out, although you could hardly miss the great hulked dome. There were other smaller islands dotted about and, in the distance, the murky outline of the Fife coast. "Gannets, lighthouse, and ruins. I think there was a prison there once."

"Have you been there?" I asked.

"No – I'd like to though. There's *so* many of these wee islands I'd like to go to. They've all got histories, and some are fascinating."

"Didn't think history was your strong point?" Liksi smiled at her.

"Oh, how cutting – but accurate, I must admit. The Bass Rock features in Stevenson's *Catriona*. The hero gets imprisoned there. I can do *that* kind of history. Oh, and it was his – Stevenson's – cousin who designed the lighthouse there. Later."

Eilidh kept us up to date on birds and lighthouses as other islands, including Fidra (linked to Treasure Island apparently), came into view. After this the Way turned its back on the coast, going due south. The scenery was unremarkable, just grass paths and tracks, and I was relieved when we got to Dirleton, a pretty little place with a few eateries to choose from. The Castle looked worth a visit on another occasion, with its butter-coloured stone walls and crumbling towers.

We settled on the Castle Inn instead, and were just in time to see Jamie Murray and his partner on the big screen as they won the Australian Open doubles before we ordered our lunch.

"He seems to change partners a lot – I can't keep up." Like so many people, I didn't follow doubles matches as much as singles.

"Huh. Pity that doesn't apply to politics too." Eilidh's change of subject was abrupt, but she was probably the most political one of the three of us. "If the Liberals had chosen a *different* partner, maybe the whole *country* wouldn't be stagnating."

"Mm." Liksi obviously didn't agree, though I was never quite sure of her politics – maybe Liberal, but sometimes Tory. Funny, although we discussed politics, we tended not to ask direct questions. I wondered idly if Alex'd have any effect on her thinking.

"It's all a bit grim just now." Eilidh was determined to make her point. "In fact – we're doomed, DOOMED!" We'd heard Eilidh's impersonation of Private Fraser from Dad's Army many times before, but it never failed to strike a chord with us and before long we were laughing away any trace of politics. We were good at this – in all our meetings we'd managed never to get so bogged down in our preferences that we upset anyone. As far as I could tell, anyway.

Looking out the window, going back out wasn't an exciting prospect. The grey sky had thickened and lowered, and from the look of the occasional huddled person who scurried past, the wind seemed to be getting up. We'd be lucky if we got to Edinburgh without rain. However, we gathered up our belongings and set out again.

Somehow, though there was supposed to be a small dogleg part of the onward trail leading from the village centre, we must've missed it and found ourselves on the main road before we knew it.

"Might as well stay on the road now." Liksi was struggling to hold the map open in the wind. "If we look for the exact trail we'll be going back on ourselves. We take the road all the way to Gullane anyway."

"What, on the official trail?" I didn't like the sound of this. "How far is it? Here, let me see - there must be another way." I held out my hand for a corner of the map and had a look.

"Two and a half miles."

"Look – if we go back up to the village centre, then take a left, it takes us through the Archerfield Estate. That cuts off a bit of the road. Might as well – it's the official trail, and from the look of this there's a lot more tarmac to come anyway." I folded up the map and gave it back to Liksi, and set off before anyone objected.

The estate bit was pleasant enough, if unexciting. At least it was softer underfoot than the road, and the trees shielded us slightly from the worst of the wind. It was getting to that dank stage – not exactly cold, but the sort of saturated damp feeling that penetrated your bones, and although it wasn't all that late in the afternoon, I just wanted to get home now. I mean, back to Edinburgh. All too soon the trail led back onto the road. This most definitely wasn't a walk I'd want to repeat – I hated walking on tarmac. However, we'd set ourselves the task of doing the John Muir Way in bits and pieces when, during the winter months, a less demanding walk within easy reach of Edinburgh or Glasgow was sensible, so there wasn't much we could do about it.

The road wasn't too busy, but there was a steady flow of traffic, and I kept thinking about what we might be breathing in. Ugh.

"Just like being back in Manchester," I said, but it fell on deaf ears as by then we were in single file on the pavement and it was difficult to hear each other over the wind.

"Look – there's Greywalls." Liksi had stopped to point out a sign on the right.

"What's Greywalls?" I asked. Everything was grey today.

"The type of place we're *not* likely to stay in on these weekends. A very posh hotel frequented by very rich golfers."

"Isn't Muirfield Golf Club around here somewhere too?" asked Eilidh. "Have they let women in yet?"

"Don't be daft." The scorn in Liksi's voice would cut through butter. "Women? Those lesser beings? Not a chance. It's probably the most exclusive golf course around here, and thinks it can only remain so if women members are barred. Oh, and Greywalls looks right onto it."

"So we wouldn't want to stay there anyway, then." Eilidh shuddered slightly. "Much better off Chez Liksi."

"Absolutely. Anyway, it was designed by Lutyens but we've been in his *castle*, so no need to visit a mere hotel to admire his talents." We looked at Liksi blankly, so she continued, "Lindisfarne – remember?"

Oh dear, I think we were all getting to the age where trivia went in one ear and out the other. We continued the trudge into Gullane village, which had a very golf-related feel about it too, being right next to the golf course and full of large and expensive-looking properties.

"Gullane Sands are nice enough – if we could get near enough to see them." Eilidh was looking between the properties towards the coast. "I went there on a field trip once."

"Field trip? What for?" Eilidh had done an Arts degree, so I couldn't see what subject would have merited a field trip.

"Principles of Biology." She looked slightly sheepish. "A science subject for non-science students. Good fun – fruit flies and genetics, and field trips. And some hunky Arts students."

"Eilidh, for goodness sake!" Liksi was laughing. "Wouldn't have thought you'd have needed a science subject, as you did French. Wasn't it science *or* a language you had to do?"

"Aye. But my father had made me do Biology and Chemistry at O Grade to 'keep my options open', so I thought Principles of Biology might be easy as I had *some* background in the subject. OK, OK, you can stop laughing now – anyway Liksi, didn't you say you did Canadian Studies at some point? How did that fit into a degree in computing?"

The banter continued until we turned off the road – at last – onto Luffness Links. Although that sounded like a golf course, it seemed to be just a path through fields and woodland. We passed a sign for Saltcoats Castle – my goodness, they liked their castles in this part of the world – and stopped to have a look at the crumbling ruins. One tall end wall was still standing, with a large arch and several small windows. Clumps of grass were growing at the top, maybe where the roof would once have been. The other walls were much smaller, of varying heights, with trees and rosebay willow herb hiding much of the stonework.

"Anyone have any idea why it's called Saltcoats when Saltcoats is in Ayrshire?" asked Eilidh.

Liksi fished the guidebook out of her pack and leafed through it. "Says here it's built on a salt marsh – although I don't know where the "coat" bit comes in. For either place. Apparently once it fell into disrepair its stones were used to build local cottages."

"It looks as if bits of it are pretty shoogly now." Eilidh frowned as she looked at it. "Still plenty of stone left, though."

"That's because some of the stones were so firmly cemented together that they couldn't break them easily. Just as well, eh – or there'd be no castle at all to brighten up this bit of the walk." Liksi made a wry face as she closed the book and put it back in her pack, just in time to miss the droplets of rain which had started to appear. We carried on, through hedgerows which would normally have had Eilidh peering into for plants or birds, but they were bare at this time of year. It wasn't long before the path reached the road, and we had to start walking along it - again.

"No choice, I'm afraid." Liksi hoisted her pack more firmly onto her shoulders. "Just have to get on with it."

What a miserable last section. The hard surface and traffic fumes were bad enough, and it was almost impossible to talk through the combination of wind and car noise, and not being able to walk three astride. When the droplets morphed into full rain and then hail, somehow it felt inevitable. We trudged along with hoods up and heads down to protect our faces, one foot after the other, for a very, very long mile and a half or so. I did wonder about the thinking behind my decision to have another walk – *this* walk - at this time of year to cheer myself up ...

At last we found ourselves at the end of today's route, in the small town of Aberlady. It was such a shame that the walk hadn't followed the coast more, especially as there was a nature reserve alongside Aberlady Bay, and an ornithological centre there. Mind you, we might have lost

Eilidh there for a while ... Instead, we took refuge in the Old Aberlady Inn. Once we'd peeled off dripping jackets, hats and gloves, and settled down with Aberlady Ale and merlot, things didn't seem so bad after all. We had another drink to fortify ourselves for the bus back to Edinburgh, and headed home to Liksi's. She quickly got herself ready, and by the time Alex came to collect her she looked stunning in a short green dress and kitten heels. They left to go to their friends' house, with many more unnecessary apologies. Eilidh and I were quite happy to spend the evening eating, drinking whisky (apparently Pete had forgotten to take his whisky with him when he left, and neither Liksi nor Alex were whisky drinkers), and watching TV – when we weren't talking.

"So, Fiona." Eilidh helped herself to another champagne truffle which Liksi'd insisted we tried – probably to salve her conscience. Oh dear, I knew what was coming ...

"How *are* you? Really."

"I am – existing," I said slowly. "I could say that there's a big gap in my life where Nathan was, but that gap's been there for years. On good days, I tell myself he was living an increasingly unhappy and desperate life and that he's now at peace. On bad days, I shut myself in our bedroom, hide under the duvet and howl."

"So hard. Are you and Olly able to talk about it?"

"Thankfully, yes. More than we used to when he was alive actually, as we'd just end up with one of us getting enraged about the whole thing, which was pointless. Olly's great, actually – he calms me down and we just try to talk things through."

"Mm. And Jack?"

"Jack's – just – Jack. He's been our source of stability all the way through, and when he comes to the house he'll often recount a story about what they got up to in childhood. It reminds us that we did have good times with them both once. He kind of keeps Nathan alive, somehow, if that doesn't sound ridiculous. But he misses him too – he saw slightly more of him than we did in recent years."

"He's a darling. I'm so glad you have him." She passed over the truffles. "What d'you say to another whisky with one of these?"

Chapter 29 – Kinder Scout (May 2016) - Eilidh

This is a circular hill walk of about 9 miles, leading up to Kinder Scout, the highest point of the Peak District at 2,077 ft. Starting in the village of Hayfield, and going through Bowden Bridge car park, the route follows the River Kinder until a path turns off to the left. This leads up through William Clough, joins the Pennine Way as it crosses the Kinder plateau to Edale Cross, comes down by Oaken Clough then back into Bowden Bridge and Hayfield.

As the train rattled its way towards Manchester, I wondered yet again what we were going to find when we got there. It'd been 15 years since Liksi and I'd stayed with Fiona. Olly'd been hale and hearty back then, and always seemed to be on his way to or from the gym when Fiona and I'd spoken on the phone. Nathan had only been about ten, and he'd been staying with a friend or something so we hadn't seen him that time. However, I'd met both boys since on the odd occasion Fiona would bring them to Glasgow en route to their Aberdeen relatives. Even as a child I hadn't taken to him – he'd been surly and hadn't responded well to my efforts to communicate – unlike Jack, who'd been a delight.

Liksi'd arrived about an hour ago, and had texted to say she'd meet me on the platform. And there she was, hair so pale gold it was almost white, and glowing with health as always. In fact, as she got closer I thought that there was more to this glow than usual - she just looked really, really happy. It made me realise how utterly miserable she must've been with Pete at times, although she'd hidden it well.

"Hi there – can you bring yourself to set foot in a tram?" Liksi held out her hand for one of my bags. "Can get one to Brooklands and Fiona'll pick us up."

"Aye, sure – trams're fine as long as they're not in Edinburgh." I settled my kit bag on my shoulder and followed her to the escalator. The tram stop was just outside the station.

Our tram arrived quickly, and we settled down to enjoy the trip through Manchester. Shoppers were out in force as we travelled through the centre and on to Chinatown, passing the Old Trafford Cricket Ground as we headed towards Sale, and finally embarked at Brooklands. I always liked to get away – it didn't matter if it was only to a different airport, train station, or town – I just enjoyed soaking up the atmosphere and the *freedom* of being away from home and in a different location. It seemed strange – but satisfying - to be back where all this had started back in 2001.

"Hi guys, how're you doing?" Fiona was waiting for us at the tram stop, and we shoved our bags into her boot. "I'm just going to take the car home. We can leave your things in the boot and go for a walk along the canal first to get the most out of the rest of the afternoon. OK?" I admired Fiona's unilateral decision-making; I was probably the very opposite – too concerned with what people might or might not want to do. I wryly reflected on Alan's regularly repeated question, 'D'you want it in writing? I've *told* you it's OK.' Oh well, probably just as well we're all different.

Fiona lived in a rather attractive cul-de-sac, which to me was typically urban English. The house was semi-detached, with the ubiquitous red brick forming the bottom half, and white-painted brick and harl on the top half. Or did they call that 'roughcast' down here? Even though I'd lived in London for six years, England still seemed like a foreign country to me sometimes, with many attractions. The entrance arch encompassed both her doorway and her neighbour's, although a huge sprawling hydrangea with dull pink flowers hid most of it from street view.

We left the car there and set off on foot for the canal, about five minutes' walk away. I loved urban canal walks – there was always so much *life* going on, in the water and alongside. Children scampered along or wobbled precariously on scooters, elderly couples ambled along for their daily stroll, dogs and their owners walked, ran or played with varying degrees of harmony. Families of ducks paddled along serenely, with mothers turning to check that their fluffy charges were still in line. A pair of swans sailed snootily past, occasionally plunging their long necks underwater, leaving their triangular butts sticking up like wobbly icebergs.

"You're so lucky with all this right beside you, Fiona." I swerved to avoid a galloping mongrel chasing a grubby tennis ball. "It's so *vibrant*."

"You think so?" She turned round with a smile. "I suppose you're right, but I get frustrated with all the *people*. It's not too bad just now, but it can get so busy that there's no pleasure in it. When you get the cyclists as well, it's mayhem."

"Is Olly able to walk here?" It was so sad to think of Olly stuck in the house most of the time, especially when Fiona was working.

"Yip, sometimes. If I can park the car near enough, we can go for a short walk together as long as I hold on to him. He has a stick, but he likes to have me on the other side."

"Poor guy, must be hard." Liksi's compassionate tone echoed my thoughts.

"It's usually OK; most people are considerate and give us a wide berth, but kids and youngsters only look out for themselves, and can knock him off balance. I have to stop myself giving them an absolute mouthful."

"I mean hard to be so isolated most of the time. Do his friends visit much?"

"Well, *my* friends do, and some of them bring husbands who know Olly. There's only a couple of his own friends who come, but they don't live all that near. You never think, do you, when you're fit and active, with a great social life, how much your life can change one day?"

Indeed. I used to envy Fiona so much – good job and big salary, lots of business travel, nice house, oozing with confidence – but what was all that when her family life was in bits? I shuddered at the thought of anything like Parkinsons happening to Alan. Fiona was actually coping remarkably well, and although she seemed quite open with us, there must be an awful lot she kept to herself too.

We had a drink in the King's Ransom, before heading back to Fiona's, where we followed her straight into the kitchen.

"Can one of you give me a hand with the chopping for the spag bol? Help yourselves to the wine on the table."

"I'll do the chopping – that's the bit I *can* do. OK, where do I start?" Liksi was doing her best to look as if being in a kitchen came naturally to her.

"I'll take a glass through to Olly, then, shall I?" I filled three glasses, and was about to fill a fourth.

"No thanks, he doesn't drink at all now." Fiona was selecting a knife from the block. "It affects his medication."

"Oh. Of course. OK, I'll go through and chat to him anyway." I felt slightly chastened not to have realised this as I wandered through to the lounge, slightly dreading what I'd find.

With some justification. The handsome, confident and very fit individual I remembered had practically disappeared. In his place, poured into a reclining chair, was a thin, worn-looking man with receding grey hair. He was wearing a worn brown jumper with a couple of stains down the front, and had just been wiping his eyes with a handkerchief and a very shaky hand. A handkerchief - Olly! Round his wrist was one of those alarm things that you could press if you fell. Beside him was a small table topped with a glass, tablets, tissues, reading glasses and a couple of books, and on the other side was a zimmer with a basket thing on top.

He turned to look at me, and as his eyes focused on what was probably a lesser version of me than he remembered, they cleared slowly and then he smiled. It was as if the invalid layer had been briefly removed, showing the real, or rather original, Olly beneath.

"Elaine, isn't it? Or no - something Gaelic –?" His speech was very hesitant, but his smile was real, if weak.

"It's Eilidh – the Highland one," I said brightly. "It's good to see you again." Oh God, was that true? Was it completely honest to say that *seeing* him like this was good?

"Yes. Eilidh. Good - for Fiona - to have you here."

"So – so how have you been? Are you keeping well just now?" Oh, God, this was difficult – was that a stupid thing to ask?

"Been better. Damn disease. Could be worse. Not in wheelchair - yet. Still got marbles – but they can't - always find each other." Much to my relief, he laughed at this and I began to relax a bit.

"Right side doesn't - behave." He stretched out this arm slowly, and raised it with difficulty, his face straining with concentration as he tried to control the shaking. "There! Major achievement."

"Well done."

Just at that minute Fiona came into the room. "Eilidh, the dinner's ready to be taken through to the dining room. I'll help Olly through, but just sit down at the table yourselves."

With some relief, I smiled at Olly and left him to go through to the kitchen, where I warned Liksi to prepare for a shock. When Olly shuffled into the room with his zimmer, her face momentarily registered her distress, then she started to burble away about how long it was since she'd seen him, did he remember first meeting her in London, how good it was to be back in Manchester again ...

Olly smiled weakly as he sat down. "Liksi. How could I forget that name?" The meal and the rest of the evening passed pleasantly, Olly contributing to the conversation where he could, although he obviously found speech difficult. When it came to going to bed, he was able to do most things by himself – they had converted the old downstairs study into a bedroom for him. It was just so sad to watch this once proud and smart man struggling with the most basic of moves. I felt the sadness of the house even more when we all went to bed – I'd been given Nathan's old room.

Having gone to bed in sombre mode, it was pleasantly disorientating to wake up with the light streaming in from the window, and a regular rumbling noise and motion coming from somewhere near my knees. I thought for a minute it might've been one of those massage things you can get for beds, and that I must've pressed a button somewhere by mistake. Flailing around to find it, the rumbling was replaced by a yowl as my hand fell on a warm fluffy body and a pair of green eyes gazed at me reproachfully. Goodness, this couldn't be Alfie or Splurge, surely, after all these years? No, it was a much younger cat – who didn't take much reassuring before nodding off again to resume his therapeutic purring.

The lighter mood continued as we headed to the start of today's walk on Kinder Scout. It was a short and pleasant drive to get there – we took the M60 briefly to Stockport, then the A6 until we turned off for a wee place called Hayfield.

"There's a small car park at the start of the walk, but I think you have to pay so we'll just park on the street." Fiona parked expertly along from a pub called The Sportsman, which looked a hopeful spot for après-walk recovery.

"Right, you northerners – what d'you know about this walk?" Fiona was looking smug as she adjusted the strap on her rucksack; sadly she was quite right in her assumption that we hadn't done our homework. I knew about Scottish walks and mountains, and a bit about the Lake District, but past that, not a lot. "OK, come on and I'll show you."

She led us along the road which followed the river to the official starting place, a car park at Bowden Bridge, where there was a commemorative plaque:

The mass trespass onto Kinder Scout started from this quarry 24th April 1932.'

"Mass trespass?" I frowned, trying to work out if this was a walking term I hadn't previously encountered.

"Some walkers, you two. This was a famous occasion, and if it hadn't happened you mightn't be doing *any* English walks. Four hundred walkers set off from here to object to the lack of access rights. They were accosted by gamekeepers, and five were arrested. The resulting outcry led to the 1939 Access to Mountains Act."

"Cool." I stared at Liksi. 'Cool'? Where'd that come from? Must be an Alex expression, unless she'd picked it up from her kids.

"Was that for Scotland too?" She carried on, oblivious.

"I don't think so," Fiona had to admit.

"I don't think we had much sensible access legislation till the Land Reform Act, in 2003." As usual, I couldn't remember all the details. "My understanding is that we might never've got proper access if it hadn't been for John Smith – remember him? - the best Prime Minister we never had?" The others nodded – who could forget him, or his untimely death? He'd been a keen hillwalker.

We'd another look round – there was an information board there too – then set off to follow the footsteps of the 'mass trespass'. The riverside greenery draped itself decorously over the rocks, above the pleasant trickle of the water, and then we found ourselves out in the country and heading up a steep cobbled path. Knowing Fiona, I assumed that "steep" was par for the course, but was pleasantly surprised when we reached a fork and she took the lower branch. However, the days of thinking I wouldn't be able to continue with climbs seemed to be well past – I was a lot fitter than I'd been in years. Thanks, probably, to becoming fixated with getting to the gym every second day now.

"Kinder Reservoir." Fiona was sweeping her arm out to indicate a large expanse of water. "Provides water for the Stockport area. Look, you can see the ridge now." Some distance away, the reservoir was backed by steep vertically ridged rocks, which formed a curve around the area. There was something unique about this place – it definitely didn't feel Scottish, and it was very different from the Lake District too. The cobbled ascent, the drystone walls, the sheep in the fields we'd passed at the beginning – even the type of walkers was different. Here there were whole families, many wearing trainers rather than boots, few with rucksacks or heavy duty jackets, and numerous dogs darting excitedly back and fore.

"I guess people just come here for an afternoon out sometimes? Like, they don't all look like climbers?" That probably sounded condescending, although I hadn't meant it to be.

"Yeah – some might just come as far as this, to the foot of the clough, and then go back. Or, they might go on to Kinder Downfall – that's a sort of waterfall – and picnic there."

"What did you say there – foot of the what?" I was glad Liksi asked, as I hadn't understood it either.

"Clough. This one's William Clough, but there's others around. It means a gorge."

I looked up at the cleft weaving in and out up the hillside, but it didn't look too challenging. The path was stony, but the stones disappeared at times, or there were so many scattered about seemingly at random that the actual path we were supposed to be following was unclear. This meant working our way through bracken till the stones would somehow regroup themselves in a recognisable manner. However, there was no way we were going to lose our way which was, very clearly, up to the top.

"A sign for the Pennine Way," Liksi shouted after a while from up ahead, and waited for us to join her.

"Yes, we follow the Pennine Way right along the plateau now, till we get to Edale Cross."

It was good flat walking for a few miles, and the views were superb – right over the reservoir and to hills and villages beyond. Tall rock formations were scattered around seemingly at random, giving a slightly surreal appearance at times. The sun was getting stronger, and I now understood why there were few 'heavy duty' jackets around. This was glorious weather – and when we stopped for lunch at some conveniently located boulders at Kinder Downfall, I leant back, closed my eyes and let the warmth bore into me.

"Mm, just leave me here, will you?" I could've stayed up there all day – it was so good to feel the *heat*. "If there's one thing I envy you English for - apart from pubs and beer, of course – it's your weather. Ow!" Something had landed on my stomach.

"Hope it hurt. You'd better put some of that on."

I picked up the tube of Piz Buin reluctantly. It was Factor 30; my usual maximum was 15, although that was getting increasingly difficult to find.

"If you don't, we'll mock you when you get a bright red hooter." Liksi laughed as she smeared cream liberally on her arms. "Or does your French blood protect you from that?"

"French blood? What French blood?" Fiona looked up as I squeezed out a small amount.

"What, hasn't she bored you with that story before now?" Liksi turned to me and laughed. "Here's your chance, Eilidh!"

"I'd a French great-great-great grandmother, from Brittany. No, honestly, I did. My great-great-great grandfather was a fisherman from the north-east, and he met her on one of his numerous trips to France." I was always happy to tell this story, passed down as family lore.

"How romantic – what happened?"

"Well, inevitably she was Catholic and he was Protestant, and her parents didn't want anything to do with him. Nothing daunted, he wheeched[10] her into his fishing boat and took her back to Scotland with him."

"That's a great story. Is it true? Were they happy ever after?"

"Of course it's true! I have no idea if they were happy together or not – but apparently she hated the Scottish weather and would never get up before midday, so got the reputation of being lazy."

"Just like Liksi – well, not the lazy bit."

"Ha. With friends like you two ..."

The banter continued through lunch, and then as we wound our way back down on the other side. We stopped briefly to look at what was left of the medieval Edale Cross. It was sheltered by a stone wall, with an information plaque beside it, but looked sadly lopsided as one arm seemed to have been broken off. We turned right there, leaving the Pennine Way to continue its path eastwards, while our route led us gently down by Oaken Clough (but avoiding the scrambling bit, which Fiona said it was known for) and alongside the river back to Bowden Bridge and Hayfield.

"Good walk, Fiona." I rested on my pole briefly, before we peeled off rucksacks and changed into lighter shoes at her car. "Great weather, great scenery – and great company. In spite of all your cheek."

---

[10] snatched or removed quickly

Recovering with glasses of Thwaite's at the Sportsman Inn, Fiona gave us another piece of local 'history'.

"Did you know that Arthur Lowe used to live in this village?" We didn't, so she continued, "He based his Dad's Army character on a local bank manager."

I couldn't help looking around to see if there were any Captain Mainwaring look-alikes in the bar, but the nearest I got to it were a couple of lads who might've been able to audition for Private Pike.

"I should add great history and cultural lessons to the list. You've done well." I raised my glass to Fiona, and Liksi followed suit.

"More culture to follow tonight." We looked at Fiona expectantly. "Eurovision Song Contest."

"Cool. Can we watch it?"

I groaned, then gawped as I realised that Liksi was serious – and so was Fiona. Oh, God, surely not – but yes, after another excellent Thai meal in Sale, that was exactly what the three of us ended the day by doing. Fiona and Liksi followed the scoring avidly, getting more and more excited as the UK ended up third or fourth last and Ukraine came top - while I watched and listened to them with growing disbelief. Olly, sensibly, had gone to bed.

Chapter 30 – Easedale Tarn and Thorn Crag (October 2016) - Liksi

Easedale Tarn - This circular Lakeland walk of 6 miles starts and finishes in the village of Grasmere, taking in Easedale Beck and Sourmilk Gill, and returning by Far Easedale Gill.
Thorn Crag – Starting from the carpark at Dungeon Gyll, the climb up to Thorn Crag (2,106 ft) is steep but straightforward. The return is made by descending slightly further over and onto the Cumbria Way, past New Dungeon Gyll and back to the carpark. The total distance is around 6 miles.

"Well done, train must have been on time." Fiona greeted Eilidh as she held the car door open for her. We were just outside Oxenholme train station in the Lake District – I'd arrived about half an hour earlier and was sitting in the back seat.

"Aye, great to see you both! Liksi, how d'you manage to get here before me? Thought we might've been on the same train."

"Got the bus." I gave a smug grin. "To Carlisle. Then another bus to here."

She stared at me with incomprehension. "Bus? Er – why?" Fiona was also shaking her head as she drove off. Honestly, these two would never dream of getting a bus if there was a train available instead.

"Because I didn't book the train early enough. By the time I got round to it, it was going to cost me three times as much as the bus." It wasn't a big deal, but since the divorce I just didn't have the same income as they did. Anyway, I genuinely did like travelling by bus, as I kept trying to tell them.

We drove through Kendal and Windermere, past the Troutbeck turnoff – prompting reminders of our night-time escapade after the Mortal Man - and up along the side of

Lake Windermere to the bustling village of Ambleside. It was a bit tricky to negotiate the narrow streets without knocking people down. Problem with the Lake District was that people went there to walk, which they did – everywhere. Grasmere was almost as bad, and it was a relief when we turned off Easedale Road, and parked near the entrance to the hostel.

"All out here, I'm afraid." Fiona turned off the engine. "You'll have to carry your bags to the hostel as you can't park any nearer."

Leaving boots, poles etc in the boot, we continued up the path to an imposing grey stone villa which looked Victorian and was to be our weekend home. A sign identified it as 'Butharlyp Howe', which sounded very grand.

"Looks like we'll be living in style this weekend." I was pretty impressed; it certainly didn't look like a hostel. "What was this in its heyday? And how on earth d'you pronounce it?"

"No idea, sorry. Anyway, I've found a good shortish walk for this afternoon, and a longer one for tomorrow. Will we just check in and head straight out?"

It was still only lunchtime when we set off. That early start had been worth it. However, before leaving Grasmere to head for the hills we went to a couple of outdoor shops for Eilidh and Fiona to get some essential gear. I left them to it for a wander round, then joined them again as they came out of the last shop.

Eilidh fished a pair of rolled-up waterproof trousers out of her rucksack and handed them to Fiona with a flourish, along with a couple of notes. Fiona gave Eilidh the pair she'd just bought, and both looked very pleased with themselves. I looked at them questioningly.

"Don't ask." Eilidh was stuffing her new trousers into her rucksack. "I've got a brand-new pair that fits, and Fiona's got an almost-new pair for a tenner."

"Honestly, you two – wouldn't it be easier to buy your *own* trousers?" I shook my head at them.

"Probably, but not so much fun. Right, ready to roll – let's go." Laughing, Fiona led us out of the village at last.

We went back up Easedale Road, past the hostel entrance and turned off at a footbridge by a sign to Easedale Tarn, which Fiona informed us was today's destination.

"Nice gentle walk – 6 miles, a warm-up for tomorrow." Sounded good.

And it was. The nip in the air meant that sweatshirts were in order, but the last of the summer sun was still there, flitting in and out of white puffy clouds. Green leaves were still clinging to the trees in the patches of woodland bordering the beginning of the path, though further afield most were well into their glorious autumn colours. I remembered some time ago discovering from crossword clues that there were scores of words to describe these, such as ochre, amber, russet, tawny, terracotta, mustard, and now I could see why. A bit like the plethora of Inuit words for snow. Or Scottish words for rain –

"Liksi! Are you with us?" Fiona's voice cut through my rambling thoughts.

"Yes, sorry, was miles away. What were you saying?"

"We were just talking about retirement again. Any more thoughts?"

"Oh no, not for a while. Don't think that'd be good for me, at all. Anyway, Alex'll be working for a good few years yet and I wouldn't want to sit at home and vegetate."

"I don't intend to *vegetate*." Eilidh sounded rather defensive. "I just want to be able to relax more, and do things I've never had time to do."

"What about you, Fiona?" I turned to her, as she stopped to adjust the length of her poles.

"I'll keep going part-time as long as Olly can manage. It helps me keep a grip on normality, and obviously I don't want to lose the income." I caught the sadness behind Fiona's words.

"And then there's this Brexit carry-on." Eilidh stabbed her pole into the ground. "Who knows where we'll be afterwards? Oh – watch out for that stone there." We were climbing up the side of a waterfall and the path was very near the edge at times.

"Is this the Tarn?" I didn't really need Fiona's "Yip" to answer my question. We'd come upon a rather idyllic scene – a small loch, or lake I suppose – sheltered cosily amongst some grassy slopes. The path led right up to the lakeside, and there were several flat grassy areas where various groups of people were lying or sitting. The sun was still strong and doing its best to give an impression of warmth, even though every so often a chill breeze would slip through. It was a textbook spot for a picnic; though we didn't have one we sat down anyway, to enjoy the scene.

"Mm, lovely." Eilidh was breathing deeply with appreciation as she handed round a bag of caramels. "I don't even mind sharing this place with other people."

"Yeah, if this is the warm-up, you've raised expectations for tomorrow." I turned to Fiona.

"That's the idea. Also, it didn't involve any more driving today, so that's always a bonus."

We stayed there, just enjoying the landscape for a while and sucking sweets. It was *so* relaxing - almost soporific, and the hills seemed to watch over us as well as the water. When we finally got going again it was with reluctance – if I'd had a book I'd have been happy to stay there all afternoon. However, we opted to continue round the lake and go over the hill to give us a different, and slightly longer, route back. Fiona did her usual and went haring off on her own, and we lost her for a while due to the bracken-covered up-and-down nature of the terrain. Once our paths eventually converged again, we followed a stone wall for a while, and crossed a footbridge before coming across a very attractive spot by Easedale Beck. We stopped to sit by the stones, and to let Fiona have a quick paddle. I remembered Pete and I doing exactly the same somewhere with the kids, all these years ago. Oh well – we did have *some* good times. Once.

It was late afternoon by the time we got back, and after showering and changing we'd a meal in the hostel. Three courses no less, thanks to the other two who couldn't resist the syrup sponge with custard – and extra custard in Fiona's case. I suppose I could have resisted ...

That left time for a pub crawl. Unfortunately, though Grasmere was a pleasant little village to wander around, there wasn't much in the way of pubs, or at least the kind of pubs we liked. We had a drink in Tweedie's, and then the Red Lion, but they were both hotel bars rather than pubs and we called it a day after that. As Eilidh said, we needed to reserve our strength for the main walk tomorrow. Sadly, this meant we were in bed by 10 and as I listened to the deep breathing of the other two I sighed, wishing they weren't always *quite* so happy to turn in early. Grumpily, I pulled the duvet over my head and gave in.

*****

"Wakey wakey! Chop chop!"

I must've gone to sleep after all. Dimly, I realised that this shrill noise could only've come from Fiona. I opened one eye, saw the streaming window and Fiona's grinning face, and promptly closed it again. "'S wet. Go away."

"Bit of rain won't do you any harm. Are you a man or a mouse?" Oh God, where'd she get these awful expressions from?

"Mouse. Give me five ..."

By the time we'd breakfast, drove to Dungeon Ghyll and parked, I was more or less awake and human again. Grasmere wasn't all that far from the Langdale Pikes as the crow flies, but there was no connecting road; we'd to go back down to Ambleside and then up again via country roads. This became a completely different kind of countryside from yesterday. The green fields and glorious trees had morphed into rougher landscape. Fields were overlooked by steep inclines, which glowered down from lofty heights obscured by thick grey cloud. I shuddered slightly, and almost wished I was back underneath the duvet.

"Oh, this is just how I remembered it." I couldn't believe Eilidh, who was looking round almost enraptured. "Forbidding, gloomy – I've always wanted to come back here. It's such an atmospheric part of the Lakes – so different from the prettiness of places like Grasmere and Windermere."

I couldn't disagree with the description, but why on earth she'd want to come back here rather than to any of these other lovely places was beyond me.

"S'pose it looks better in decent weather." This was the best I could offer. "Can't say it looks enticing at the moment." We'd parked, but were still sitting in the car, looking round at the stone walls, miserable-looking sheep and trees whose remaining leaves looked weighted down with rain. Visibility was poor – we could see about a thousand feet up, but Fiona'd said that the tops were more than double that. Not quite Furth Munros, but still significant.

"I can't see us getting up to the tops today." Eilidh was looking doubtfully up at the crags. "What route had you in mind exactly, Fiona?"

"We're going to head up to Thorn Crag and the top of Dungeon Gyll, and then on to Harrison Stickle if we can. That's the highest Pike, about 2,400 ft. We can come down in a circuit from there. Come on, let's go." She opened the car door and stepped out into the elements.

"Look." She was pointing over to the east. "There's a break in the clouds over there, and I think the rain's lifting."

The two of them were getting into their waterproof trousers, Eilidh jumping about on one leg before collapsing against the side of the car, while the loose leg dropped in the puddle beside her.

"Oh, God, I thought it'd be easier getting into the bigger pair – well, it is, but it's still not *easy*." Balanced against the car, she'd another go and finally beamed at us triumphantly as she pulled them up. "Fiona, how d'you manage to do that so effortlessly? Liksi, are you not getting into yours?"

"No, left them at home. I'll be fine, don't worry." I didn't want them fussing, but I did feel rather stupid that I'd forgotten them. Well actually, I hadn't forgotten them – I was just trying to carry as little as possible, and the forecast had been quite good. More fool me. By now the other two looked as if they were wearing black hazmat suits, so I did what I could and put my hood up over my hat and pulled the cords as tightly as I could.

"Ready." Whatever else, I was still looking forward to the exercise, and we set off with no great hopes of achieving much. The rain had kind of stopped now, but there was still so much dampness in the air that it didn't take long for my trousers to get pretty dank. The path led up from the New Dungeon Ghyll Hotel and then we took a left fork to sweep round and upwards.

"God, this is steep – but it takes my mind off the rain! Or is this just mist?" Eilidh shouted up to us as we climbed steadily.

"Where's that break in the clouds you mentioned?" I shouted up to Fiona, but she just laughed as she ploughed on. We kept going, Eilidh keeping up with us but through the drips off her hood she was looking increasingly anxious.

I could imagine how she was feeling – we all wanted to walk, but Fiona sometimes took risks and both Eilidh and I were usually too wimpish to hold her back. This really wasn't much fun – the rain crept back stealthily and I couldn't remember getting as wet as this since Bute – usually we'd been pretty lucky with the weather. As we got higher, the sky just seemed to become more leaden, and worse, it was getting really misty and visibility was diminishing rapidly. At last, we seemed to have reached a summit and Fiona stopped. We tried to find shelter round the crag, but nothing could diminish the relentless cold blanket of mist, and we could hardly see each other, let alone a glimpse of any view.

"OK, what d'you want to do?" Fiona's wet face turned to us under her hood.

"Go back. This is too dangerous – we don't know where we're going." Eilidh's response was rapid and definite.

"Oh, I know where we're going." Fiona's tone was defensive. "Dungeon Ghyll is just down there, and Harrison Stickle is round that way."

"I'm with Eilidh." For once, I was going to stand firm. "This is not fun and I'd rather *see* where we're going, or even where we've *been*." I was by now absolutely frozen, and my trousers were soaked through. Why had I been so stupid as to leave the waterproof ones at home?

"Oh well, if that's what you want." Fiona gave the impression that she would've preferred to go on, but at least she was giving us the choice.

"What's Dungeon Ghyll anyway?" I asked. "Another peak?"

"It's a waterfall." Eilidh was pulling the drawstrings of her hood as tight as she could. "And a ravine – very tall, and I don't fancy falling into it. I think we should go back the same way we came, just in case." She was about to start back, when Fiona stopped her.

"We could, if you want, go back down and when we get off the craggy bit head for the Cumbria Way? It's a low-level path, and at least we can keep walking without worrying about getting lost?"

"Fine." I started back, with the others following. I wasn't sure about more walking in these bloody trousers, but once we were halfway down we emerged from the mist and found that the sun *had* come through, and everything was looking fresh and more appealing. As Fiona directed us to the join with the Cumbria Way, I decided that wet trousers were a reasonable price to pay for a good walk after all.

"I can hardly believe this." Eilidh swivelled round as she took in the new vistas. "It's as if we've arrived in a completely different place – it's much more like yesterday."

I knew what she meant – the grimness of our first sightings of the Langdale area'd been replaced with sunny snapshots of green fields fringed with burnished bracken mounds, and the bleak slopes in the background were now revealed to be heather-clad and much less sinister. Like the landscape yesterday, there were patches of autumn-tinged trees side by side with those determined to hang onto their summer greenness as long as possible. A ribbon of water sparkled slightly in the distance, and further back still a body of water could just be made out, cushioned between the hills.

"And what lovely *sheep*!" I turned to Eilidh to see what on earth could be lovely about sheep, but she was right. Small animals with soft dark fleeces had turned their white faces to eye us warily, whilst sitting chewing contentedly on still luscious-looking grassy banks. Even I had to admit that they really were very attractive.

"I'm used to the opposite type – there's blackface sheep all over the highlands and in Lewis, but only my Auntie Mary Ann could ever call them 'lovely'. Oops!" Eilidh'd been so busy admiring the sheep that she'd walked right into a gatepost. She laughed at herself as she rubbed her forehead, before wriggling through the gap of the swing gate.

The Cumbria Way was really very pleasant, and reminded me of parts of the West Highland Way – hills all round, but very easy walking. I still felt pretty soggy in my trousers, but they were beginning to dry off and at least I didn't feel so cold. By the time we reached the end – or the beginning? - of the Way, I was looking forward to going to the pub that Eilidh had promised us to finish off the warming-up procedure properly.

"This is the New Dungeon Ghyll." Eilidh waved her hand at the entrance to a pleasant stone hotel. "It's got a good bar for walkers."

"OK, Eilidh, you're the expert," said Fiona. "We can get the car and go back to it."

Which we did. Eilidh led us into the Hikers' Bar – as she had promised, it was full of character. Comfortable, the kind of place that welcomed muddy boots – or soggy trousers – and had beer of a standard that kept Eilidh happy. In fact, she was in her element – the star turn was a litter of black Labrador puppies and their proud mother, trying to keep an eye on them as they waddled – and widdled - all over the place. The barman didn't seem to mind that he'd to mop the floor every few minutes – at least it was that kind of floor.

With difficulty, we extricated Eilidh from the puppies in order to visit the nearby Sticklebarn pub for one for the road. She'd not been there before, but had done her research and it was a very appealing place. Not as rustic as the Hikers' Bar, but warm and hearty, with an interesting menu.

"It's a National Trust pub," said Eilidh before swallowing her first mouthful of whatever local brew she'd found.

"Didn't know there were any." I looked around. "Thought the National Trust was just stately homes."

"The only other National Trust pub I know of is the Crown in Belfast," said Eilidh. "I was over there on business a couple of years ago – what a fantastic place. It's got a beautiful ceiling which only came to light properly when they cleaned it once the smoking ban came into play."

"I'm sure there must've been a few others in that situation." Fiona laughed. "I'm not sure about Scotland, but there are some National Trust pubs around south of the border - remember the George Inn in London? The night of Elaine's infamous party?"

"Oh God yes, how could I forget? Wasn't that the time that ...?"

Oh, these girls were wonderful. For the rest of the night I don't think I missed Alex even once – except maybe when yet again I found myself in bed before 10, with the other two sound asleep.

Chapter 31 – Scarborough to Filey (February 2017) - Fiona

This is a 12-mile coastal walk starting at the youth hostel, just off the A165 north of Scarborough, and ending in the centre of Filey. It follows the Cleveland Way and hugs the coast for the most part, taking in Scarborough's north and south bays, and the dramatic peninsula of Filey Brigg.

Both here – see you in The Tap at the Station. X

I shoved the phone back in my bag with a sigh of relief. So Eilidh'd made it to York after all. Thank goodness; I just hoped her father wouldn't deteriorate dramatically over the course of the weekend and she'd feel obliged to cut the trip short. It'd been difficult enough to work out the logistics of this trip, and it'd be a real hassle to have to re-arrange everything, including the hired car. Not to mention how awful Eilidh would feel. She'd been terribly stressed about this whole weekend, and had been on the verge of cancelling it. However, as she said herself, if there was any chance of her making it, it would probably do her the world of good.

Anyway, I could relax now. I turned back to my iPad to look at a few more emails. *Relax!* I snorted. Working three days a week was all very well, but my boss was only too aware that I'd probably pack at least four days into the three whenever possible. In one way I resented this assumption, but in another, as she'd probably worked out, I was happy to do the work if it took my mind off Olly's needs and our changed circumstances.

However, when the train pulled into York I snapped the iPad shut with relief and switched to leisure mode. I found The Tap easily, and followed the sound of Liksi's gutsy laugh to locate the two of them tucked away in a corner of the station bar.

"I see you've been enjoying yourselves already?" I nodded at the table, laden with glasses and strewn with empty crisp packets, whilst exchanging the usual hugs.

"Absolutely – but can I just emphasise that these are not all ours? And don't bother raising that eyebrow of yours. What can I get you?" Liksi got up to go to the bar, but I pressed her back down.

"Thanks, but no thanks. Not yet, anyway – I'm going to have to drive and I need to keep my wits about me."

"No worries – we'll just drink up and then we can be off." True to her word, Eilidh drained about half a pint without blinking an eye, then stood up and gathered all her things together. Liksi sat back and watched her, shaking her head. It was good to see Eilidh smiling, although she looked pale and drawn compared to her usual bursting-with-health freshness.

"Right, let's go – Liksi, are you going to finish that wine?" Oh, they were so different – Eilidh at the ready, and Liksi completely laid back. She elected to leave the rest of her glass, saying she'd had quite enough already, bearing in mind it was only lunchtime. We headed off to check in with Europcar, which was just a street or so away from the station. The paperwork seemed interminable, and all for a mere Citroen Cactus, and it was a good half hour before we were ready to go.

"This is good of you, Fiona." Eilidh sat back with a sigh of relief as we set off. "We'd have been bankrupted if we'd all gone to Scarborough by train."

"Yip, this was the only sensible way to get to Scarborough really." I was keeping my eyes peeled for road signs. "I just thought it would be good to do a bit of the Cleveland Way and get a sight of the sea for a change. Oh, damn, I forgot to bring a roadmap with me – can one of you look up Google Maps when we get nearer Scarborough?"

"Eilidh, sorry but can you do it? My phone's out of charge." Liksi put the phone back in her bag.

"Er, well, I'll try, but I've only used Google Maps to print maps out." Eilidh fished out her phone and pressed a few buttons. "Here, Liksi, can you do it for me?" She held it out behind her.

"Sorry, but these are new glasses and I need to get them adjusted. I could *try*."

"Oh, for goodness sake – go into my bag and get my phone and I'll do it myself." I was starting to laugh. "I know we're getting on in years, but ..." Eilidh had picked up my bag and retrieved my phone. "Thanks, I -"

"Oh no!" This from Eilidh, as the phone slipped out of her hands and disappeared somewhere under my seat. "Oh, sorry, sorry!"

I started to laugh, which was just as well as Eilidh had looked rather distressed. I guess she wasn't quite wired to hilarity these days. However, Liksi joined in and before long Eilidh had a weak smile on her face too.

"IT skills, eyes, motor co-ordination – I guess this is just a precursor of what's to come." I stopped the car just before Scarborough, retrieved the phone and set Google Maps for the youth hostel. After only a couple of wrong turns, we found the incredibly tight turn-off and arrived there in one piece. The solidly built white building dated back to the 1600s, and was originally a water mill. It might've lacked some of the facilities found in other hostels, but it had plenty of character and was in a quiet spot beside the river. I parked beside an apple tree, which was next to one of these pines with branches curving upwards.

After sorting our stuff out, we were all keen to get out and see the sea. We walked back to the main road, followed it north for a short time then crossed it, and followed the path down to the coast. It was so good to get to the sea again, and to breath in the salty air. No urban pollution, just fresh healthy air – I could feel my lungs expanding already. When the path came to a T-junction, we turned right onto the Cleveland Way, following the coast via a steep up-and-down section which led us up to a pub, the Old Scalby Mill. However, we held back our thirst and agreed to carry on, as we could see that Scarborough town centre had a lofty position overlooking the sea. We toiled up a *very* steep slope and arrived at a row of grand-looking white buildings.

"I thought this was supposed to be a recce, not a training session!" Eilidh was puffing hard but it was good to see her smiling too.

"That's the hard work over – now you get your reward." I was as glad as she was to search out a pub I'd found on the internet, and it wasn't long before we were enjoying the local ales in the North Riding Brew. The clientele seemed to be mainly regulars, and took quite an interest in us – what we were doing in Scarborough, and our proposed route tomorrow.

"Have you noticed," I said when we had a moment to ourselves, "that their interest is born out of curiosity rather than admiration?"

Eilidh snorted. "Long gone are the days when our appearance in a pub would cause a stir due to our stunning looks," she said, holding out a strand of her greying locks.

"If it ever did." I shook my head. "Ah well."

Our new friends weren't backwards in making suggestions as to where we should go to eat, so we settled on a diner located about halfway along the road back to the hostel. The meal at the Tunny Catch was uninspiring but adequate, and we were all – even Liksi – happy to turn in not long afterwards.

Gathering outside after breakfast the next day, we took a bit more notice of our immediate surroundings – the hostel was in a secluded spot beside a small river, which flowed below a bank with a dense covering of wildflowers and other vegetation, although the ubiquitous rosebay willowherb was winning out. Even in this sheltered location, the flowers and trees were bending at steep angles in the wind.

"This is NOT going to be warm, sunny English weather." Liksi was wrapping that scarf thing of hers round her neck, already huddled into her fleece collar until only the tops of her ears were visible. "You do know, Fiona, that we only come south of the Border to get the sun."

"Yes, you've lured us here under false pretences." Eilidh joined in, also looking as if she was prepared for a polar expedition with her eyes peering out from under a woolly hat.

"Come on, wimps. Thought you were supposed to be hardy up there. Anyway, it's early yet." I led them at a brisk pace back the way we'd gone last night, and retraced our steps to Scarborough along the coast. By the time we'd climbed up the steps to the Old Scalby Mill again, everyone seemed to have warmed up, at least for the time being. We walked along the front this time, glad not to be repeating last night's climb. There were quite a few people about, mostly families or older people rather than walkers.

"This must get packed in the summer." Eilidh had a look of slight disapproval on her face.

"Yes, it does, but it's not nearly as popular as it used to be." I found Scarborough interesting, but not somewhere I'd want to spend much time in. "Look – surfers." The waves weren't particularly big, but there were some hopeful souls trying to catch a rare wave, and the usual groups of onlookers. We were more interested in the far end of the bay though, as we wanted to climb up to the castle, although it wasn't strictly speaking directly on the Way. It was, however, well worth the climb to the extensive walled area housing the tall, ruined tower and other crumbling structures, some dating from the 12th century.

We spent a few minutes speaking to the very friendly staff in the castle shop, who did their best to locate a Cleveland Way map for us without success. Liksi got engrossed in a historical discussion about the origins of the castle, which lost me almost immediately. Eilidh was anxious to get back out into the fresh air and it wasn't long before I followed her, with Liksi close behind. The views from the Castle were superb, and give us a much better idea of the layout of Scarborough. With the help of the limited printouts of the maps we did have, we could see that the castle promontory split the town in half. Looking back the way we came, we could see the length of North Bay extending back to Old Scalby Mill, and on the other side was South Bay. This was more built up and framed an extensive curve of reddish grey sand, which is where we headed down to next. Cafes, tearooms, ice cream parlours and gift shops faced the esplanade. Each of them, located closely together in different types and colours of buildings, seemed to extend several stories upwards.

"This has such a different to feel to anywhere in Scotland." Eilidh was right – we were walking alongside the immense Grand Hotel and ubiquitous (in England, anyway) seaside arcades. "The *size* of these places!"

"I know, it's faded grandeur at its best." I felt sad for the town; in its heyday it was *the* place to holiday for thousands of people. Now, at this time of year anyway, these forlorn monoliths were like towering empty shells – still-beautiful facades, but it was easy to imagine a network of ghostly corridors criss-crossing the interior to link countless empty rooms. Having said that, most of them still struggled along, helped by Groupon and bus-party deals. The promenade came to an end at a large circular area, which turned out to be a Star Disk of some significance (something to do with stars and sunrises), but I just felt sad that its original use as a huge open-air pool was no longer feasible.

Out of Scarborough, the path climbed above and away from the town, and headed inland briefly before turning back to the grassy clifftop. After the calm of the sheltered promenades, it was invigorating to be buffeted by the wind again. Interesting as the town was, we all relished being out in the open countryside, and inhaling all that fresh air. The path was easy to follow, but we'd to watch as there were muddy patches in places. There wasn't much conversation, as it was almost impossible to hear each other above the wind, so when the path led down to the beginning of Cayton Sands and we came across Lucy's Beach Shack it was a unanimous decision to have a stop there, in spite of the gale.

"Scones, or scones?" Eilidh shouted at us from the serving window of what was, definitely, a wooden shack. A Walls ice cream flag flapped wildly about above the hatch, and boxes of beach balls and fishing nets were balanced rather precariously – and optimistically – outside.

"Scones. With butter and jam ..." Liksi was pulling in some chairs round the sole wooden table positioned just off the path above the shack, and we huddled down to wait for Eilidh to come back. When the scones and tea arrived, we grabbed anything that was likely to blow away before spreading liberal quantities of cream (even better) and strawberry jam on what were possibly the best scones I'd ever had.

"Mm." Eilidh raised her face to the wind with appreciation. "Battered by the elements, scones that melt in your mouth, surrounded by your best pals – what more could a gal want? I needed this, big time."

"How are things with your Dad now?" I had forgotten to ask her earlier. Well, not exactly forgotten – I wanted *her* to be able to forget about things for a while. Much as I sympathised with her, she did tend to dwell on things sometimes and I didn't want her to sink into a gloomy fugue.

"Grim." The answer came back as I'd expected, as Eilidh turned back to us, putting her cup down. "The staff do what they can, but they can hardly get him out of bed now – he gets quite distressed when they try, and he's so weak that he can hardly keep upright in a chair anyway."

"And your Mum?" Good for Liksi – I'd almost forgotten about Eilidh's mother, as there'd been so much worry over her father recently.

"Very distressed. She spends every afternoon with him now – they wheel her over after her lunch, and she just sits there, talking to him and watching him and just – just – it's awful. It can't be long now, surely – it's *so* unfair that older people have to go through this. What have they ever done to deserve it? And it's worse for Mum than it is for Dad."

"And awful for you too." Liksi tried unsuccessfully to lick a bit of jam off her face. "Seeing them like that."

"And wishing for the end – but the next minute thinking no, that's awful, how can I think that way? I really, really shouldn't be here – so far away, if anything happens." Eilidh's eyes were filling up and she turned away again as Liksi put a hand on her shoulder.

"Eilidh, don't give yourself a hard time – you need a break or *you'll* start to crack up and be no use to your Mum."

"I know, I know. I'm trying to see it that way – and don't get me wrong, it's wonderful to be here. I just couldn't forgive myself if he goes before I get back to see him."

"Have you thought of taking some time off work and just going up there?" I was sure the college would let her go without question.

"Oh, but the students," Eilidh looked alarmed. "I know I'll have to go up near the end, and for the funeral, when it comes, but if I go now I could be away for weeks. I couldn't do that."

"Eilidh, you could," I said firmly. "No-one's indispensable. When've you last been off work? Everyone would understand."

"No, I – I'll think about it. Honestly." She blew her nose loudly – an Eilidh speciality. "Thanks, both of you. Sorry to be like this." Before we could protest, she stood up and reached for her pack, giving us a weak smile. "Time to go."

Good girl. Poor thing, you just wanted to cuddle her but I was glad to see she was pulling herself together, and we set off down the concrete steps to the shore. There were loads of dogs charging about, and trying to make friends with all of them took her mind off things a bit as we walked along, before climbing back up onto the clifftop.

"Phew!" Liksi gasped as we reached the top again and stood a bit to recover. "Think this is what you call 'bracing'. In capital letters."

"The wind's certainly much stronger up here. Be careful – I'm staying well away from the edge." Eilidh proceeded to do just that as we carried on. I wasn't worried, and I liked going to the edge to look down on the ochre rock formations below, although I suspected Eilidh was angst-ridden watching me. When we got to the Blue Dolphin Holiday Park, the Way had a diversion away from the cliffs due to some erosion.

"Don't fancy living here – d'you?" This was Liksi, pointing to the houses nearby. They did seem precariously near the edge – and probably getting nearer year by year.

"All these houses in what would previously have been really desirable spots – clifftops, down by the shore, on riversides." I used to envy the inhabitants of such places their views, but now only too often they suffered badly from the increasingly capricious elements.

"I know – when there's yet another spell of bad flooding in the UK, I'm always grateful I live on top of a hill." Eilidh was trying to keep the hair out of her eyes as she spoke.

"Mind you, I don't always feel that when I pech[11] my way up it after a late night and the train home."

"That's what keeps your stunning figure in trim." Liksi laughed as Eilidh threatened to batter her with her pole.

"I wish!"

The wind kept up as we wound our way back to the grassy fields which went right up to the cliff edge. There must have been a bit of rain recently, and some areas were pretty dodgy, so we had to divert a little inland to avoid the slippy bits at the very edge.

"Watch out." I turned back to warn them. "Cows have been here before us." One or two beasts were placidly chewing as they watched us from a short distance away.

"As long as there's none with horns, eh Fiona – oh!" A yell came from Liksi and the next minute she was on her backside, in exactly the patch I was referring to. "Oh no – oh, my God – *yeuch*!" She gasped, helpless, and then screwed up her nose as she took in her predicament properly. "Christ, what a smell - help me up! Quick!"

Eilidh and I grabbed an arm each, being careful not to join her in the mud – or should it be mire? - and hauled her to her feet. As she twisted round to inspect the damage, Eilidh and I looked at each other and back at Liksi and couldn't contain ourselves. Her plight was greatly enhanced by the fact that once again, Liksi was wearing that pair of light beige trousers. Why on earth did she wear light coloured trousers for walks?

"What're you two laughing about?" An indignant Liksi had started to laugh too, not helped by the two of us backing off and holding our noses theatrically. "You've got to put up with me for the rest of the day. Any suggestions? I can't strip off here!"

---

[11] to breathe with noisy deep gasps

"You could have my waterproof trousers." Eilidh was trying hard to control herself and be helpful. "But you'll need to wait till we get to somewhere more suitable to change. And they'll be far too big for you."

"Don't care – they'll do – but where the hell am I going to change? Look!"

She was right – the way ahead was flat as far as we could see, and although there were some gorse bushes and tall grasses in places, there was nothing that would afford any privacy. Added to that, a stream of walkers was making its way towards us, although we hadn't seen many braving the winds up till now.

Well, we managed. Sort of. There was nowhere to hide, at all, but we got to a bench where Liksi sat after taking her trousers down to her knees. She had to wrestle with her mud-caked boots to tug them off without getting too much of the gunk on her hands, then slipped her trousers off completely – just as a runner appeared out of nowhere.

"Quick! Give me something – anything – for God's sake, you two –" She snatched up her rucksack and sat with it on her lap and hunched over it till the runner had passed, not without bemused looks aimed in our direction. By this time Eilidh and I were doubled up and Eilidh was actually crying helplessly with laughter. We were, as Liksi stated forcefully, less than useless, and could only watch through streaming eyes as she pulled on the clean trousers.

"Not – useless! Gave – you – my – breeks!" Eilidh could hardly get the words out. "No gratitude - at all. Oh – ha ha ha – *look* at you!"

Liksi looked down at her calves – she'd had to roll the trousers up by about a foot and the waist was gaping.

"Don't care – at least I'm clean and don't smell. Too much, anyway – can't do anything about my boots. Just have to keep hold of the waist in case they fall down. Anyone got a plastic bag?" She rolled up her filthy trousers and put them in a Tesco bag that Eilidh found somewhere, and we got going again, hampered every so often by someone breaking into another fit of laughing.

We still managed to admire the spectacular cliff formations which were now visible in both directions, but particularly ahead, at Filey Brigg, which was the official end of the Cleveland Way. I'd vaguely imagined that this would be some kind of bridge, but in fact it was a long thin promontory with high, steep cliffs. The horizontal layers of mainly reddish sandstone must've provided loads of nesting opportunities for the seabirds flying about. It would've been invigorating to walk right down to its tip, to feel the full strength of the wind and look back at the coast in both directions, but time was moving on and we'd still about a mile to go to get to Filey itself. So reluctantly, we carried on along the cliffs till the path finally headed down to the promenade leading into the town.

"A quick refreshment?" Eilidh looked at us hopefully, as I got out my phone to check for bus times.

"What? Can't go into a pub looking like this!" Liksi stuck out a leg to remind us of her new look.

"Yes you can!" When Eilidh wanted a drink it was hard to refuse her. Anyway, she deserved it just now.

"There isn't a bus for half an hour, so we might as well. Anyway, we need to eat too. Come on, Liksi – how about The Imperial over there? If Eilidh and I go in first, you can sort of sidle in behind us."

"Well, you'd better hide me properly. This is the time to find out who your friends really are." Liksi did her best to make herself inconspicuous as we went in. We moved towards a table in a huddle, and she sunk down and wriggled into the corner.

"That was actually a ploy on my part to get you to buy the beers," she said. "Shandy please."

Eilidh shook her head at the thought of anyone wanting to waste good beer by putting lemonade in it, so I got the guest beer for us two.

"Oh, I wonder who won the rugby?" Liksi suddenly noticed the TV screen.

"Your lot beat Wales 29-13." A burly bearded guy standing at the bar turned round to offer this information. "Played well, they did."

"Good God – *really?*" It took a second for this unusual state of affairs to sink in.

"*That's* a turnup for the books."

"Fantastic, can't believe it!"

"Great Scottish defence, and Russell played a blinder. Pity you missed it."

A couple of other guys had joined our friend, and they all seemed genuinely happy for us, even raising their glasses in tribute.

"Now all we need is for England to lose tomorrow and we might even get the Triple Crown."

"Er, Liksi, not sure if everyone here will feel the same." Eilidh was torn between a laugh and an apologetic look towards the guys.

"Oh, sorry – old habits die hard." Liksi was only slightly shame-faced. "So unused to winning that we get carried away."

"Sure do – another one?" Eilidh went up for another round and we settled in for an enjoyable banter session with the guys. After another drink we moved on to Tikka Tikka for a celebratory curry. As we were getting ready to leave afterwards, Liksi emerged from the loo with an exaggeratedly careful walk that certainly didn't help her attempt to blend into the scenery.

"Oh, God, I should've remembered what happened to you at Loch Katrine; I've just done the same thing." She bent down to show us the problem. "I unzipped my legs for some stupid reason, got the zip of one leg stuck and I've had to fasten it with the side poppers. I'm scared to move in case they all burst open!"

Needless to say, the resulting merriment didn't help her case either, and it only increased when the bus driver got an unexpected eyeful. By the time we got back to the hostel we were worn out with laughing; as soon as she could, Liksi got out of her makeshift ensemble and headed for the shower. Looking at Eilidh, I could see that for now at least, thoughts of her Dad were set aside, as she re-claimed her waterproof trousers and put them in a bag in the far corner of the room.

Chapter 32 – John Muir Way 3 (July 2017) - Eilidh

This 15-mile walk starts at Linlithgow train station, skirts Linlithgow Loch and goes briefly north along the A706 before turning left and picking up the John Muir Way. At Kinneil House it borders Kinneil Nature Reserve, then follows the coast through Bo'ness to Blackness Castle, skirts Hopetown House and finishes in South Queensferry.

"Have you noticed that all our Edinburgh-based trips involve public transport, and the other ones involve cars?" I said idly, as we waited at Waverley for the Linlithgow train.

"Are you complaining?" Liksi gave me a mock-upset look.

"No, no, not complaining at all. Just *observing*. At least you don't make us go on trams."

"Oh *please* not trams again!" Fiona pleaded. "I couldn't bear it – thank God, here's the train – we need to be over there."

We moved along the platform and waited till everyone got off the incoming train. Oh, this gentle backchat was *so* comforting, like a favourite glove. In fact, last night'd been the same – off the train, up to the Halfway House, drinks with Alex, then an excellent curry in Voujon, somewhere up Newington Road en route to Liksi's. I needed this *so much*.

Since we last met, I'd lost my father, and then my mother – she only survived him by ten weeks. Six weeks ago, I became an orphan. I felt battered, bruised, and found myself welling up in the most inappropriate places. A kind word from a student in a class, a sympathetic touch on the shoulder from a colleague in the workroom, and I was off again. The horror of that phone call from the care home – "Your mother's had a bad fall. You might want to get up here as soon as you can. She's in Raigmore Hospital." Stark, shocking. No, it couldn't be - my mother'd been fine – she seemed to have been coping amazingly well with the void that my father's death had left. Numbly, I'd raced up the A9 again to Inverness, only on arrival at Raigmore to be taken aside by the senior nurse who told me gently that I was too late. In spite of being told that my mother hadn't regained consciousness at all, I could never be sure in myself, and nothing could stop me feeling that I'd let her down.

"How're things, Eilidh?" Liksi ushered me into the corner seat as the train took off. "Been back up again since the funeral?"

"No – I decided to leave it till the holidays, then go and blitz the house."

"Good idea - give yourself a break first." Fiona was always telling me to look after myself, but it was hard at times – certain things just needed doing and I had to get on with them.

"Well, it's not so much that. It's just that I can't really face it." I couldn't take in that Mum had been fine, then she was gone, just like that – with nothing in between. That I was there for, anyway. "I'm even dreading the drive up – it'll be the first time ever with neither one of them there, I mean at home."

"It's a shame you've got to face that on your own."

I'm sure Liksi was remembering when *her* father died. Her brother'd been at the other side of the world and although he'd managed to get over for the funeral, he'd had to go back to work immediately afterwards – but at least her mother had been there. And still was – doing very well. I shivered slightly as I brushed away the fleeting feeling of envy – my mother had been in a care home, not wrapped in the comfort of her own home. Was it *so* awful for her, who had been so close to my father, not to be alive any more? That was another of the futile questions I found myself asking.

"I'll be OK." I pulled myself together – but then I remembered how I'd felt after the funeral. Alan, my big, jovial, wonderful Alan was so supportive and had been with me since the day after Mum died, but after hugging all my relatives at the end of the day, I felt my coming isolation so powerfully. I was going back to Alan, but there was no younger generation to keep up the family genes on my side. Did that mean that after all these years I regretted not having had children?

To my relief, hardly any time passed before we were alighting at Linlithgow, and it wasn't hard to put these soul-searching questions aside as we strolled along the main street of the douce[12] wee town. It was the first time I'd been in it – having only ever passed through on the train before – and it really was very attractive, peppered with what looked like historically important buildings. I made a mental note to visit Linlithgow Palace with Alan one day, and some of these pubs looked worth a visit too.

It was turning out to be a glorious day, and much as the town had impressed me, I was glad when we turned off the road onto a path which led along the side of Linlithgow Loch. Moorhens, coots and the ubiquitous mallards and swans were puttering along on the sky-coloured water, with the sun glinting in their wake. On another day it would've been good just to sit here and watch them for a while, just thinking …

Fiona, however, was directing proceedings. Even though she'd never been here before either, she was oozing confidence as she led us away from the lake and onto minor roads to head towards the coast.

"You know, Fiona, I'm happy to just follow you blindly now." Liksi voiced my thoughts exactly. "I know that you'll always get us there."

---

[12] sober and sedate

"Yes, and if you don't you can always blame me and feel virtuous. But seriously, you should've a look at the maps too, just in case." She was absolutely right, but I wasn't going to tell her that, and anyway I was too lazy. I'd always known I was more of a follower than a leader, and was happy to remain that way.

We walked past farmlands where cows grazed serenely, and along hedgerows full of colourful wildflowers. I could feel the sun warming my arms and was glad I'd decided to wear a sleeveless top.

"Anyone got suncream?" Liksi was hugging her arms round her chest. "Going to turn into a lobster otherwise."

"Here." I fished out a tube and handed it to her.

"What's this? Factor 15? That's just like putting body lotion on!" Liksi stared at it in disbelief.

"Well, it's better than nothing – it works for me." I knew I sounded a bit defensive.

"Thought they didn't make anything below Factor 30 any more." Having ascertained that Fiona didn't have any at all, Liksi gave in and slathered it on as thickly as possible. I put a bit on my nose and neck and left it at that, as Liksi shook her head at me.

"Stop bickering, you two – look, the sea!" The expanse of the Firth of Forth had come into view in the near distance. What was it about the sea, and the coast, that had such a pull? We all stopped to take in the panorama, right across to Fife at the other side. Longannet's tower, and its smoking power station, was not quite in the same category as the scenic coastal path further round, but it was still by the *sea*, and even though I'd lived in cities for almost all my working life I still missed having it on my doorstep.

Continuing with some reluctance, we lost the view for a short time, but in the grounds of Kinneil House there were plenty of other items of interest. An unassuming ruined cottage turned out to be James Watt's old workshop, with a cylinder for one of his engines outside it, and Kinneil House itself was a lovely old stone building which was part-museum.

"You know, I didn't even know James Watt'd lived anywhere near here." Once again, I reflected on my limited knowledge of important historical people or events.

"Nor me – and I never thought for one minute that the Antonine Wall would go through here either." Liksi pointed to a sign. Oh good – if our historian didn't know these things, then it was no shame that I didn't either.

We followed a long avenue to leave the Kinneil Estate, and turned onto the wonderfully named Snab Lane, then Snab Brae which led to a small car park.

"Wonder what all this's about?" Liksi drew our attention to the fact there were two parked police cars, and a police dog and handler right in our path. "Hope this doesn't mean we can't go any further."

"Hi there – can I just stop you for a minute?" The man was reining in his dog with apparent difficulty, and much as I love dogs I didn't fancy getting too near this one, an extremely powerful German Shepherd. Handsome beast, though.

"Just wanted to ask – have you seen this man recently?" A sheet of paper with different images and sketches was thrust in front of us. We took a good look; he didn't look particularly scary, but I couldn't remember ever being asked this question before. And what do mass murderers look like these days anyway?

"Nothing to worry about; just continue with your walk, but if you see him could you contact this number please?" He pointed to the number at the bottom of the page. "We just want to know that he's OK."

As he and the dog left, following the path we were about to take, we looked at each other.

"So, not a serial killer then." Fiona sounded relieved.

"That's good." I was joking, but there was still that wee frisson at the unexpected. We crossed a railway line and carried on, and I'm sure the others were peering into all the bushes just as I was – you never knew.

A seaweedy, slightly fishy smell was getting stronger, and the gulls wheeling and squawking above told us that we were nearing the foreshore. There, the curlews were picking their way delicately along the grey sands, like plump, well-dressed ladies trying not to get their feet dirty. Little ringed plovers scuttled busily about, ignoring them, and oystercatchers darted noisily overhead, seemingly determined to get noticed with their piercing cries.

Liksi, looking inland, drew our attention to clouds of steam, which turned out to be from a train on the Bo'ness and Kinneil Steam Railway. We stopped to watch – it was quite a dramatic sight as it chugged along, belching out thick dense clouds.

"Wouldn't like to be the owner of that over there." Liksi laughed as she pointed out a line of washing emerging gradually from the steam. "Not the wisest of moves, I'd have thought."

"Yip, you'd think the locals would know when to put out their washing – or not. Maybe it's a form of steam cleaning ..." At least Fiona'd the grace to make a face at her own weak joke.

By this time we were starving, so decided to head into Bo'ness for something to eat. However, this proved more difficult than it should've been. There was no pub that we could see that looked enticing enough to try, and no cosy cafés either. The main street was dingy and depressing, with paint peeling off doors and windows, and people going about their business with their heads down. Many of the sad-looking shop fronts had doors that were firmly closed.

"Look – photo of the man in the police notice." Liksi'd stopped at a shop window and was reading something taped to it. "Apparently he's a local man who's recently gone missing, and they're worried that something might've happened to him."

"So, not a mass murderer then. That's a relief – but poor man." I hoped he was all right – someone in distress, all on their own outside, did not bode well.

"I thought this was supposed to be a holiday town?" Fiona was mildly despairing, as we came back from yet another wild goose chase down what'd seemed to be a promising side street.

"*Was.* In the 50s or 60s, I'd guess. Seems to've been left behind now." Liksi was dead right – it was almost like the town that time forgot.

"Even worse than Rothesay." Fiona was peering inside the only cafe we'd been able to find. I glared at her, wishing I could get it into their thick heads that Rothesay, or at least the island of Bute, *were* attractive places.

After fortifying ourselves with run-of-the-mill filled rolls and coffee, we were glad to get back into the sunshine and head for the coast again. Bo'ness was a disappointment, but as I'd actually not known anything about it in the first place, it didn't really matter. Our spirits rose as we left the uninspiring town behind, and as we looked across the Forth I reflected that this really was an interesting walk today.

"There's Longannet power station over there." I pointed to a lightish-coloured tower silhouetted in the distance, back towards the west. "And that must be Dumyat sticking up."

"Dum-what?" Liksi asked, trying to follow where I was pointing.

"Dumyat. It's a hill in the Ochils, near Stirling. It's a good wee walk, actually, with great views. I remember it being a pain to find though – lots of driving about wee twisty roads."

"Walking? Without us? Surely not." Fiona gave me a mock glare.

"Yes, I do have other friends, you know. Some. People from work, actually." I often felt that I must've been a collie in a previous life – I'd go for a walk with anyone who'd take me.

The path continued to follow the shore, and we walked along without incident to the next place of interest – the imposing mass of Blackness Castle. We could see it well before we got there, jutting out from the shore within its protective walls, on its own small headland.

"I only know that's Blackness Castle from the map – I can't believe we're going through so many places today that I've never heard of, or haven't been to before." I was actually quite ashamed that my knowledge of this coast was so poor.

"Think I might've been here with Pete and the kids." Liksi frowned. "It was a long time ago and I don't really remember it being so impressive. Probably too busy trying to keep the kids under control."

It was more likely that she'd been trying to keep Pete under control – her children'd never been a problem. As we walked into the walled castle grounds, I went straight into the visitor shop and bought ice creams, which we consumed sitting at one of the wooden benches placed on the grass.

"Lovely spot." Fiona was scraping the bottom of her carton regretfully. "That castle looks indestructible, it's so solid and well-built. Good to see a castle that age, that's not a ruin."

"Yes, very impressive – great stonework." Liksi looked up from the leaflet she'd picked up in the shop. "Fifteenth century – they don't make them like that now."

"No indeed." I said this with feeling. "I heard recently that the new housing development going up near us is only expected to have a lifespan of 50 years. Cheap and quick – that's all that seems to matter." I could never understand why people would pay that kind of money when there was hardly a car's length between the houses.

"The castle was built as a home for the Crighton family, then used as a prison for a while." Liksi continued with her history lesson.

"Can't have been all that bad to've been incarcerated here." I looked up at the windows, imagining prisoners staring hopefully out at the coastline. "At least they'd have been able to see the sea, and ships arriving ..."

"Not if they were kept in the dungeons." This from Liksi, and she was probably right. Still, it was a great spot for resting walkers, and especially welcome after the depressing vibes in downtown Bo'ness. I could've stayed here, savouring the atmosphere, for hours, but –

"Time to go. Come on, enough loitering – another 4 miles yet." I grudgingly knew that Fiona was right, so pushed back unkind thoughts and got to my feet. It was unlikely that Alan and I'd come here in the near future – we were both always so busy, and any free time was either spent catching up with friends, or going on holidays to more distant locations. Not that I'd a problem with the latter – we'd be heading off to the Rockies and Vancouver in three weeks' time and my head was full of lakes, glaciers, wolves and bears ...

We picked up the path behind the castle, and soon found ourselves in thick woodland, though still with glimpses of the Forth through lightly swaying branches of beech, birch and oak. Not long after that we found ourselves in the well-manicured grounds of Hopetoun House. A light rumbling noise alerted us to the wonderful sight of a large herd of red deer sprinting in our direction down the grassy slope. They swerved to avoid us and continued their dash along the field until they disappeared into another patch of woodland in the distance.

"Wow, if I was American I'd say that was 'aaawesome'." Liksi was still staring after them, or at least where they'd last been. "What d'you think they were running from?"

"Or to?" I suggested. "Maybe it's tea-time. If I'd four legs I'd probably run like that at the prospect of food."

"I have no doubt of that." Cruel Fiona. "But maybe we just scared them."

"But they started by running *towards* us, not away from us. Hope we didn't get in the way of their dinner though." Lovely animals – such an unexpected sight. I just hope they weren't kept to be converted into venison for the House's grand banquets. The house faced east, in an imposing stone semi-circle; our route took us from the back of the building then round by the side; at the front we had another brief stop to admire the scale and lines of the magnificent Georgian building and gardens.

"Bit different from Blackness Castle." Liksi's tone was of reverence.

"Sure is – but just as imposing." Fiona leafed through the guide she'd pulled out of her bag. "It's about 250 years younger."

"*Still* built to last." I couldn't stop the comparison with modern buildings. "But imagine somewhere this size being built to house one family. There must've been many more servants than family."

"Puts Downton Abbey into the shade, doesn't it?" Actually, I thought Liksi had missed the point – it was *very* like Downton Abbey.

"You know, I'm not going to remember much about the history or details of any of these buildings, but it's been a real education today." I looked at the others to see if they felt the same. "I tend to think of a 'walk' as being out in the hills or along a beach, but this's been completely different. So interesting."

"It's more your territory than ours, Liksi," said Fiona. "Guess you've seen it all at some stage."

"Maybe, but not like this – not all at the same time. And you don't take things in to the same extent when you're younger."

"*Or* when you are older." I forgot things only too easily these days.

Even then, we hadn't finished admiring impressive constructions. When we emerged from Hopetoun Estate, the path led along the road next to the shoreline, and ahead of us lay the impressive spans of the three Forth crossings.

"When's the new bridge due to open? What's it called again?" Fiona asked.

"Queensferry Crossing – August some time, I believe. Unless there are any delays. But –" Liksi turned and looked at us smugly, "Alex and I will be walking across it *after* that."

Fiona and I looked at each other, shrugged, then waited for her to explain this statement.

"*We* are going to be walking across it on the 2nd of September. Alex and I – and about 25,000 others."

"Er, how come? I thought it was opening in August? Is there a wide pavement or something?" My grip of dates, space and logistics wasn't great at the best of times, and I'd no idea why she was so pleased with herself.

"We entered a ballot – they're going to close the bridge to let us all walk across on that day or the next."

"Oh." It would probably be quite a spectacle, but I did wonder if they'd be better just getting on with the business of transporting vehicles rather than people, as it'd originally been scheduled to open *last* year. However, as our weary feet took us into South Queensferry and past the various marinas, it was quite humbling and actually rather awe-inspiring to walk under the path of the silvery sails of the new Queensferry Crossing, and then under the path of the more familiar towers of the Forth Road Bridge. I would've appreciated them even more if my feet hadn't been so sore by then – we hadn't done a 15-miler for some time. It was still warm and sunny, though approaching late afternoon, and although we (well, me anyway) wanted to sit down somewhere with a drink as soon as possible we still wanted to remain outside. Of course, this meant traipsing up and down the main street till we found somewhere that suited everyone – did these two *never* get properly tired?

"Down here, look." Fiona was making her way down some stone steps beside the Boat House for a recce. "Tables outside. Perfect."

It was. Round metal tables placed on a concrete terrace, right above the shore. Children were paddling or sifting through pebbles, dogs were racing about chasing something only dogs understood, and the odd tourist was taking photos of the bridges. *What* a relief it was to sit down – maybe not the most comfortable of seats, but so what. There was that warming, embracing "end of day" ambience – still bright but with a mellow feel, and the beginning of a chill in the air.

"Drinks?" A waitress had appeared – what luxury, we didn't even have to go to the bar ourselves. A long, cool sip of IPA hit the mark and set me on the road to recovery.

"You know, I've just realised something." I put the glass down slowly as I thought this through. "I don't think I've thought about Mum and Dad since we last spoke about them. Not once."

"That's the idea." Liksi smiled at me with sympathy. "You needed this."

"And don't start feeling guilty." Fiona knew me only too well. "You know they'd have thoroughly approved of your having a day like this. You did need it."

I tightened the muscles in my face to stop the prickling behind my eyes developing into tears. They were absolutely right, I knew that, but somehow feeling so fulfilled and content seemed wrong, and disloyal to the memories of my wonderful parents. They'd been real outdoor people, and would've loved a walk like this – there'd been so much to see which would have interested them too. I'm sure Blackness Castle would've prompted a speel about Dad's time at Fort George on a different Firth, and Mum would've been able to identify all the birds, and, and ... I also knew that this feeling would lessen over time – but did I want it to? I missed them so, so much ...

I managed to hold myself together while we'd another drink; after that it was getting too chilly to think about eating outside so we went back up the steps to the main street to look for a restaurant called Orocco, which Liksi'd recommended. It wasn't far, and the airy spacious dining area looked out onto the Forth so we still had the views.

Afterwards, we didn't have long to wait for a bus, and once again I enjoyed the trip back into the centre of Edinburgh. Like anywhere you haven't seen for a while, everything's interesting, even though it's just streets that you used to traipse up and down as a student. And Princes Street itself – what a truly wonderful location, taken for granted all these years ago.

"Any chance of a drink in town before we go home?" I asked. I wasn't in Edinburgh very often, and it was too good an opportunity.

"Great idea." Fiona was equally enthusiastic, and Liksi led us without hesitation to the Café Royale. *What* a great pub – like so many in Edinburgh. It was mobbed, but a group of guys moved closer together and freed up some seating for us. We had a good chat with them before they moved on, then had the space to ourselves for a time.

"Too young for us, sadly." Fiona pulled a face.

"Still, we can always hope ..."

"Liksi! You've just *got* yourself a new man. How could you even think about it?" As I pretended to be shocked, I reflected on how easy we all were in male company. Also, there'd never been any jostling to be noticed; we just enjoyed the banter. One of the advantages of being ladies of a certain age, maybe. Talking of which –

"Right, you two ancients." I loved this bit. "In case you've forgotten, or thought it would go unnoticed, you're going to be occupationally pensionable in the next few months. Unlike me, being a mere youngster."

"Is that even a proper term?" Fiona asked. "We won't be *pensioners* though till we're 66."

"Thanks, I'm trying to forget all that." Liksi threw her arms out in despair. "Did you *have* to bring it up?"

"Oh yes. Being the baby, I'll need to get used to looking after you two in your dotage. Anyway, I just wondered – your choice of where to go for our next walk this year, to celebrate."

"Oh, we know where that's going to be, don't we Fiona?" They looked at each other and grinned, then back at me.

"Sure – a very special destination." This was Fiona. "Now, get those calendars out …"

Chapter 33 – Ben Nevis (September 2017) - Liksi

Ben Nevis, at 4,413 ft, is the UK's highest mountain. This 10.5-mile route is the most popular and least challenging one, commonly known as the Mountain Path. Opposite the Glen Nevis Youth Hostel, a path crosses the river and soon joins the main route to the top. The descent takes the same route, although on this occasion near the end, instead of turning off to the hostel, the walk continues on the main path to the Ben Nevis Inn.

Fiona's amused glance made me only too aware that I probably had a soppy look on my face as I watched Alex saying goodbye to Alan. Alex had driven me over to Bearsden, and this was the first time the pair had encountered each other. Quite a contrast – Edinburgh public schoolboy meeting rough'n'tumble Lanarkshire boy. Should've known they'd get on fine though – Alan was like an oversized puppy, always glad to have someone new to play with, and Alex was just – Alex. Totally, totally wonderful.

Fiona and I'd decided that the ascent of Britain's highest mountain was an appropriate challenge for the celebration of our 60th birthdays, and Eilidh'd offered to drive us up there.

I reluctantly said goodbye to Alex after he put my pack in the boot.

"See you on Sunday." He kissed me gently. "Take care – and have a good time." I leaned into his neck, savouring his scent and wishing I could take it with me.

"Good luck." Alan addressed us all then folded Eilidh into a bearhug. She laughed and winced at the same time as she disentangled herself, and watched with slight concern as he moved on to Fiona to repeat the exercise with equal enthusiasm.

"These two can manage themselves – couldn't leave *you* out of things!" was his excuse for squashing Fiona's spare frame as he nodded in our direction. I *think* she enjoyed the experience ...

There was a snort from Eilidh, before she asked, "So, what did you two ancients do for your birthdays?"

Oh, God, I'd been dreading this – but Fiona got in first.

"Oh, it was lovely – a few friends came round for fizz and canapé things in the afternoon." Poor soul; the old Fiona would've wanted a full-scale blast, I'm sure. "Jack and Marta came up for it, and Jack cooked the dinner for the four of us. Delicious, it was, too."

"Nice. What about you, Liksi?"

"Er, well, I – we - went up Ben Nevis." As expected, there was a stunned silence.

"Wh-at?" They were both staring at me with disbelief. Oh, God, I hoped they wouldn't take this the wrong way.

"Didn't tell you earlier because I didn't want it to change any of our plans for this weekend. Not long after the South Queensferry trip, Alex told me to keep the weekend before my birthday free, but wouldn't say what for."

"Hadn't you told him about *our* plans?" Eilidh sounded a bit plaintive.

"No - somehow they just got lost, what with work and other things, then I got quite excited about whatever Alex was planning. Joe and Julie arrived the night before, then I was told to pack walking gear, and off we all went north. Was only near Glencoe that I got an inkling of what he was planning."

"So what did he say when you told him about our trip?" This was Fiona.

"I – I didn't, until afterwards. Couldn't spoil it for him. The four of us went up together, and we'd champagne and salmon sandwiches at the top. It *was* lovely." I knew I was sounding a bit defensive, but it had been a complete coincidence.

"Oh. Well, at least we won't need Fiona to lead us this time. You'll know exactly where to go." Eilidh, I was relieved to see, was smiling.

"Don't think *anyone*'d need help finding their way up Ben Nevis – it's like a motorway. But listen, guys – I'm *really* looking forward to going up again." I'd had to make light of it all when I told Alex, though it'd all been rather unfortunate in some ways. "To get to the top once was great, but to get there twice in two months, specially with you guys, will be absolutely amazing. *Honestly.*"

"Well, well, you kept that one quiet." Fiona shook her head, but she too had a smile on her face. I did feel very bad about it all though.

The talk soon turned to safer topics, and I began to relax into the journey. It was unusual for us to be driving the full distance in the one car to get to our starting point, and I enjoyed the backseat views – unlike Fiona, who struggled with nausea as we navigated the bends along the top end of Loch Lomond, and she didn't improve much until we neared the more gentle outskirts of Fort William. We found the minor road that led to Ben Nevis, following the river, and the smart wooden Glen Nevis Youth Hostel soon appeared on the right-hand side of the road, just after a metal footbridge across the water. There was a handy car park at the back, and we lugged our gear round to the front entrance.

"And there's the Ben." Eilidh's voice was almost reverent as we stopped to look across the road at the looming mass. I'd to take her word for it, as I hadn't seen it quite from this angle before. Anyway, the top half was completely obscured in heavy mist, and there was a light drizzle by now which was a fair indicator that in a few hours' time there would be practically nothing to see of our nation's highest mountain.

"We were OK till near the top, then the mist came down and we didn't see a thing." I shivered slightly.

"Actually, we're not likely to see anything from the top either – apparently there's only something like 14 days a year when there's no mist at the summit. One interpretation of the Gaelic meaning of 'Ben Nevis' is 'mountain with its head in the clouds' – love it."

"Thanks, Eilidh. Very encouraging." Fiona laughed as she shook her head.

"You're welcome. I'd better not tell you what the other definition is. Come on, time to eat."

We'd walked the short distance back to the Glen Nevis Bar and Restaurant, and were waiting for a table, before Eilidh disclosed the other definition – 'venomous mountain'.

"Oh dear. You really know how to motivate people. Having its head in the clouds doesn't sound so bad after all." I picked up my drink, ready to move.

"How long did it take you – up and down?" asked Eilidh.

"Not sure – maybe eight hours or so? Weren't exactly trying to break any records, and Alex kept stopping to take photos." I could've kicked myself as that was likely to give Fiona the incentive to want to break my humble record – why hadn't I said nine hours? I caught Eilidh's eye and knew she was thinking the same thing. Never mind.

Eventually we headed back to the hostel and to bed – even I didn't read long this time before putting the light out.

The next morning, Fiona was up and looking out of the window as Eilidh and I came to slowly. "Come on, you two – up! Look – no mist! Unbelievable."

I tried to reconcile snatches of dreams/thoughts of Alex/remembering where we were and what was ahead. Screwing up my eyes, I tried to see the Ben through the sun streaming in through the windows. It did look enticing, with the purplish grey hulk softened by areas of green and gold in the sun – though once outside it was quite chilly, and there were patches of grey murk in the otherwise bluish sky.

"Good God, are we really going up there?" Eilidh looked in awe at the mass in front of us. "It's a lot higher than any of the other Munros we've been up. Ben Lawyers was the nearest – and Ben Lomond's only a baby at just over 3,000 ft."

"Yup – 4,412 ft of rock and hillside." Fiona'd obviously been doing her homework. Although it was only three weeks since I'd been up, I'd forgotten the stats already. Some of the finer points of the climb'd been lost on us – well, on me, anyway.

We crossed the road and the footbridge over the river, and followed the woodland path until it joined the one from the Visitor Centre, where I was on familiar territory. After a while the path became one of large boulders, sometimes usefully laid out like steps, but at other times just awkward buggers to get round or over. The terrain opened out; the sun was still pretty strong, and jackets and fleeces were soon discarded.

"T-shirt weather!" Eilidh proclaimed blissfully, stretching out her bare arms and lifting her face up to get the heat directly.

"Yup, just now – but look." Fiona pointed to the murky bank of cloud, which seemed larger and definitely much nearer now. However, there were also large fluffy clouds milling about, and in fact one of them had already draped itself over the top of the mountain. "Guess there'll be no views from the top, right enough."

The panorama from where we were now was terrific, though. We could look back over Loch Linnhe and the Mamores, and countless other mountains that I still couldn't identify. When we got to a small loch we stopped to savour the peaceful location in a plateau between slopes. The ripples on the surface were only slightly more pronounced than they'd been last time, and the couple of small tents we'd seen had gone, replaced by one or two groups of walkers having a picnic. It was quite airy though, as if the plateau served as a bit of a wind tunnel.

"Lochan Meall an t-Suidhe." Fiona enunciated this carefully, looking up from the map. "Excuse awful pronunciation. What's it mean, Eilidh?"

"Don't ask me," Eilidh replied, making a face. "Hold on – I might get a signal – oh, didn't expect to – seems to be something like 'Loch of the Hill of the Resting Place'." She peered into her phone.

"Guess that's the hill." I looked at the slope on the other side. "Quite a good name, really. Starts to become a bit more of a trudge from now on, if I remember."

"If you remember? It was only three weeks ago, you said!"

"Eilidh, I can't remember what I did yesterday, far less three weeks ago."

"That's what comes of paying more attention to Alex than your surroundings." Fiona'd that annoying grin on her face. Before I could object (although possibly without reason, if I was honest), Eilidh butted in:

"I expect I'll just have to get used to more of this kind of thing, with you two."

"What – gentle teasing?" Fiona raised her eyebrows in amusement.

"No – senility. Memory, eyes, ears – I'll be looking out for the signs from now on."

"Nonsense! Leave me out of it – I might be the oldest by all of two weeks, but I'm not having you put me in the 'has-been' box just yet. Come on, up!" Fiona'd her backpack on again and was buckling it up.

"I'm putting that phrase on your gravestone, Fiona." I laughed at her as I obediently got to my feet.

"Well, I hope that'll be a while yet. Come on, we need to get going – not even half-way up yet." And she marched ahead, leaving us to shake our heads and follow her. There was little vegetation by now, and after crossing the tumbling burn which cascaded down the hillside below from its lofty beginning somewhere above the path, the short green grasses soon gave way to scrub and stones. We concentrated on the climb now – this next bit was something to be endured, whereas earlier, however steep and sometimes awkward, it had been attractive and varied. This was *not* part of the climb I remembered fondly. The path crawled its way up in long zigzags through what was really just scree now. Loose, sometimes jaggy, sometimes slidey – and *always* uncomfortable to walk on. We caught up with Fiona from time to time when she waited for us, in case we lost each other before getting to the top. Eilidh and I'd slowed down – suppose I could've gone a bit faster, but I didn't particularly want to – partly for Eilidh's sake, but I was comfortable with the slower pace too. We stopped a few times and exchanged pleasantries with other walkers; there was always that camaraderie in the hills, based on a shared love of the outdoors, and a shared empathy when the going got tough.

And now, another change – we seemed to have caught up with the murk, which had insidiously thickened and wound its way round everything. Apart from brief glimpses, the views had gone, and we'd to concentrate more and more on the line of the path, and following other walkers. We put our jackets on again, although we were still too warm to put the hoods up against the thickening mist. Up, up, inexorably up. I'd been looking out for the drop at Five Finger Gully, and sure enough we were able to see it on our right as we passed by, making sure we were as far away from the edge as possible. So easy to miss that in weather conditions not much worse than this – and this was still summer. Just. Five Finger Gully was the name I could remember, but really the vertical drops on the other side were even more scary – and I'd no Alex gripping on to me this time.

Finally, the outline of Fiona appeared ahead of us, flapping her arms about.

"I think this is it," she announced. "Liksi?"

I peered ahead, vaguely making out groups of people, cairns and other stone structures. Through the mist, it all looked rather eerie – it'd been a much thinner mist last time and the actual top'd been a bit more obvious.

"Yes, this is what they call the 'summit plateau'," I said. "There's a cairn about somewhere – the other things are memorials, or shelters that people've built up. All a bit messy." I hadn't wanted to tell them that beforehand, as half of the thrill of climbing is the thought of being at the top, view or no view, but quite honestly the top of Britain's highest mountain isn't somewhere I'd want to spend too much time.

"What's that?" Eilidh was pointing to the highest structure.

"Old observatory, now an emergency shelter. Come on, let's find the cairn." We moved towards the shape with the most people round it, then had to wait our turn and ask someone to take a photo. Even our wet and sweaty faces couldn't hide our grins of achievement as we lined up with Eilidh in the middle – 'an oldie on each side' as she styled it. OK, all these other people'd done it too – and so'd I three weeks ago – but I still felt elated, to be here with these two, and I knew they'd feel the same.

"Come on, we need to find a sheltered spot for lunch." Fiona started picking her way over the boulders to examine some of the mini shelters.

"How about here?" Eilidh had stopped at one of them. "Mm, no, it's a bit niffy. Keep looking."

We finally found a shelter that was just being vacated, and settled in cautiously.

"Right, time to celebrate." Fiona brought out three of these plastic champagne flutes that you click onto a stem, and I was already starting to uncork one of the 3 small bottles of Prosecco I'd brought.

"Cheers!" We clinked glasses and I took a long draft of my second glass of fizz at the top of the Ben. I could get used to this.

"Here's to you two – happy 60th birthdays, and may you survive another year at least to help me celebrate mine next year." Eilidh downed hers in two gulps.

"Looking forward to it already – but you can stop the smug, baby of the group stuff," I said, washing a mouthful of ham salad roll down with more Prosecco.

"Good to have got up here, after all these years. Should've been a doddle for you, second time round." Fiona looked at me questioningly.

"Don't think it would ever be a doddle, however many times you went up." I said this with feeling.

"It wasn't an *arduous* climb, just a long slog. I don't feel too bad really." Eilidh was right – because the path's so well defined, and there are so many people, it was just a case of following the crowds. It was still a real trudge though.

"I think I'm going to be very glad to get away from here – it's not exactly fragrant." Fiona, wrinkling her nose and looking at the swelling crowds with disdain, started to pack away our glasses. There was no dissent from us. There was no view, except fuzzy outlines of other walkers, and of makeshift shelters and cairns. So, in spite of our plans to relax and enjoy the moment – 60 and still walking, and very much still together – it wasn't long before we started downhill again. At least we'd a lot to look forward to on the way down – smells, mist and crowds receding, giving way to warmth and sunshine, glorious views, and the prospect of a good evening to finish off a memorable day.

We made good progress down the zigzags, and stopped at the tumbling burn, which Eilidh could now tell us was called the Red Burn, presumably due to the colour of the peaty water at times. It was a very pretty spot, with the water gurgling down the hillside above us, then trickling down the other side. Boulders were scattered up the slope, forming ideal seats for groups of walkers enjoying a rest and taking in the scenery. We polished off the other two bottles of Prosecco – well, they *were* small - and watched as a young guy hobbled up to the burn and started to wash an alarming amount of blood off his leg. He seemed all right otherwise, and it wasn't long before he limped back onto the path, and passed in front of us.

"You OK?" I called out. "Got a First Aid kit if you need it." After our first few walks, Alan had always insisted that Eilidh carried one with her, but we'd hardly ever used it other than for the odd blister plaster.

The guy stopped and turned round. "Yeah, no worries. Thanks. I'll get it seen to when I get down." With a smile and a dismissive wave, he was off.

"Pity. Sure we'd have enjoyed looking after him." I watched as he negotiated his way lopsidedly down the loose stones. "Looks painful."

"Just as well he didn't take you up on the First Aid." Eilidh was laughing as she turned round.

"What d'you mean?" I looked at her, puzzled.

"Have you *seen* our First Aid kit recently? There's hardly anything in it he could've used, except maybe a grimy bandage and some dried-up antiseptic wipes."

"Oh well, was worth a shot. I'd just have blamed you for not keeping it up to date."

As there were no other young injured males in need of attention, we set off downhill shortly afterwards. The loch was just as peaceful as it'd been on the way up, and the views were even better. The next bit over the boulders however, was much more painful going down than up. This was partly because it was trickier to negotiate them going downhill when the momentum could carry you forward too quickly, but also my knees were starting to scream. I was relying heavily on my single pole by now. I didn't often use it, and never uphill – but it certainly took at least some of the pressure off the knees on the way down. Fiona was doing her Iron Woman bit and didn't seem bothered in the least, but Eilidh was also going slowly and carefully, often placing her feet sideways to get a better purchase.

"Thank God for poles." She was leaning on hers heavily. "I'd be in some state without them. Heavens, where are all these people coming from?" We all stopped to stare at what seemed like scores of people, mainly youngsters, coming towards us, chattering brightly as they walked past.

"What on earth are they doing starting the climb at this time?" It seemed madness to me.

"It's 5 o'clock, and it's taken us nearly seven hours – they'll be coming down in the dark. Insane." Fiona had checked her watch, and was looking back up the hillside at them. They didn't have the look of normal walkers – too sociable, walking in groups, and not always with suitable footwear. Oh well, they were young, they'd soon learn.

It was good to get off the boulders and back down into the woodland, where the path became much easier, and eventually arrived at the branch for the hostel straight ahead, or the Nevis Inn to the right. It was a no-brainer – in spite of adding half a mile or so, and being badly in need of showers, we just *had* to have a drink at the end of today, so we plodded on to the place we'd fond memories of from the end of our West Highland Way trip. Unfortunately, the beer garden at the back was full, although hardly unexpected on a day like this.

"Might be quieter inside." Fiona went up the steps to the entrance. "We need to go in to get a drink anyway."

"Och, no, not *steps*." Eilidh groaned as she forced her weary legs into one last effort, before collapsing onto a stool as soon as Fiona found us a table. Mind you, she soon got up again to check out the beers on tap when I went up to order.

"The body can always rise to a life-or-death challenge, and getting a decent pint of beer now is definitely one of these times." She looked through the whole range before asking me for Skye Red. Unusually, she went straight back to sit down at the table, without engaging the barman in a conversation about the finer points of the beer.

"Were you at the top today?" He looked up from pulling the pint.

"Yeah – mist on the top third, but otherwise great conditions. We're just down – met hundreds of youngsters just starting up though. Hope they know what they're doing – they'll be coming down in the dark."

"Oh, aye, that lot. They'll be linked to some kind of organisation, or charity, so they should be reasonably prepared – but there's always the odd one who goes up without any rain gear, or in a T-shirt with nothing else to put on when it gets cold. We get loads of these large groups, almost every day from March to October."

I relayed this news to the others as I went back with the drinks. "He also said that several of these groups do the 'Three Peaks Challenge' - that's Ben Nevis, Scafell Pike and Snowdon in 24 hours."

I was pretty impressed, but Eilidh had a look of slight disdain on her face. "Eh?" That's sheer madness. What on earth would you put yourself through that for? There'd be no chance at all to enjoy the views or – or just take in the setting."

"So I take it you're not in favour of the Three Peaks Challenge for our 70ths then, Eilidh?" Fiona winked at me. "Oh – it's OK, I wouldn't ..." Eilidh was making a disgusted face as she put down her beer hurriedly.

"No, it's not that – this beer's terrible! I'm sure it must be off –" and away she was up at the bar again, while Fiona and

I exchanged amused glances. When she finally came back with something she deemed acceptable, we'd a couple more drinks then moved upstairs for something to eat. By that time we didn't care about our unshowered state, and a meal and a couple of bottles of wine to finish off our celebrations seemed much more immediate. Later – much later – we started to think about getting back to the hostel.

"You know, I didn't think I'd say this, but I'm really looking forward to getting outside again." Eilidh did sound a bit fuzzy. "It's so *hot* up here."

It was, and she was right – as we stumbled outside, forcing those tired legs to work again, the fresh air was welcome, although I think we could all've done without the extra walk. However, the woodland smells, animal rustlings and gurgling stream were welcome accompaniments as we traipsed wearily back through the trees to the hostel in the dwindling light. Just before we went inside, we paused to look back at the mountain – and there, twinkling in a slow-moving ribbon down the slope, were the lights from countless head torches.

"Rather magical, isn't it?" Eilidh voiced all our thoughts as we watched them for a while.

"A fitting end to a special occasion." I meant every word.

Chapter 34 – Blairgowrie to Kirkmichael (May 2018) - Fiona

The Cateran Trail is a 64-mile loop through Perthshire and Angus tracks and drove roads. This 16-mile stretch starts at the small town of Blairgowrie, following the River Ericht, leading over Cochrage Muir to Bridge of Cally, then through Strathardle Glen and Blackcraig Forest to the village of Kirkmichael.

"D'you think the car'll be OK here?" asked Eilidh, looking back rather anxiously at her new Honda as we headed to the Kirkmichael Hotel with our bags. She'd picked me up at Pitlochry station, and we'd taken a series of minor roads to get to this small village. We'd parked the car over the bridge in a small car park, as there didn't seem to be any room nearer the hotel.

"It'll be *fine*. It's not exactly a city centre crime hotspot here." God, Eilidh could be so anxiety-ridden sometimes.

"I know, but still. I could try and move it later on if a space appears."

"That'll need to be before your second pint, then." The hotel was just across the small bridge, and as we approached we could see Liksi waving from a window on the first floor. With a bit of luck it would look out over the car park so Eilidh would stop fretting.

"You just come in that door there and up the stairs," Liksi shouted down. Her instructions led us to the family room that I'd booked a couple of months earlier. I looked round with approval at the 3 beds and opened the door to the en-suite.

"Comfortable, clean and definitely a step up from our usual hostel accommodation," was my verdict. "So, Liksi, how'd your bus tours go?" Liksi had done her usual – arrived here via at least two buses.

"Absolutely *fine*, thanks. You needn't laugh – I'm now an expert on local buses so we're all fixed for tomorrow." She waved a handful of timetables at us. Soon afterwards, we headed downstairs to start the weekend properly, settling down at a shiny wooden table beside the window.

"So, what d'you think –" I stopped in mid-sentence as a tanned, silver-haired man came up to our table.

"Hiya, girls." *Girls?* He gave us a broad, slightly proprietorial, smile. "How's the room?"

"Er, hi." Eilidh looked rather taken aback.

"Good thanks." Liksi returned the smile. "These're the other two. This gentleman checked me in." Ah. The mid-Atlantic twang had thrown me.

"Tek. Pleased to meet y'all. Your pal here said you're doing the Cateran Trail tomorrow?"

"Just one part of it." Eilidh was quick to make this clear. "We'll do the rest another time."

"Good stuff. You can eat here or through there in the dining room. Have fun." He nodded to us and went off round the corner in the direction of the small Reception area.

"Tek?" I asked, raising an eyebrow as I looked at Liksi.

"I *think* that might be his name. Seems to run the place. Was very welcoming when I arrived, anyway."

We'd a decent meal in the bar not long after that, and stayed for a few drinks, but Tek didn't make a further appearance even though the bar was very lively. A number of young males came in one after another, and got louder and louder as bottle after bottle was drained. When the shots started appearing and disappearing with equal rapidity, we feared the worse.

"I don't think I've ever seen people trying to get drunk so quickly." Eilidh had to shout above the noise.

"That's probably because you can't remember most of your student years." Liksi shouted back.

"Ha, very funny. They seem pretty happy, though, don't they?" Eilidh looked back at the bar, which was rapidly becoming an essential prop for many of them in an attempt to keep upright. It was actually rather pleasant to watch them enjoying themselves – they all appeared to know each other pretty well. Then I inadvertently caught the eye of one of them, having been admiring his flowing black locks, and suddenly he was lurching over to us and collapsing on a nearby chair.

"'Lo ladies." He beamed at us all beatifically. "Lovely ladies." He raised his bottle to us, then realised it was empty, so yelled over to one of his mates for another one.

"Is this a celebration or a normal Friday night?" I asked him. Heavens, if this was normal, Kirkmichael must be quite a place. And where on earth did all these young guys come from?

"Finished! Home tomorrow - lasht night!" He swept his arm expansively to indicate his mates, and I grabbed hold of my glass. "Oops!" He put his hand to his mouth in mock apology.

"Davy! Get back over here and leave the lassies alone." As our friend aimed a vacant look towards the source of the voice, a small wiry chap picked up a full shot glass and held it up. "Come on – your drink's here."

"Mus' go." Davy hauled himself to his feet with difficulty, beamed at us again and staggered back to the bar, where he was welcomed back into his raucous group of friends.

"Well, and there was me thinking I'd got a lumber – to borrow your phrase, Eilidh."

"What d'you mean, *you* thought you'd got a lumber?" Liksi laughed. "I thought he was heading over for *me*."

"Right – and *I* think it's high time we went to bed." I was none too steady myself. It didn't take much to set me off these days, and we'd over fifteen miles ahead of us the next day. We left the lads to their celebrations and went upstairs.

The next morning at breakfast, we were served by a familiar face. After we'd been waiting for quite a while, a rather harassed Tek appeared to take our order.

"Sorry for the delay – short staffed. Hard to get staff here – small place." Judging from the length of time it took for our breakfasts to arrive, he seemed to be cooking as well as waiting on tables.

"Hope the noise from the bar didn't keep you up all night." He put the toast on the table.

"No, not at all – but they were certainly having a good time. D'you know what they were celebrating?" I vaguely remembered our friend trying to tell us last night.

"Oh yes – they've been here on a three-month contract working on the wind turbines. That's them finished – they'll be on their way home this morning."

"If they're fit to travel - there'll be a few sore heads." Liksi passed over some of the other dishes.

"I have to ask." Eilidh leaned over. "Where's that accent from?"

"Ah, well – I'm actually from round here." He smiled at the rather incredulous looks we gave him. Turned out he'd spent time in the States as a police detective. At least that explained his name, but not why he was now running a hotel in Kirkmichael.

He didn't re-appear, so we set aside all thoughts of the US police and our intriguing host and instead concentrated on the maps for the day's walk, as none of us were familiar with the area. We decided to get the bus to Blairgowrie, and walk back towards Kirkmichael. The journey only took about half an hour, but it was good to get off the bus into the bright, bustling little town, ready to start.

"Nice." Eilidh was looking round at the well-kept floral displays and twee shop windows. "I don't remember ever having been here before."

"We used to come here in the holidays sometimes." I remembered being dragged here as a sulky teenager, when the last thing I wanted was to be detached from my friends and our inane ploys. My poor parents had been trying to do the best for me – but I didn't want to go too far down that road as it led to our own relationship with Nathan. *Had* we done the best for him? We'd never know.

At the bridge, we went down the steps and took the path upstream along the Ericht. I was just settling into a rhythm, when there was a yell from Eilidh, and as I turned round to see what was going on, there was another yell from Liksi as she careened into her.

"No! I don't believe it!" Eilidh was looking down with horror.

"What is it? What's wrong?" I don't know what I was expecting to see – a snake or something?

"Look! My feet!" She held out a foot and pointed to it, hopping about on the other leg.

"My FEET! Look at them!" Even then it didn't quite dawn on us.

"Boots! I haven't got my boots on!" A closer inspection revealed that she was sporting suede slip-on shoes which, although rather comfy looking, were definitely not walking boots.

"Oh, right enough." I began to laugh. "Can you walk in them?"

"Well, I'm just going to have to – I can't go back now. Oh, what an *idiot*! I must've forgotten to change them after breakfast, when I went to check on the car."

"Just be glad it wasn't your slippers you were wearing!" Liksi teased her as she inspected their soles. "At least they've got a bit of a grip. Sure you're OK to continue?"

"We'll soon find out. Will you two stop laughing? You won't be doing that when you've got to carry me over burns and bogs!"

"No indeed – though I thought you said you'd lost weight recently?" Liksi wiped her eyes. "Good one, Eilidh!"

With a lot of hilarity, and further expressions of self-disgust from Eilidh, we carried on until we got to a viewing platform where we paused to look down over the tumbling white froth below.

"I think this must be Cargill's Leap." I referred to the walkhighlands printout which I was reading whilst trying to avoid strangling Eilidh, as it was still in the plastic holder round her neck.

"Was Cargill a Cateran?" Liksi was trying to read the printout too. "In fact, what *is* a Cateran?"

"I think they were fierce cattle-raiders. No, Cargill was a minister and a Covenanter according to this. You'd *think* that he wouldn't be in the habit of stealing anything, but then you never know ..."

This was another of the many reasons why the three of us got on so well. We were interested in some of the back stories we came across in our walks, but didn't make a big deal of them. Snippets of history, geography or biology were fine, and interesting to everyone, but more complex explanations would've been too heavy for the blanket of friendship we had wrapped around ourselves over the years. Learning about each other's lives, and supporting each other through them, was much more important.

The trail continued past farm buildings and through fields, and alongside wooden fences and ancient stone dykes, with the odd cattle grid thrown in. Eilidh seemed to be managing fine, although I did wonder how she'd deal with this muddy bit I'd just got through. You could plough through it with reasonable confidence in boots, but it would be easy to put a shoe-clad foot down in the wrong place and find you'd a shoe full of sludge.

"Need a hand?" I called back, but Liksi was taking care of it, walking carefully in front of Eilidh and testing each foothold out first. It was slow going, but at least the muddy bit wasn't too extensive.

"I made it!" Eilidh placed a second foot carefully beside the first one on a solid-looking tussock of grass and grinned at us. "Thanks, Liksi – that made all the difference."

"Feet still OK?" Liksi asked her, moving to stand on another tussock beside her.

"Aye – dry, and only a slight pre-blister feeling on my wee toe so far."

We carried on, the path moving from farmland to moorland, then back into woodland where we came up against a gate with a rather unwelcoming notice beside it.

"They're felling trees and don't want people coming in," Eilidh told us, being the nearest to the notice.

"Oh well – why don't we do a slight detour to the Bridge of Cally Hotel anyway?" I'd seen the sign to the hotel, hidden in the trees. "We can work out what to do over lunch."

"Good idea – and I can sort out my almost-blister too."

It didn't take long to backtrack slightly and divert to the hotel, which was situated on the road just before the bridge. We were well used to stopping off at watering holes en route, but as soon as we got up the ramped entrance and through the door, we realised from the elegant décor and general ambience that this was rather more of an upmarket establishment than we normally frequented.

"Oh dear, I don't think they're used to walkers in here," Eilidh almost whispered, after we'd received a rather disdainful look from a woman in a smart belted dress as we trooped past. There were a few occupied tables in the main bar area, all of whom seemed to have equally well-turned-out adults or designer-clad children sitting there – but Liksi led us through to a more distant area which was empty of customers, and I headed for a table by the window, overlooking a grassy lawn with the river beyond.

"I'm sure the rest of the clientele will be happy that we're tucked here out of the way." I sat down and looked out at the slow-moving river. My thought was reinforced when Eilidh came back from the bar – after an interminable time away.

"Sorry that took so long." She placed our drinks carefully on the table. "All *very* polite, but at least three bar people gave me one of those forced smiles, said they'd be with me shortly – and then promptly ignored me as they served other tables."

"Guess they worked out that we'd not be having much, and that we don't look like future overnight guests." Liksi picked up her glass. "Anyway, who cares? We're here – and these are comfy seats." She wriggled into the back of her chair, and stretched back luxuriously.

We'd a look at the menu and ordered biscuits and cheese, risking another trip to the bar (me this time), and then relaxed and just enjoyed the view at last. It was certainly a lovely spot – but definitely not my type of place. I like luxury, but not stuffiness. Luxury for me is quality surroundings, but where I feel comfortable enough to be myself and not put on a false persona.

"I can't believe that my feet are holding up so well." Eilidh carefully stuck a precautionary Compeed round her toe. "Maybe I didn't need to spend all that money on my last pair of boots – I could've been using these all the time instead."

"What are they again – your boots, I mean?" asked Liksi.

"Salomon. Got quite a bit off them in Tiso's sale last August – because they were the winter version, rather than the summer one. That meant, apparently, that they were brown instead of pale blue – honestly!"

"Ah, Eilidh, you'll never be a shopper." I shook my head at her in mock despair. "No vagaries of fashion for you. Sound common sense will never make a shopper."

We didn't linger there after our lunch, although that lawn, with the clear water rippling its way past, was very seductive.

It would've been good to just sit there reading a book all afternoon – some other time. On a different bit of the river, without the hotel.

We'd a look at the map to see how we could proceed without going through the gate which had the notice beside it, but there was no obvious alternative.

"We'll just have to go through the gate and hope for the best." I noted Eilidh's alarmed look but chose to ignore it. "Otherwise we'd have to walk along the road, from here to Kirkmichael, and that would be quite a bit longer."

"Don't fancy that – at all." Liksi settled it. As it happened, when we got to the gate and read the notice properly, it was vehicular access that was prohibited, not pedestrian. Duh. Trust Eilidh to err on the *far* side of caution – although she did have the grace to accept her mistake. However, the walking was easy and I kept the pace up as we moved from forest track to paths delineated by drystane dykes, and then to more open moorland again. We'd a bad stretch when I hared off in the wrong direction just as the waymarkers did a vanishing act, and of course that had to coincide with another muddy patch. It took two or three goes, and frequent consultations over maps, before we found ourselves back on the right route again.

"Feet still OK?" Liksi asked, looking down at Eilidh's shoes, which were looking considerably less presentable than they'd been when we first noticed them.

"OK, if a bit tight-feeling now, but I don't think these'll ever be the same again." Eilidh held out a foot, looking at her shoe rather mournfully. "They weren't designed to be completely covered in thick mud, and they must be pretty mucky inside too by now."

She perked up as we rounded Dalvey Loch, the pine-sheltered water a welcome addition to the scenery, and home to enough avian wildlife to take her mind off muddy shoes. A couple of miles or so later, we plodded wearily into

Kirkmichael's tarred streets. After checking that Eilidh's car hadn't done a disappearing act since the morning, we went back over the bridge towards our hotel, but on my suggestion we carried on a few hundred yards to the right to reach the Strathardle Inn. It was always good to try out different places – and its cosy bar bore this out.

"If we have a drink here, we can see if we want to eat here as well or go back to the Kirkmichael." I dragged a third chair to the table, then plonked myself down with relief. Goodness, this being 60 business was taking its toll – not that I'd admit it to the others.

"Eilidh, you can't have long to go now." I took off my fleece with relief before looking up at her..

"Sounds as if she's pregnant." Liksi laughed as Eilidh spluttered into her beer.

"Now that *would* be a miracle – but you're right. I don't have long to go, if you're talking about retirement. Three months yesterday, in fact. I can - not - wait."

"Really?" Liksi opened a bag of crisps and handed them round. "I know you've been talking about it for ages, but I'm still surprised – you always seemed to be working, even at weekends."

"I know, I know – but I overdid it really. The last two years I've just been ready to go. Burnt out, I suppose. I can't wait, I really can't. Getting up at 8 instead of 6, having time to read the paper over a coffee before deciding what to do with the day – bliss!"

"You'll be travelling quite a bit, though, isn't that the plan?" I felt a stab of jealousy; that was just not possible for Olly and me now. We'd both had big retirement plans – together and separately – but I'd just have to accept that things – many things - would need to be different.

"Aye, hope to get to New Zealand later this year to visit some cousins, and maybe back to South America after that.

We've always given cruises a body swerve, but I'm trying to persuade Alan to go on one that follows Darwin's footsteps."

"Cool. Yeah, s'pose a specialist cruise should be OK, with a smaller ship. Can't imagine you on one of those monstrosities with millions of people." Liksi shuddered. "Always think they're going to topple over one day."

"Oh, I know. Imagine us and 'the entertainment' on board! That's just not what we'd ever want from a holiday."

"Never say never. You don't know what life will hold." I reflected sadly that all my grandiose working plans had gradually faded too, as other aspects of my life had taken priority.

"Can't imagine me getting to the female equivalent of the pipe and slippers stage." Liksi had always been sure about this. "Not that I love my job, exactly – but I just can't imagine ever not working."

"You wait – once *we've* stopped you'll think differently." I'd felt the same as Liksi until very recently.

"'We'? Don't tell me *you're* going to retire soon as well?" Liksi looked at me in amazement. "Thought you said you were going to keep going."

"I – I don't know." I looked down at my drink. "Work gets me away from the situation at home, and it is interesting, and challenging. But Olly's got so many medical appointments, and needs so much done for him, that I feel I'm constantly juggling. And dropping balls more often." I smiled at them, hoping to remove any element of pity. There'd be time enough for that. "We'll see."

"Oh, just *look* at this!" Liksi was staring at something under the table, and when I bent down to investigate I found a pair of liquid brown eyes, with an adoring gaze moving from one of us to the other in turn, and a feathery tail thumping the floor in excitement.

"Look at those eyelashes! I've never seen a dog with eyelashes like that." Eilidh was immediately smitten, and started fondling the cockapoo's silky ears while indulging in fulsome dog-talk, earning herself a devoted look as the animal's sleek body rippled from left to right with sheer delight.

"Hamish! Stop mooching!" This came from a guy at the neighbouring table, who made a move towards us. "I'm sorry, I'll get him – he's got dreadful table manners."

"No, he's all right, honestly. In fact, he's *gorgeous*," I added, as the guy sat down again with a look of relief. I didn't normally fall for dogs, at least not in the way Eilidh did, but this one was something else. He was a beautiful golden honey colour, and just oozed friendliness and zest for life. As we made a fuss of the dog, his owner was joined by a bearded friend. It turned out that they – and Hamish - were doing the Cateran Way too, all of it, and this was their second – and middle – day.

"He looks as if he could do it all again right now," Liksi was lost in admiration. It crossed my mind that it said something about us that we were more interested in the dog than his owners – another sign of age? Reluctantly, we soon had to go next door when our table was called, leaving Hamish to sniff out other potential admirers.

"So, you oldies, I'll be as ancient as you in a couple of months. Hope you've booked the ferry OK?" asked Eilidh between mouthfuls of chicken something. She'd planned a big trip for us.

"Absolutely. Can't wait to see this place – you've been talking about it for so long." I looked at Liksi, who nodded. Next time we met, Eilidh would be 60 and retired, and we'd be walking out to the place that meant more to her than anywhere else, except possibly her own home. And who knows – maybe I'd have called it a day work-wise, too.

Chapter 35 – Rubha Mor (July 2018) - Eilidh

This walk takes place in the remote parish of Uig, on the Isle of Lewis near the border with Harris. The exact location and some local placenames have been left out or changed. 'Rubha Mor' is the name used to refer to the house, the croft and the immediate area around it. Part of the walk is on an estate track, and the actual house has new owners now. The return walk would be about 16 miles, all over rough ground.

"You could sit here forever and look at that view." There was something approaching reverence in Liksi's voice as she gazed out the conservatory window at the gathering dusk, while the oversized glass of Merlot on the table beside her remained untouched.

We were in my cousin's old crofthouse, situated in an enviable position above the vast expanse of white sands in a remote part of Uig, on the west coast of Lewis. Almost every year of my childhood, my father had brought us here for Easter or summer holidays; this house had been his home for a brief period after his parents had left Rubha Mor. Weeks were spent running along these sands, poking about in rock pools, climbing the hills, ruining the sheepdogs with affection and playing with a myriad of small cousins. It'd been paradise then, even before I was old enough to appreciate it as I do now. After leaving school, other holiday activities such as earning money or basking with various boyfriends on Greek islands had been more appealing, but when I came back from my back-packing stint round Australia many years ago, I re-discovered it, drawn back by my network of wonderful relatives and the haunting scenery.

"You wouldn't believe the colours could change so much." Even Fiona appeared mesmerised, and her voice was almost a whisper. "Look - the water from the river has gone red to match the sunset now." A rusty brown swirl had furrowed its way into the sands, giving a depth of tone to the amber-red patterns vying with the grey-tinged clouds above.

"We should really be at the other side of the headland to see the sun going down behind the wee beach." I smiled lazily, knowing that nothing was going to prise me from my current position. Having spent countless evenings over the years looking out at the sands as they moved in and out with the tides, fringed by the hills of Suaineabhal and Mealaisbhal, every time was different and the older I got the more I treasured the uniqueness of every single occasion. I swirled the Talisker round in my glass before taking another sip, thinking how well its peaty aroma and burning sensation matched the sights and scents of the location.

"This is just magic." Liksi picked up her glass without moving her gaze. "Thought the view from the dining room at Ullapool was great, but this, this ..."

"I know. I feel so privileged to be part of it – Lewis is in my blood, in spite of never having lived here. And I can't tell you how much it means to me to be here with you two this year, of all years."

"And we're honoured you asked us." Fiona turned to look at me. "Honestly. I know that sounds corny, but it's true. What a wonderful place."

I'd just had my 60th birthday a few days ago, with a handful of close friends and local relatives. The long spell of glorious weather had enabled us to transform our lawn into a beer garden – well, actually a *champagne* garden – and the crowning glory was the cake that Alan had designed for me. The icing outlined a map of Lewis, with key place names, and miniature boots and poles positioned in strategic places. It was an absolute masterpiece.

"And now that you're retired, you could come here any time." Liksi took a long slow sip of wine.

"Guess so, although I haven't thought that bit through yet." I was just so very, very happy and savouring 'being in the moment'; any future plans could wait.

"What d'you think then, about tomorrow?" asked Liksi, waving at the sky. "Red sky at night, etc?"

"Well, Auntie Mary Ann says tomorrow will be fine - the oracle has spoken. I just hope Peigi will agree with her." For the first time in our walking history, we were going to be accompanied on the trek out to Rubha Mor. My second cousin Seonaid and her husband Jim were on holiday here and had asked to join us, and Peigi was Seonaid's friend who lived in another village overlooking the sands. I was grateful to have local knowledge involved, as I'd only been out to Rubha Mor on three previous occasions, mostly when I was much younger, and there wasn't a defined trail. The island's weather could change in minutes, and I didn't want to take any chances in what could be very inhospitable terrain. Anyway, I loved all my cousins to bits, and any opportunity to be in their company, or that of their friends, was a bonus.

"Indeed." Fiona was a bit on edge, as she was uncomfortable leaving Olly for any length of time now, and wasn't sure how many days she'd be able to stay. The sooner we could get out there, the better.

"Well, it was hardly a hardship not to've gone today." Liksi'd taken the whole week off and she was determined to make the most of it. "We had a nice little warm-up, and another gorgeous beach. You are so *lucky*."

The weather'd been very overcast this morning, and both Auntie Mary Ann and Peigi had warned against tackling the hilly trip to Rubha Mor today. Instead, we'd walked the seven-mile loop round the island of Great Bernera. Far from merely passing the time, it took in a flattened cottage, washing hung out on a Sunday[13] (must remember to tell my

---

[13] Religion plays an important part in Lewis; any work on a

aunt!), the identification of countless machair[14] flowers and trying to get these two townies to remember their names, a picture-perfect beach, an iron-age house and a Time and Tide Bell. Not bad for a warm-up.

I was almost scared to wake up the next morning. Flinging the curtains open, and for once ignoring the vast expanse of sand, I looked anxiously at the sky. It was still grey, but maybe, maybe not quite so heavy? Just then, the phone rang and I raced down the stairs.

"It's on. Meet you at the second parking bit on the old road at 9.30." Seonaid was off the phone before I could exchange any pleasantries.

"It's on!" I shouted up the stairs. "Out of your pits, you two – today's the day!"

Even Liksi was up almost before I'd finished speaking, and we were all dressed and downstairs in record time. After eating Fiona's porridge and toast, I made up tuna mayonnaise rolls while Liksi gathered whatever fruit and biscuits she could find – after all, there'd be no welcoming pubs or cosy cafes where we were going. We threw our stuff in the car and set off along the rough single-track road, going into a passing-place once to let a car past.

"D'you know that person?" asked Liksi. "He seemed to know you."

"No – well, maybe he did. The locals'll know we're here and most of them knew my father, but I don't always recognise everyone. Anyway, you always wave in passing places. Island etiquette."

We drove through a couple of places too small to be called villages, each with a scattering of houses. Most were croft houses, but several were occupied by people too elderly to be able to do much in the way of crofting any more. A vehicle

---

Sunday is frowned upon

[14] Grassy and sandy low-level coastal plain, often with an extensive carpet of wildflowers

track to the right, over the heathery soil, led to the peat bank where Auntie Mary Ann cut her peats. Many of the islanders cut their own peat; I still loved the smoky aroma of peat fires – they were part of the heady scent of the island. At the end of the second village, the road became narrower, and tufts of sturdy grass with the odd sea pink grew in the raised bump along the centre of the road.

Seonaid, Jim and Peigi were already waiting for us as I pulled into a cleared area and drew up beside their battered Volvo. We got out of the car and I made the introductions as we pulled on rucksacks and adjusted walking poles.

"Peigi makes the best ice-cream on the island. You'll need to have some at the café before you go home." Peigi waved away the compliment, smiling in spite of herself. Another example of Alan's belief that Scottish women don't know how to take compliments. "She's also spent her life walking these hills, so we're in good hands."

"Oh now, I don't know if I can take the responsibility. Island weather can take me by surprise too."

"Nonsense – if anyone knows weather, you do. And Mary Ann, of course. Your aunt spent *years* looking after sheep on these hills." Seonaid gave her bootlace a last tug, and we were ready.

"And she'd be here today too, if she could." I had absolutely no doubt of that.

"Oh, and I forgot to say – if the wind stays off, Johnny from No 10 is going to pick us up from the Rubha Mor jetty about 4 o'clock." Seonaid was looking at me as if she'd pulled a rabbit out of a hat, but I looked at her, and the others, in confusion.

"Pick us up? By boat?" We'd not discussed this possibility at all; we'd been looking forward to walking the whole, 16-odd mile round trip. Fiona gave me a rather panicked look – I think she'd said once that she was worse in boats than cars.

"Aye – don't worry, it's big enough. They used to use it to get the sheep out to Scarp in the summer." Scarp was an island just off the Harris coast, just south of Rubha Mor.

"Oh – that's, er, very kind of him." I looked at the other two uncertainly. Fiona nobly managed a 'well, if we have to' look, and Liksi seemed quite intrigued at the prospect, so I risked a smile of thanks. I could just imagine Johnny, whose father'd been at school with mine, being intrigued by our trek and wanting to help in any way he could, and it would've been terribly rude to refuse. Something else just struck me – Johnny must be in his eighties. Was this really a good idea?

"Right, now look up there to the right, to that slight dip in the skyline." Peigi pointed up to the purplish grey slopes in the near distance. "That's where we're heading, but at an angle. We need to get up this bit first, then work our way round. We keep low; there's a loch this side of the dip and we should keep to the left of it. OK?"

There were no objections to this plan, and we set off quickly, my head still reeling with the prospect of a boat trip back. It would certainly make the whole day a lot less tiring, but I hoped the others wouldn't feel cheated of their long walk.

The first stage involved a stiff but not difficult climb – there was no path through the purple carpet of heather though, and I picked my way through the tough tussocks carefully, in the hope of avoiding rabbit-holes. A twisted ankle at this stage would not be a good idea. Seonaid and Peigi, who were slightly ahead, stopped at the ruins of an old house, which Peigi informed us was an old sheiling.

"The men used to come up here with the cows in the summer, and leave the lower pastures for winter grazing." She was looking around carefully, maybe to check that nothing had changed since she'd last been here. "Probably not your father, but definitely your grandfather and the others."

I stepped through a gap and into what would have been the inside of the dwelling. A blackened alcove indicated the position of the old fireplace, and an old rusted kettle lay on its side nearby. Gazing around, I tried to imagine what it'd been like staying here overnight – far away from the villages, and with only one or two other men for company. Did they appreciate the solitude, and the stunning views back over Uig bay? Or was it all part of the annual cycle of croft work, taken for granted? There were no cows around now, only the ubiquitous sheep chewing steadily whilst keeping a wary eye on us.

"Look over there." I pointed out a line of grey shapes on the horizon to Fiona and Liksi. "Those are the Flannan Isles, where three lighthouse keepers disappeared from in 1900." I left it to Seonaid to tell them the story of the tragic mystery which'd always fired my imagination.

Having got our breath back, we set off again – a slight descent, then a steady climb in the direction of the steely glimmer of the loch which had now come into view. Rocks and boulders were strewn everywhere, with sparse patches of green scattered amidst the heathery slopes. Clusters of bog myrtle scented the air, and yellow splashes of bog asphodel vied for space amongst swaying tufts of bog cotton.

As we worked our way down the slope to the loch, the boulders became more densely packed. I concentrated on picking my way between them carefully, so as not to dislodge the smaller ones which might've rolled down on top of the others. It was quite hard going for a while – there was no shoreline to walk along, so we just had to keep going over the rocks, until we reached the grassy patch at the far end of the loch, where we stopped briefly for lunch.

"We're over half way there now." Peigi unscrewed a flask, and poured something hot into the cup. "Easier walking from now on."

"That's what I like to hear," said Liksi, reaching for an apple. "My goodness, they must've been hardy in those days."

"What d'you mean?" I laughed. "They still are! I'm sure these two could out-walk us any day." Peigi and Seonaid gave modest headshakes at the compliment.

"Of course, yeah – but y'know what I mean. Didn't you say that your Dad had to walk miles to school over these hills?"

"Yes, but only twice a week – he stayed with his grandparents during the week, as they were in the village where the school was. But yes, he was a great walker – and wasn't the least impressed by me going to the gym three times a week. That wasn't *real* exercise, in his book."

"I can't imagine what it must've been like walking through all this as a child, and on your own." Fiona was looking thoughtfully back the way we'd come.

"I know – *I'm* a bit spooked, and we've great company, and good weather." Liksi laughed, but I knew exactly what she meant. I felt very close to my father, and my roots, here, but couldn't help contrasting my hard-won level of average fitness, with the robust vigour and stamina of my ancestors.

Peigi was anxious to get going again in case the weather changed, but the thick bank of cloud didn't get any darker as it hovered above us, keeping us company for the rest of the route. The wee freshwater loch gave way to one of the west coast's magnificent sea lochs, and this time we could walk along the long shoreline for a while, winding our way in and out of the seaweed-strewn pebbles and clumps of sea pinks. The odd lobster creel or discarded buoy indicated that there was still some fishing done locally, although any commercial fishing was unlikely to be landed anywhere other than Stornoway or Tarbert. Lobster fishing'd been the main source of income for my grandfather. I remember my father telling me how all the lobsters got measured; if they were over a certain length they'd get sent to Billingsgate, but shorter ones were enjoyed by the family on a regular basis. Lucky them.

We walked right round the loch, and followed the burn for a while, crossing over on a rickety piece of wood then following a trail up into the heather. Peigi led us over the moorland and up a small hill, and when she got to the top she waved triumphantly down as we joined her breathlessly, one by one.

"There it is – Rubha Mor!" A long rugged headland lay stretched out before us. At the foot of the hill there was a solid-looking stone house in a cleared grassy area of land, overlooking the loch, the cliffs at the other side and the open sea. There were the ruins of further buildings to the left of the house, and a number of crumbling stone walls, disappearing into the undergrowth.

"Oh, my God."

"Wow."

"What a fantastic place!"

"No wonder you wanted to come here for your birthday walk!" Liksi turned to me with a mixture of awe and envy on her face. The familiar vista unfolded magically as it had every other time I'd been here, and I felt a lump in my throat as I took in the fact that my friends were also stunned by the beauty and peace of the setting.

This was the house that my grandfather had built. There was the glen, with the ribbon of waterfall tumbling down past the single rowan tree, bent sideways now after decades of the relentless Uig gales. The land round about had been the playground for my father and his three sisters, as well as the source of much of their livelihood. Those tumbledown drystone walls delineated fields or areas of the croft where my aunts had worked with the sheep – lambing, feeding, shearing, branding. A short winding path led from the house down to the jetty, with the sturdy stone shed beside it.

There was no boat tied up there now, but this was where my father had spent countless hours – maintaining boats and nets, taking in the lobster creels, gutting fish, baiting lines. Oystercatchers, unmistakeable with their piebald bodies and bright orange bills, claimed their territory with their shrill cries as they swooped and circled overhead. The tang of seaweed and sheep mingled with the sweeter scent of the bog myrtle, bringing back more memories of happy childhood and my father's tales.

"Glorious isolation." Fiona's spoke in an awed whisper.

"Is Rubha Mor the name of the house? Or the croft?" Liksi asked.

"Well, everything really. It means 'Big Headland', and both the original house, and the 'new' one, have always just been referred to as Rubha Mor. Look, see the ruin at the side of the path down there? That was the original house - Dad lived there till he was five, and remembers watching his father building the new one. The original house was a blackhouse."

"Blackhouse?" asked Liksi.

"A two-roomed house with a hole in the middle of the roof for the smoke to get out. The animals lived in one half, and the people in the other." It always took me by surprise that some of my friends knew so little about life in the highlands – but then, what did I know of Glasgow's past?

"Oh my God, the new house must've seemed like a palace." Fiona shuddered.

"It did. Come on, come and see it properly." We scrambled down the hill, and spent the next half hour wandering about, peering in the windows of the new house, and going in and out of the ruins of the old house. For me, the most poignant part was bending down under the lintel of the old house, and picking my way round the thick nettles which had colonised the inside. The fireplace was still there in the middle, and most of the walls were still standing, up to about head-height. It was almost impossible to imagine what it must've been like for a family of six to have lived there. Outside the door, another lone rowan guarded the entrance by warding off evil spirits.

One by one, we ended up down by the jetty, the three of us finding places to sit on the grassy mound just above the water. Peigi, Seonaid and Jim were away at the tip of the headland – they'd all been here several times before, and no doubt Peigi and Seonaid had tales of their own family history. They'd lived on the island – Peigi still did – and would know other equally poignant or atmospheric spots, but this was *mine*. Mine.

I sat there hugging my knees and just taking it all in. The waves lapped at the shore, drawing the pebbles towards the tidemark of still-wet seaweed, and drawing them back out again. Across the loch was the faint outline of the track we'd followed down to the shore; it had also been the main route for my father and his ancestors when they walked to the nearest village, all of eight miles away. I didn't realise my face was wet till Liksi gave me a hug and a look of sympathy.

"Sorry, sorry, I'm just a bit overwhelmed by it all." I dashed the tears away with a rather embarrassed laugh.

"No wonder – what a beautiful place. But so isolated – must've been very lonely for them all out here." Liksi looked back up at the house. "And how did they manage for food?"

"No problem with food – they'd their own sheep, hens and a cow for milk. Then there were rabbits, deer – er, unofficially, of course – and salmon too, also unofficially. And obviously, all the fish they could eat – they were much more plentiful in those days."

"I just can't imagine being so far from civilisation." Fiona seemed mesmerised by the place though. "However lovely."

"Well, apparently this was a very sociable place, although it's hard to believe now. Uig was much more heavily populated then, and there were boats going in and out of all the sea lochs. Dad used to say that at certain times of the year hardly a day went by without a visitor, and one room was always kept to house any unexpected guests. After all, you couldn't exactly phone to give warning of your arrival."

"There's a visitor now!" Liksi stood up to get a better view – the gentle purr of a motor had alerted her to a boat which had just come into sight at the end of the headland. The figure sitting at the outboard motor raised a hand to wave at Seonaid and the others, still at the far end, and after returning the greeting they started to make their way back towards us, following the boat inland.

"Johnny, I guess." I hadn't seen him for a number of years, but I knew it must be him. We watched as the boat bobbed its way slowly towards the jetty.

"Oh, God, I'm dreading this." Fiona watched its progress anxiously. "Although, I have to admit that I'm quite glad we don't have to walk all the way back. It's tricky terrain, and it's getting a bit cloudy."

"You'll be fine in the boat, Fiona, just watch the horizon. At least it's not windy – yet, at least." I wasn't as confident as I sounded, but felt I had to try. I'd never been seasick in my life, but it must be awful and I didn't want her day to be spoiled.

A tall, rangy man with a weathered complexion and a shock of white hair climbed nimbly out holding a rope, which he tied round a metal post. I was amazed and relieved at the same time – this was a fit man, whatever his age.

"So you got here," he said by way of greeting, treating us to a wide grin which exposed a mouthful of crooked teeth – a perfect example of what Alan'd call a set of burglar's tools. Although I hadn't seen him for many years, I would've recognised him anywhere.

"Johnny, how are you? This is just so good of you." I grasped the dry, calloused hand which he held out firmly.

"Ach, no, what else would I be doing these days? Always good to come to Rubha Mor anyway." He turned to the others and exchanged a few words in Gaelic with Peigi and Seonaid, then sat down and took something out of his pocket. Unscrewing the top, he handed round a half bottle of Bells. "To your father – he'd be very happy you're here."

My eyes filled up again, as I watched everyone else take a swig – or pretend to, out of politeness. Even Liksi managed a semblance of enjoyment, and she hated whisky with a passion.

"Anyone need seasickness pills?" I looked at Seonaid in surprise as she pulled a battered strip of something out of her pocket. "They're a bit old, but they might be useful?"

"Yes *please*." Fiona's fervent thanks brought a wide grin to Johnny's face. He passed her the bottle back to 'wash them down with', and she carried out his instructions without needing to be asked again. "D'you mind if I've another swig?"

"Of course, of course." He waved aside her thanks and his eyes lit up as Jim produced a hip flask from his rucksack. "Finish it; there's more here!"

By the time we clambered into the boat, falling over each other with the motion and getting in Johnny's way, Fiona'd a glazed look in her eyes and Johnny was alarmingly uproarious. Who knows how much he'd had before he arrived – it was Liksi and I who looked at each other nervously now, as Johnny pulled at the outboard motor starter and the boat began to putter gently backwards and away from the jetty. However, as we pulled away from Rubha Mor and I watched the house become ever more distant, a sense of peace and well-being descended on me and I relaxed into the exhilaration of being in an open boat, in the hands of a seasoned sailor, who had probably done this same journey with my father as a passenger many years ago. We headed out to sea, and followed the outline of the coast right round to near where we'd left the cars. With a heartfelt mixture of thanks, hugs, and handshakes, we said goodbye to these wonderful people who'd helped to make the day happen.

Alone again, we looked at each other with tired but happy smiles.

"Magic." Liksi shook her head with wonder. "What an amazing day."

"Brilliant. And I didn't even get seasick."

"You've probably got the whisky to thank for that, rather than the pills." I laughed at Fiona's still slightly off-kilter gaze. "And I'm jealous – come on, let's get home so that I can catch up with you drouths!"

Later, we settled again in the conservatory, waiting for our salmon (courtesy of Auntie Mary Ann) to cook. Both faces were watching expectantly as I slowly twisted the cork in the bottle, relaxing once it popped and I was able to pour the bubbles into the waiting glasses.

"This is the real stuff, girls, left over from my birthday. No prosecco this time! A toast – to all our 60th birthdays past and present, and to the best walking companions in the world, in the most beautiful place in the world."

"And to another decade of walks and our 70th birthdays!" Liksi grinned cheerily as we clinked glasses and drank.

"And then our 80ths ..." Fiona's soft voice tailed off as we turned to watch the night falling over the silvery sands.

Acknowledgements

This page has to start with a huge thanks to my great friends, the real Fiona and Liksi - they know who they are. There would be no book without them: we have shared ALL these walks along with many others, and we are still walking. They encouraged me to put our experiences down on paper, and have put up with years of 'could you read this bit to see what you think?', 'can you remember if there was much of a view from the path up to ...?' As if that wasn't enough, I've been guilty of significant character assassination (or at the very least, alteration). I can't thank them enough for their support and friendship over the years. Special thanks must go to 'Fiona', who was my first reader, and who painstakingly kept me on the right path (no pun intended).

And what can I say to the real Liksi's husband, 'Pete', for agreeing to be the villain of the piece? His only stipulation was that I gave him a Racing Green Aston Martin - it seemed a small price to pay.

My first foray into creative writing was a workshop run by the author Linda Cracknell. This excellent event was followed by several courses in creative writing run by the amazing David Pettigrew, at the University of Strathclyde. His enthusiasm, experience and tolerance of my initial efforts encouraged me to move forward. Thanks too to all the class members and their supportive critiques. In particular, I am so grateful to our small group which has continued to meet long after the classes ended - Richard Louden for his wealth of experience; John MacDonald for his often quirky but wonderfully fresh ideas, not to mention keeping me right on the finer points of English; John Parker for noticing things I've missed; Ann Scott for her encouragement and suggestions, and also Maggie Brady, Michael Gallagher and Mary Attenborough for their remote support. Special thanks to group member Margaret McMillan, my second reader, who worked her way nobly through every chapter, offering invaluable advice and suggestions throughout.

Bearsden Writers has provided support via its key aim of facilitating publications by local authors. I am immensely grateful to Marion Macdonald for sharing her own publishing experience with me.

Closer to home, thanks to my talented cousin Susan Johnston for embarking on the writing experience alongside me, and for providing mutual support and insightful critiques. Much of my inspiration has come from my father, John MacDonald, who published his own book at the age of 83. Both he and my mother Mary passed on their love of the countryside to me at a very early age.

And finally, to my husband Norman, to whom I owe everything. I could not have done this without him. He has provided support and encouragement all the way, propping me up when I needed it and believing in me unconditionally.

About the Author

Helen Williamson

Helen was brought up in the north of Scotland. Her childhood holidays were spent camping and walking all over Scotland; this love of the outdoors has remained with her all her life.

After a career in further education, Helen is now retired and able to devote time to one of her other interests, writing. This is her first book.

She lives near Glasgow with her husband, and still goes walking whenever the opportunity arises.

Printed in Great Britain
by Amazon